Freud, Psychoanalysis and Death

Was "death" a lacuna at the heart of Sigmund Freud's work? Liran Razinsky argues that the question of death is repressed, rejected and avoided by Freud, therefore resulting in an impairment of the entire theoretical structure of psychoanalysis. Razinsky supports his claim through a series of close readings of psychoanalytic texts (including not just Freud, but Klein, Kohut, Jung and Lacan, among others) that explore psychoanalysis' inattention to this fundamental human concern. The readings are combined to form an overall critique of psychoanalysis—one that remains sympathetic but calls for a rethinking of the issue of death. In presenting a fresh and persuasive interpretation of the Freudian corpus, this book will be of interest to scholars of Freud's thought and psychoanalysis, literary scholars, analysts, clinicians and all those curious about death's psychic life.

LIRAN RAZINSKY is a Lecturer in the Department of Hermeneutics and Cultural Studies at Bar-Ilan University, Israel. He works in both French and comparative literature, and critical theory, as well as in theoretical psychoanalysis.

Freud, Psychoanalysis and Death

Liran Razinsky

CAMBRIDGE
UNIVERSITY PRESS

University Printing House, Cambridge CB2 8BS, United Kingdom

One Liberty Plaza, 20th Floor, New York, NY 10006, USA

477 Williamstown Road, Port Melbourne, VIC 3207, Australia

314-321, 3rd Floor, Plot 3, Splendor Forum, Jasola District Centre, New Delhi - 110025, India

103 Penang Road, #05-06/07, Visioncrest Commercial, Singapore 238467

Cambridge University Press is part of the University of Cambridge.

It furthers the University's mission by disseminating knowledge in the pursuit of education, learning and research at the highest international levels of excellence.

www.cambridge.org
Information on this title: www.cambridge.org/9781107009721

© Liran Razinsky 2013

This publication is in copyright. Subject to statutory exception and to the provisions of relevant collective licensing agreements, no reproduction of any part may take place without the written permission of Cambridge University Press.

First published 2013
First paperback edition 2014

A catalogue record for this publication is available from the British Library

Library of Congress Cataloging in Publication data
Razinsky, Liran.
  Freud, psychoanalysis and death / Liran Razinsky.
    pages cm
  Includes bibliographical references.
  ISBN 978-1-107-00972-1
  1. Death–Psychological aspects. 2. Psychoanalysis. 3. Freud, Sigmund, 1856–1939. I. Title.
  BF789.D4.R39 2013
  150.19′52–dc23

2012018825

ISBN 978-1-107-00972-1 Hardback
ISBN 978-1-107-47844-2 Paperback

Cambridge University Press has no responsibility for the persistence or accuracy of URLs for external or third-party internet websites referred to in this publication, and does not guarantee that any content on such websites is, or will remain, accurate or appropriate.

Contents

Acknowledgments		*page* ix
Introduction		1
	Death in theory	5
	Death in the clinic	9
	The structure of the book	12
Chapter 1:	Against death: Freud and the question of death's psychic presence	15
	The case against representation	15
	The desiring machine (hits the wall of reality)	24
	The I of the beholder	26
	The case against fear	30
	Doubt and hesitation	37
Chapter 2:	"Most of the time life appears so uncertain to me": Death as a concern in Freud's life	40
Chapter 3:	The dream of death: *The Interpretation of Dreams*	46
	Opening: Death representable and irrepresentable	46
	Dying the death of the other	50
	Non vixit	52
	Dying in one's dreams	56
	Finally he melted away	56
	A castle by the sea	59
	Autopsy-choanalyzing oneself	62
	How much time?	64
	I must not go yet? A visit to the underworld	67
	Concern for others	67
	Limping, pale, and seriously ill. Irma	69
Chapter 4:	To dream, perchance to die: A further exploration of *The Interpretation of Dreams*	75
	Death and ambition	75
	The man with the beard	76
	Non vixit	77
	Rome	78
	"I must not delay any longer"	81

	Late in life	82
	The Botanical Monograph	83
	Method in the madness	85
	The "1851 and 1856" dream	86
	Aspire – expire	87
	Death, an absurdity	89
	Father on his death-bed	90
	Death: Between denial and recognition	92
	For dust thou art	93
	Night of the living dead	97
	Anxiety and wish	98
	Conclusions: Death and dreams	101
Chapter 5:	Death and anxiety	105
Chapter 6:	A struggle with the concept of death: "Thoughts for the Times on War and Death"	112
	Giving death the place which is its due	114
	But what is the place which is death's due?	117
	The highest stake in the game of living	120
	The direct encounter with death	124
	The influence of war	126
	Freud's hesitation	127
Chapter 7:	Driving death away: Freud's theory of the death drive	131
	The death drive and death	133
	Dying your own death	142
	Critiques of the death drive	146
	Recasting the death drive as an existential concept	149
	The death drive, Freud, and death: Further considerations	152
Chapter 8:	Death and culture: Death as a central motif in Freud's cultural and literary analyses	155
	The dead and us	155
	Immortality	155
	The uncanny	158
	Totem and Taboo	160
	Transient lives	161
	Further thoughts on "Thoughts"	162
	On Transience	164
Chapter 9:	Avoidance and reduction of death in psychoanalysis	170
	Reduction	170
	Generalization and non-specification	173
	Sexualization of death	175
	Rendering death a wish and activizing the subject in death	176
	Concretizing death	177
	Pathologization of the psychic reaction to death	178
	A negative moral judgment	180
	Overlooking death	182

Contents vii

	Intermezzo: Dying without death—Mourning and Melancholia	183
	Treating death as a problem of the ill and elderly	189
	"So what?"	189
Chapter 10:	The post-Freudians in the labyrinth of death	191
	The Kleinians	191
	The Kleinian understanding of the fear of death	193
	The theory's application	195
	Erikson	197
	Kohut	201
	Jung	204
	Winnicott	206
Chapter 11:	Lacan	208
	The symbolic, the imaginary, and the real	209
	The symbolic	209
	The imaginary	211
	The real	213
	Tragic paths and the death drive	215
	The nature of desire	216
	Das Ding	218
	The concrete fear of death	219
	Conclusion: Talking about death	220
Chapter 12:	Attempts at reconciliation	222
	Rank and Becker	222
	Piven	224
	Lifton	225
	Death equivalents	226
	Yalom and clinical approaches	228
	Facing the abyss and surviving it	230
	Existential psychoanalysis: Handling otherness	232
	Bridges to one's past	233
Chapter 13:	Sources of the clash: The conflict between analytic ideas and concern with death	236
	Where does the problem lie? Some analytic tenets that hinder the integration of death	236
	The deterministic-mechanistic model	237
	The focus on the past	238
	The detachability of affect and content	238
	The interdependence of psychic events	239
	The instinctual model	240
	The focus on presence	240
	Explaining the external in terms of the internal	241
	The analytic perspective on reality	242
	The focus on relational aspects	243
	Recoiling from the "high": Against philosophy	243
	Generality versus idiosyncrasy I: Universal explanations	245
	Therapeutic pessimism	246

		Aspects of death that lie—or do they? Beyond psychoanalysis	247
		Death and the meaning of life	247
		Analytic sensibilities helpful to the integration of death	248
		"Freudian pessimism"	249
		Truth and illusion	249
		Generality versus idiosyncrasy II: Idiosyncratic explorations	249
Chapter 14:	Death in life		253
		Death in praxis	254
		The psychic life of death	257
		Death anxiety and the thought of death	260
		On not knowing death: Defenses and distortions	261
		Death as a dynamic absence	265
		To be with not-to-be	274
		Knowledge of death and the encounter with it	276

Final thoughts 279

References 286
Index 299

Acknowledgments

The current study, as well as my entire thinking about psychoanalysis, owes a great deal to Rachel Blass, who through her comments on my texts and countless personal meetings, has helped me to think about these issues and give them form. The intellectual dialog with her has continuously advanced my ideas.

This book originated from a PhD dissertation begun over a decade ago. For a long time, I was amused by the fact that the university authorized a project that overlapped to a large extent with my frequent discussions with my good friend Eran Dorfman. These long discussions on life and death, meaning, and existential concerns were not a professional matter of course, but a personal inquiry for us both. We have both come a long way since then. One discussion in particular, where we wondered whether psychoanalytic issues are the same as existential ones, put me on track for this work.

My dear sister, Hili Razinsky has always been able to illuminate issues, expose things not sufficiently clarified, and develop my ideas and push them forward.

The person who has accompanied my work most intimately has been my beloved wife, Tehila Mishor. Through her advice and support, she has always helped me get on with it. Whenever in doubt or in need of exchange of ideas, I would turn to her. Her intelligence and clear thinking enabled her to see through my mistakes and problems, and helped me make decisions, something never easy for me. Above all, she was always there, and made this long period a pleasant one.

I wish to thank my past teachers to whom I feel indebted. First, Betty Rojtman, with whom I share many intellectual interests, and whose delicate and nuanced thought enriched my thinking on death. My consideration of psychoanalysis has evolved in various contexts. Vladimir Marinov helped to deepen my investigation, and in many discussions engaged me in a rigorous examination of aspects of psychoanalysis' relation to death. Julia Kristeva taught me much about the strong and weak points of psychoanalysis, and helped me develop a more existential approach. Ruth Ginsburg was the first to teach me that Freud can be read in a literary way, that is, as a text, and fostered my keenness for diving into Freud in search of pearls. Rivka Eifermann taught me how to listen with an analytic ear.

I owe many of the improvements and changes to Cathy Caruth, Jose Brunner, and three anonymous Cambridge reviewers, all of whom were extremely helpful with their close attention to my text, and with evaluating the overall project and pointing out strengths, and weaknesses to be worked on. I am very grateful to Hetty Reid from CUP for believing in this book and putting this belief into practice, and to Carrie Parkinson, Josephine Lane, Sally Seehafer, and Chris Miller for being so helpful with its production.

Mark Joseph was much more than an English editor, although he also performed this job tremendously. He was the first reader of the work in its current version and alerted me to all those places which were theoretically unclear or fuzzy. Many of his important comments are now incorporated in the book.

Much gratitude goes to Lia Levy and Batya Razinsky for their valuable help in taking care of organizing the bibliography.

I wrote this study over the course of several years in the cafés of Jerusalem. Specifically, I wish to thank the wonderful staff of Nocturno, Uganda, and the Qawehouse for having created the kind of environment that could make the potentially tedious work of writing a book pleasant.

★ ★ ★

The work was partly supported by scholarships from the Sigmund Freud Center for Research in Psychoanalysis (Salinski Fund) and from the Center for Austrian Studies, both at the Hebrew University of Jerusalem.

Some chapters and sections have previously appeared (with alterations) as articles or as book chapters, and I wish to thank the journals and editors for granting me permission to reprint them here. Part of Chapter 1 appeared as "Against Death's Representability: Freud and the Question of Death's Psychic Presence," in *The Psychoanalytic Study of the Child*, 65, 2011. Chapter 6 appeared as "A Psychoanalytic Struggle with the Concept of Death: A New Reading of Freud's 'Thoughts for the Times on War and Death,'" in *The Psychoanalytic Review*, 94, 355–387, 2007, and is used here with the permission of the National Psychological Assiciation for Psychanalysis, and Chapter 7 appeared as "Driving Death Away: Death and Freud's Theory of the Death Drive," in *Psychoanalytic Review*, 97, 393–424, 2010. The section on ambition from Chapter 4 first appeared as "Death and Ambition in Freud's *The*

Interpretation of Dreams," in A Kasher (Ed.), *Making Sense of Dying and Death,* published by the Inter-Disciplinary Press, Oxford, 2011. A shortened version of which was also published in the e-book *Mortality, Dying, and Death*, edited by C. Edwards and C. Haliburton.

A few passages appeared in "How to Look Death in the Eyes Rather Than Shunning It: Freud and Bataille," published in *SubStance. A Review of Theory and Literary Criticism* 38, 63–88, 2009. © 2009 by the Board of Regents of the University of Wisconsin System. Reproduced courtesy of the University of Wisconsin Press. Other Passages were included in the review "On the Strange Case of the Attitude of Psychoanalysis Towards Death," *Contemporary Psychoanalysis*, 43, 149–164, 2007.

A very short summary of this work in its initial stages appeared as "What Freud Did Not Say: The Absence of Death in Freud's Writings," in A. Suppan & R. Lein (Eds.), *From the Habsburgs to Central Europe. Europa Orientalis*, 6, 239–249, 2008.

All Freud's citations are from *The Standard Edition of The Complete Psychological Works of Sigmund Freud*, translated and edited by James Strachey © 2010 James Strachey. Reprinted by permission of the Random House Group Limited, the Marsh Agency on behalf of Sigmund Freud Copyrights, Basic Books, a member of the Perseus Books Group, and W.W. Norton.

Introduction

> *All cognition of the All originates in death, in the fear of death. Philosophy takes it upon itself to throw off the fear of things earthly, to rob death of its poisonous sting, and Hades of its pestilential breath ... Without ceasing, the womb of the indefatigable earth gives birth to what is new, each bound to die, each awaiting the day of its journey into darkness with fear and trembling. But philosophy denies these fears of the earth. It bears us over the grave which yawns at our feet with every step.* (Franz Rosenzweig, 1971 [1921], p. 3)
>
> *[H]ere the philosophers are thinking too philosophically ...* (Sigmund Freud, 1915, p. 293)

Around the same time Rosenzweig was beginning to formulate these words as a soldier during World War I, another Jewish thinker writing in German was taking a completely different stance: "The high-sounding phrase, 'every fear is ultimately the fear of death', has hardly any meaning, and at any rate cannot be justified" (Freud, 1923, p. 57). Freud's words, here and elsewhere, constituted merely the first steps in what has become a long-lasting psychoanalytic journey. They express much more than the occasional concrete remark and bear witness to, rather, a fundamental and mostly hidden tendency. In psychoanalysis, the greatest effort thus far to "map" the human psyche, death seems to occupy, as I hope to show, only a marginal place. A thorough reading of analytic writings reveals a sort of a "denial of death," or at least a reluctance to acknowledge death as a constituting factor in mental life. Sometimes death anxiety is reduced to other fears and mental states. At other times death's significance in psychic life is denied, or death is simply ignored. This book explores the theme of death and death anxiety in psychoanalysis, and the existence of a lacuna, an act of repression, in psychoanalysis' handling of death. It aims to show how and why death has been marginalized or repressed in psychoanalysis.

It all starts from a few statements by Freud about death's inaccessibility to the unconscious (1915, pp. 289, 296–7; 1923, pp. 57–9; 1926, pp. 129–30, 140). Death is negative, abstract, it involves time, and cannot, therefore, be part of unconscious thought. Accordingly, if people are afraid of death, these fears should be understood as secondary, as indications of another "deeper" problem, mostly castration. This is where it all starts but not where it all ends. For this position reverberates throughout the history of psychoanalysis, finding various expressions. It consists in a kind of disbelief in death, an unwillingness to recognize death as a possibly influential psychic factor.

While it deals with the psychoanalytic approach to death in general, the focus of this book is Freud. I examine some of the central Freudian texts with the aim of exploring the role of death in psychic life. Freud's importance here is much more than historical, for several reasons. His position with regard to death had a tremendous influence on future generations of theoreticians. In fact, interestingly, in very few areas did Freud's views endure with such little challenge and undergo so little revision. The reiterations and variations of his position amount to a psychoanalytic "common sense" regarding the secondary nature of the fear of death. An exploration of Freud's writings thus goes straight to the heart of the problem.

However, as sometimes happens, Freud's position on death is more ambivalent, vacillating, and complex than the positions of many of his followers. Even when reductionistic, it is multifariously so. Freud's work, particularly in its less reductionistic manifestations, contains fruitful intuitions and sharp insights into the nature of our attitude toward death. It often betrays a tension between reductionistic tendencies and attempts to attribute the utmost significance to death. Many times, only Freud's more reductionistic statements were adopted by future generations of theoreticians and analysts. In Freud, psychoanalysis is captured in its *status nascendi*, allowing us to examine the psychoanalytic approach in its formative stages, and observe its initial structure and fractures. A close reading of Freud's texts enables us also to question the justification and inevitability of psychoanalytic accounts of death, and to ask whether there is another way.

There certainly is another way, for Freud actually had two significant points of view on death. The one, much more prominent, is evident throughout his work, and does not regard death as a psychic motive or death anxiety as a factor in mental life. It finds expression in both explicit statements and implicit presumptions, constructions, and biases, the uncovering of which constitutes much of the work of the current study. The second point of view, less dominant and often hidden, regards death as central, and often reflects a personal belief held by Freud, rather than his "professional" views. The two positions undermine and displace each other. Oftentimes, what looks like a clear expression of one turns out upon examination to disclose the other. Places where Freud seems

Introduction

to explicitly accept death as a psychic factor are sometimes revealed at bottom to be further cases of neglect or repression of death, and vice versa.

This ambivalence, this wavering, is manifest throughout this book. It is reflected in the movement between Chapters 1 and 2, from Freud's theoretical resistance to death to his personal engagement with it, and in the hesitations and doubts that accompanied the forming of that theoretical resistance in the first place (Chapter 1). It comes into play in Freud's major essay on death, "Thoughts for the Times on War and Death" (Chapter 6), a text where the two thoughts on death are all the time at war. It sometimes displays itself as a kind of return of the repressed, as is the case in *The Interpretation of Dreams*, where death simply keeps asserting itself over and over but is ignored on the theoretical level (Chapters 3 and 4). The theory itself keeps coming back to death, be it in sporadic gestures that acknowledge its importance, mostly in Freud's cultural writings (Chapter 8), or in the direct attempt to conceptualize it and not let it remain outside the cathedral of theory, Freud's notion of the death drive, which again, we shall see (Chapter 7) fails to acknowledge death in the very attempt to do so. In fact, this pattern is so dominant that it could be said to be structuring Freud's psychoanalytic theory.

It does, in effect, go on after Freud: Theorists declare death important but fail to integrate it well into the theory. While the overall picture allows death meager space (see Chapter 9), we witness repeated attempts throughout the history of psychoanalysis to address this theoretical lack (Chapters 10, 11, and 12). If it is almost always the reductionistic or evasive position that has the upper hand, this has perhaps to do with reasons embedded deeply within the psychoanalytic worldview, addressed in Chapter 13. The theory, on the whole, fails in its attempts to incorporate death, and showing how this takes place is my main task in this book.

Throughout the history of psychoanalysis several thinkers have made the claim that the psychoanalytic approach to death is reductionistic (Rank, 1950 [1945]; Klein, 1948; Brown, 1959; Searles, 1965 [1961]; Becker, 1973; Meyer, 1975 [1973]; Lifton, 1979; Hoffman, 1979, 1998; Yalom, 1980; Lachmann, 1985; Bonasia, 1988,[1] and more

---

[1] Bonasia's (1988) paper, one of the best on the subject, has only come to my knowledge in the very final stages of preparing the manuscript (probably due the journal's recent inclusion in PEP) and therefore is regretably not analyzed or alluded to in this work. Its analysis of the death drive is expecially pertinent and bears close resemblence to the one offered in Chapter 7.

recently Piven, 2004. It has also been suggested more marginally by Stern, 1968a, 1968b, Jonte-Pace, 2001, and a few others). As Lifton (1979) points out: "Psychological theory has tended either to neglect death or to render it a kind of foreign body, to separate death from the general motivations of life" (p. 4).

In examining the problem more closely than has been done to date, this book exposes different modes of reduction and shows that they are multiple, complex, and often hidden. Freud's texts and those of others are carefully read, and their approach to death is analyzed in detail. Many times we shall see, death is ignored, even when nothing is stated explicitly. Even in places where supposedly analytic texts do attribute some importance to death, they often do so in ways that distort its existential significance. Reduction in these cases is elusive and covert, yet persistently active.

Through exposing the specific ways in which death and death anxiety are constructed in analytic theory, and aiming to find out what is *implied* by them, the adequacy and validity of those constructions is questioned. We shall see how reduction distorts the fact of death itself, how it creates contradictions and dead-ends in the theory. However, the contrary will also be shown: not only how Freud has dispersed throughout his writings sharp intuitions regarding death, but how death reasserts itself constantly in the texts and refuses to be silenced, how the psychical phenomena related to death defy reduction. The theory, I suggest, must be taken seriously to show why its treatment of death is lacking. It cannot be simply dismissed as inadequate. In probing its unintended constructions and its inconsistencies, I show how they reflect a fundamental problem with the psychoanalytic approach to death.

I give a close reading of Freud's key texts, and analyze the role death plays in them or the attitude toward it expressed in them. In most of them the question of death had not so far been studied attentively or has been subject to misinterpretations and clichéd reading. The present study is also one of the first to comprehensively review Freud's ideas on death.[2]

My analysis also does not stop at Freud. It deals with various psychoanalytic currents to demonstrate the pervasiveness of the neglect of death throughout psychoanalysis' development.

The current study, unlike most existing work on the subject, calls attention not only to psychoanalysis' obliviousness to death, but also to its deep relation to the psychoanalytic attitude. Such obliviousness or

---

[2] Only Piven (2004), to my knowledge, has done so previously (Hoffman's, 1979, study is also important, but very brief). Piven's overall perspective, while intriguing, seems not always critical enough in its approach to the Freudian texts.

active belittling of death's importance is not treated here as a minor blind spot, or a phenomenon confined to isolated passages, but rather as a deep-rooted, pervasive stance, embedded in psychoanalytic thought. The reductive approach cannot be simply brushed under the carpet by passing over several problematic passages.

Curiously, the few critiques made so far on the analytic approach to death have not been integrated or incorporated into analytic thought. They are hardly referred to, and there is no real network of discussion around them. They remain islands within analytic thought, and indeed, islands rarely frequented. Moreover, analysts do not seem to think that the psychoanalytic attitude to death is problematic at all. This fact, that the relevant critiques have been rejected or ignored, is another symptom of the problem, and necessitates a further, more elaborate enquiry into the causes.

The interest in critically examining psychoanalytic theory is twofold. It lies both in the fact that psychoanalysis is the most overarching theory of the human psyche, and hence should not be blind to a central dimension of life, and in the influence of psychoanalysis on clinical contexts, as part of the worldview of therapists.

Clearly, to some extent death is already a part of psychoanalysis: It is present in analytic discussions of loss, trauma, masochism, suicide, war neurosis or the Holocaust and is part of many clinicians' awareness. But these are isolated areas, theoretical patches, bypassing the deeper position against death. The fundamental problem remains, and needs to be addressed directly. This would help make the theory more truthful and alive.

Death in theory

Our idea of death evolves both from the fact of death itself and from images and perspectives on death, perspectives which are cultural-historical: "[i]n American society, a high number of automobile deaths is acceptable; a high number of crib deaths is not" (Stephenson, 1985, p. 2). Of course, the psychoanalytic view of death is only part of larger historical transformations in the perception of death, due to the changing intellectual climate, the decline of the influence of religions, mass death events in the twentieth century and the development of medicine and institutionalization, to name just a few salient factors. Nevertheless, it is also important in itself, for its ideas, for its representativeness of cultural trends, for its role in ideological transformation, and for its ongoing influence through therapeutic practice. What kind of picture does psychoanalytic theory present of death?

Theory creates blindness. Even useful, fruitful theories bring about a certain blindness. In illuminating reality, they ipso facto relegate other parts of it to the darkness. Concepts we use sharpen our perception of certain aspects of reality, but necessarily blind us as to others.

Of course, the psychoanalytic world has a well-based tradition of constantly putting its premises in question and updating them. Many times, however, in what concerns death, even when certain faults or lacks are explicitly recognized, and an attitude that deviates from the dominant theory is expressed, one is still limited in the extent to which one is able to recognize the nature of the problem. One may notice the problem, but not see how deep it goes. Alternatively, one tries to correct the theory, but still carries it on one's back, and part of reality remains hidden in the shadow of theory.

The current study tries to illuminate a basic lack in analytic theory with respect to death, an aspect of human life that largely remains outside its understanding of the human subject. It attempts to shed some light on some things hidden in the dark.

Yet, one may ask, does death anxiety really exist? Is death in general part of psychic life? It is my contention that it does and that it is. It is not the goal of this book though to demonstrate this. Anyone who thinks otherwise, or believes her finitude has no relevance for her life, is kindly asked to go and sincerely examine the nearest mirror before going on reading. Broad expositions of death's central role in psychic life, and specifically of death anxiety, can be found in Becker (1973) and Yalom (1980), while Heidegger (1996 [1927]) offers perhaps the most profound philosophical argumentation for death's centrality for the human being. I try in general not to use the idea of the "existence" of death anxiety or death's psychic influence as an argument in itself, but to examine the psychoanalytic approach to death on its own terms. It is true though that on a certain level the existence of death anxiety is also a matter of belief: not that there is no evidence or argumentation for it, but one could always counter them if one's mind is set on it.[3]

---

[3] There are two essential sources for the idea that death anxiety exists, and one marginal source. The two essential ones are a simple consideration of the human condition and sincere introspection. Can one honestly dismiss, upon thinking of the human's basic situation in the world, that one's finitude is completely without psychic consequences? And do we not know, from our own experience, even if only vaguely, that the knowledge of the future event of death deeply affects us? Even if it is rarely on our minds, even if we do not normally experience the anxiety of it, do we not sense it, albeit in brief, fleeting flashes of awareness?

The less important source of support is the empirical study of death anxiety and depression. One can cite numerous experiments that examine psychic responses to

Interestingly, one person for whom death and death anxiety were certainly significant was Freud himself. As I shall describe in Chapters 2, 3, and 4, in his private life, death was a constant worry for Freud, and death anxiety a daily experience. At all times aware of his mortality, he can be said to have lived his life under the shadow of death, the same shadow he claimed in his writings to be but an insignificant specter. Asking, therefore, if death receives a sufficient place in Freud's work derives a basic justification from this gap between what he tells us in writing and what he tells his friends in private.

Because I claim that the analytic approach to death is problematic, something must perhaps be said as to what kind of approach to death would be less problematic. As I said, I do not set about here to advance the view that death anxiety or death is a troublesome issue for people. However, this intuitive, common sense notion is so widespread among diverse schools of thought, not to mention laypeople, and finds such frequent expression in mythology, art, literature, etc., that in some respect, the burden of proof falls on those who claim that death is not significant. The support the analytic arguments provide for this claim is, as I shall show in the first chapter, insufficient. Much of the examination of the analytic approach is carried out here, then, vis-à-vis a common sense approach, which I believe is available to anyone.

Moreover, even without supposing any alternative view, it is still possible to demonstrate the problematic nature of the current state of affairs concerning the psychoanalytic approach to death. As I said, I expose inconsistencies and contradictions in the theory, showing that it does not hold up as is, that the phenomena it seeks to explain remain unexplained, and that internal tensions undermine the effort to understand death in the usual analytic terms. I also show how death stubbornly "rises from the grave" after ostensibly being put to death by existing explanations. Death simply will not be silenced.

death across age, sex and ethnic groups and that look at various related factors (e.g., Feifel & Branscomb, 1973; Feifel & Hermann, 1973; Hoelter, 1979; Persinger, 1985; Alvarado, Templer, Bresler, & Thomas-Dobson, 1992–1993; Maglio & Robinson, 1994; Neimeyer, 1997–1998; Galt & Hayslip, 1998; Rasmussen, Templer, Kenkel, & Cannon, 1998; Fortner, Neimeyer, & Rybarczyk, 2000; Thorson & Powell, 2000; Tomer & Eliason, 2000; Tomer & Eliason, 2005; Lehto & Stein, 2009). If I refer to empirical research as less important, it is because the first two considerations are so fundamental that even if empirical studies were to find no death anxiety or depression at all, one would still have reasons to regard them as fundamental human possibilities and concerns.

Of special importance are experiments in Terror Management Theory (TMT) showing how influential the awareness of death, death anxiety and the defense against them are in shaping and supporting cultural belief systems and ideologies, as well as self-esteem (see Solomon, Greenberg, & Pyszczynski, 1998).

In addition, as I have said already, much of the approach to death I expose is inexplicit and unintended. Thus, rather than directly attack the analytic claims that diminish the importance of death, I show how death, or significant aspects of it, are disregarded even when this is not the aim. The obliviousness to death in psychoanalysis is, to anticipate later conclusions, more a part of a worldview, the result of a network of ideas, than merely a position in itself. To sum up these points, ignoring death can be shown to be problematic without any view external to psychoanalysis.

This notwithstanding, an alternative conception is built up step by step, and not explicitly at first, as we proceed through an examination of the analytic corpus. Through a systematic inquiry into the shortcomings of existing analytic understandings of death, it will gradually become clearer what a more adequate approach to death could look like. In the final chapter, I address the issue more directly and attempt to delineate more specifically the various aspects of death and death's repercussions in psychic life, which should be addressed.

It is still perhaps worthwhile here to note why some conceptions of death are perceived as flawed or lacking. They are lacking not necessarily with regard to a specific alternative understanding, but rather in the measure to which they succeed in accounting for the phenomena themselves. First and foremost, the problem with many analytic understandings of death is that they dismiss the phenomenon of death anxiety itself. They purport to account for it, but render it something else.

Similarly, the reality of death is often not acknowledged. Death's influence is not recognized as such; the event of death as a real thing in the world, that will take place, is forgotten.

In addition, specific dimensions of this fact of life are left unaddressed, especially those harder and more threatening to incorporate. For example, that we know about it in advance, and acknowledge its inevitability. Another important example is death's imminence, the fact that it could come at any moment. If we do not address this fact, we have failed to address death's influence. Similarly, that death is an event external to us is often blurred in analytic explanations.

More common are specific understandings of death, which leave out many of its more general influences. Psychoanalytic studies often refer to very particular cases of death or annihilation anxiety. Rarely is the deeper impact of the fact we are finite brought into account.

In sum, such psychoanalytic conceptions of death's psychic impact often fail to contribute to our understanding of it, and neglect significant parts of psychic life.

Death in the clinic

For me, then, to a large extent there is no real question whether death is part of psychic life. Clinicians, however, might feel troubled by two subtler concerns I wish to address here. Readers untroubled by these clinical questions might move directly to the next section. The first possible reservation is that clinically, "in reality," death is simply not an issue. The second is that it is an issue but that analysts take good care of it, and that they do not reduce it when it comes to the anxious patient.

Is death a clinical issue? In the works of those who do seem to be aware of the issue of death, one can find numerous descriptions of cases where death is a central theme; for example, Stern (1968a), Rosenthal (1973a [1963]), Meyer (1975 [1973]), Lifton, (1979), Yalom (1980), Lachmann (1985), Hulsey & Frost (1995), Hoffman (1979, 1998), Langs (1997), and De Masi (2004). Langs (1997, pp. 30–3) and Yalom (1980) insist on how abundant death references actually are in therapies. It can be shown that even in Freud's own case histories death is ubiquitous: in some cases in Freud and Breuer's *Studies in Hysteria* (Yalom, 1980, pp. 59–64; Breger, 1981, pp. 112–13; Lifton, 1979, p. 205), in the case of the Rat Man (Lifton, 1979, pp. 207–10) and of Little Hans (pp. 213–9; Stern, 1968a, pp. 5–6) or the Wolf Man (Piven, 2004, pp. 125–39). Valuable analyses and descriptions of the role death plays in psychopathology can found in Rank (1950 [1945] pp. 119–33), Brown (1959, pp. 87–134), Searles (1965 [1961]), Leclaire (1971), Becker (1973, pp. 208–52), Meyer (1975 [1973]), Lifton (1979), Yalom (1980, pp. 110–58), and Piven (2004).

After citing numerous cases where death is a central theme, Yalom (1980) concludes that in fact, in light of all he encounters in the clinic and the importance death has in people's lives, the absence of discussions of death in the clinical literature seems to amount to a "conspiracy of silence" (p. 55). He cannot understand how it is that what repeatedly comes up in the clinical context is so scarce in the literature. Elements of the clinical exchange pertaining to death are either dropped from discussion, mentioned but ignored, or translated into other psychological terms (*ibid.*).

Indeed, while one can understand a theoretical reluctance to deal with death, it would be odd if death were also absent from the clinical exchanges themselves. As Yalom (1980) asserts, it is not that death concerns do not come up, but often rather that "the therapist is not prepared to hear them" (p. 57). If the therapist is receptive to death, she will frequently recognize it in what patients say (*ibid.*). However, when the ear is obstructed, no mention of death by a patient, no matter how direct and imposing, will be heard.

In addition, the claim of some analysts that they simply do not encounter death-related issues in their therapies sounds to me very unanalytic. Since when does one rely in psychoanalysis solely, and without further examination, on the direct account of patients? Do patients normally speak openly about their castration fears? Death is never an easy issue for anyone, and naturally death anxiety is not readily admitted; yet it is easily repressed. Clinicians should deal with death as they deal with other issues in psychoanalysis, follow their suspicions, and go beyond the defenses. The problem is that "when mortality does not stare the analytic dyad in the face, we tend not to invite it into the room" (Frommer, 2005, p. 485).

To unresolved death fears in the therapist, Yalom adds the general inattention to death in psychological theory, regarding which he suggests some interesting preliminary ideas. My work is solely concerned with the second of these issues. I focus on the negligence of death on the theoretical level, the ways in which it is excluded, denied, ignored, reduced, pathologized, and rejected. The key for an improved clinical attention to death is directing more theoretical attention, not only to the issue of death, but also to the way this issue has been rejected.

The theory is crucial here. Death cannot remain a matter of personal preference alone. Because it is not an issue, one will rarely look for it. Analysts will often look for issues when guided by theory: hidden channels of aggression, sources of gratification, narcissistic injuries. If the "official" theory remains silent about death, one will not be on the lookout for it (Moreover, when practitioners do not look for death, the patients might adapt themselves, just as Freudian patients have Freudian dreams and Jungian patients have Jungian dreams. If death is not an important issue for therapists, it will be brought up less by patients).

This gains special importance from the fact that the role finitude plays in our life is not restricted to concrete manifestations of affect such as anxiety and depression. Death affects us in profound ways, as I shall show. It guides our global evaluation of life. It is a shadow behind our perspective on things, behind choices, behind our basic sense of presence in the world, behind our feelings and commitments. Concern about death is often something that operates silently, something fundamental to human existence, a question posed which precedes life, so to speak, and accompanies it. It is like a background to life, a basis on which psychic life is erected. As such, it does not always find direct concrete expression. Unless the theory says something about it, a substantial part of the most inner substrates of the psyche risks remaining in the dark.

We now come to the second objection. Some readers who practice psychoanalytic or psychodynamic therapy might contest the above characterization of the analytic attitude, and claim that in actual practice things look different, and never read the book as a result. Because that would be lamentable, let me look at this claim. They might argue that practitioners are well aware of death and its importance, and deal with it frequently. Death anxiety, so the argument goes, will not be attributed today to castration anxiety or treated in a reductionistic manner. A prominent analyst, whose opinion I highly respect, once told me that she believes death is brought up in every significant analysis, or rather should be brought up, and when it is not, this testifies to a flaw in the analysis.

My response to such claims is twofold. But first, let us note that this second objection directly opposes the first one, that death anxiety simply does not comprise a part of patients' complaints or experiences. Having heard or read both these kinds of objections from practicing analysts, this confusion, or unacknowledged point of disagreement—some find death prevalent and see it as part of analytic work, while others say it is not an issue in therapy—seems to me in itself already indicative.

The authentic claims of some analysts about their own practice should not be underestimated, and I will turn to them shortly. But overall, such claims should be accepted only to a limited degree. The tendency to reduce death anxiety to other issues (separation, castration, guilt) is still prevalent. In other cases, fear of death is not accounted for through castration anxiety, but other reductive or transforming tendencies are still at play. As we shall see, the ways in which death anxiety is not recognized for what it is are numerous and often much deeper and more subtle than the simple claim "death equals castration." The marginalizing-reductive approach to death is well rooted, and is, as I endeavor to show in this study, inherent to psychoanalytic thinking. The claim that the problem is already solved seems premature if it takes, as I believe, reading the analysis in this book to see how deep the problem is in the first place.

Returning to the claims of practitioners that they do deal with death in their work, I feel that this state of affairs further supports my criticism of psychoanalytic theory. That there is a difference and tension between the official theory and private theories of analysts has already been demonstrated (Sandler, 1983). Sandler even suggests the motivational role of non-instinctual anxiety, and of external threats that are not related to drives, as places where personal theories sharply differ from the official ones (p. 42), and one can probably include death anxiety among these issues. However, the fact that such a tension exists on such a large scale means that something is lacking in the theory. If, as some practitioners claim, their practice deviates from theoretical guidelines, what is the approach that guides them when they deal with the subject of death? Are they using another theory? Standard psychoanalytic theories regarding death do not account for the importance of death in people's lives, as we shall see. The few alternative psychoanalytic modes of understanding have not been accepted on a large scale. How many analysts have read Becker's (1973) *Denial of Death*, for example? How many of the ideas of the authors who have dealt with the topic have permeated instruction and training frameworks? The feeling of some analysts that they do deal with death extensively only serves to highlight further the fact that, on the theoretical level, there is a lacuna within psychoanalysis in all that regards death. This theoretical lack of reference is, of course, quickly transposed into the modes of thought of practitioners, students, candidates, and analysts, in such a way that one has to be particularly inclined toward questions of death to notice them in actual practice.[4] Once again then, the clinical objection leads us to the role of theory and to the need to carefully examine theory, a mission that this book undertakes.

At any rate, I think there is necessarily, in significant dynamic psychotherapy, an encounter of one kind or other with death's inevitability and life's limitedness. If there is a practical aspect to this theoretical study, it is to help prevent this encounter from being a missed one.

The structure of the book

More specifically, the book is structured as follows.

We begin, in Chapter 1 with an examination of Freud's overt claims against the psychic presence of death, and in support of the view that the fear of death is secondary. These arguments serve as the basis for the psychoanalytic conviction that death is not a significant psychic factor, and we shall examine their validity.

Chapter 2 briefly discusses Freud's approach to death in his private life, where death's importance seems to have played a greater role.

The Interpretation of Dreams occupies us in Chapters 3 and 4, where a close reading demonstrates how death repeatedly, stubbornly, and in various ways surfaces in Freud dreams. The example of Freud's own dreams and associations reveals that contrary to his claims elsewhere against death,

---

[4] Thus, the analyst just mentioned admitted that she was only beginning to become aware of death in recent years, with her own advancing age.

death is in fact abundant in the psychic world. Ignoring the issue of death would actually result in misunderstanding Freud's book.

In the fifth chapter, I examine Freud's theories on anxiety to determine whether they are constructed, even before they refer to death at all, in such a way that can accommodate death anxiety and acknowledge its importance.

A sixth chapter then deals with Freud's most important essay on death, "Thoughts for the Times on War and Death," which is often taken to reflect a more existential spirit. Through a close reading of this text, we see how self-contradictory it is, with reductionist and existentialist views locked in a struggle.

We then move to a seventh chapter where Freud's theory of the death drive is considered. Again, it seems that what could have been treated as an acknowledgment of the psychic importance of death, and indeed has been by many, is found to be yet another case of a profound denial of death, or defense against it.

Freud, I have said, alongside his suspicious approach toward death, has another position on it in which he deems it a central human concern. One site where this second position tends to appear is his cultural and literary texts, examined in Chapter 8, where he often treats death as significant. However, there too death does not find a home within analytic theory: alongside several poignant intuitions about death, where death is indeed considered as a central issue, Freud's reductive tendency is revealed to be no less active, albeit in more covert forms.

We then move on, in Chapter 9, to a survey of the psychoanalytic literature beyond Freud, and pinpoint the ways in which death is overlooked, dismissed, pathologized or constructed in a reductive manner. The problem, we shall see, goes beyond the specific denial of death's psychic importance. Citing examples from the literature, while also ascertaining a general picture, I show how embedded the refusal of death is in the analytic mode of thought.

The swing of attempted attention to death and falling into familiar traps continues well beyond Freud. Chapters 10 and 11 examine more thoroughly the ideas of some later psychoanalytic thinkers, focusing on those instances in which death is ostensibly ascribed the greater importance. The Kleinian school, it will be claimed, supposedly assigns death a cardinal place, but the ideas it has on death are merely a different manifestation of earlier reductive tendencies in Freud. As for Erikson and Kohut, Jung, and Winnicott, the theoretical place they seem to reserve for death or the fear of death is mitigated by newer, more sophisticated forms of reduction, which take the sting out of death. Different is the case of Lacanian theory (Chapter 11), where more than in any other major analytic school, death can really be said to be central and dealt with in a non-reductionistic manner. We shall question, however, whether something about death is not still lost in these ideas.

Chapter 12 examines several authors who have addressed the insufficient treatment of death in prior analytic understandings, particularly Becker, Lifton, Yalom, Hoffman, and Piven. Several models for the integration of death within a psychoanalytic perspective are discussed through these authors, as well as independently.

We then abandon textual analysis to ask, first, in Chapter 13, what are the underlying psychoanalytic premises or modes of thought that impede proper attention to death, and what, on the other hand, are those that might be more conducive to it.

In Chapter 14, we direct our attention to the more general influence of death in psychic life, insisting on how widespread, hidden, thorough, and continuously active death's presence is in life. The chapter aims to determine which ideas a psychological theory of death would have to face up to, if it wished to account for it, and offers some broad guidelines for how this can be done.

1 Against death: Freud and the question of death's psychic presence

The best place to begin our exploration of the analytic approach to death is where the cards are laid on the table: Freud's arguments as to why death is not of psychic significance. There are basically two kinds of claims: those concerning the representation of death, and claims about the fear of death. In the first case it is asserted that death, as a concept, idea, or phenomenon, has no access to the mind. Death, Freud says, cannot be represented and specifically so in the unconscious. The second line of argument explains the fear of death as something else. The two claims, of course, are part of one logical move: if there is no representation of death in the unconscious, then death cannot be a primary source of concern, and fear of death is hence secondary to other factors. We shall look closely at both positions. Arguments for the first, I will suggest, are either invalid or unnecessary. Statements of the second are also either unsound or unjustified, or they distort the phenomenon of death, constructing it in ways remote from the thing they wish to clarify.

The case against representation

The cornerstone of Freud's objection to the validity of the fear of death is his position regarding death's irrepresentability or unavailability to the mind. The more important statements concerning death's absence from the mind occur in three passages, one in "Thoughts for the Times on War and Death" (1915, pp. 289, 296–7), one in *The Ego and the Id* (1923, pp. 57–9), and one in *Inhibitions, Symptoms and Anxiety* (1926, pp. 129–30, 140).[1] These passages being relatively incidental (in two of the texts) we can skip formalities and begin *in medias res*, with the claims themselves.

---

[1] The discussion of "Thoughts for the Times" will be more partial, since the entire text is the focus of another chapter, and expresses a more complex position.

Freud uses six arguments to ground his claim. Four of them refer to the impossibility of death being part of the unconscious. "Death is [1] an abstract concept with [2] negative content," Freud (1923, p. 58) notes, and [3] it involves reference to time, while the unconscious, it is argued, cannot contain abstract or negative ideas, and time has no sway in it. A fourth argument, perhaps a summation of the previous three concerning time, negation, and abstractness, is that the fear of death has no correlative in instinctual or unconscious life. Taken together it means that, Freud concludes: "in the unconscious every one of us is convinced of his own immortality" (1915, p. 291). The fifth argument is empirical-developmental: we have never experienced anything like death, and, therefore, cannot grasp it. The sixth argument is philosophical: we cannot represent our own death because in trying to do so, we are always still left as spectators.

Let us examine each of these arguments, one by one, beginning with a brief discussion of the first three: the negative nature of death, the fact that death has to do with time, and death's abstractness. Yes, death is the negation of life, and is thus indeed a negative concept. Yet it is important to note that it is only as a concept that death is negative, only on an abstract level. First, from a psychological point of view, it is quite unclear in what sense exactly death can be said to be truly a negation, or to have negative logical attributes. The very notion of negativity as it relates to death, namely the idea that death is the logical negation of life, is itself a category that far exceeds the cognitive abilities attributed by Freud to the unconscious. It cannot, therefore, be a reason why the unconscious ignores death. Second, indeed, as something that occurs, death is not really a negation of life. It is also a state in itself, or it is an end, a cessation, something of which the unconscious can have a presentiment through experience.

The problem with speaking of death as a negation can be shown from a different angle: what actually, we may ask, is negated by death? Death might be a negation of life, but do we have a representation of life in the unconscious, or even the conscious mind, that can be negated by it? Alternatively, we can speak of death as negating who we are, the life that is ours, our identity—but do we have such an unconscious representation of ourselves, and will it not, if we posit such a representation, necessarily include a reference to time (itself, according to Freud, absent from the unconscious)?

Besides, is negation completely foreign to unconscious thought? In his paper on negation (1925), Freud, while reiterating his claim about the absence of negation from the unconscious, actually describes the way negation is already found at the level of "the oldest—the oral—instinctual impulses," as an act of ejection (by the pleasure-ego) (p. 237).[2]

Let us now move to the question of time. That there is no time in the unconscious according to Freud should hardly exclude death altogether from the unconscious. For although death is related to being in time, time is not essential to the concept of death itself as a state. Death can be conceived of as a state, without reference to time.

Freud at any rate, believes death is absent from the unconscious because it involves time. But is death really unique in involving time? Hoffman for example claims (1998, pp. 45–6) that there should not be any difference with regard to time between death anxiety and the anxieties of castration or object loss to which death anxiety should supposedly be reduced. In all three instances it is not enough to notice a loss to produce the anxiety: the idea of the permanence of the loss should equally be grasped. This permanence is impossible to imagine, for it is not a given in experience, and involves a cognitive leap, and this impossibility pertains to all three. Yet Freud insists on it only in the case of death anxiety.[3]

Actually, similar logic applies beyond the issue of permanence. In a sense, most wishes are related to time. There is a will to change a current situation; there is a recognition of the separateness of states. How can one be sorry for the loss of anything, any object, if it is not because there is some reference to a future, to time at some level? Wanting assumes time or futurity. One wants what one does not have or the prolongation of what one does have. Instincts themselves, says Matte Blanco (2005 [1973]), as processes, as movement, inherently involve time and thus run counter to the idea of the timeless unconscious (p. 1473).[4] In fact,

---

[2] One could also argue that at a certain level of description, all human drives are negation, in the sense that they transform nature and transcend it. This is the view of Hegel for example, for whom negation, in the above sense, is the essence of human desire. Or, if we take the analytic model of tension and discharge, how can one want to drink when thirsty without there being a negative side to it? One wants something that opposes or negates the current state of affairs.

[3] In light of these considerations and following Schimek's (1975) critique of Freud's theoretical premise that representations are originally formed through an unbiased registration of reality (presented below, footnote 6), Hoffman (1998. p. 45) contests the whole focus on the possibility of concrete representation in the unconscious as a criterion for the influence of death in the mind. Hoffman also argues that if unconscious processes are timeless as Freud claims, there could be no belief either in mortality or in immortality, for both require the notion of time, and therefore we can not be, as Freud claims, convinced of our immortality (pp. 34–5).

[4] Matte Blanco (2005 [1973]) has an interesting solution: the deep unconscious really has no time, and instincts are therefore absent from it as well. They are translations into higher levels of thought.

instincts also involve a span of time at a more intrinsic level: there is the time lapse between the tension and its discharge, a time lapse inherent to the instinctual demand itself. One does not only want discharge, but discharge preceded by tension: Wanting to drink is not wanting-not-to-be-thirsty. In addition, a drive refers to action and not only to a state of things. One does not want something to be so, but to do something. This is a process that involves recognition of time. If, then, the idea that time is completely absent from the unconscious had been strictly applied, much more would have been precluded from the unconscious than the mere idea of death.

To this we should also add the self-preservation instincts, which cling to life, and seem to involve a projection forward in time. We will turn to this issue shortly.

In fact, in a late revision, Freud himself (1933a [1932], p. 74) decides to attribute timelessness to the id rather than to the unconscious, yet this does not lead to a change in his views about death, nor in those of others who wrote about death basing themselves on him, as noted by Hoffman (1998, p. 40–1).

Regarding Freud's third argument, about the abstract nature of death, one may ask if death is more abstract than, let us say, castration, whose result might perhaps be a specific mutilation but which, as a threat, is abstract and formless.[5] Or to take another example, the sexual ideas of children are described by Freud as vague and abstract. The male child senses "obscure impulses" within him "to press in," "to tear open a hole somewhere," "impulsions which [he] cannot account for," yet he remains in "helpless perplexity" for lack of knowledge of the vagina (1908, p. 218; see also 1909, pp. 134–5). My claim is not that death is not abstract—in fact, concretizing it is sometimes used in analytic texts as a strategy to reduce it (see for example Hárnik, 1930, Brodsky, 1959, p. 108, Lewin, 1950, pp. 115–6, or Wahl 1959 [1958], p. 24)—but rather that this is not a consideration that bothers Freud in other contexts.[6]

---

[5] The comparison with castration, concerning abstractness, is of course related to Freud's fifth argument, tackled below, that nothing like death has ever been experienced, unlike the case of castration.

[6] In some of its aspects, however, and from an opposing angle, death is really not that abstract, but rather quite concrete. Death is when biological life stops, and it is difficult to imagine something more concrete than a dead body, especially if it was alive a minute ago.

The question of abstractness also brings up Freud's theory of representation in general; a theory that Schimek (1975) criticizes mainly for its premise that representations are originally formed through an unbiased, passive perception and registration of reality, an assumption that he believes does not stand up to contemporary ideas on perception.

The case against representation

Before moving on to Freud's fourth argument, I wish to make a point relevant to the three previous ones. A serious objection to Freud's claims against the psychic presence of death is that if death cannot be pictured in the unconscious, it cannot be represented in the case of the other's death either. Freud, however, denies the psychic presence of death only in one's own case, and specifically claims that the unconscious acknowledges death in the case of another person, the enemy, and indeed, that death is the only punishment the unconscious knows (1915, pp. 296–7).[7] He even states this in the same passage as his claims against death's representation, only lines away from them. Yet all the above arguments apply equally to the death of the other: death is no less negation, an abstract concept, or one that pertains to time, when it applies to an other than when it is our own death.

Freud's fourth argument, that "the unconscious seems to contain nothing that could give any content to our concept of the annihilation of life" (1926, pp. 129), or that "no unconscious correlative can be found" to it (1923, p. 58) could be seen, and so it is used by Freud, as a summary of the other statements. At one point, however, Freud phrases it differently, and perhaps intends something else: "there is nothing instinctual in us which responds to a belief in death" (1915, p. 296). The secret of acts of heroism, he adds, is that at bottom the unconscious does not believe in its death. It is worthwhile examining the claim concerning the absence of an instinctual correlative to death.

It is doubtful, first of all, what the historical status of the claim is, when in 1920 Freud posits a death drive, and thus something instinctual which responds, albeit in a complex manner, to a belief in death. Indeed, this argument (put in terms of instinct) is missing from the 1923 and 1926 passages.[8]

While on the subject of the death drive, it should also be noted that most of the other arguments as well are thrown into question by that concept. As two of the passages we are dealing with are later than its formulation (1923 and 1926), it is puzzling how these arguments could have been made with no reference to it in the first place, and it is unclear

---

Freud's grounding of his theoretical reference to death's psychic influence in the notion of representation is therefore problematic in that it rests on an outmoded epistemology.

[7] The dynamics (e.g., narcissism, externalization of aggression) that supposedly lead to this representation of the other's death are irrelevant; what matters here is that Freud judges this representation possible whereas his own arguments should have precluded it, or alternatively, the existence of such a representation should have led to a reconsideration of the arguments.

[8] The variation of the claim in Freud's text of 1926, the requirement of involvement of "the deeper levels of the mental apparatus" and of sexuality (p. 129) is discussed below.

to what extent Freud actually stands behind them.[9] Is there for example really nothing negative now in the unconscious?

Reflections on the death instinct aside, Freud's own thoughts on what lies in the unconscious should have allowed him more space. Just before the phrase on "nothing instinctual in us which responds to a belief in death" he defines the unconscious as "made of instinctual impulses" (1915, p. 296), and accordingly, death cannot be part of the unconscious. And yet obviously Freud always attributed to the unconscious a variety of contents other then instinctual impulses per se, from repressed memories, to internalized objects, aspects of reality that we prefer not to recognize, and unexperienced traumas. In his later work, he speaks of the disavowal of parts of reality (1940 [1938], pp. 202–4),[10] a notion that could have served as a theoretical mode of explanation for the attitude to death, but did not (Hoffman, 1998, p. 36; Piven, 2004, pp. 23–4). As a matter of fact, ideas about the disregard and distortion of reality can be found quite early in Freud (1901, pp. 227–9, for example).[11] The important thing is that while elsewhere, in his early writings on dreams or the psychopathology of everyday life for example, Freud applies his theoretical model with a certain ease to the phenomena, leaving a space between the "official" theoretical requirement and its application to clinical matters, here, in the case of death, he demands the strictest and most literal adherence to the instinctual explanatory model.

Among unconscious contents there is one of specific importance for our discussion, namely annihilation. Hurvich (2003, pp. 591–2) for example stresses that concerns about annihilation can form part of unconscious fantasies, and that the latter are not limited to wishes of a sexual or aggressive nature, as is often suggested in the literature.

With regard to death as something that is not instinctual, Freud (1915, p. 296) notes that, in contrast to our own death, we acknowledge the death of others, and that the instinctual element which responds to that belief is found in the wish for the death of the other. Yet not only, as was claimed above, does grasping the other's death involve the same problems that pertain to one's own, but we can also find an equivalent of the "instinctual" element—the death wish toward the other—in death

---

[9] Although, of course, there is a difference between a tendency in the organism to reduce tension to zero, or to unbinding – two linkages between death instinct and death – and a psychic representation of death.

[10] Although even here he still holds that the basis of the disavowal is instinctual, the example being the disavowal of the female lack of penis in the case of fetishism.

[11] As psychoanalysis develops, the list of unconscious contents grows much larger and varies according to schools.

wishes toward the self, which are well recognized by Freudian theory, and could meet the requirement for an instinctual basis for the belief in our own death.

But beyond death instincts and death wishes, the Freudian system contains a very simple instinctual correlative of the fear of death in the instincts of self-preservation. The organism wishes to continue existing, and the threat from without is antagonistic to this desire. Beyond purely somatic experience, wishing to exist testifies to a recognition of the possibility of non-existence, and moreover, not in an abstract sense, but as a concrete possibility.[12]

It is a simple answer, and Freud is aware of it. His reluctance to accept it is worth examining. Freud's consideration of death in *Inhibitions, Symptoms and Anxiety* actually begins with the possibility that war neurosis ensues from a direct exposure to danger. Freud says that some may use it to counter his theory of sexuality as the basis of neurosis, but that this is misguided, because the instincts of self-preservation are themselves libidinal, in that they are a form of narcissistic cathexis. Freud opposes the possibility that the "objective presence of danger" can lead to neurosis, "without any participation of the deeper levels of the mental apparatus" (1926, p. 129). Yet this immediately follows his recognition of the instincts of self-preservation, and moreover, his insistence that they *are* sexual. Thus, he already has this instinctual basis, this participation of "deeper levels," at hand, but wants something else. This relates, I think, to a limitation Freud has in recognizing a certain dimension of existence which does not involve activity in the ego or the notion of past and is related to the wish of the organism to simply live on. We will discuss this problem further in Chapter 5.

If we look at the problem from the opposite direction, what appears to be at issue here, beyond the reluctance to admit death into the system, is the instinctual expression of desires, which, according to the theory, cannot form part of the contents of the unconscious. A death instinct is posited, yet death is supposedly not part of the unconscious. Ego instincts of self-preservation are suggested, but almost without explanation for the wish of the unconscious to simply live, to prolong its existence. Similarly, in the sexual domain, there is a difficulty in that the sexual instinct in the male child is directed toward an aim that is incongruous with his lack of knowledge of his mother's anatomy.

---

[12] Zilboorg (1943, p. 467) sees the fear of death as the affective aspect of self-preservation. The organism expends a great amount of psychological energy to stay alive, and this is because it is always exposed, albeit not consciously, to fear of death. See also Rheingold (1967, p. 64)

As described above, the boy's infantile unconscious does not know of the vagina, yet he has impulses to penetrate and have intercourse with his mother. There is a discordance between what are considered on the one hand as unconscious contents, and on the other as instinctual desires.[13]

In sum, it is doubtful whether Freud can really use the demand for a direct correspondence of instincts and unconscious contents as a condition for psychic presence, because there are, in his own theory, both instincts without an equivalent content and contents without an equivalent instinct.

Freud's fifth argument is that nothing like death has ever been experienced, and, therefore, it cannot be a content of the unconscious:

> [T]he unconscious seems to contain nothing that could give any content to our concept of the annihilation of life. Castration can be pictured on the basis of the daily experience of the faeces being separated from the body or on the basis of losing the mother's breast at weaning. But nothing resembling death can ever have been experienced; or if it has, as in fainting, it has left no observable traces behind. I am therefore inclined to adhere to the view that the fear of death should be regarded as analogous to the fear of castration. (1926, pp. 129–30)

Several points should be made. First, the argument itself, that in order for something to be a content of the unconscious something like it should have been experienced, is strange. It is not a standard claim in psychoanalysis. Although the notion of anticipation is fundamental to the psychoanalytic worldview—the finding of the object is the re-finding of it, and transference shows how the emotional world repeats prior experiences—these notions, like the rest of Freud's views, are based on the power of fantasy, and on the mutability of experiences. It is not that the male analyst really resembles the mother. It is enough that a specific, marginal aspect or trait of him reminds the patient of her. That Freud here, in the context of his discussion of death, insists on a precise resemblance of experience is unusual. The implication of this would be that mental life is very limited in the kind of displacement and free play it can create, that the reality of objects or perceptions is more important

---

[13] In "On the sexual theories of children" (Freud, 1908, p. 218) and in the case of little Hans (1909, pp. 134–5), one can see both an Oedipal wish that includes intercourse with the mother and penetrative impulses, and conversely, an insistence on the unavailability of knowledge about women's genitals to the little boy. Chasseguet Smirgel (1988) notices the existence of these impulses and the discrepancy, and uses the latter to claim that the theory of phallic monism is the result of repression or a split rather than of lack of knowledge. More than a question of acquired knowledge about the vagina, the absence of such a content from the unconscious is probably related to an unconscious refusal to acknowledge anatomical difference. This reversal can be applied to death as well, where it seems to be a case of not wanting to know, rather than a structural absence from the unconscious.

than the work of the mind. This of course would be to undermine much of the analytic structure, and it makes Freud's claim here unconvincing, *from a psychoanalytic point of view.*

But suppose we accept the criterion of earlier experience. The counterexample of fainting (and sleep, which is not mentioned) is obvious, and Freud quickly adds, as if to refute it, that fainting does not leave traces, another ad hoc criterion against the representation of death. Yet even if we accept the requirement of an earlier experience, one can question the notion of resemblance. Is separation from feces or the breast really closer to castration than fainting or even sleep is to death?[14]

Another variation of the lack of prior experience argument insists on the factor of age.

Children know nothing of the horrors of corruption, of freezing in the ice-cold grave, of the terrors of eternal nothingness—ideas which grown-up people find it so hard to tolerate, as is proved by all the myths of a future life. The fear of death has no meaning to a child. (Freud, 1900, p. 254)

In addition to the empirical question of whether Freud is right in describing the child's idea of death (see Anthony, 1971, and Yalom, 1980, pp. 75–109), it is questionable whether this argument can be adequately wielded against the influence of death in the mind, as it is almost self-refuting. Piven comments accurately that if children do not know of "freezing in the ice-cold grave," it is almost directly suggested that adults do know about it (2004, p. 22).

It is interesting to note how even in Freud's characterization here of children's lack of knowledge of death one can already make out a defensive position. "The horrors of corruption," and "freezing in the ice-cold grave," both relate to what happens after death rather than to the fact of having to die. These images, Freud suggests, are hard to tolerate even for adults, and that is why myths of afterlife were devised. An afterlife, then, is a myth to help assuage tormenting fears. Yet amusingly, the fears or experiences Freud mentions, themselves actually presuppose a life after death. To feel the coldness of the grave, the horrors of corruption, or eternal nothingness one has after all to be there to experience them. And if one is there, one is really not dead as such. So it seems that death is not really admitted in this description, which, although it is probably only a case of Freud getting carried away by a metaphor, is still significant in what it says and what it does not say.

---

[14] It is worthwhile noting that in Freud's 1926 citation he talks of analogy ("als Analogon," Freud, G. W., XIV, p. 160), and although it is clear he means "reducible to" or "a derivative of" (1915, p. 296; 1923, p. 58), the idea that the two entities are analogous does not establish either a timeline or a hierarchical relation.

The desiring machine (hits the wall of reality)

Before embarking on a consideration of Freud's sixth, philosophical, argument against the representation of death, an argument of a different nature, let us first draw some conclusions from what we have seen so far.[15]

At bottom, Freud's claims against the presence of death in the mind are simply unconvincing. Sometimes they are unsound, sometimes they seem ad hoc, sometimes they do not appear to reflect concerns that should have occupied Freud, and occasionally a plausible answer seems to have been at Freud's finger tips, had he only wanted it. The arguments discussed above seem more to be part of an attempt to justify a broader theoretical stance—that the fear of death is not a dominant psychic factor—a stance that precedes the arguments rather than emanates from them.[16]

For some critics of the analytic approach to death (Zilboorg, 1943; Becker, 1973; Yalom, 1980; Hoffman, 1998; Piven, 2004), human avoidance of death is clearly motivated by an acknowledgment of death at the deepest levels of our mind. Hoffman (1998) for example, commenting on Freud's arguments against the presence of death in the unconscious, finds that "the language of cognitive limitation is hopelessly entangled with the language of defensive avoidance" (p. 35). It seems to him less that within the unconscious there lies a deep-seated belief in immortality than that the unconscious is very much aware of death, and that consciously and defensively we retain a belief in immortality.

---

[15] One might object to the focus here on the issue of representation, in that I do not give enough importance to the link between Freud's ideas on representation and the instincts: namely the notion that representation is how the drives become known and available to awareness, as derivatives, and the idea that representation is biased by the drives and never simple. But note, first, that Freud does not refer to this more specifically analytic notion of representation, turning instead to standard notions of representation, and evoking for example "a *belief* in death," or "our *concept* of the annihilation of life." Second, and from the opposite direction, Freud's analytic notion of representation is in a sense precisely the problem for him. It is through that very drive-biased representation model that, we shall soon see, he finds he cannot account for death's psychic presence. This is why he says that fear of death "presents a difficult problem to psychoanalysis" (1923, p. 58).

[16] Interesting in this regard is Freud's need to accumulate arguments. If the claims concerning timelessness and lack of abstraction and negation in the unconscious are really what troubles him, and these are the ones most often cited, why does he feel the need to add the claim about prior experience and the philosophical spectators argument?

The case against representation

One could interpret Freud's attitude toward death as a logical result of his premises. Death does not exist in the unconscious, because it is negative, abstract, and involves reference to time. It might play a role in conscious thought, but conscious motives are not the important ones in Freud's view. Therefore, death concerns are not psychically significant. Yet, of course, such a way of looking at things fails to explain anything; it fails to explain why those premises about psychic life—and actually about death too—were adopted in the first place, why alternative theoretical frameworks Freud had at his disposal were insulated from this attitude and why Freud's explicit position remained unaltered throughout the many years of his life's work, in contrast to his constant changes of mind on other issues, especially given the shaky ground upon which it stood.

An example of something that could have been modified concerns the instincts of self-preservation. I have mentioned them as an element within Freud's theory that could have been used as a vehicle for a discussion of death. The theory concerning ego instincts, of which self-preservation is one, was revised several times in Freud's work. In none of the versions was self-preservation given serious consideration. While in the beginning, the ego instincts were identified with the need for self-preservation, hunger being the prototype of such an instinct, they were severely neglected in comparison to the sexual instincts, their counterpart. Moreover, in later reconceptualizations (see Bibring, 1941 for an ample discussion), self-preservation was minimized in favor of aggression. Freud's difficulty in arriving at a satisfactory result on the question of the counterpart to the sexual instincts—the duality of the instinctual world being one of the most fundamental issues for him—is perhaps another consequence of his lack of willingness to take death seriously. More importantly, however, it could have served him as an indication of a problem in the theory that needed to be addressed.

In a sense, even if some of the arguments are open to dispute, it seems we can understand what Freud has in mind when he claims that there is no place for death in the unconscious. He seems to be thinking of something like a pure id experience, which consists solely of wanting. This most archetypal of psychic structures lives in a continuous present, is totally oriented toward the aim of desire, and is focused on immediate discharge (Pollock, 1971b, p. 438), and as such knows no negativity. In such an entity, Freud says, there can be no fear of death. My claim is that all this hardly precludes death's psychic presence, because both in Freud's own view and the views of later psychoanalysts, the psyche consists of much more. The purely desiring entity is but one part of our psychic construction and does not even make up the entire unconscious world.

Moreover, negation is implicit even in pure wanting. When something is desired, it is because of its absence in oneself. One wants what one does not have. When one desires the prolongation of a current state of affairs, it is this future that one does not have. Even the pure id experience is not as whole and total as it sounds. Such experience is differentiated from something else. Insufficiency and logical negation are directly involved.

Of particular interest here is the interaction between this desiring machine and reality. We can extend this desirous entity to the longing for something absolute, infinite: absolute power, absolute life, absolute control of reality. Maybe in saying that in our unconscious we are all immortal Freud means that we wish to be so. Reality, then, creates suffering because it necessarily frustrates these demands: "[T]he most touchy point in the narcissistic system, the immortality of the ego, ... is so hard pressed by reality" (Freud, 1914, p. 91). Against these demands for the absolute, reality sets limits—to our control, to our power, to our life. This is the source of misery, of the construction of the psyche, of conflict, repression, and development. In the case of death, even on the level of the perception of the threat of annihilation, reality is always part of the psychic equation, as is the case with every analytic discussion of unconscious phenomena.

If libido is so central for Freud, why did he avoid acknowledging theoretically the most fundamental, inevitable frustration of the libido, which awaits all of us?

The I of the beholder

We now come to the sixth and final argument against the representation of death, Freud's philosophical assertion concerning death's psychical presence:

> It is indeed impossible to imagine our own death; and whenever we attempt to do so we can perceive that we are in fact still present as spectators. Hence the psychoanalytic school could venture on the assertion that at bottom no one believes in his own death, or, to put the same thing in another way, that in the unconscious every one of us is convinced of his own immortality. (Freud, 1915, p. 291)

The basic claim, that death, our death, is ungraspable, has been made repeatedly in philosophy. Freud's variation of the argument is built like the Cartesian *cogito*: I think, therefore, I am. Try as one might to shake oneself free of oneself, one will not be able to get rid of one's presence as carrier of that very effort; trying to imagine ourselves dead still assumes that we are alive.

The argument creates a split within the personality. One attempts to imagine oneself dead, but is very alive in doing so. One cannot be both the object and the subject of the thought at the same time, when being an object means being a dead one. The self is presented as a spectator (*Zuschauer*), with all the distance this position entails between the one that sees and the objects of his or her perception.

While some authors find this argument to be flawed (Edwards, 1967), or naïve (Hoffman, 1998, p. 37) their conclusions seem premature. The argument is in fact quite powerful. There is a special problem with one's own death, something totally ungraspable in it. What we should consider first, however, is how significant this philosophical argument is for Freud.

One question is how such an argument is compatible with Freud's view, developed in *The Ego and the Id* (1923, p. 57), that what the ego fears in anxiety is annihilation. The argument seems no less valid for annihilation than it is for death: if one cannot fear one's demise because one cannot think of it without being present, in what sense can annihilation be the ultimate threat?

Note that the argument concerns more the possibility of death in the conscious mind than the unconscious mind. It deals with what we can imagine and what we perceive. As Hoffman (1998, p. 34) comments, while the first part of the argument concerns conscious cognitive limitations, the conclusion asserts that there is no death in the unconscious. Freud's swift move between the two parts ("to put the same thing in another way") is unjustified.

However, the problem Freud refers to is not a mere cognitive limitation. It posits consciousness as the problem in itself: grasping death is a problem because consciousness always remains, because we are always also spectators. The argument is based precisely on the centrality of the conscious mind. Beyond the fact that it is a philosophical argument, one is probably justified in asking to what extent it fits the general Freudian scheme.

But perhaps we should take a step back to see what is really at stake. The problem here is different from that of trying to imagine, say, a very big number. What Freud insists on here is that our acknowledgment of death must in some way remain superficial. He says that we readily admit to it but we do not believe it. The problem he poses is that death is inaccessible to the mind. Death slides on the mind like oil on water and cannot penetrate its deeper levels.

Death, Freud is saying, is incompatible with one's subjectivity, and as such, is ungraspable. When claiming that "at bottom no one believes in his own death" (1915, p. 291), "belief" is perhaps a misleading choice of word: If what is at stake is the possibility of imagining death, then the problem is that one cannot even pose the question of one's mortality. One simply does not understand what death is. The claim amounts to a difficulty within life, within subjectivity, of entertaining the idea of a world without oneself.

The philosophical argument is different from the others in that it expresses a problem that has to do specifically with *one's own* death. It does not exist when it comes to the death of another. The claim made earlier that if death cannot be pictured in the unconscious, it is equally irrepresentable in the case of the other, is not valid here. The value of this last argument is exactly that it highlights the uniqueness of one's own death. We consider it, but then forget that we will really no longer exist when we die.

Thus, the only strong argument in Freud's quiver is one that does not deal with the unconscious at all. The only strong position against admission of death in psychoanalysis is not a psychoanalytic one and does not pertain to anything specific to psychoanalysis.[17] It has to do with the wider difficulty of integrating death within subjectivity. That in itself is a reason to put in question some widespread convictions about why death could not be a theoretical element in psychoanalysis. It also allows for a broadening of our perspective in the attempt to think about death's psychic presence and its psychoanalytic implications.

Perhaps, the way out of Freud's paradox is to question his basic assumption, not explicitly stated, that death is given to us through reflection, and that we must grasp it, imagine it, and represent it. If we fail to conceptualize death, it is destined to remain unavailable to us. Yet there are other, more direct and immediate, possibilities; the appropriation of the fact that one dies seems to occur more through direct affective channels. Death could be available in states of mind, exposure to death, or the mediation of another's death. It can be highly present to us when it penetrates our world. Reflection on death is not necessarily the crucial factor.

Death can have an impact on us through its influence on other psychic elements, in its effecting the rest of psychic life. This would actually be a more psychoanalytic way to think about death, in that it puts the stress on links between different psychic elements.

Death can also influence us through the very lack of clear and stable representation. Death's resistance to representation is precisely what makes it, in my view, so influential in psychic life. Death operates

---

[17] In another paper I discuss Freud's argument alongside the ideas of George Bataille on a similar paradox in Hegel (Razinsky, 2009).

precisely as a kind of unknown, an absurdity, a nothingness. It is the absence of a clear imaginable object that makes death such a persistent trigger of dread and alertness, a source of psychic work, rather than something that precludes it. This absence is not a simple, neutral inexistence: we know that we do not know; we know something is missing.

Moreover, the attempt to cognitively grasp death, to clothe it with sense, distorts the idea of death in some way. The cognitive attempt does not mean grasping death itself, but rather death-as-meaningful (Razinsky, 2009, p. 83), and this is where part of the problem lies. In a way, if we were able to represent it, death would no longer be death, but something else. To know death is not to know it. As Weber puts it, "[t]o "think" of death in this way, as representation, is to idealize it," "to transform it into a spectacle and ourselves into spectators" (1997, p. 97).

I mentioned earlier that we have no representation of life, one that could, therefore, be negated by death. But we do have an apprehension of the possibility of annihilation. On various levels, our identity, our feeling of ourselves, our going-on being, and even to some extent our consciousness, not to mention our self-preservative instincts, are all threatened by the possibility of death. A threat to these aspects of ourselves is enough to give a presentiment of death. If what is negated are not representations, there need not be a representation to negate them—merely a threat, and this is something that is very well accessible to us, in the form of fear of annihilation.

Heidegger (1996 [1927], pp. 224–31, 241–2) argues that to think of one's death as a thing is misguided. Death is a possibility, never a finished product, which one can ponder. This, he says, makes death accessible to us only through its linkage to our lives. There is no point in trying to ponder it, as it were, separately, because it is a possibility that belongs to oneself. It is not a question of death's existence or being, but rather of one's own. We exist as beings who will one day cease to exist. One never actually asks about death except in the context of questions about life—mortal life, finite life, whose end is necessarily death.

And yet the very *attempt* to grasp death cognitively is nevertheless already part of the solution. Whether death is available to us or not, the important thing is that we attempt to come closer to it, to bring it into our thoughts. To leave it outside our mental life has too high a price. I will come back to this point in the concluding chapter.

Death can also have a profound impact upon us even when only dimly understood. Even when we do not believe in it at bottom, or when we resist such knowledge, it has some hold on us, and this hold can be manifested in much of what we do or think, much more perhaps than we are willing to acknowledge. Even a vague awareness of death changes fundamental aspects of our experience and approach to life.

Death is undoubtedly difficult to grasp, and this difficulty is part of what shapes our attitude to it. Freud's philosophical argument about remaining a spectator captures some of the turmoil we run into when we try to figure out death for ourselves. But death's resistance to representation gives it a heavy influence in psychic life. We will return to this line of thought in the last chapter, but we should perhaps keep it in mind in reading the following part, which discusses Freud's shift from the impossibility of representation to the marginality of the fear of death.

The case against fear

If death has no representation in the mind, no psychic presence, then the fear of it would not have much importance, and would not be primary. This seems to be the gist of Freud's arguments against the psychic presence of death. Thus, in the three passages we will deal with here, where he puts forth his position on death, fear of death is said to be "something secondary ... usually the outcome of a sense of guilt" (1915, 297), a derivative of the fear of castration (1926, pp. 129–30), that is, a variation of the fear of the superego (p. 140) or the feeling of being deserted by it (1923, p. 58).[18]

Such explicit rejections of death's direct psychic influence are critical junction points where the analytic approach to death is shaped and we need, therefore, to study them closely. In doing so, we will also look at the kind of conceptualization of death that is implied by them. What we need to ask is whether fear of death is indeed explained by Freud, and whether the entire move of rejection is justified. Before we do so, however, let us note that to many, the very idea that fear of death is reducible to castration anxiety seems untenable. There is a pervasive intuition, among both classic psychoanalysts and existentially minded authors, that fear of death is the primary fear, and that castration anxiety is a secondary manifestation or transformation of it (Chadwick, 1973 [1929]; Klein, 1948, p. 117; Money-Kyrle, 1957, pp. 501–2; Brown, 1959, pp. 114–20; Rosenthal, 1973a [1963], pp. 171–2; Stern, 1968b; Becker, 1973; Meyer, 1975 [1973], pp. 9–10, 23–30; Lifton, 1979, pp. 48–9, 214–5; Yalom, 1980; Bronfen, 1992, pp. 34, 54; Eigen, 1995, p. 280; Hurvich, 2003). Even

---

[18] I follow Freud in using "fear" and "anxiety" almost synonymously in discussing death. As Choron (1972 [1964], p. 208) notes, although Freud distinguishes fear (*Furcht*) and anxiety (*Angst*), he uses them indiscriminately when it comes to death.

The case against fear

within psychoanalytic terminology, the alternative to Freud's view is easily conceivable and is probably more intuitive.

Chadwick for instance believes castration may represent the loss of self, the male ego being identified with the penis (1973 [1929], pp. 75–6). Stern (1968a, p. 25) suggests castration anxiety might be defensive, warding off and displacing the fear of death, and according to Rosenthal (1973a [1963], pp. 171–2), castration is only a partial loss, while death is a total loss.

Becker gives the broadest formulation: "The horror of castration is not the horror of punishment for incestuous sexuality, the threat of the Oedipus complex; it is rather the existential anxiety of life and death finding its focus on the animal body" (1973, pp. 223–4).[19]

For Freud, however, fear of death is secondary to other issues. What needs to be examined first is the logical status of this position as a necessary conclusion. If, according to analytic theory, death cannot be part of the unconscious, as Freud puts it, and if fear of death in fact exists, then it must be ascribed to something else, namely guilt, castration anxiety, or fear of the superego, or of being deserted by it. Yet, of course, there is no real deduction here. Freud recognizes the existence of the phenomenon he seeks to explain, the fear of death. If something in the theory prevents him from accounting for it, namely that he presumes death cannot be represented by the unconscious, he could have chosen other courses of action. He could have, for example, questioned some of his premises, such as the idea that *every* important psychic element comes from the unconscious, that *every* fear has its roots there. Or, as I suggested, he could have proposed that the lack of psychic presence might be exactly what is responsible for this fear. Alternatively, the assumption that there is a fear of death with no corresponding unconscious presence could have been a riddle to be solved. Something important cannot be explained: the influence death has on us, or the phenomenon of the fear of death. If the unconscious ignores time, and cannot grasp death, then perhaps unconscious involvement is an insufficient explanation for all of psychic life after all. The analytic theory of Freud's time is perhaps limited in its ability to encompass more holistic issues, issues that involve a more conscious mode of thought, that involve cognitive abilities and secondary processes, that necessitate

---

[19] Although these critiques are important, we shall see later that psychoanalytic theory's problem with death goes much deeper than the question of what is to be reduced to what, death to castration or castration to death. The problem is seen, for example, in the fact that even among authors who see castration as a derivative of the fear of death, some retain the tendency to reduce death, only in different ways.

knowledge that is not available at birth, namely, the fact that everyone dies, all issues that are part of psychic life as well. The question of death and the difficulty accounting for it could have been both an internal motive for change and development within Freud's psychoanalysis, and a test case for its limits.

In any case, nothing logically compels Freud to conclude from the absence of death in the unconscious that fear of death is something else, or that it is secondary. This is evident, for example, in the fact that the specific details are not deduced logically: fear of death exists, but death in the unconscious does not. So the former must be secondary—but secondary to what? To which of the elements of the unconscious? Freud offers more than one possibility. These possibilities are interconnected but not identical. Some of Freud's followers have added other possibilities, to which unconscious element death can be reduced (see Chapter 9). Examples include fear of orgasm (Fenichel, 1945, pp. 208–9, 544; Keiser, 1952), "fear of a state where the usual conceptions of time are invalid" (Fenichel, 1945, 285), a concrete fear of suffocation (Hárnik, 1930), or the "dread of turning into feces" (Brodsky, 1959, p. 108). The arbitrariness with which this element is determined puts the justification of the deduction in doubt.

Another, related problem is involved: the reduction does not necessarily supply us with an explanation. If we fear death, and yet simply cannot believe in it in the unconscious, the explanation that it is secondary will not help. How do we fear it at all, as primary or as derivative? We think we fear death, Freud might say, but we actually fear something else. Yet he recognizes an experience of fear that has death as its specific object, and hence should explain why our fear is so centrally directed to it. Why, even if all that talk of death by people is hot air, does it deal specifically with death, and not with say, little marshmallow men? Why does the fact that we humans die get so much of our attention? There is a shift, which remains unclear, from the "something else" in the unconscious to a conscious death fear. They are not the same. In addition, Freud believes that even on the conscious level, we are incapable of grasping death (the spectators argument). So how is fear of death explained as a fact of consciousness, even allowing that something else supposedly lies behind it?[20]

The reduction of death anxiety to earlier anxieties is not so much the conclusion of an argument as it is a position Freud simply holds, and as I shall claim, one bound up with much of psychoanalytic thought. For

---

[20] These claims apply, to some extent, to other issues, such as morality, and are not unique to the issue of death.

example, in *Inhibitions, Symptoms and Anxiety*, Freud (1926, pp. 138–40) proposes a developmental theory of anxiety, where the determinant of anxiety changes with every developmental phase. It is within this context that he speaks of death anxiety as a transformation of the fear of the superego. The main point is that fear of death is reducible to fear of the superego, to castration anxiety (p. 130), and is not primary. And yet if the different transformations of anxiety are reducible to each other, if what is later is never primary, then the same logic should have been applied to castration itself. Castration too, Freud says, is a transformation of an earlier anxiety, and can be traced to separation from the mother (p. 139, 151). Yet in Freud's theory, this fact, the idea that castration has a history, a prior development, does not change anything regarding its status. As late as 1937, Freud considers it the bedrock of psychic functioning (Freud, 1937, pp. 250–2).[21] In the case of death, by contrast, this history serves to render death anxiety secondary. Thus, regarding death, what is earlier is more important; regarding castration, although it too has anticipations, what is important is the later formation, castration, which is really a significant nodal point in itself.

The 1923 discussion of death (pp. 57–9) immediately follows, in Freud's text, an attempt at specifying the response of the ego to anxiety. Now, animals often flee when they feel their lives are under threat. Could it be that what the ego fears in anxiety is its extinction? Actually, Freud tends here to agree: what the ego fears, in external or libidinal danger, "cannot be specified," but "we know that the fear is of being overwhelmed or annihilated" (p. 57). And then a second reservation: "but it cannot be grasped analytically." "On the other hand," Freud continues, "we can tell what is hidden behind the ego's dread of the super-ego," by which he means, of course, castration (p. 57). In the next paragraph, he claims that fear of death is between ego and superego, and is actually a later incarnation of the fear of castration. The logic of the argument exhibits the nature of the problem. What it is that the ego fears (death! annihilation!) we cannot know or accommodate. It might be being overwhelmed, or annihilation, but we cannot grasp it analytically. However, we can grasp other kinds of fear, like fear of castration. Would it not be easier to grasp things "analytically" if we were to construe fear of death as fear of castration? There is a joke about a man looking for a key under a street light. "Did you lose it here?" someone asks him. "No," he replies, "a bit further down the street, but here there is light." This

---

[21] Freud (1909, pp. 8–9n, a comment added in 1923) stresses the independence of castration and its relation specifically to the loss of the penis, with regard to earlier anticipations.

seems to be what Freud does. A problem that is difficult to grasp is replaced by a problem analytic theory does know how to handle, even acknowledging this will not provide the sought for answer.

Freud (1923) follows up the above passage with a surprising new one that starts with: "The high-sounding phrase, 'every fear is ultimately the fear of death,' has hardly any meaning, and at any rate cannot be justified" (p. 57). Death abruptly barges in. The statement seems to come out of the blue; nothing has called for it. Unless, that is, something compels Freud to raise the issue of the fear of death at that specific point. As if he knows very well what it is that "could not be specified" or "grasped analytically." The whole dynamic here recalls the one described in "On Negation" (1925, p. 235): "Who was this figure in the dream? Certainly not my mother." Anyway, once such an antithetical view has snuck in, it must be refuted. So, it "has hardly any meaning." Yet Freud then seems to reconsider the accuracy of such a remark, adding the argument: "and at any rate cannot be justified."

Freud then begins his discussion of the fear of death, but admits "it presents a difficult problem to psychoanalysis," because death is abstract, and negative, and has no unconscious correlative (1923, p. 58). However, the text then seems to entirely negate it as a real phenomenon, and renders it instead something between the ego and the superego, a case of disturbance in libidinal cathexis (we shall turn to this subject shortly). What "presents a difficult problem to psychoanalysis" no longer does so, because it is reconceptualized in analytic terms which may enable its discussion, but strip it of much of its essence.

Freud claims that the mechanism of fear of death "can only be" that the ego gives up a great deal of its narcissistic libidinal cathexis, "gives up itself, just as it gives up some *external* object in other cases in which it feels anxiety" (1923, p. 58, emphasis in the original). It is enough to ponder death for a moment, to realize the oddness of such a contention, and the extent to which death itself—death as an external event, as an ultimate danger to the self—is denied. Fear of death in this description is a willing action of the ego, an internal event, related to the love of the ego for itself. It is as if the mechanism of life depended completely upon a constant fueling of libidinal energy, and when the fueling ceases, one dies. Not that this is not the case—it might be true that some such cathexis is needed to endure the struggles of life—but it is certainly not the only thing needed to prolong life, and in most cases, death comes to the individual from the outside. The contention is all the more remarkable when what we have in mind is temporal finitude on a more abstract level. It is a very peculiar position to construct our eventual demise as depending on ourselves; it is indeed a rather narcissistic position to construe it as a matter of narcissism. Of course, Freud is speaking about the fear of death, and not about death itself, as depending on the ego, but his description of the fear negates the impact of death. There is, after all, the possibility that people are afraid because they know they will die someday, or feel threatened at this very moment.[22]

Fear of death can arise, Freud continues, as a response to either an external threat or an internal process; the example of the latter he provides is melancholia. He explains what happens in melancholia, and extrapolates the explanation to the case of external danger. "The neurotic manifestation," Freud suggests, will help to explain the normal one. In melancholia, the ego feels deserted by the superego, and because living for it means being loved (by the superego), losing the latter's love is a death sentence. Analogically, when the ego faces "an excessive real danger," which it is "unable to overcome by its own strength," it "draw[s] the same conclusion": it feels abandoned by the superego and "lets itself die." The same situation underlies separation anxiety and anxiety at birth (1923, p. 58).

Freud acknowledges the existence of the fear of death in melancholia and in external danger.[23] However, what he describes in both cases is a fear of a symbolic, affective death—"If you do not love me, I will die"— rather than of real death.

Taking a look at how fear of death is constructed in Freud's presentation, we can see that fear of death is:

1. An internal affair. Even in the case of external danger, the fear is not because of the danger, but a result of the feeling of being deserted by the one whom the ego has put its trust in.
2. An act of volition. The ego draws conclusions, "gives itself up," and "lets itself die." Fear of death is a choice.
3. A result of defeatism. The ego gives up and does not fight, reframing the dangerous situation as one it cannot overcome by itself—it is as if Freud is reproaching a disobedient or cowardly soldier. The tone is critical and judgmental. Fear of death is a result of lack of will, lack of motivation to fight, or softness.

---

[22] Note in passing Freud's claim for the exclusivity of his explanation: "the mechanism of the fear of death can only be that ... " (1923, p. 58). Freud is not offering us one possibility among many for the formation of the fear of death, but rather presents a single solution, in which it is an internal event.
[23] The possibility Freud recognizes here, that fear of death might be a part of melancholia, is significantly absent from his "Mourning and Melancholia" (1917 [1915]), which we will examine later (Chapter 9).

4. A neurotic manifestation. Fear of death is seen as a result of melancholia (and not, for example, as an apprehension of the human condition). Moreover, melancholia as a neurosis serves as a template for the case of external danger, where the same dynamics are involved.

These constructions are reiterated again and again in psychoanalytic accounts of the fear of death, as we will see further on in this study. One can also observe them earlier in Freud's explanation in *The Ego and the Id* (1923), in the discussion that precedes the one on the fear of death: "The ego's work of sublimation" assists the death instincts in gaining control and unleashes aggressive tendencies in the superego. Thus, Freud says, the ego risks falling prey to the results of its own work, like microorganisms that are destroyed by their own products of decomposition (p. 57). The whole thing is envisioned as internal, and the weak ego is responsible for its own demise.

In addition, death is conceived in these passages as a form of loss. The ego "sees itself deserted by all protecting forces," and the situation is the same as separation from the mother (Freud, 1923, p. 58), or, in 1926: "the situation to which the ego is reacting is one of being abandoned by the protecting superego—the powers of destiny" (Freud, 1926, p. 130). To be sure, loss is one situation in which people grasp that death is an ongoing threat to life, but Freud here likens death, our death, to a state of loss. Yet in my death, it is *I* who am lost. It is as if Freud, unable to analyze directly the issue of *one's own* death, diverts it to the more comfortable question of another's death—the loss of another.

Schur (1972) criticizes Freud's explanation—that the ego relinquishes itself—from a different perspective. The problem with it, he claims, is that it simply explains something else, rather than the fear of death. It explains perhaps the wish to die, or "a lack of *will to live*," but not the fear of death (pp. 372–3).

Another consideration is the issue of danger. What Freud's argument goes back to, in both *The Ego and the Id* and *Inhibitions, Symptoms and Anxiety*, is that in the fear of death, the ego feels deserted; it feels it has lost the protection, love, or support of the superego or of destiny. Yet Freud here merely circumvents the question, because once the protection is gone, what is actually feared? Or, to put it differently, what is threatening in the loss of protection? Is it not the danger to life? Freud's argument never gets there. Freud starts out ostensibly discussing the fear of death, and as I have shown, proceeds to construct it in a way in which it is transformed into something else. Yet even his own argument, deliberately intended to dismiss the question of the fear of death altogether, and explicitly claiming it is secondary, ends up, once again, confronting Freud and his readers with the question of the fear of death itself, this time in a more real, concrete, form. When the protection is gone and we are left alone facing the danger, what do we fear then? As Freud (1926) notes: "[T]he situation to which the ego is reacting [in the fear of death] is one of being abandoned by the protecting super-ego—the powers of destiny—so that it has no longer any safeguard against all the dangers that surround it" (p. 130). The problem of remaining without a safeguard is of course unsettling, but are not "the dangers that surround" (or in 1923: "an excessive real danger," p. 58) also a bit of a threat? Is not the fear of being left unprotected at least sometimes a byproduct of the real threat itself? Why should these dangers not be considered a threat in the first place? What have we explained if we are constantly led back in a circle to the same danger we started with?

Doubt and hesitation

Freud's passages discussed in this section have had a tremendous influence on the history of psychoanalytic thought about death. Piven (2004, pp. 3–6) rightly observes that analysts have tended to focus on them as the sole expression of Freud's ideas about death, and have reiterated or recycled them at the expense of alternative ideas. In short, they have become canonical, the final judgment on death. However, when we look at Freud's texts themselves, we see how full they are of reservations and personal expressions regarding the subjective nature of the response: "I am inclined to adhere to the view" (that fear of death is fear of castration); "it seems to me" (that fear of death is a transformation of the fear of the super-ego) (1926, pp. 130, 140); "I believe that" (fear of death is between the ego and the superego); "it seems to me" (that fear of death should be distinguished from realistic anxiety). Fear of death "presents a difficult problem to psychoanalysis" the considerations discussed above "make it possible to regard" (fear of death as fear of castration); the significance of guilt in neurosis "makes it conceivable that" (common neurotic anxiety is reinforced by anxiety relations between ego and super-ego which could be fear of death). What exactly one does fear in danger "cannot be specified" and "cannot be grasped analytically" (1923, pp. 57–9). Even in retrospect, the derivation of the fear of death from the fear of the superego is seen as a mere "attempt" (Freud, 1924b, 168).[24] Of course, in later

---

[24] All the expressions of doubt and hesitation cited above are equally valid in German: *"Ich halte darum an der Vermutung fest...," "....ist mir....erschienen," "[i]ch meine, daß....," "Es scheint mir....," "[s]ie gibt der Psychoanalyse ein schweres Problem auf," "kann also.... aufgefaßt werden," "ist es auch nicht von der Hand zu weisen, daß," "läßt sich nicht angeben," "es ist analystisch nicht zu fassen," "[i]ch habe...den Versuch gemacht"* (Freud, G.W., XIII, pp. 288–9, XIV, pp. 160, 170).

analytic texts on death (see Chapter 9), these reservations and tentative expressions are no longer heard: what was earlier "conceivable" is now a "fact," and where it was then "possible" to regard fear as something, it is now impossible to regard it differently.

I have commented above on Freud's passage where he suggests that the fear of death "presents a difficult problem to psychoanalysis, for death is an abstract concept ... " and explains that "the mechanism of the fear of death can only be that the ego relinquishes its narcissistic libidinal cathexis." As I have pointed out, fear of *death* is not really accounted for in this explanation. Yet perhaps we should also look at these formulations differently. Freud almost admits at least a temporary defeat before the riddle. That death plays such an important part in psychic life is not itself refuted. What is difficult, however, is to supply a psychoanalytic explanation for it, because in analytic terms, Freud fails to understand it. It is as if he were saying: "I know very well it is there, but I do not understand how, since based on my current knowledge, it has no place in the unconscious. It cannot be a real psychic content, but nevertheless is." Thus, we are left with a big hole in the analytic view of the human being and her psychic world. The riddle remains without an answer. All we can make of it is to subject it to other concepts, but when we do try to apply a strictly psychoanalytic view, we find ourselves with rather strange and unconvincing explanations.

The problem is that even if this reframing is partially correct, it has not been evident in the history of analytic literature. The navel of mystery, if you will, in the abdomen of the analytic world, was over the years simply forgotten. Freud himself hardly ever returns to it, and his followers left it largely untouched. Freud's expressions of failure to understand death psychoanalytically were taken literally, as an answer rather than as a call for further inquiry. It was too often assumed that death cannot be represented. It is denied a place in the unconscious, and hence, to some extent, it is seen as an empty concept for psychoanalysis.

Before concluding, two general remarks about the entire preceding discussion. It is a mistake, as I have said, to focus on representation of death as the sole criterion for death's presence. Likewise, it is a mistake to focus on fear of death as a sole criterion for death's influence. We can react to death without directly experiencing the fear of it, and the knowledge of finitude can be behind much of what we do or think even when we do not acknowledge it. The a priori limiting of the discussion of death's psychic impact to a conscious fear of death has shaped the ways in which this impact has been discussed, while other possible manifestations of death's psychic importance were left in the shadows. But more on this in the last chapter.

My second general remark involves supposing that Freud was correct in claiming that the child is wholly ignorant of death (1900, p. 254). And suppose that on the basis of this assumption, we conclude that death has no value for the child.[25] Still, the problem of the adult fear of death is left unresolved, because the child might not know about death, but one day she will in fact learn of it. One day she will learn that death is not merely a long vacation, that it is irreversible, inevitable, and will happen to everyone, including her parents and herself. She will learn that she will decline, degenerate, and finally, one day, be gone. Is it not justified to expect at least some emotional response to this knowledge? Can this adult, conscious apprehension of finitude really be dismissed as a non-event, always secondary, from a psychical point of view? That is, even if we accept the Freudian claim that everything essential is already shaped in childhood, and that conscious thought and knowledge are never to be counted among crucial things, what are we to do with newly acquired knowledge of finitude? Can one really suppose we are indifferent to it, that the knowledge has no independent influence on our minds and lives? We know of our own finitude. This is significant knowledge, worthy of being theoretically and clinically considered. Failing to account for it is a problem that should have troubled everyone involved in psychoanalysis.

---

[25] We might even go one step further and adopt Piven's (2004) idea that the mature fear of death is built on templates of fear that originate in many childhood traumata and annihilating experiences (p. 11). It still remains to bring the acquired knowledge of death into account.

2 "Most of the time life appears so uncertain to me": Death as a concern in Freud's life

The theoretical rejection of death in Freud and in the psychoanalytic world, which we have only begun to think about, is all the more remarkable when we come to consider Freud himself. It would be odd if someone of such deep insights and psychological attentiveness as Freud were actually blind to the possibility of death. Indeed, while one might have maintained the view that death is absent from Freud's writings simply because it was unimportant for him, just as it was apparently unimportant for many others, and perhaps because fear of death was not within his range of experiences, such claims would be rapidly dispelled by knowing just how dominant death was for Freud in his own life. Jones (1957) writes in his biography that Freud:

> seems to have been prepossessed by thoughts about death, more so than any other great man I can think of ... He had the disconcerting habit of parting with the words "good bye; you may never see me again". There were the repeated attacks of what he called *Todesangst* (dread of death). He hated growing old as early as his forties ... He once said he thought of it [death] every day of his life, which is certainly unusual. (pp. 301–2)

In Freud's own life, death occupies a much more central place than in his theory. In his letters, death is revealed as a persistent issue, central to his psychic life. He does not, most of the time, minimize or reduce it in any way. In his consolation of others, in his confessions about himself, death is fully recognized. Death is, in fact, so central to him that Schur, his personal doctor, chooses to entitle his biography *Freud: Living and Dying* (1972), and to have it follow a historical thread related to death in Freud's life. "Most of the time life appears so uncertain to me that I am inclined not to postpone long-held wishes any longer," Freud writes to Fliess (June 22, 1894, Masson, 1985, p. 84), and his letters contain many similar thoughts. There are also indications of fear of death, concern about and awareness of death, gloom, uncertainty, acceptance, and encouragement. "I think about the possibility of death everyday,"

Freud admits to a patient. "It is a good practice" (to Smiley Blanton, in 1930, cited in Breger, 2000, pp. 267–8).[1]

In the first years of his correspondence with Fliess, the years of the formulation of his first discoveries, Freud was suffering from cardiac problems, which made him fear for his life. Thus, for example, he writes to Fliess: "As for me, I note migraine, nasal secretion, and attacks of fears of dying" (Letter of April 16, 1896, Masson, 1985, p. 181). (Disclosing perhaps the somewhat mechanistic side to his thinking about the fear of dying, seen as something at the level of headaches to rid oneself of.)

Then there is the strange case of Freud's preoccupation with the age at which he will die. Throughout much of his life and to varying degrees, Freud maintains a belief in a predetermined age for his death. It evolves, strengthens, and weakens around his relationship with Fliess. Fliess's theories of biological cycles are at the root of the odd mathematical calculations which determine the feared date. At various stages, Freud considered the ages 40, 41, and 42, later more intensively 51, then 61, 62, and finally 81½ predetermined for him (Schur, 1972, pp. 104, 159). 51 for example would be 23 plus 28, Fliess's masculine and feminine cycles. It is hard to ascertain the exact degree of seriousness behind these beliefs, which seems to waver between a self-amused peculiarity and apprehensive concern. At times, having the "expiry date" almost signifies a relief.[2] Finally, Freud survives all these dreaded dates, and dies at the rather neutral and unexpected age of 83.[3]

Funnily enough Freud's obsession with the age at which he will die is both a manifestation of the fear of death and an attempt to refute it. It clearly expresses the fear and can also perhaps intensify it as the expected date draws nearer. Yet calculating and anticipating one's own death can also serve as an opposition to death. It is an attempt to control death: to anticipate it in advance and thus to limit it, that is to deny the arbitrariness of its timing. Death is troubling not only for its inevitability, but also

---

[1] To cite another example: Freud writes to his friends, in between two operations in his mouth: "The uncertainty that hovers over a man of sixty-seven has now found its material expression. I don't take it very hard; one will defend oneself for a while with the help of modern medicine and then remember Bernard Shaw's warning: Don't try to live forever, you will not succeed" (letter to Katá and Lajos Levy, June 22, 1894, cited in Schur, 1972, p. 358).
Choron (1972 [1964], pp. 151–2) believes Freud's two well-known fainting spells were both related to death (as finitude, not as patricide) and fear of death.

[2] "The superstition that has limited my life to around February 1918 seems downright friendly to me," Freud writes to Ferenczi on November 20, 1917 (Falzeder and Brabant, 1993–2000, Vol. 2, p. 249).

[3] See Schur (1972, pp. 153–98) for a more ample description of Freud's fatalistic belief, and Schur's entire book for a discussion of Freud's personal approach to death.

for the indefiniteness and haphazard nature of its timing. For Meyer (1975 [1973], pp. 1–2) and Heidegger (1996 [1927], p. 238), the peculiar combination of complete certitude regarding the fact that death will come and incertitude as to its specific timing, is responsible for much of death's menace. Having, as Freud would like it, a preset, fully known date of death eliminates and neutralizes a serious source of distress. Thus, for example, both the fear and the assurance find expression in Freud's letter of September 29, 1896 (Masson, 1985, p. 198), where he relates how sick he was and says: "I would like so much to hold out until that famous age limit of approximately fifty-one, but I had one day that made me feel it was unlikely."

The conception of death as resulting from biological cycles also makes dying a completely internal affair, as if at a certain point the system, like a can of food, goes over its shelf-life. Such a belief seems to immunize the subject from an external death, removing any possibility of suffering a death inflicted from the outside.

Just because you are paranoid doesn't mean they're not out to get you, and just because Freud was obsessive about his death concerns doesn't mean these concerns did not have some basis in reality. For example, his cardiac problems in the 1890s heightened his apprehensions about death. Thus, Freud writes to Fliess toward the end of their friendship how in a time when he "had reason to believe that [he] was very close to the end of [his] life," "it was [Fliess's] confidence that kept [him] going" (letter of June 9, 1901, Masson, 1985, p. 442).

Later, it was ageing. For example, 2 days after his 65th birthday, he writes: "On March 13 of this year I very suddenly took a step toward really getting old. *Since then the thought of death no longer leaves me at all*, and sometimes I have the feeling that seven organs are vying with one another for the honor of being allowed to make an end to my life" (letter to Ferenczi, May 8, 1921, Falzeder & Brabant, 1993–2000, Vol. 3, p. 56).

During the last two decades of his life, the cancer he was suffering from joined old age as a source of thoughts about death. In these years, his celebrated serenity in facing death was crystallized, and although fear was still dominant, there was an accompanying tendency to combat the fear and to look boldly into the eyes of death. This, together with a certain tiredness with living, characterized Freud's attitude till his dying day. For Loewenberg (1992), Freud's approach to his death—"forthright, without sentimentality or self-pity, but with a full consciousness of reality"—is a truly stoic position, in line with Freud's general approach of resignation to his inexorable fate. Loewenberg sees continuity between the personal and the theoretical position, but only because he fails to take into account Freud's theoretical neglect of death.

Death as a concern in Freud's life 43

Freud's serenity in the face of death is famously recognized as the "dignified" response of a great man to the necessities of life.[4] Although it is clear that Freud fully accepted death in his own life, the fact that he was engaged in a project that might win him symbolic immortality, that is, the establishment of psychoanalysis (Lifton, 1979, p. 16; Becker, pp. 47–66), certainly contributed greatly to his acceptance of death. Upon the death of Abraham in 1925, Freud writes to Jones how no one is irreplaceable for psychoanalysis, and although he himself and others will soon vanish, the cause, psychoanalysis, must continue, and compared with it, the specific individuals, Freud and his friends, are insignificant (letter to Jones, December 30, 1925, Paskauskas, 1993, p. 591). This is not to underestimate his heroic battle with the cancer, 16 years of continuous threat and pain, which marked the final phase of his life.[5]

The recognition of death is often ambivalent.[6] Phillips (2000), who presents Freud as a mentor in mortality, notes Freud's dislike and lack of trust of biographers, as manifested in the burning of his letters in 1885, following which Freud contentedly announced to his fiancée that the biographers would have to work much harder if they wished to squeeze him into their books. For Phillips, this act represents Freud's wish to be the sole master and author of his story (pp. 69, 71). However, we should note that it has another side. To imagine, as Freud did at the age of 29, before having any serious scientific or philosophical achievement to his credit, that one day biographers would be interested in his personal letters, suggests of course that he believed he would become important enough for biographers to show such interest. Such a vision assumes that one's work will be great enough to achieve some form of symbolic immortality. One's work will be one's monument. It is a stance that involves both recognition of death, and its antidote denial.

Unlike others who he believes treated Freud's reflection on death as a part of his neurosis, as a symptom, Nachman (1981) makes Freud's individual preoccupation with death into a theoretical position. Freud, he says, "dreaded death because he believed that death is too important, too significant for us, to be accepted without a tremor, as if it did not matter at all. For if your dying does not matter, neither does our life"

---

[4] The serenity was of course not without a measure of negative feelings. In a letter to Jones (May 3, 1928, cited in Jones, 1957, p. 149), Freud writes that there is precious little consolation regarding death: "As an unbelieving fatalist I can only let my arms sink before the terrors of death."

[5] A struggle well described by Schur (1972) and Golub (1981–1982).

[6] Freud's fear was not free of denial, as I claim above. Wangh (1989, pp. 6–7) also finds that Freud had trouble recognizing his fear of death. Freud's attempt to admit death to himself, he argues, is always combined with an attempt to obscure it.

["our" in the original] (p. 552). While others either affirmed life but rejected death, or, vice versa, Freud is unique, to Nachman's mind, in upholding both to the highest degree: "The individual was important because of, not in spite of, his mortality" (p. 552).

Nachman's position is appealing at first glance, but I am not sure if it holds water. Most of his discussion mistakes Freud's emotional, sometimes unconscious, attitude for a fully thought-out theoretical position. He does so to avoid the diagnosis of the fear as a neurotic symptom. Yet, a symptom or a worked out position are not the only possibilities. Freud's fear might very well have been an existential recognition of death and its inevitability, rather than a neurotic symptom, but it does not follow that this is a theoretical position. At any rate, Freud's personal relation to death vacillated between dread and serenity, and at times the two are inseparable, as if they are two sides of the same coin. It is highly significant that the theoretical stance Nachman refers to, where mortality is significant, is rare in Freud's writings.

In fact, the discrepancy between the place death occupied in Freud's private life and the one given to it in his writings is nothing less than astonishing. Certainly, it is not the case that Freud was simply unaware of death's psychic presence, and, therefore, failed to deal with it. The fact that he was so aware of it, and yet in his writings repeatedly underestimates death's importance, or explicitly dismisses it as a byproduct, is remarkable and serves to highlight how his theoretical views fail to conform not only to human reality in general, but to the psychic reality of their author.

To think, for example, that the person who wrote the passages discussed above in 1923 and 1926, where it is claimed that the mind is impervious to death, was not only quite old, but was suffering from cancer (although the first 1923 operation took place after the paper was written), leaves us perplexed.

Freud's struggles with death are good stuff, but it is not Freud the man but rather Freud's texts and psychoanalytic theory that are my focus in this book. It is not Freud's personal quirk or his neurosis that lead to the inclusion or exclusion of death in analytic theory, certainly not in later analytic writing. What clearly emerges, from this brief discussion at any rate, is a strong ambivalence about death which the theory acts out as well, as we shall repeatedly see. It is an ambivalence already hinted at in the tension between theoretical rejection (seen in the previous chapter) and Freud's own lifelong struggle with death.

We now move, in the next six chapters, to a textual examination of several texts by Freud, where death is an issue, explicitly or in a more covert way. We shall see that even there Freud has difficulty relating to death. The examination will allow us, on the one hand, to trace the full extent of the repression of death in his thought, which has become an integral part of analytic thought ever since. On the other hand, we will also see that death's importance is not easily dismissed. In particular, the two chapters we now turn to examine the place of death in *The Interpretation of Dreams* and question Freud's ideas opposing the psychic significance of death in the context of his own dreams. They demonstrate, contrary to his claims against the psychic presence of death, the role of death itself in unconscious thoughts and psychic life, together with its intricate links to other psychic issues.

3 The dream of death: *The Interpretation of Dreams*

Opening: Death representable and irrepresentable

As pointed out in Chapter 1, one of Freud's major claims regarding death is that of non-representability. This irrepresentability extends across all levels of mental life—the unconscious and the conscious, the primitive and the civilized, the child and the adult. For all, death remains foreign and inaccessible.

A second basic position of Freud's, influenced of course by the first, is that death is not an important factor in mental life. Fear of death, Freud (1915, p. 297) tells us, is something secondary. Sexuality always has primacy where motives for our actions or mental constructions are considered. Anxiety is not about death or existential concerns, but is rather an effect of excitations or excessive libido.

Even though clear formulations of these attitudes only appear later in Freud's writings, they are active from the very beginning. Death, Freud seems to say, is of marginal importance in understanding the psyche. For example, he tells us in *The Interpretation of Dreams* that death has little meaning or value for the child, for whom it is the equivalent of a long absence or trip, and, therefore, the child is not influenced by it. Fear of death in particular "has no meaning" for him (1900, p. 254). The extension of this notion from the child to the adult, whose unconscious also fails to recognize death, is clear.

Yet what if these claims are refuted in Freud's own texts? What if his own writings fail to substantiate these claims, and portray instead a very different picture concerning death's role in the psyche and the possibility of its representation? What if as a test case for the validity of these claims we take Freud's most important theoretical and clinical book, *The Interpretation of Dreams*?

The current chapter and the following offer a new reading of *The Interpretation of Dreams*, a reading which aims at uncovering a hidden theme of death as a motive force in Freud's dreams, associations, and interpretations. They show that death is in fact a pivotal theme in the book, and lay stress on how Freud's general approach to death articulated above not only fails to stand up to external criticism, but also to the facts of his own mental life as reflected in his dreams, and his ideas as an author-interpreter. Death has a central place in Freud's dreams, yet on the theoretical level he seems to have overlooked if not explicitly refuted this fact.

The Interpretation of Dreams is used here then both as a general example of how dreams and psychic life can have to do with death, and as part of a discussion of Freud's work.[1] We shall see for instance that his position regarding death contains multiple layers. The influence of finitude may be acknowledged on one level and denied on another. Death is sometimes at the heart of his discussion, but more often its presence is ignored or dismissed.

These two chapters examine death in *The Interpretation of Dreams* from several vantage points. The first deals with the direct or implied death of the individual as it appears in dreams. The discussion starts from dreams where another dies, and shows that both theoretically and in Freud's dreams and associations, the death of the other, be it a death that was wished for or one met with sorrow, involves a recognition on some level of one's own fragility. It is then demonstrated how Freud's own death is often directly represented in his dreams, rather than through the death of others. Occasionally Freud gives this some acknowledgment, but he does not draw the appropriate theoretical conclusions.

A shorter, second subchapter deals mainly with the dream of "Irma's injection," and addresses the issue of concern for others. While in Freud's discussion this concern almost always turns out to be illusory and spurious, I wish to restore its more everyday meaning, and insist on its genuine character. This concern testifies to a deep recognition of human fragility and finitude, and thus cannot be so easily dismissed.

The next chapter examines the most recurrent theme in Freud's book, namely ambition, arguing that it is closely intertwined with death, and that this link must be recognized to understand ambition more fully. On a more general level this discussion serves to show that death, even when not directly represented, is active in the mind and has an influence on other domains in mental life, such as ambition or sexuality. Death is an issue that cannot be isolated. Whether one recognizes it as important or

---

[1] My intention is not so much to analyze Freud's personality as to generalize his ideas, in the same way that *The Interpretation of Dreams* itself is intended to be a general psychic account rather than a confession. Freud is used here as an example. The discrepancy between his ideas and his theory only serves to show how much the latter fails to account for even the most basic facts that were involved in its construction.

not, it is a mistake to treat it as a kind of psychic island, and ignore the interplay between it and other issues.

A short section about the specific class of absurd dreams follows, claiming that such dreams revolve around the absurdity of dying itself, the absurdity of the transition from life to death. Before concluding, we shall look at several other issues to do with the dynamics of recognition and denial of death.

The various dreams, associations, and concerns discussed ultimately lead to a very different conclusion from the one normally drawn regarding the role of death in *The Interpretation of Dreams*. Death is here found to be a central motivation.[2] Accordingly, we must alter our perception regarding the role of death in dreams and mental life in general: Given the significance of this book for psychoanalysis—perhaps the most important book in the history of the psychoanalytic movement, and surely its foundational text, from which many of its themes are drawn— the fact that it can be shown to revolve around death has implications beyond the specific enquiry into dreams and their interpretation. Death emerges here not as a secondary psychic issue but as central to the psyche, specifically in unconscious formations and manifestations.

Because in some of Freud's dreams the issue of death is explicit, one would not expect that this issue would go completely unnoticed. And some remarks about death's appearances in the book can indeed be found in the literature, but they tend to be either very general, or deal only with explicit references to it. Sometimes the death-related motifs in Freud's dreams are seen as expressions of his mourning for his father (Buxbaum, 1951). Other authors (Anzieu, 1986 [1975]; de M'Uzan, 1977 [1968]) who are more sensitive to the role of death in the book tend to interpret it as resulting from Freud's mid-life crisis or from a pathological obsession with death. A few authors have addressed death in specific dreams (Breger, 2000, pp. 138–40), most famously perhaps Lacan (1978, pp. 186, 196; 1988b, pp. 154–5, 164) in his analysis of the "Irma" dream, and a few others have considered death's role in a more general manner (Grinstein, 1968; Schur, 1972; Anzieu, 1986 [1975]; Nachman, 1981; Kofman, 1985, pp. 20–32; Piven, 2004, pp. 29–31).[3]

---

[2] It is not that interpretations in the psychoanalytic literature hold that death is unimportant in the book, but rather that the book is rarely considered from the perspective of death.

[3] Breger (2000, pp. 138–40) points out that Freud's discussion of the "Non Vixit" dream obscures death-related meanings. He does not, however, demonstrate the extent and sophistication of the role of death-related concerns in this dream, which we will explore below.

These observations are important pointers, but restricted. The current and next chapters attempt to go beyond them in several ways. First, in scope. The whole of Freud's text is examined here with the aim of systematically exposing and articulating a broader picture of death's role in *The Interpretation of Dreams*. Second, in depth. The discussion that follows observes the intricacies of death's involvement in the production and analysis of dreams in much greater detail and looks at various links between it and other issues. Third, in going beyond what is overt. Rather than settling for those instances where Freud is explicit about death in his associations, the attempt here is to expose more hidden cases where death-related thoughts and feelings are active. Fourth, death is not subordinated here to other issues, transformed into them or treated as a personal or pathological problem. Fifth, the role of death in dreams is theoretically elaborated, rather than simply pointed at. Rather than settle for general remarks about death's involvement, we shall explore the intricate ways in which it plays a role in psychic life. The overall picture that emerges is very different from common understandings of Freud's book, which have been quite blind to the significance of death in

---

Kofman (1985) is perhaps the author most sensitive to death's role in Freud's dreams, mainly in those involving ambition. She carefully picks up many of the threads leading to death but they lead her more to the question of guilt toward the father (pp. 24–5) and fear of exposing the incestuous imaginary relationship with the mother (pp. 27–30).

Nachman (1981) offers an interesting, albeit provisional, exception to common interpretations. His short paper deals with death in Freud's dreams, and stresses indications of the fear of death and denial of death within them. He claims Freud's dreams reveal a denial of death, which the conscious Freud uncovers and refutes, although as we shall see the dreams reflect much more than mere denial of death, and often contain a recognition of death. Nachman presents the fear as a part of a theoretical stance that values attachment to this world (to my mind failing to distinguish between recognition on a personal level and a theoretical stance, and thereby blurring the very nature of the problem). Piven (2004, pp. 29–31) as well notes that while Freud contended that death cannot be part of the unconscious, such a contention is thrown into question by the fact that some of his dreams express fear of dying and a need to deny it. Although he only briefly develops this point, he does add the perspective that in order to take part in a dream, death must be transformed into a pleasurable fantasy. It is part of his overall view that death is the source of the creation of fantasy and illusions, because it is unacceptable.

Even among the sparse exceptions where death is noted, the reductive tendency which will be explored below is sometimes at play. In Schur's *Freud, Living and Dying* (1972), Freud's attitude towards death is the focus of the narrative of his whole life history. Schur discusses some of Freud's death-related dreams, but does not go into depth and strangely enough his interpretations seem to focus more on the relationship with Fliess than on the problem of death, which as his title suggests, is supposed to be at the center of his book. Anzieu stresses the presence of death in Freud's thoughts and dreams, but sees it primarily, as mentioned above, as a manifestation of a mid-life crisis Freud was allegedly going through (1986 [1975], pp. 114–18, 212), ignoring death in the more general sense. Moreover his discussion of death often succumbs to the familiar tendency to put stress on more common psychoanalytic issues.

it, and different too from those few studies which have pointed to some limited role for death.

For the most part, I will confine myself to Freud's own dreams. Rather than "Irma," Freud's specimen dream, mine is the one Freud calls "Non Vixit," which will open most of the succeeding sections. Interpreting Freud's dreams against Freud is not easy: The text at our disposal is fragmentary and biased; all we have are the details Freud chose to include and which serve his interpretations, details which we, therefore, must try and exploit to the full.

To allow psychoanalysis to recover from its own illnesses, to bridge its own lacunas, we have to find the potential for it within itself, to put Freud to work against Freud, paraphrasing Laplanche (1992, p. 434). This task is much easier in a book as plural and diverse as *The Interpretation of Dreams* where the examples are always threatening to spill outside the frame of the theoretical elements and where the argumentative side is easily invaded by the imagery and language of the dreams, disrespectful of theoretical constraints. Death speaks itself there in abundance. In looking at his own dreams Freud is often conscious of their link to death—he is much more conscious of their real meaning than his overall conclusions seem to suggest. The material that surfaces in the associations engages the reader again and again with an undeniable centrality of death. These elements are dropped in the larger theoretical synthesis but we can seize hold of them here and use them with and against Freud.

Dying the death of the other

Let us begin by pointing to a small and surprising fact about *The Interpretation of Dreams*, which has perhaps not received enough attention. In his first important book, the one that has remained the cornerstone of his work, Freud presents the Oedipus complex, his major contribution, in a rather strange way: as a detour and a sideline, branching out from another discussion—that of death in dreams. Dreams about the death of someone close serve as a launching point for Freud to talk about the Oedipus complex, with implications regarding not only infantile sexuality, but also fraternal rivalry and the egoism characteristic of the psychic life of children, later to be called narcissism. All these are presented as merely serving the discussion of the death of relatives in dreams (Freud, 1900, pp. 248–67). This already seems to testify to an unconscious and unintended set of priorities, different from Freud's standard view that subordinates death to psychoanalytic concepts.

One would at first glance tend to regard the framing of such crucial questions in the context of dreams about the death of others as coincidental and devoid of meaning. Yet it is worth a second thought. Freud (1900) tells us on the one hand that the fear of death has no sway in the mental life of small children, and on the other hand that the death wish toward the other is common, and is a frequent means of punishment (pp. 254–5). There seems, however, to be a link between the death of the other and one's own death or survival: in contexts of rivalry, and also in general, the death of the other often has the unconscious significance of outliving him, and serves as proof of narcissistic victory. Zilboorg (1943) aptly recognizes these dynamics. The normal interest in fatal accidents and executions hides, in addition to the obvious sadistic gratification, "an unconscious reaction of egocentric self-delight: . . . 'It is not I who was executed last night; it is not I who was killed in this automobile accident or train wreck or earthquake'" (pp. 468–9).

The death of the other can even serve, in psychic life, as a substitute, a sacrifice immolated to appease death, as if the monster would be less eager to have more if it has this one victim in its possession. In a related manner, the death of the other can serve as a sort of barrier against death, a proof of one's vitality. Do we not feel more alive when we have just visited a house where somebody died, knowing the satisfaction of the survivor?

On the other hand, on the simplest level, the real death of the other rattles our defenses against the acknowledgment of death. Any death in our surroundings reminds us of the fact of death. It shakes our beliefs about the constancy of our world, even if only minimally, and reminds us of the ephemeral nature of our existence. What was ignored or dismissed as unreal must now be admitted. Yalom (1980, p. 56) recounts a hallucination of a patient after his father died, a voice coming from above telling him: "You're next!"

Bronfen, in her study on representations of dead women, lays stress on the dual functioning of the representation of death: "any articulation of another's death, it seems, invariably returns to the surviving speaker" (1992, p.15), but at the same time, "[e]very representation of dying . . . implies the safe position of the spectator" (p. 44).

Whether we are reassured or unnerved, the death of the other involves us. Whether as triumphant survivors or reminded of our own frailty, we are personally implicated.

In addition, narcissism, when understood in its wider existential, non-pathological, and non-technical senses, could be seen as the force with which the individual asserts him- or herself in the world, against all odds, nullity, insignificance, and the sad truth that one is made of dust. Against all these, one claims: I am here and I am significant. This applies even more to sibling rivalry. I will kill whoever dares to threaten my uniqueness, my place in my family, whoever dares to compete for the love of my parents. And if the other disappears, unconscious voices might cheerfully whisper "I am here, and he is not. I survived him." Beyond this lurks the recognition of one's insignificance.[4]

Let me say in parenthesis that the Oedipus complex as well, involving attachment to one parent and conflict with and fear of the other, is related to one's place vis-à-vis the other and to one's vulnerability. One parent's love is necessary for sustaining life, and the other's imagined hostility could be seen as possibly detrimental to it. In an attempt to rethink psychoanalytic issues from an existential perspective, Brown (1959, pp. 110–34) and Becker (1973, pp. 25–46) see the core of the Oedipal situation in the will of the subject to become his *causa-sui*—his own reason and ground (Brown, 1959, p. 118). Sleeping with one's mother means being one's own father, and thus ostensibly overcoming death (Becker, 1973, p. 36). Hence, there is something about Oedipal striving that is actually aimed at sustaining oneself beyond natural limits and involves an attempt to transcend death.

From this perspective it does not seem coincidental that the innovations concerning egoism-narcissism and Oedipus, as well as sibling and other rivalries (which according to Freud should end with the death of the rival and survival of the self) are inserted into the discussion about the death of the other. It is indicative of the relationship between these issues. Dreams in which another dies or is dead should be understood, I propose, as related to thoughts about one's own death, as the following example is intended to show.

Non vixit

One dream where the death of others—or in a way, the killing of others—is involved is Freud's "Non Vixit" dream. Whether we are talking about death or killing is not clear, the victim being, so to speak, already dead at the time of the murder. Here is the dream itself:

I had gone to Brücke's laboratory at night, and, in response to a gentle knock on the door, I opened it to (the late) Professor Fleischl, who came in with a number of strangers and, after exchanging a few words, sat down at his table.

---

[4] The brief characterization of narcissism and rivalry I have presented here is specifically connected to death in dreams, and will be echoed in the following discussion of Freud's "Non Vixit" dream. Other links between narcissism and death can be found in Becker (1973) and Brown (1959).

This was followed by a second dream. My friend Fl. [Fliess] had come to Vienna unobtrusively in July. I met him in the street in conversation with my (deceased) friend P., and went with them to some place where they sat opposite each other as though they were at a small table. I sat in front at its narrow end. Fl. spoke about his sister and said that in three-quarters of an hour she was dead, and added some such words as "that was the threshold". As P. failed to understand him, Fl. turned to me and asked me how much I had told P. about his affairs. Whereupon, overcome by strange emotions, I tried to explain to Fl. that P. (could not understand anything at all, of course, because he) was not alive. But what I actually said—and I myself noticed the mistake—was, "NON VIXIT." I then gave P. a piercing look. Under my gaze he turned pale; his form grew indistinct and his eyes a sickly blue—and finally he melted away. I was highly delighted at this and I now realized that Ernst Fleischl, too, had been no more than an apparition, a "revenant"; and it seemed to me quite possible that people of that kind only existed as long as one liked and could be got rid of if someone else wished it. (Freud, 1900, p. 421)

The associations spun out by this dream are numerous, and I will just mention a few facts here. Freud tells us how he was concerned about the health of his friend Fliess, who was undergoing an operation. Moreover, though Freud does not mention it, Fliess chose to do so exactly on his 40th birthday, which he deemed fatal for him, by reason of his numerological theories about the end of life (Schur, 1972, pp. 158–9; Anzieu, 1986 [1975], p. 377). Freud was planning to come and see him, but was afraid he would arrive too late. Fliess, he feared, was too weak and might die (Freud, 1900, pp. 480–1). The association I wish to emphasize here is one in which Freud recalls the funeral of his friend P. The orator had implied that without P, the world would come to an end. A remark, made by someone to protest that proposition, is behind a series of dream-thoughts: "'It's quite true that no one's truly irreplaceable. How many people I've followed to the grave already! But I am still alive. I've survived them all'" (p. 485). Freud says that such a thought, at a moment when he feared he would not arrive in time to be with his friend Fliess, who might die, has only one meaning:

I was delighted because I had once more survived someone, because it was *he* and not I who had died, because I was left in possession of the field, as I had been in the phantasied scene from my childhood. [Freud refers here to a dispute he had with his nephew as a child, and where, since he was the stronger one, he was left in a position of supremacy.] This satisfaction, infantile in origin, at being in possession of the field constituted the major part of the affect that appeared in the dream. I was delighted to survive. (p. 485)

Freud compares the naïve egoism he felt to that expressed in the joke about one person in a couple saying to the other: "'If one of us dies,

I shall move to Paris.' So obvious was it to me that I should not be the one to die" (p. 485).

Let us take a moment to examine this enlightening discussion. It is a rare instance where Freud seems to be conscious, at least in part, of the hidden death-related sources of his fantasies and dream-thoughts. Yet it seems their meaning is still unrecognized. The important element is the aforementioned issue of survival. When another dies—even someone close—one's own death is likely to be implicated as well. Focusing on the issue of rivalry, of "being in possession of the field" as Freud does, not only conceals the meanings related to personal death, it also prevents us from seeing how the two issues—the threat of personal death and rivalry—are in fact closely related; how wishing the death of the other, for example, immediately exposes the wisher (not necessarily through guilt) to her own transience. If I can wish so can the other, and if he can disappear so easily, perhaps I can as well. More importantly, because it is an either/or situation, if he dies, the implied meaning is that *I* did not. I am directly involved as a survivor, acutely conscious of the risk to me, as death has just crossed my path and might do so again.

First, reciprocity: "'I hit him'cos he hit me,'" Freud notes, citing himself in the childhood scene with his nephew (1900, p. 484). The game is dual and reciprocal, he knows. This, however, has implications. If the world is full of evil wishes for the death of others, we know that some of them will be directed against us. After all, the other's mind is not so different from our own. This brings to mind the joke about two policemen in a totalitarian regime where one asks the other, "What do you think of our government?" And the other replies, "Just about what you do—more or less the same." "I will have to arrest you then," replies the first. In addition, we note that if no one is irreplaceable, as per Freud's dream-thought, then the speaker, i.e. Freud, is not excluded. He is replaceable like everyone else.

Second, survival: "'How many people I've followed to the grave already! But I am still alive. I've survived them all'" (p. 485). The theme of survival could not be more prominent, and yet it is not developed theoretically, or taken into account in further analysis of the dream-thoughts. In a letter to Fliess (September 21, 1899), Freud tells him: "In the 'Non Vixit' dream I am delighted to have outlived you" (Masson, 1985, p. 374). It is not that the other dies but that the self survives which is important here. There is a double implication regarding death wishes in dreams. First, the actual wish to kill might be a response to a fear of dying and the will to survive. Second, even if the order is reversed, an acknowledgment of death is an almost instantaneous byproduct of the wish. "I am *still* alive" is far from being an expression of ignorance of death. There is a full recognition that time is limited, yet this does not find expression in Freud's theory.[5]

In any event even when Freud in this rare example exclaims, "'But I'm still alive,'" he does not integrate it with his thought. He tends in general to see only what is related to his core psychoanalytic attitudes: wishes, sexuality, ambivalence. And here too, it is only the wish that interests him. In a subsequent passage he asks why the censorship has not suppressed these egoistic thoughts, but refers only to the wish for the other to be dead, and for the victory of the enduring self. He does not seem to recognize the ego's potential discomfort with the implication that it will inevitably die too, that it might have escaped this time, but not forever.

Freud draws no such conclusions, and there is almost no link between the material brought up in his associations, almost self-evident in this case, and the weight it receives in his theoretical elaborations.

Although materials such as these come up in dreams, they are likely to go unrecognized as long as concerns about finitude are left out of mainstream analytic theories. Commonly, the order of causality will be reversed and the idea of death will be seen as a punishment for strong feelings of rivalry and ambition. Such, for example, is Anzieu's (1986 [1975], pp. 375–88) interpretation of the "Non Vixit" dream. In Anzieu's words: "He who wishes to kill his rivals will be punished with death" (p. 388), "failure and death lie in wait for the ambitious" (p. 382). Although this is a plausible line of thought which could very well describe a specific unconscious fantasy, it still seems to involve a more complex series of unconscious thoughts, and to follow less directly the more basic human attitudes in response to the death of another person, than the tendencies described above where one's own existence is under threat. More importantly, the use of this kind of reasoning, common in psychoanalysis, with its origins in Freud and then developed by Klein, tends to imply that death anxiety itself is only secondary. It puts ambition and rivalry at the center, focuses on death wishes toward the other, and relegates death to the status of a side effect lacking significance in its own right.

---

[5] The link Freud makes to the infantile world is also important. The same dialectics are at work in the mind of the infant as in that of the adult. The implications regarding the self, namely, a reminder of fragility, or a reaffirmation of vitality, are not the result of a later acquisition. Freud claims that the satisfaction felt at survival is infantile in its origin.

Dying in one's dreams

Finally he melted away

I have elaborated on the death of self as arising from the death of others, because it runs counter to the more habitual psychoanalytic understanding which focuses on the death of others, stressing murderousness and aggressiveness, and neglects the death of self. There is in the death of the other, whether wishful or not, an implied recognition by the self of his or her own death; the one entails the other.

It seems, however, that death takes an even more prominent part in the "Non Vixit" dream than we have hitherto seen, and in a more intimate way: Freud's death is symbolized directly, and not only through the issue of surviving others.

Two dead persons figure in the dream: "(the late) Professor Fleischl" and Freud's "(deceased) friend P." Both are Freud's colleagues in Brücke's laboratory. Both actually died within a short period (1890–1). Could the superstitious Freud refrain from thinking about himself in relation to their deaths?

Indeed, an examination of the characters figuring in Freud's dream and dream-thoughts points at Freud as the true protagonist of the dream, that is, the one who plays the role of the dead. Among these characters we find Freud's teachers (Brücke and Breuer), his senior colleague (Fleischl), and his junior colleague and successor (Josef Paneth) at the Brücke Laboratory, and Fliess, of course, his best friend and intellectual twin. It seems that Freud is surrounded here by a swarm of doubles and equivalents. They all fulfill one of his categories of narcissistic love, listed in "On Narcissism," according to which a person may love what he is, was, would like to be, or what was once part of himself (Freud, 1914, p. 90). It is as if Freud's person is indicated by the presence of every one of them. The death of a double, as numerous literary works illustrate (e.g., Maupassant's *The Horla*, Nabokov's *Despair*, Poe's *William Wilson*, Rye and Wegener's film *The Student of Prague*), is never satisfying or pleasant. It brings to mind the fragility of one's own existence. One's own death is always implied by it. (The double in Poe's *William Wilson* tells the original Wilson, with his final breath after he is defeated in a duel: "You have conquered, and I yield. Yet, henceforward art thou also dead," 1958, p. 292.)

Freud seems to identify with these characters. That identification is involved here is actually reported by Freud himself who says, in a footnote about Josef Paneth, that he finds it easy to identify with people named Josef, or as he puts it, "my own ego finds it very easy to hide itself behind people of that name," because of the biblical Joseph, the emblematic figure of the dream interpreter (1900, p. 484n). Joseph in this dream is not only Paneth or Breuer, but also Kaiser Josef, whose memorial plays a major part in the dream. Memorials, by the way and as we shall see, loom large in the dream, the tormenting question for Freud being whether there will one day be a memorial for him as well.

Just a few pages after the "Non Vixit" dream, Freud (1900, p. 431) discusses dreams about dead people in almost the only instance in the book where he acknowledges death on a theoretical level. He offers the following rule for their interpretation. If, in the dream, the fact that the other person is dead is not mentioned, then "the dreamer is equating himself with him: he is dreaming of his own death." However, continues Freud, if "in the course of the dream the dreamer suddenly says to himself 'why, he died ever so long ago', he is repudiating this equation and is denying that the dream signifies his own death" (p. 431). Incidentally, one may also note that Freud also confesses immediately thereafter that the full nature of dreams of this kind is not yet wholly known to him.

Freud curiously refrains from applying this rule to the dream he has just discussed, and where dead people play such an important role, but we can do so ourselves.[6] In the dream Fl asks Freud about P, who does not understand him, "Whereupon, overcome by strange emotions, I tried to explain to Fl that P (could not understand anything at all, of course, because he) was not alive" (1900, p. 423). So the elements are all there: surprise, astonishment, and a sudden insistence on the fact that the person in the dream is actually dead. Applied to his own dream, Freud's theory about dreams of dead people would suggest that Freud the dreamer is repudiating the equation of himself and the dead person, and "is denying that the dream signifies his own death."

Freud (1900, pp. 480–7) devotes yet another discussion to the "Non Vixit" dream, in which he refers to the piercing look he gave P in the dream, a gaze that made him melt away. He says here that the gaze was taken from a real scene where he was the object of this gaze. Brücke, his teacher gave Freud the same look with his blue eyes for coming to the laboratory too late. The blue eyes then remained the other's (P's) eyes, "but the annihilating role was allotted to me—a reversal which was obviously the work of wish fulfillment" (p. 481). Brücke's look was a reproachful one, in the real scene reproduced in the dream. However, it

---

[6] The discussion of the meaning of dreams in which people alternate between dead and alive was only added to the book in 1919, so to apply the rule involves a certain anachronism. However, it was available for Freud in his own revisions of the other parts of his book.

seems that the wish fulfillment that reversed the roles was motivated not only by a will to lift the burden of reproach from Freud, as he seems to interpret it, but by a will to reverse the roles on the more important matter at stake: annihilation. Freud clearly prefers here to be on the annihilating side of the equation, rather than the annihilated. There is indeed a wish fulfillment involved, that it will be others who die and not himself.[7]

The suggestion that the person sentenced to death in the dream is actually Freud himself is further reinforced by the link Freud (1900) makes between his own physical condition and that of Fliess. While Fliess is the one undergoing the operation (and as we saw, on a date Freud and Fliess superstitiously thought was dangerous for him) and whose condition stirs up Freud's anxiety, Freud's own health is quickly brought up as well. Freud receives only indirect news of Fliess's condition. "I should have much preferred to go to him myself," he says, "but just at that time I was the victim of a painful complaint which made movement of any kind a torture to me" (pp. 480–1). Freud is referring to a large boil he was suffering from. Further indications regarding Freud's health are supplied by Anzieu (1986 [1975], p. 372), who describes how Freud's physical condition around the time of the dream was poor: he suffered from an infection resulting from a recent influenza epidemic, had difficulty breathing, and was afraid the cardiac problems he had suffered from some years earlier might recur. It is reasonable to suppose that these concerns played a role in the construction of the dream. These hints become even more manifest upon reading Freud's letter to Fliess, shortly after having the dream, which discloses Freud's deep sentiment of affinity and twinship between them. "As a consequence," the letter opens, "of the secret biological sympathy of which you have often spoken, both of us felt the surgeon's knife in our bodies at about the same time, and on precisely the same days moaned and groaned because of the pain." Specifically in reference to the boil Freud says: "In my case it was a large furuncle on the raphe scroti which reminded me of my kinship with you" (letter of November 6, 1898, Masson, 1985, pp. 333–4). Thus, Freud too goes under the surgeon's knife. Gathered together, these indications seem to point to the "Non Vixit" dream as representing, alongside other issues, Freud's own death.

---

[7] This, incidentally, may be a more general explanation for some dreams entailing killing, a mechanism involving a double reversal, from passive to active and from self to other. Instead of the self having to die, the self kills the other.

We now proceed to another instance in *The Interpretation of Dreams* where Freud dreams his own death. This time, he seems much more aware of this implication of the dream.

A castle by the sea

"A Castle by the Sea," Freud says, is his "most vivid and beautiful dream" (1900, p. 546). In the dream, Freud is a naval officer, attached to a garrison at a seaside castle. A war is raging, and an attack by enemy ships is anticipated. The governor of the castle gives Freud, the officer next in rank, some instructions. The governor then turns to go, but suddenly falls dead. His death seems to evoke no sentiment. Freud in the dream thinks that maybe a question he asked put a great deal of strain upon the governor, but other than that, everything continues as usual. The castle, of which Freud is now the commandant, prepares for the onslaught of enemy ships, which are already in sight. Toward the end, the dream turns comic. A strange ship appears, and Freud and his brother, who is suddenly standing beside him, shout "That's the breakfast-ship" (pp. 463–4).

This dream could be discussed through the prism of death of the self as implicit in the death of the other. Yet it is perhaps more accurately a demonstration of the direct representation of the death of the self, because the nature of the dead other (the governor) as straw man is here all too transparent.

The governor dies, but his death continues to be present in the dream in the form of the questions "I wondered whether his widow would remain in the castle, whether I should report his death to the Higher Command, and whether I should take over command of the castle as being next in order of rank" (Freud, 1900, p. 464). Death is also prefigured in the allusions to the governor's wife's disability and the Governor's respiratory difficulties, in the redundant indications of the fact that he "intended to leave," and "turned to go," and in the fact that instructions are being given regarding what to do "if the event that we feared took place." The threat to the castle, "the dark water," the fear of bombardment, and the arrival of the ships are all further indications of dread, creating "a tense and sinister impression" (*ibid.*).

Imagery of death continues to permeate the dream in the theoretical discussion that follows. Associations regarding the "breakfast-ship" which appears at the end of the dream, lead to mourning dress and funeral boats "in which in early times dead bodies were placed and committed to the sea for burial," as well as to a line from Schiller's allegory of life and death, about the old man who sails his ship into the port (Freud, 1900. p. 465–6).

60 The dream of death: *The Interpretation of Dreams*

So who exactly is being buried?

Freud (1900) analyzes this dream in the context of his discussion of affect in dreams. He uses it as an example of the displacement of the affect from the idea linked to it to another point in the dream, and the displacement of an important conclusion from its true place in the dream-thoughts to some other content in the dream itself. In his analysis, Freud notices that the affects in the dream were distributed in a way that more or less converged with its content. It is true that the Governor's death left no impression on him, but there was no reason why it should have. It is no less logical that he would be frightened at the sight of the approaching enemy ships, because he was now commander of the castle. But analysis of the dream reveals a different picture:

The analysis showed, however, that Herr P. [the castle's governor] was only a substitute for my own self. (In the dream *I* was the substitute for *him*.) *I* was the Governor who suddenly died. The dream-thoughts dealt with the future of my family after my premature death. This was the only distressing one among the dream-thoughts; and it must have been from it that the fright was detached and brought into connection in the dream with the sight of the warship. (pp. 464–5)

This dream is the only one in *The Interpretation of Dreams* in which Freud is so explicit about the role of thoughts about his own death in a dream. As he openly admits, this is a dream about his own death. This fact supports the attempt to interpret other dreams in the book as hinting at Freud's own death. And yet even concerning this dream, death's centrality is not always recognized. Anzieu (1986 [1975]) for example, while noting Freud's explicit remarks and acknowledging that "the fear of imminent death now occupied a central position" (p. 317), also supplies an Oedipal interpretation of the dream. The Oedipalizing machine is also at work in Buxbaum's (1951) analysis, also mentioned by Anzieu. Buxbaum focuses on the relationship with Fliess and with Freud's (now dead) father. She sees Freud's fear of dying and being unable to take care of his children as a consequence of, an unconscious punishment for, his death wishes toward his father and toward Fliess. In Buxbaum's words, "Who wishes to kill will be killed himself" (p. 207). Again we meet the idea of death as a punishment for rivalry and ambition, the dominant line of thought among psychoanalytic thinkers when they occasionally stumble on the issue of death. That death is an issue in the dream, one cannot deny. After all, Freud himself says so explicitly. Yet even when this is the case, the tendency is not to give death an independent place, but to use it as an indication of some other, more classical psychoanalytic theme. Why must death be a punishment for incestuous murderous wishes involving rivalry and Oedipal feelings?

Dying in one's dreams 61

One of the arguments Freud uses to diminish the role of death in the psychic world is, as we saw, that "[i]t is indeed impossible to imagine our own death; and whenever we attempt to do so we can perceive that we are in fact still present as spectators" (1915, p. 289). A central aim of the current and following chapters is to show that death is present in dreams, that it has a place in unconscious life, and can be represented in many ways. Now, "A Castle by the Sea" concurs well with Freud's argument. Freud indeed imagines his own death, but only as a spectator. Nevertheless, the subterfuge of the unconscious, of replacing one person with another, allows us to see more than that: The dreaming Freud is totally indifferent to the death of the governor, who represents himself, but the dream work displaces the affect of fear to the ships that are imperiling the castle. And not only the fear, but the whole situation seems to be expressing anticipatory thought, acknowledgment, emotion, and self-mourning related to the knowledge of one's own death. Waiting for the barbarian ships, the stress seems to be laid on the fear and anticipation of the dreadful event that is about to take place. Freud can be both already dead (at least his substitute in the dream is) and still alive. He is alive not only as witness and survivor, *after the event*, but also as the protagonist of the drama *before* the event took place, as the living human being who is in the existentially emblematic situation of waiting for his own death. Thus, the dream work, in which time is not a factor, artfully manages to simultaneously reproduce by condensation the anticipatory fear and grief, the death itself, and finally the mourning or survival in the wake of death.[8]

While Freud's dream work is ingenious, and while in this particular case, his analysis does not fall short of partially recognizing the true nature of the dream, his discussion of death nevertheless seems to be limited, in that he avoids touching on death as a problem in itself. In the case of "A Castle by the Sea," Freud (1900), following the acknowledgment of his role in the dream, says: "The dream-thoughts dealt with the future of my family after my premature death." He then goes on to assert, as if to remove any doubt, "This was the *only* distressing one among the dream-thoughts" (p. 465, emphasis added). Neither the fact of his death, nor the fear of it (in contrast to the fear for the future of his family), nor the revolt against it are acknowledged. The fact of death itself has been stifled. Freud is as

---

[8] If the inhibition and displacement of affects is indeed, as Freud tells us, the work of censorship, and if the dream work displaces them between elements, it follows that the element to be banned is well known to the censorship. It cannot be absent from the unconscious thought.

indifferent to the possibility of his own death in his analysis, as he was to the death of the Governor in the dream.

This dream is also relevant to the issue of death and ambition discussed below. In "A Castle by the Sea" Freud is the "next in order of rank," and when the Governor drops dead he takes command. The issue of arriving at a higher position is entangled with that of death: the death of the other on the manifest level; latently, the death of the self.

Autopsy-choanalyzing oneself

Another of Freud's dreams where his death is an issue is "The Dissection of the Pelvis." Freud (1900) devotes only a short passage to the analysis of the dream, and does not develop it fully, but his dissection-discussion is enough to give us some important hints:

> Old Brücke must have set me some task; STRANGELY ENOUGH, it related to a dissection of the lower part of my own body, my pelvis and legs, which I saw before me as though in the dissecting-room, but without noticing their absence in myself and also without a trace of any gruesome feeling. ... I was then once more in possession of my legs ... I was making a journey ... with an Alpine guide who was carrying my belongings. Part of the way he carried me too ... At last we reached a small wooden house at the end of which was an open window. There the guide ... laid two wooden boards ... upon the window-sill, so as to bridge the chasm which had to be crossed over from the window. ... I saw two grown-up men lying on wooden benches ... I awoke in a mental fright. (pp. 452–3)

Freud's main conclusion regarding the dream is that the self-dissection is self-analysis, which seems fairly reasonable. Yet the dream also arouses, even upon an initial reading, the suspicion of an underlying death theme. And indeed, Freud writes that the thought that must have accompanied the tiredness in his legs was "'How much longer will my legs carry me?'" (1900, p. 454). And he immediately evokes the end of the Rider Haggard novel, *She*, mentioned among the associations of the dream, in which "the guide, instead of finding immortality for herself and the others, perishes in the mysterious subterranean fire," and states that "a fear of that kind was unmistakably active in the dream-thoughts" (*ibid.*). In the dream, Freud is led by a guide, who at a certain point even carries him "out of consideration for [his] tired legs" (p. 453).[9] This image of being

---

[9] Grinstein (1968, pp. 395–422) underlines several themes in the two books by Haggard Freud alludes to, mostly sexuality, punishment for forbidden incestuous impulses and the image of woman as a threat to men. Among them he mentions the idea in *She* that "there is no death but only change," or that it is "possible to put off one's own death for thousands of years" (p. 401).

carried, and Freud's allusion to Haggard's novel where, as he stresses (p. 454), the guide is originally a woman (in his dream as well, a woman, Louise N, assists in the dissection), bring to mind his discussion in "The Theme of the Three Caskets" (1913b) of the dead hero being carried by the goddess of death or the Valkyrie: "the third of the Fates alone, the silent Goddess of Death, will take him into her arms" (p. 301). So, returning to Freud's dream, an image of death, of being carried by an agent of death, is represented. "How much longer will my legs carry me?," means essentially "how much time do I have left before I die?" Hence, within a general atmosphere of dread—"I woke up in mental fright" (p. 453)—the dream seems to revolve around the fear of impending death. "The wooden house," which appears in the dream as the final destination, or rather the relay station for some mysterious adventure, the crossing of a chasm, is according to Freud, "no doubt, a coffin, that is to say, the grave (p. 454)."

"But," says Freud (1900), "the dream-work achieved a masterpiece in its representation of this most unwished-for of all thoughts by a wish fulfillment." He goes on:

I had already been in a grave once, but it was an excavated Etruscan grave near Orvieto, a narrow chamber with two stone benches along its walls, on which the skeletons of two grown-up men were lying. The inside of the wooden house in the dream looked exactly like it ... The dream seems to have been saying: "if you must rest in the grave, let it be the Etruscan one." And, by making this replacement, it transformed the gloomiest of expectations into one that was highly desirable. Unluckily, ... a dream can turn into its opposite the *idea* accompanying an affect but not always the affect itself. Accordingly, I woke up in a "*mental fright*," even after the successful emergence of the idea that children may perhaps achieve what their father has failed to—a fresh allusion to the strange novel in which a person's identity is retained through a series of generations for over two thousand years. (pp. 454–5)

Years later, in *The Future of an Illusion*, Freud (1927) returns to this dream as an example of wish-fulfillment that attempts to overcome a feeling of helplessness: "The sleeper may be seized with a presentiment of death, which threatens to place him in the grave," but the dream-work cleverly places him in an Etruscan grave and makes it into the fulfillment of a wish (p. 17).

In sum, the dream is quite plausibly a representation, in Freud's mind, of his own death, through various symbols and associations. He is his own surgeon, and he dissects himself as one only dissects a corpse. His march with the guide is a voyage to the other side, across the chasm, into the realm of death. He is unable to carry himself. It is his time to die.

Coming back once more to Freud's (1915, p. 289) claim regarding the impossibility of imagining death because we find that we are still present as spectators: It is hard to imagine a better representation of the impossibility of representation than the image of dissection of one's own pelvis: while the dead body is immobile on the operating table, the representing part, the thinking ego, is active in its very dissection. Thus, a dis-section,[10] a cutting apart, of the person who represents his own death, that is of the represented self and the representing self, is evident here.[11]

How much time?

"'How much longer will my legs carry me?'" Freud (1900, p. 454) asks, and indeed this question reverberates in several of his dreams, including one which he calls an "absurd dream about a dead father" (p. 435), but which is also an absurd dream about his own death:

I received a communication from the town council of my birthplace concerning the fees due for someone's maintenance in the hospital in the year 1851, which had been necessitated by an attack he had had in my house. I was amused by this since, in the first place, I was not yet alive in 1851 and, in the second place, my father, to whom it might have related, was already dead. I went to him in the next room, where he was lying in his bed, and told him about it. To my surprise, he recollected that in 1851 he had once got drunk and had had to be locked up or detained. It was at a time at which he had been working for the firm of T——. "So you used to drink as well?" I asked; "did you get married soon after that?" I calculated that, of course, I was born in 1856, which seemed to be the year which immediately followed the year in question. (pp. 435–6)

Freud's interpretation concludes that the dream's aim was to protest against the accusation, and probably the feeling, that he was not progressing fast enough in the treatment of a patient which had already lasted 5 years. The message in the dream is a simple one, he says. From the fact that 1851 equals 1856, or 51 equals 56, the conclusion to be drawn is that 5 years are nothing. There is no problem in a treatment lasting 5 years, because 5 years are not too long a time. And more importantly, there is still time: "What are four or five years in comparison with a life-time ... ?" (1900, pp. 438–9).

Five years are, Freud tells us, as well as the duration of his longest treatment, also the time of his engagement, the time of his studies, and

---

[10] The German terms used, "*Seiziersaal*," "*präparation*," do not render that literal meaning, but support the overall morbid image.
[11] According to Owens (2004, p. 29), Freud's dream and his interpretation of it paint a picture very similar to the Christian resurrection narrative: from dissolution and disintegration to resurrection of a perfected body and immortality.

the time he was supported by a friend before he stood on his own feet. "I have time enough in front of me," is how he sums it up (1900, p. 438).

Time for what? On the manifest level, Freud means time for the treatment, time to develop his theory and advance in his research, time to get a professorship. To this I would add the obvious: time to live. Death is still in the distant future.

One minor detail is presented only in the final lines of the interpretation, as if it were an insignificant addition. The number 51, says Freud, is also determined in another way: "51 is the age which seems to be a particularly dangerous one to men; I have known colleagues who have died suddenly at that age; and amongst them one who, after long delays, had been appointed to professorship only a few days before his death" (1900, 438–9). The comment seems to be marginal here, but its importance is actually crucial. The number 51 testifies to the more serious pressure of time. Is there still time in front of me? Will I live long enough? And in relation to success and attaining a professorship—will I achieve it before I die?

Of course Freud does not tell us here about his obsession with the age of 51, in other words his belief that he will die at that age, as discussed in Chapter 2. It is an age that is dangerous not just for colleagues or people in general, but most importantly, for Freud himself.

Freud's rule for interpretation of dreams involving people who are alive when they are supposed to be dead, makes an appearance just a few pages before the analysis of the "*1851 and 1856*" dream and again seems useful: When there is a dead man in a dream who appears to be alive, "the dreamer is equating himself with him: he is dreaming of his own death." And whenever in the dream the dreamer says to himself "why, he died ever so long ago," he is expressing a rebellion against this equation (p. 431).

It would then not be too farfetched to apply this to the "1851 and 1856" dream, and claim that Freud is equating himself with his father, and is dreaming of his own death. After all, Freud (1900, p. 436) tells us that his father, dead in reality but alive in the dream, was only a straw man, standing for someone else. This someone else might very well be Freud himself. There is also an implicit equation between them: in the dream Freud knows that in the year in question, 1851, his father was already dead, and he himself was not yet alive, *non vixit*.[12] Neither of them could have been hurried to the hospital. The confident affirmation

---

[12] Concerning the dream's relation to not living, Freud also alludes to the parody some of his patients used to make of his views, when they suggested that they not only look for recollections from a very young age, as he wanted, but also for recollections from the time "at which they were not yet alive" (1900, pp. 451–2).

that his father was indeed already dead seems to be an attempt to repudiate the equation, to insist that he, Freud, is not dead yet, and still has time.[13]

It is interesting to note that almost the entire chapter on absurd dreams, from which this dream is taken and which will be discussed below, consists of dreams of death, specifically the death of a father. Of course Freud's mourning of his father is reflected here, but the series additionally demonstrates that the death of the father conjures up thoughts about death in general, and the death of the son in particular. "The loss of a parent represents the removal of a buffer against death" (Moss and Moss, 1983, p. 72). Because the parent is supposed to die before the child, the adult child feels protected as long as his or her two parents are alive.

When Freud mentions this dream again later in *The Interpretation of Dreams*, he now takes for granted what was not said in the interpretation itself, and treats it as a center of the dream: "there was a *second* line of thought in the latent content of the dream leading to the number 51; and along this track we arrived at my fears of 51 years being the limit of *my* life [emphasis added], in glaring contrast to the dream's dominant train of thought which was lavish in boasts of a long life" (1900, p. 513).[14]

Beyond death itself, the "1851 and 1856" dream also deals with the experience of time. It seems to ask whether time is moving slowly (Freud is not moving fast enough, everything takes so much time—his studies, the long engagement before marriage), or rapidly ("what are four or five years")? It manifests how years can be erased in seconds (1851? no, it was 1856) or last a long time. There was time before Freud was born, and after his father's death. There might even have been a time, 5 years, the dream suggests, when Freud was not yet born but his father had already died. It is an uncanny time, an impossible time. Who was kept in the hospital before Freud was born? Was it him as a baby? The dream seems to be asking if time is purely subjective, or rather extends

---

[13] Note that the dream comprises two issues around the father's death: that he is alive while known to be dead – one can even speak with him – and also that he "was already dead" at the time mentioned. Thus we have fulfilled the two requirements of Freud's rule.

[14] Anzieu (1986 [1975]) tends here and elsewhere to highlight the "positive" and reassuring aspects in this dream, which, like others, gave Freud strength to deal with this anxiety, by allegedly revealing its meaning. "Death would seem more acceptable to him as long as he had time (five years) ... to make a great discovery and publish it" (p. 441). This line of thought only blurs the incessant preoccupation of Freud with death. It obscures the fact that Freud's book is governed by the fear of death and thoughts of death and is written hastily, in a race against time.

backward, to before one's birth and forward to after one's death. And if the latter, how is it related to one's subjective time?

I must not go yet? A visit to the underworld

The issue of time left in one's life reappears in the "Hall with Machines" dream where Freud is summoned to an inquiry in a kind of private sanatorium. Freud, convinced of his innocence, enters a hall of hellish punishment machines, on one of which a colleague of his is stretched out. Finally, he says, "I was then told I could go. But I could not find my hat, and could not go after all" (1900, p. 336).

In a footnote suggesting a secondary meaning of the dream, Freud mentions an association to the closing sentences ("I was then told I could go"): the saying, taken from Schiller, "The Moor has done its duty, the Moor *can go*" (1900, p. 337n). Freud then recalls that he was called a Moor as a child, due to his blackish hair. He is the Moor then, who was told that he could go. Freud continues: "The end of this dream also concealed a rejection of some melancholy thoughts about death: 'I am far from having done my duty, so I must not go yet'" (*ibid.*). We have then both dread (he has done his duty, so he can go; gloomy death is all that is waiting for him) and the revolt against it (I have not done my duty, and, therefore, I must not yet go). Without his hat, Freud really could not go.

Beyond this and the dream's somewhat morbid content which Freud seems to overlook (the hall with machines "reminds [him] of an Inferno"), the dream also entails a comparison with colleagues: Freud sees a colleague stretched out on one of the "hellish instruments of punishment," and at that minute is told he can go (1900, p. 336). A contrast is made here: the colleague is doomed to be in the inferno and will perhaps die, while Freud will not and is free to go. He still has time.

Freud has not, however, always shown himself so indifferent or narcissistically content with the suffering of others. In fact, as we shall see in the next section, one manifestation of death's presence in his dreams is rather concern for others.

Concern for others

Whether he likes it or not, Freud's associations often show him concerned or anxious about the well being of others. On reading *The Interpretation of Dreams* one is struck by the amount of concern over his own health and that of his dear ones. Yet none of this concern for others is acknowledged by Freud as a motive force for a dream.

The "Non Vixit" dream could once again serve as an example. "The exciting cause of the dream," which "was of great importance," was that Fliess was undergoing an operation, and the first reports of his condition were not optimistic. Freud is concerned with Fliess's health, all the more so because the operation was on precisely the day that Fliess was supposedly destined to die according to his numerical theories, as I mentioned above. Moreover, Fliess's sister died very young, after a short illness, and Freud thought Fliess's "constitution" was probably as fragile as his sister's: "The dream-thoughts informed me that I feared for my friend's life" (1900, p. 481).

Yet Freud refuses to follow up on this concern for the life of the other. He is unwilling to accept it, here and elsewhere, as a motive force for the dream. Time and again he notes such concern, but tends to invalidate it in his interpretation, often turning it on its head. It is deemed either imaginary or as concealing a more powerful, more basic force. In the thoughts that led to the "Non Vixit" dream, Freud was so worried about his friend Fliess that he thought that if he received more bad reports about Fliess's health, he would go to Berlin to visit him after all. However, his mention of this thought is followed by the fantasy that he will get there "too late," and will "never cease to reproach" himself. Freud tells us that this guilt-ridden self-reproach for not arriving in time "became the central point of the dream" (1900, p. 481). This theme in turn, including the need to counter or overcome the feelings of shame and guilt ("the need I felt to consider that I was excused by my illness," *ibid.*), combines with the infantile satisfaction at surviving Fliess, to obscure what is perhaps the real, tormenting concern in the interpretation of the dream. Similarly, Breger (2000, pp. 138–40) finds that Freud's interpretation of the dream as involving guilt over rivalry is used as a means of mastering and overcoming the more threatening issue of death and loss.

Freud's concern for the health of people close to him is also subordinated to other factors in other dream interpretations: In the dream of "News of Son from the Front" (1900, pp. 558–60), for example, the very real anxiety and lack of certitude over the son's condition ("we had once more been without news of our son at the front for over a week," p. 559) are only admitted because they hide the deeper satisfaction resulting from Freud's own good health (p. 560). Another dream that one might consider an anxious dream about the well being of another is Freud's childhood dream about his mother being carried by two people with bird beaks, in which Freud is relieved only when he sees the face of his mother, indicating that she is alive (pp. 583–4). Yet even here, the death of the mother is found by Freud to be only a defensive interpretation in the dream itself, against a sexual desire. This tendency is also active in the discussion of "The May Beetle" dream of one of his patients (pp. 289–92), where worries about the absent husband are interpreted by Freud as carrying sexual meanings, as well as in the dream of "Otto Was Looking Ill" (pp. 269–71).

Limping, pale, and seriously ill. Irma

Nowhere, however, is this concern for the basic safety of himself and others more salient than in Freud's (1900) specimen dream, "Irma's Injection." In a reception in a large hall, Freud is talking to his patient Irma. She tells him that she is suffering tremendous pain. Looking down her throat, Freud sees a big white patch and some other bizarre structures. He calls a friend, Dr. M, and together with two other friends, they examine her (pp. 106–7). A discussion ensues concerning the origin of her illness, or the more burning question of who is to be blamed for it. Freud's analysis, in turn, leads to a wish to exculpate himself from Irma's condition: "I am not responsible for the persistence of Irma's pains" (p. 316).

The concern for other people is salient in the dream associations. But even before dwelling on the dream material one might raise the objection that the issue at hand is not sheer concern with another's well being, but a feeling of guilt, which is also of course the primary meaning of the dream—medical malpractice, guilt over not discerning Irma's true illness etc. While guilt is undeniably central here, it does not cover the full extent of concern for others' health and others' lives, as revealed in Freud's associations. These lead him well beyond the issue of medical malpractice, and closer to himself and to true human concern.

In the dream concern over Irma's health is expressed, and elicits anxiety. Irma is looking pale. She is in pain. Something is choking her. When Freud hears this he is "alarmed." Dr. M examines her, and then Freud notes that he was looking "quite different from usual; he was very pale" (Freud, 1900, p. 107). It is as if Irma's paleness is transferred to whoever looks at her.

In the dream Dr. M "was pale, had a clean-shaven chin and walked with a limp." Freud comments that "this [presumably his paleness] was true to the extent that his unhealthy appearance often caused his friends anxiety" (1900, p. 112).

One of the day residues of the dream relates to an injection Otto gave Irma in the dream when she was feeling unwell. Freud recalls having heard from Otto that during his stay with Irma (in reality) he was called to some hotel to give an injection to "someone who had suddenly felt unwell" (1900, p. 115). Another association that comes to Freud's mind is that of a bottle of liqueur, given to him and his wife by Otto, which they opened the evening of the dream. The liqueur had such a bad smell that Freud refused to touch it. He also turned down his wife's suggestion of giving it to the servants: "There was no need for *them* to be poisoned either" (pp. 115–6). Once again, the endangering of someone's life is evoked. Of course, the "them" (emphasized in the original) and "either" point to whose life was actually being threatened.

The issue of ageing is also raised: the examination in the dream reminds Freud of another examination he carried out, of a governess who, although "at a first glance ... seemed a picture of youthful beauty," on opening her mouth "had taken measures to conceal her plates" (1900, p. 109).

The word "dysentery" calls up a young man Freud had treated who had "remarkable difficulties associated with defaecating" which Freud diagnoses as hysteria. Subsequently, however, this man actually contracted dysentery. Freud also speaks about a notion that "morbid matter can be eliminated through the bowels" (1900, p. 114). Irma also reminds Freud of a patient of his "who succumbed to poisoning" (pp. 111–12, 292), induced by a drug Freud himself had prescribed for her. Thus, more and more of Freud's associations involve people whose health was threatened and allusions to possible threats. These do not remain on a general level and involve, as we shall immediately see, specific individuals dear to him.

Freud sees the Irma dream as an example of condensation. Irma was much more than his patient, he says, and "the pathological changes" in her throat involved "allusions to a whole series of other figures" (1900, p. 292). It is precisely the lack of health that connects her with the other figures, and these are numerous: Irma brings to mind a lady friend of hers, who Freud suspects is also a hysteric, and who suffers, like Irma, from hysterical choking; an old woman of 82, about whom Freud received news that she was then suffering from phlebitis; and a child examined in the neurological department (significantly the transition is enabled by the figure of Freud's own child) (*ibid.*).

The concerns about the health of others come closer and closer to Freud's inner circle, to Freud himself. Another association is related to Freud's feelings of guilt surrounding the death from cocaine abuse of his "dear Friend" Fleischl von Marxow (Freud, 1900, p. 111), who is referred to as "my unfortunate friend who had poisoned himself with cocaine" (p. 115).

Dr. M's limp was true in reality, but the limp, together with M's external appearance bring to Freud's mind his own brother, whom

Dr. M resembled in the dream. Freud was informed some days earlier that his brother was "walking with a limp, owing to an arthritic affection of his hip" (1900, p. 112).

Things move closer still to Freud, and become more and more serious. Everyone around him seems to be stricken by some physical illness. Disease and infirmity encircle him. His insistence on feelings of guilt seems defensive. There is guilt, but there is also apprehension, fear, and even alarm. "What is it with everyone?," Freud seems to ask. "Why does everyone's body fail?"

Yet other associations evoke concern for the health of Fliess, who "suffered himself from suppurative rhinitis, which caused me anxiety" (Freud, 1900, p. 117). A year before the dream Fliess "was seriously ill" (p. 294) and Freud went to visit him, presumably out of concern.

Freud's family is not immune either. One association links Irma to Freud's wife, who was also looking pale and puffy and suffered, again like Irma in the dream, from "pains in the abdomen" (Freud, 1900, p. 110n). The phlebitis of the old woman mentioned above, Freud says, also brought his associations back to his wife "who suffered from thrombosis during one of her pregnancies" (p. 118).

The associations continue to come closer to home and the possible threats more grave. The white patches in Irma's throat remind Freud of a serious illness of his daughter some 2 years earlier. He is reminded of "the fright [he] had had in those anxious days" (1900, p. 111). In recalling the woman he had inadvertently poisoned (pp. 111–12, 292), he is suddenly struck by the fact that she bears the same name as his daughter.

Yet more than his daughter's health is at stake: "The scabs on the turbinal bones recalled a worry about my own state of health" (Freud, 1900, p. 111). Having used cocaine extensively to reduce nasal swelling, he is afraid that he might develop a necrosis of the nasal membrane, as one of his patients did following the same procedure. Is it only the necrosis of the nasal membrane which is at issue, or is a different kind of "necrosis" at stake? As we recall, he is also reminded of the death of a close friend resulting from the use of this drug (p. 111).

Freud's associations then conjure a crowd of characters, an assembly of personages, all sick, in danger, hurt or malfunctioning in some way. Some are remote, others are as close as can be. Freud is concerned, alarmed, and anxious about the health of others. The threat of illness and death always looms, it seems. And he himself is not exempt.

This vast amalgam of concerns and anxieties, so copiously abundant in the associations of "Irma's Injection," evaporates almost completely in the process of determining the final meaning of the dream. In the end it mainly comes down to the fulfillment of one preconscious wish—Freud's desire to exculpate himself from Irma's affliction: "*I* was not to blame for Irma's pains" (1900, p. 119). It is not only in the conclusion that these themes are minimized. While they are plentiful in the associations, Freud remains perplexingly blind to them in his discussion, and his best effort is to divert them to the issue of medical malpractice—that is to guilt, which is again safe ground for him. When at the very end of his discussion of the dream (p. 120), Freud again raises his concern with the health of others and himself, and actually lists many of the cases discussed here, he once again quickly dismisses them as subordinate to his wish for self-presentation as "highly conscientious." He says that they could be categorized as "concern about my own and other people's health—professional conscientiousness." The leap and the reduction enacted through the dash between the two parts of this phrase tell much of the story. The thoughts about others' health are relegated to evidence used by the defense, presented to refute a felt accusation of lack of professional conscientiousness or medical malpractice (p. 120). The possibility that they had their own influence on the dream, or that they really form a kernel of meaning, is not considered.

It nevertheless seems highly improbable that such recurrent and obsessive references to the health deficiencies of the people around him, and to the danger they might be subject to, is merely a cover for something else, and that the anxious days at the bedside of his mortally ill daughter or the experience of his own illness, which might awaken concerns regarding his own mortality, carry only secondary meanings. Moreover, what happened to the affects that accompanied all these real life events and circumstances? Is it more logical to suppose that the real danger for his own child, wife, best friend, and himself was only used to express something else? Did all the emotion simply dissolve in the process of fabricating the dream?

It seems unlikely. Death seems to be involved in the dream of "Irma's Injection" in a much more central manner. This is also Jacques Lacan's conclusion in his famous analysis of the dream. He starts by recalling that Freud's main wish in the dream, namely to absolve himself of any responsibility for the failure of the treatment, is only preconscious or conscious, and cannot in itself explain why Freud regards this dream as so crucial. What was it that Freud saw in the depth of Irma's throat?

"A horrendous sight," he answers, elaborating:

Everything blends ... in this image, from the mouth to the female sexual organ ... There's a horrendous discovery here, that of the flesh one never sees, the foundation of things, the other side of the head, of the face, ... the flesh from which everything exudes, at the very heart of the mystery, the flesh in as much as it is suffering, is formless, in as much as its form in itself is something which

Concern for others 73

provokes anxiety. Spectre of anxiety, identification of anxiety, the final revelation of *you are this—You are this, which is far from you, this which is the ultimate formlessness.* (1978, p. 186; 1988b, pp. 154–5)

This part of the dream led:

to the apparition of the terrifying anxiety-provoking image, to this real Medusa's head, to the revelation of this something which properly speaking is unnamable, the back of the throat, the complex unlocatable form, ... the abyss of the feminine organ from which all life emerges, this gulf of the mouth, in which everything is swallowed up, and no less the image of death in which everything comes to its end. (1978, p. 196; 1988b, p. 164)

Lacan goes on to mention the possibly fatal illness of Freud's daughter, and the death of his patient. He recalls the three Fates, whose significance Freud (1913b) analyzed in his "The Theme of the Three Caskets," the youngest of whom, Irma in the dream, signifies death, and summarizes: "Hence there is an anxiety-provoking apparition of the image ... of the real lacking any possible mediation, of the ultimate real ... this something faced with which all words cease and all categories fail, the object of anxiety par excellence" (1978, p. 196; 1988b, p. 164).

It is at this point in the dream that Freud's ego recedes into the background and is decomposed into its successive identifications. Then comes a second climax in the dream, the appearance of the symbolic order in its total, inexplicable form, eluding significance. It is the irruption of the real, in the form of the "whitish grey scabs" (Freud, 1900, p. 107), which alarms Freud so much and necessitates the introduction of the symbolic, which covers the real and initiates the order of culture and language, enabling us to forget. Yet at bottom, when the veil is lifted, what we see is the horror of death.

The concern for others, to sum up, involves recognition of the fragility of human life, and can reach a very high degree of fear, which acknowledges the ongoing vulnerability of our bodies. Freud acknowledges the fact that the Irma dream was not fully analyzed, that a gap remained in his understanding of it (1900, p. 121). Just what the nature of this lack is he does not indicate. It now seems that the issue of death is central to this gap. This same gap reverberates through many other dreams in the book, as it does through life itself, and remains, for Freud, a continuous blind spot.[15]

---

[15] One cannot discuss the Irma dream without mentioning a very real and legitimate cause for concern around it, which stretches far beyond Freud's declared vacillations over whether Irma's illness is organic or not. We now know (Masson, 1984, pp. 55–106; 1985, pp. 106–127) the detail Freud omitted from his discussion: that Fliess has forgotten, during an operation on one of Freud's patients, Emma Eckstein (represented

We gradually come to see that death is recurrent in Freud's dream book in a way that was not initially evident. It emerges as a continuous concern behind many of his dreams, both directly present or indirectly and in disguise. But our exploration of death's role in the book does not end here. We shall see in the next chapter that death's presence is even wider and that it runs through many more dreams, including ones where nobody actually dies. I shall, therefore, postpone my conclusions to the end of the next chapter, where I hope death's centrality to the book will be further established.

---

by Irma in the dream) a half-meter long gauze in her nasal cavity. When it was taken out, "a flood of blood" burst out, Emma "turned white, her eyes bulged, and she had no pulse" (letter to Fliess, March 8, 1895, Masson, 1985, p. 117). The danger to Emma's life seems to have been very real (pp. 117, p. 121), and it no doubt unnerved Freud considerably.

4 To dream, perchance to die: A further exploration of *The Interpretation of Dreams*

Freud's most intimate text, *The Interpretation of Dreams*, we see, is itself strong evidence against his position that death is marginal in psychic life. Both his claim about the irrepresentability of death in the unconscious, and his belief that death concerns are always superfluous and secondary to other psychic motives seem to be put in question by what slowly emerges, through our reading, as the constant and deep presence of death in Freud's own dreams. We have seen how behind cases of the death of others, there are often glimpses of Freud's own death, how this death is even sometimes directly implicated in his dreams, and how genuine concern for other people's lives is sometimes apparent. In what follows, we will see how death is intricately entangled in Freud's psychic life, and how in fact any reading of the book that does not acknowledge the role death plays in it will necessarily remain partial. Death is not an isolated issue figuring in this or that dream, but the essence of the material of which Freud's dreams are made, a constant concern that finds repeated expressions in his dreams. We shall begin with exploring the centrality of death in Freud's ambitious strivings, move on to a rereading of the essence of absurd dreams, and end with a closer look into the dynamics of denial and recognition of death.

Death and ambition

The theme of death may be most salient in *The Interpretation of Dreams* in the context of ambition. Freud's ambition constitutes a thread running through the book. It is the hidden wish behind many of the dreams, and ties into several childhood memories and determinants. Specific manifestations of his ambition are related to his wish to become a professor, and the whole cluster of related themes (anti-Semitism, jealousy, feelings of superiority, etc.), and even to doubts concerning the publication of *The Interpretation of Dreams* and the possible glory that might result from it.[1]

---

[1] All of these aspects are subsumed under my use in this chapter of the term "ambition."

While the book remains silent about the role of death in mental life, we shall see that death has a very strong influence on the ostensibly unrelated theme of ambition. If the issues of ambition, achievement, fame, reputation, and the future of his work trouble Freud, they do so because of their relation to death. It is from this link to the issue of mortality that they draw most of their motive force.

The man with the beard

A first hint at the intrinsic link between ambition and the hourglass can be found in one of the first dreams analyzed in the book, namely "Uncle with the Yellow Beard" (Freud, 1900, p. 137). The dream consists of not much more than an image: Freud's friend R is Freud's uncle in the dream, his face is somewhat changed, and he has a very noticeable yellow beard. The real life trigger to the dream was a meeting with R., who had long been awaiting a professorial appointment, the delay being, as the friend suspected, due to anti-Semitic discrimination. Just before visiting Freud he succeeded in obtaining certain evidence confirming his suspicions. Freud himself was only recently recommended as *professor extraordinarius*, but was warned not to get his hopes up, as the chances were slim that the ministry would approve the appointment. The dream associations lead him to the following conclusion. Both R and another friend are condensed into the image of the uncle, and are thus represented as either simpletons or criminals, for the uncle was both. And if their character traits are responsible for the fact that neither attained professorships, then Freud can be reassured that no anti-Semitic considerations were involved, and, therefore, retain the hope that things may turn out differently in his case (pp. 137–45). The discussion repeatedly raises the question of ambition and renown, including childhood memories where Freud was foretold he would become an important person.

Yet what about the yellow beard? In reality, the uncle did not have one. The hair of Freud's friend "had originally been extremely dark." "But," says Freud, "when black-haired people begin to turn grey, they pay for the splendour of their youth. Hair by hair, their black beards go through an unpleasing change of colour: first they turn to a reddish brown, then to a yellowish brown, and only then to a definite grey. My friend R's beard was at that time passing through this stage—and so, incidentally, was my own, as I had noticed with dissatisfaction" (1900, pp. 138–9).

It is hard to ignore the issue of passage of time in this association. The continuous delays cannot be ignored, because as the graying of one's hair signifies, time presses on, death is closing in, and one might never win that appointment at all, or achieve it too late.

Non vixit

Ambition is a manifest theme in the by now familiar "Non Vixit" dream. Freud discusses it primarily in relation to the death wish toward others. He twice cites Brutus' lines in Shakespeare's *Julius Caesar*: "As he was ambitious, I slew him" (1900, pp. 424, 484). "Wherever there is rank and promotion the way lies open for wishes that call for suppression," he continues. "Shakespeare's Prince Hal could not, even at his father's sickbed, resist the temptation of trying on the crown" (p. 484; Freud refers to *Henry IV, Part II*: IV, 5). The issue here looks like no more than self-promotion with a concomitant death wish toward others, but as we dig further we discover that this is not quite so. Freud is fond of citing another line from *Henry IV* (*Part I*: V, 1), where Prince Hal tells Falstaff: "Thou owest God a death." Prince Hal does not only wish for the death of his father to succeed him on the crown; he is also keenly aware of his own ephemeral nature. He knows that every ambition always has one eye turned toward death.

The words that Freud pronounces in the dream, "non vixit," were taken from a memorial for Kaiser Josef: "For the well being of his country he lived not long but wholly" ("Saluti publicae vixit non diu sed totus") (1900, pp. 422–3). Dying is related here to the question of having lived wholly or partially. Leaving early means not finishing what should have been finished (as is indicated by the use of "but," *sed*).[2] It is as if one has to live either a long life or to live it fully if one is to earn a memorial.

But the question of memorials is even more central to the *non vixit* dream. A few days before having this dream Freud attends the ceremony where the memorial for his deceased colleague Fleischl is unveiled. He sees another memorial there, this time for his old, illustrious teacher, Brücke, and it makes him think about his friend P (Josef Paneth). The dream, then, elicits a series of memorials—for those who lived long enough to fulfill their role in the world, and for those who did not: "The premature death of my brilliant friend P., whose whole life had

---

[2] Freud (1900, p. 423) actually misquotes the Kaiser Josef memorial. He writes '*patriae*' instead of '*publicae*.' Wittels interpreted this mistake, and Freud (1900, p. 423) admits he is probably right. One should note that in the course of his interpretation Wittels says that "Freud is a quiet citizen who would like to live and die at peace.... the champions of the enlightenment did not live to see the revolution; and Martin Luther died before the Thirty Years War" (1924, pp. 100–1, cited from Grinstein, 1968, pp. 285–6).

Of course, it is impossible to know if it is this part that Freud approved of, but it certainly goes very well with our emphasis in what follows on the fear of dying before achieving one's life goal, and that one will never enter the promised land.

been devoted to science, had robbed him of a well-merited claim to a memorial in these same precincts. Accordingly, I gave him this memorial in my dream" (1900, 423).

Who could that "brilliant" researcher "whose whole life had been devoted to science" possibly be? Is there a need to recall Freud's comment (mentioned above) about his identification with Paneth, and in general with people bearing the name Joseph (1900, p. 484n)? The obvious and harrowing question behind the thought is whether Freud himself will have a memorial. Does he merit one? "Do you suppose," he asks in his famous letter to Fliess (June 12, 1900), after visiting the house where he had the dream of "Irma's Injection," "that someday one will read on a marble tablet on this house—'Here, on July 24, 1895, the secret of the dream revealed itself to Dr. Sigm. Freud.' So far there is little prospect of it" (Masson, 1985, p. 417). Among the three Josephs evoked by the dream (Paneth, Breuer, Kaiser Josef) and the three memorials (Kaiser Josef's, Brücke's, and Fleischl's), Freud is thinking about the fourth memorial, his own. The memorial not built for Paneth is a memorial not built for Freud himself.

It seems that the dream reflects a series of thoughts revolving around the issue of leaving a mark on the world which will endure after one is gone ("'It's quite true that no one's truly irreplaceable,'" Freud, 1900, p. 485), and around the value of the life lived. These concerns seem to provide a better explanation than that of Freud for the slip at the center of the dream—"Non vixit" instead of "Non vivit," "did not live" instead of "is not living." The more threatening question is not if Fl, or any other self-equivalent person is alive, but whether he has ever really lived at all. Is an unfulfilled life enough to ascertain that one has even been alive? The threat for Freud is that he will die too soon, thus rendering his life meaningless. The meaning of one's death is directly related for him to one's accomplishments, and in Freud's case, to what he has achieved in his research, and consequently to the possible claim to symbolic immortality.

Rome

The series of dreams on Freud's "longing to visit Rome" is overdetermined, he says, that is it was elicited from multiple sources, including the issue of Jewishness, his friendship with Fliess, and his relationship with his father. It is also, it seems, the arena where the link between ambition and death and finitude is played out. From the beginning of the discussion, Rome is already situated as unattainable, and in a way that directly links it with a threat to Freud's health: "For a long time to come, no

Death and ambition

doubt, I shall have to continue to satisfy that longing in my dreams: for at the season of the year when it is possible for me to travel, residence in Rome must be avoided for reasons of health" (Freud, 1900, pp. 193–4). So Rome is longed for, but feared because it is dangerous. In one dream, Freud sees Rome "half-shrouded in mist," from a hill and comments that "[t]here was more in the content of this dream than I feel prepared to detail; but the theme of "the promised land seen from afar" was obvious in it" (p. 194). We have here both a reminder of Freud's lifelong identification with the figure of Moses and an allusion to the question of dying before achieving one's life mission. Moses sees the Promised Land from afar, but dies in the wilderness. The question seems to be raised for Freud whether he will get to fulfill his wish, or die before it is carried out.

What is it that Freud does not wish to tell? Anzieu (1986 [1975], p. 185) seems to give a plausible explanation. Freud says that he was reminded of the city of Lübeck, which he first saw shrouded in mist. According to Jones (1953, p. 165), this city was where Freud and his wife Martha went on their honeymoon. It is also a city where Martha had a fantasy of drowning (Anzieu, 1986 [1975], p. 185; Jones, 1953, p. 146). Anzieu, therefore, refers to Rome "half shrouded in mist" as a "metonymical substitute for 'Martha drowned in the sea at Lübeck,'" and to the latent thought as "Martha might have died before I possessed her" (p. 185). Freud wrote to Martha after she told him her fantasy that her death would be "the end of the world, at least the world so far as I am concerned" (cited in Jones, 1953, p. 146). It would also be his own end, as he hints sometime later, for he would then have taken his own life (p. 146).

A second place mentioned in the dream—the spa at Gleichenberg—is even more pertinent to our discussion. It was there that Freud visited the fiancé of Martha's sister, Minna, who was seriously ill. Realizing he is doomed, the fiancé asks Minna to break off the engagement, but she refuses (Anzieu, 1986 [1975], p. 185). When Freud learns of this he writes to Martha: "And you wouldn't behave differently, wouldn't leave me before I died, if it looked as though I were going to die. And I certainly wouldn't give up what is most precious to me as long as I am alive" (letter of June 23, 1885. E. Freud, 1960, p. 155). So, while the hidden content of the dreams seems to have a sexual meaning, this meaning is also closely linked to the issue of death and of fulfilling one's aspirations before one's life ends. There is a desire involved, but the deeper question is whether this desire will be consummated before one dies.

The whole series is saturated with imagery of dying—trains, a stream of dark water with black cliffs on one side and meadows with white flowers on the other—related perhaps to the image of the river Styx one has to cross.

The landscape of dark cliffs reminds Freud of Karlsbad, and he comes to see two Jewish jokes as part of the dream material. The first one he calls "the '*constitution*' story":

An impecunious Jew had stowed himself away without a ticket in the fast train to Karlsbad. He was caught, and each time tickets were inspected he was taken out of the train and treated more and more severely. At one of the stations on his *via dolorosa* he met an acquaintance, who asked him where he was traveling to. 'To Karlsbad,' was his reply, 'if my constitution can stand it.' (1900, p. 195)

The theme of endangering one's health, one's constitution if you like, which was linked with traveling to Rome at the beginning of Freud's discussion, is further reinforced here. One might never make it to Rome, for one's constitution might not stand it. It is a race between two movements—the ever-weakening constitution, and the closing in on one's goal. The constitution is ever too weak. It is a "via dolorosa," and such a "via" has only one possible end.[3]

When in reality Freud gets to within fifty miles of Rome and then turns back, he understands how the longing for Rome is related to some of his youthful experiences. He is reminded of Hannibal, who, like him, "had been fated not to see Rome" (1900, p. 195), and he tells the reader about his identification as a child with him, an identification that is intertwined with issues of Judaism, Christianity, and anti-Semitism. Apart from being a Semitic leader who fought against Rome, which later became identified with the church, Hannibal was a "great man," whose lifelong ambition to enter Rome had been frustrated. Freud also mentions Massena, who as Grinstein (1968, pp. 82–9) indicates, is yet another example of not achieving one's lofty goal, the conquest of Lisbon in Massena's case. In these two examples, as in the case of Moses, the magnitude of the figure and the fact that his life ended before his ultimate goal had been reached are linked, and this is precisely what seems to trouble Freud. He aspires to be like these larger-than-life characters, but is afraid that his constitution will not stand it. He is afraid that he will see the Promised Land only from afar, and die before entering Rome, or on a more mundane level, before publishing his book on the interpretation of dreams. It is only after the book is finished in 1901 that Freud is able to surmount his internal resistance and visit Rome.

---

[3] Karlsbad was itself another place related to health problems – Freud (1900, p. 195) says that doctors, including him, used to prescribe treatment there for people suffering from diabetes.

Winckelmann, also mentioned in Freud's association (in relation with Hannibal), is another figure who paid with his life for aspiring to Rome. Actually, he pays for the fulfillment of that wish. As Grinstein (1968, p. 77) points out, Winckelmann got to live some time in Rome, where he was appointed a cardinal's librarian, but was then murdered. The nuance here is different. The fear is not of failing to attain one's life's goal, but rather of having to pay dearly for achieving one's ambition. Alongside a notion of punishment clearly at work here, there is another active train of thought: the possibility that achieving one's goal means the end of the story. Life goes on as long as the goal is unattained and one's desires remain unfulfilled. By repeatedly postponing the fulfillment of the wish, the realization of one's ambition, one in a way postpones death.[4] Rome is not only a goal but also a threat, and death is not only a possible risk on the way, but also the potential consequence of the very attainment of the goal.

"I must not delay any longer"

"The Dissection of the Pelvis" dream, discussed in the preceding chapter as representing Freud's own death, is yet another dream in which the themes of ambition and death are inseparable. Freud (1900) easily sees the link between the dissection of his own body and his self-analysis, the task of analyzing his own psyche (p. 454). The thought in the background of the dream, "'How much longer will my legs carry me?'" (p. 454), we saw, means "how much time do I have left before I die?" It is a question about time needed versus time remaining. This is the time needed to complete one's work and to have it recognized. Freud is troubled about the success of this enterprise which is taking too long—he had himself postponed the printing of the dreams book for over a year (p. 477). He recalls an earlier discovery of his that had waited far too long before publication. Freud then notes that the absence of a gruesome feeling in the dream (*Grauen*), which should have perhaps accompanied the dissection of the pelvis, was the fulfillment of a wish because he "should also have been very glad to miss growing grey—'*Grauen*' ... I was already growing quite grey, and the grey of my hair was another

---

[4] In his dream Freud asks someone for the way, later seeing this as another allusion to Rome, for all roads lead there. But Rome's association with death also comes up here, for it is not the only place many roads lead to: "[A]s we say in Vienna," Freud writes to Fliess in a different context, "there are many roads to the Central Cemetery" (May 28, 1888, Masson, 1985, p. 22).

Grinstein (1968, p. 72) explains that in the Karlsbad spa one used to drink a lot of the mineral water with a laxative effect, and so one had to rush to the bathroom time after time; and so the joke "if my constitution can stand it" refers, in addition to the difficulty getting to the wished for place, to the possible consequences of arriving.

reminder that I must not delay any longer. And, as we have seen," he continues, "the thought that I should have to leave it to my children to reach the goal of my difficult journey forced its way through to representation at the end of the dream" (pp. 477–8). Once again, the issue of finishing one's work and achieving a goal is intimately connected to the fear of time, which, flowing relentlessly, might undermine one's work or its value, or prevent it from being fully carried out.

The day event that occasioned the dream, Freud (1900) tells us, was a conversation with a woman who asked Freud for something to read. He gave her Haggard's *She*, and in response to her somewhat nagging question, "Have you nothing of your own?" he replies: "No, my own immortal works have not yet been written" (p. 453). Thus, it is the work, the self-analysis that will become a book and a theory, which is supposed to secure immortality. Let us also recall that Freud draws an association between the tired feeling in his legs, accompanied by the question "How much longer will my legs carry me?" and the end of Haggard's book where "the guide, instead of finding immortality for herself and the others, perishes...," and states that "[a] fear of that kind was unmistakably active in the dream-thoughts" (p. 454) (Freud additionally sees himself, in his role as an author, precisely as a guide for his readers in their imaginary walk through his book. See his letter to Fliess, August 6, 1899, Masson, 1985, pp. 365–6).[5] Hence, despite the fact that immortality might be achieved through work, one might fail, because while one is dallying or limping along, time is racing forward. Premature death is not only a threat, however, but also an impetus to proceed: "I must not delay any longer" (p. 477).[6]

Late in life

Freud's (1900, pp. 269–71) brief dream about his friend Otto looking ill once again links life's temporality with the theme of ambition. Otto was asked by Freud to watch over Freud's children's physical education "in case anything happens to [him]" (p. 270). Otto is represented in the dream as a certain Baron L, who proved himself to be an untrustworthy helper. Freud, in contrast, is identified with Professor R who "resembled me [Freud] in having followed an independent path outside the

---

[5] On the metaphor of the book as a journey and Freud as guide, and in general on the literary and rhetorical aspects of the book, see Hyman (1981).

[6] Harmonizing Freud's delays in publishing work which might make him immortal with his very wish for immortality, Kofman (1985) suggests the delays had to do with guilt, lest Freud succeed where his father had not: "I deny myself immortality and bequeath it only to my children out of guilt toward my father, who was unable to attain it himself for lack of heroism" (p. 25)

academic world" and "had only achieved his well-merited title late in life." "So once again I was wanting to be a professor!" Freud exclaims. "Indeed the words 'late in life' were themselves a wish fulfillment; for they implied that I should live long enough to see my boys through the age of puberty myself" (p. 271).

As in so many of his dreams we are again witness to Freud's ambition to become a professor, achieve glory, and have his work recognized as valuable. And these wishes are again bound up with the fundamental, harrowing question of whether he will fulfill them before he dies. Freud does not trust Otto in the dream. He knows that something might indeed happen to him (Freud) and is thus aware of death. It is on this basis that he perceives a wish fulfillment behind the words "late in life"—because it means he would live long enough to watch over his children's education himself. Being a professor and living long enough are even more intricately linked here than they normally are in the book, since here, being a professor, like professor R, actually signifies living long enough. That professor R achieves his glory late in life is reassuring. Being a professor "late in life" means that ipso facto one had had a long life.

The Botanical Monograph

Another dream where the question of death seems to hover in the background of issues of ambition and academic success is "The Botanical Monograph," which, at face value, does not seem to be related to death at all:

I had written a monograph on a certain plant. The book lay before me and I was at the moment turning over a folded coloured plate. Bound up in each copy there was a dried specimen of the plant, as though it had been taken from a herbarium. (p. 169)

The monograph, as Freud (1900) interprets it, is his own work—either the monograph on the coca-plant, or more importantly, the dream book itself from which this dream is taken. Fliess writes to him that he can see the dream book "lying finished" before him, and him "turning over its pages." Freud envies him, for he is still only in the midst of writing it: "If only I could have seen it lying finished before me!" (p. 172). So this dream is another one in which Freud is concerned about his own success and achievements. He wonders if the book will ever be finished. Prospects for it are not very clear at this time. And there is the history of the cocaine monograph. There, Freud had a chance to enter the pantheon of glory, and feels he missed the chance. Another person achieved fame, while he remained relatively unknown. The dream seems to be preoccupied with the question of whether the dream book will finally bring him glory. Will Freud be the famous author of a monograph? (See my discussion of the specific link of writing and death in *The Interpretation of Dreams* in Razinsky, 2013.)

Other indications in the dream shift the issue away from fame in itself, and closer to the more troubling question of leaving one's thumbprint on the world before passing away, and the relationship between death and our life's work. Something in the dream images themselves raises a suspicion, beginning perhaps with the dried plant specimen. Freud's associations to "herbarium" lead him to a memory where he and other students are asked to clean the school's herbarium, which is infected with worms, book-worms. In fact, he says, he himself was a book-worm (Freud, 1900, pp. 171–2). So now we have a dead plant, and worms eating through it, thus suggesting worms in the grave, which eat not the product of a person but the person himself.

More death imagery emerges when we examine what is on Freud's mind when he recounts the dream, that is, the unconscious associations of his associations. In trying to account for the link between the dream and the day residues, Freud (1900) says that background thoughts of the previous day are not enough to evoke a dream. And, for seemingly no reason, he quotes Horatio in *Hamlet*: "There needs no ghost, my lord, come from the grave to tell us this" (p. 175). So the grave seems to come up again, without really being required by the context itself.

In another section of the book, Freud (1900) again momentarily evokes the dream of "The Botanical Monograph" to demonstrate that a dream contains less affect than the dream-thought behind it. While the thought behind "The Botanical Monograph" dream consisted of "a passionately agitated plea on behalf of my liberty to act as I chose," the dream itself has "an indifferent ring about it." "This reminds one," Freud then says, "of the peace that had descended upon a battlefield strewn with corpses; no trace is left of the struggle which raged over it" (p. 467). Death is once again evoked.

"The Botanical Monograph," however, has an even deeper relation to death. The day following the dream Freud has a peculiar daydream: He fantasizes that should he ever get glaucoma, he would undergo an operation by a surgeon in Fliess's house. He would go there incognito, and the surgeon would boast how easily such operations can be performed ever since the introduction of cocaine; "and I should not give the slightest hint that I myself had had a share in the discovery," adds Freud. He then continues: "This phantasy had led on to reflections of how awkward it is, when all is said and done, for a physician to ask for medical treatment for himself from his professional colleagues." The surgeon would not know who Freud is, and Freud "should be able to pay his fees like anyone else" (1900, p. 170).

That this fantasy involves both Freud's emotions regarding the discovery of the anaesthetic properties of cocaine, and his relationship with Fliess, is clear. Yet it is also clear that there is more to it. It is indeed awkward for a doctor to fall ill, and to require treatment; for the curer to be powerless when it comes to his own body. This fantasy involves an acknowledgment by Freud of his non-immunity to health problems, of his own fragility, vulnerability, impotence, and mortality. He is not omnipotent, even if he did write the monograph on cocaine. He is indeed "like anyone else." He too can run up a fee, he too has a debt to pay. He too "owe(s) nature a death," as he likes to quote (Freud, 1915, p. 289). Achieving academic or career-related aims alone will not prevent death. Even within a completed monograph, all that remains are some dried flowers. One's books will be like the specimens in the herbarium. They will not make their author any more vivid or alive, once he is dead. Symbolic immortality through one's life work is hereby negated. Whether or not Freud will one day be Freud, the well-known author who changed the world, Freud the conquistador of the mind, in the face of death he will still be, as in his daydream, "incognito."

The monograph dream then binds together, literally, the doubts surrounding the publication of the book and potential glory with the recognition of human fragility and mortality. It also goes a step further and negates the possibility of achieving immortality through one's work. The race is futile, because one is doomed to lose, whether or not one becomes famous.

Method in the madness

Similar issues come into play in a letter to Jung of April 16, 1909, which pertains to the same period. Freud discusses his (by now old) belief that he will die at 61 or 62. The conviction, he says, first appeared in 1899, when two events occurred: he finished *The Interpretation of Dreams,* and received a new phone number, 14362. He was 43 years old. Freud writes:

> Thus it was plausible to suppose that the other figures [following the 43] signified the end of my life, hence 61 or 62. Suddenly method entered into my madness. The superstitious notion that I would die between the ages of 61 and 62 proves to coincide with the conviction that with *The Interpretation of Dreams* I had completed my life work, that there was nothing more for me to do and that I might just as well lie down and die. (McGuire, 1974, Letter 139, p. 219)

The completion of the tremendous effort put into his *magnum opus* is for Freud a reason to assume his life is about to end. On the one hand, his work completed; he can now rest his mind. On the other hand, Freud does not accept so easily the superstitious belief in a predestined age of death. Instead, another unconscious thought might be at work: Earlier, Freud's work gave him the horizon of a future. But now that his work is finished, what will keep him going? Freud must now reengage himself, and assume new, death-repelling projects.[7]

Yet there is still another dynamic involved. We explored above Freud's fear that he will die before completing his work. His calm acceptance of dying when the book is finished seems to be, on the one hand, a defensive displacement of the fear of death: the fear is not of death, even a premature death, but of not finishing a specific task. It seems that if only he can finish this work, Freud will be rendered indifferent, or immune, to the fact of death itself. On the other hand, however, let us recall Freud's reply to the woman who asked him for a book of his own (in the context of the "Dissection of the Pelvis" dream): "my own immortal works have not yet been written" (1900, p. 453). *The Interpretation of Dreams* is Freud's claim to symbolic immortality, and this renders dying in the wake of its completion somehow less significant, something less than dying. Dying before it is completed is far more frightening, because it implies final and irreversible death. That is maybe the way to understand Freud's (1901) frank remark, in his interleaved copy of the 1904 edition of *The Psychopathology of Everyday Life*, that his preoccupation with the possible dates of his death was related to a "suppressed ambition (immortality)" and was a displacement of the normal fear of death (p. 260 n. 3).

The "1851 and 1856" dream

The "1851 and 1856" dream discussed earlier can be interpreted, we saw, as referring to Freud's own death. But Freud's interpretation also turns on the theme of ambition and the will to succeed. The trigger for the dream where the years 1851 and 1856 are confounded is a reproach Breuer makes to Freud for still treating the same patient after 5 years. Freud says that the dream-thought was a protest against the accusation that he "was not getting on faster"—with the patient of course, but then in other domains as well. "Was he not aware," he asks, that "conditions

---

[7] See Freud's "2467" example from *The Psychopathology of Everyday Life* (1901, p. 242), where finishing the manuscript of *The Interpretation of Dreams* is intimately related to a concern lest this signifies the end of his life.

of that kind are altogether incurable and last a lifetime? What were *four or five* years in comparison with a whole lifetime?" (1900, p. 437).

So Freud's work is slow going; it takes him too long to produce results and there is no real certainty that success is even possible. This theme cannot be separated from the issue of Freud's death, that the dream also deals with, because the source of Freud's anxiety is the likelihood that of the two events toward which he is moving, success and death, the latter shall come first.

Success means not only the success of the specific analysis, but of Freud in general. His (1900) dream-thought tells us: "if only I had been the second generation, the son of a professor ... I should certainly have *got on faster*" (p. 438, emphasis in the original). Being a second generation professor means, of course, having wanted to be a professor oneself. Freud reassures himself that he still has time, but the associations quickly lead him to recall the significance of the age of 51 as a dangerous age. Not only does he know colleagues who died at that age, but also, among these colleagues is, as I cited before, "one who, after long delays, had been appointed to professorship only a few days before his death" (p. 439).

Aspire – expire

We find then that death and ambition are very much interrelated in *The Interpretation of Dreams*. Behind every reference to Freud's professorial aspirations, in every vacillation between doubt and reassurance about his work's future, is the shadow of death, the stark reminder that life is finite. The time one has left to accomplish one's aims is uncertain, and this fact enters every consideration, every expectation. These are not marginal, sporadic or isolated thoughts, but pertinacious, tormenting concerns.[8]

Overall, there seems to be a close interaction between the question of the value of life (and one's life work) and temporal finitude running through Freud's text. This is manifested on different levels. It is implied that one's deeds in this life may grant one a form of immortality. Such immortality would be a sort of answer to the fact of death, which threatens to render life valueless. Yet the value of immortality is fragile,

---

[8] In his famous interpretation of the Irma dream Erik Erikson lays stress on Freud's ambition, namely his wish to become a "somebody" (1954, pp. 41–3), and sees the dream as originating in internal conflicts over generativity: Freud's wish to generate new thought and the accompanying internal and external doubts and reproaches (36). Having seen in the previous chapter how death too is central to this dream, and in light of the exploration of the interrelatedness of death and ambition, we can perhaps now see how death sharpens the ambitious strivings or is pulled into the dream by them.

because it is always under the risk of crumbling once it is recalled that it is only symbolic. A memorial plaque is nice, but it does not warm us as we are "freezing in the ice cold grave," to use Freud's (1900, p. 254) phrase, too dead to enjoy such immortality. Posthumous glory is, therefore, of no use to Freud if the importance of his work is not also recognized within his lifetime, and so he feels the need for signs of this recognition, a professorship being just one of them.[9]

The question of life's value, however, is not only relevant to securing immortality, but has a more intrinsic aspect. Life itself might be related to as valuable or valueless, and value is often a question, as we have seen, of whether we perceive ourselves as having fully lived our lives or not. Death's relation to life's internal value is also double-edged. We noted above the motif of a race against time/death, and what appears to be a continuous oscillation on the question of life's value. Death is an impetus to act, to live fully, but on the other hand always threatens to undermine that which is achieved. "If both of us are still granted a few more years for quiet work, we shall certainly leave behind something that can justify our existence," Freud writes to Fliess on April 1896 (Letter from April 2, 1896, Masson, 1985, p. 180), expressing in a condensed form how work can both vanquish death and be vanquished by it.[10] Both stances discussed in Freud's short essay, "On Transience" (1916 [1915]), that finitude can render life either meaningful or meaningless, come into play in *The Interpretation of Dreams*.

Considered from a different angle ambition might be risky. One might pay for it, as a punishment, in some unconscious fantasy. Alternatively, attaining one's objective might be dangerous, because it might leave one with nothing more to aspire to. Life would effectively reach its conclusion. Death is warded off as long as one is working toward one's goal. This may lead to a desire to defer, delay, or hamper the attainment of success, so as to postpone death. This may also apply to "those wrecked by success," a character type Freud (1916) describes in a different context some years later.

Ambition is linked to death because it is related to the planning of future time, because one's projects are always limited, and because ambition involves the issue of self-worth in its deepest sense, against a background of finitude. Becker (1973) believes man's fundamental

---

[9] The narcissism-serving element in such signs, like a professorship, is not irrelevant here, but it should be understood within a larger frame, since the question is that of a basic value to one's existence rather than the simple satisfactions of narcissistic wishes.

[10] Note that existence must be justified for Freud, a belief that is itself related to an attitude to death.

desire, in the face of finitude, is to stand out, to count more: we may just wish for a little more money in the bank or a brighter child, "[b]ut underneath throbs the ache of cosmic specialness" (p. 4).

The exact psychic meaning of death might vary for different people, but it has meaning, and this meaning comes into play with the rest of psychic life. We saw above how it is entangled with the major wish of the dream book, with the persistent motivational force expressed time and again in it. Even if Freud could claim that only wishes are the true instigators of dreams, and even if he could maintain his very dubious position that death is not represented in the unconscious, it would still seem that he should have recognized the way *death interacts with other factors and colors them*. Even if not represented, even as a non-entity from a psychic point of view, the line death draws delimits other psychical contents and gives them form. Even if death cannot act as a wish, it colors and emphasizes other mental states, wishes, feelings, and thoughts. Even if not present, it is nonetheless present, as absence, and influences the rest of psychic life. Death is the light, or rather the shadow that is cast over all other psychic entities. Sometimes it is futile to look for it as a separate element in the picture. One can perhaps better discern it upon examining other psychical contents or issues that may be easier to represent, feel or think.

In this regard, ambition is not only an issue in itself, which as we saw is closely linked with death, but also an example of the way death acts upon and influences psychic life in general. The knot of death and ambition shows how the question of direct representation, so dear to Freud and many of his followers, is sometimes simply irrelevant, and how death can operate in the background, or even form the background of other wishes, thoughts, and feelings, even when it is itself transparent. The concluding chapter of this work presents a fuller elaboration of death as the void at the center of our entire mental life.

Death, an absurdity

The "1851 and 1856" dream is a dream about the death of a father. It is a part of a series of absurd dreams to which we now turn. The dream is absurd not only because of the incongruence of the dates involved (that the year 1851 is identical with 1856, Freud's cause for classifying it as an absurd dream), but also because Freud's dead father lies in the other room and can be asked questions. The absurdity of the manifest content of the dream serves to hide precisely this deeper layer of absurdity.

The whole series of dreams by which Freud demonstrates the issue of the absurd in dreams consists mostly of examples where the death of a father is involved.[11] Freud is not blind to this fact, and tries to explain it through the internal conditions that lead to an absurd dream, conditions that typify the ambivalent relation that is felt toward one's father (1900, p. 435).

The short discussion that follows tries to illuminate the issue of absurd dreams from a different angle. The absurd, at least in the series of examples Freud gives, is that of death itself, or rather, of the transition between life and death. People known to be dead appear to be alive in the dream, and then it is recalled that they are actually dead. What is at play here is the absurdity of the transformation, so difficult to represent. Something remains utterly meaningless, incomprehensible, illogical in this moment of transition, when one minute a person is a living being and the next minute he or she is organic matter. The liminal condition or the moment of transition is a basis for questioning the very nature of the two states and their mutual exclusivity or binary opposition. It brings to mind the question of what it means to be dead, and looming over that, the larger riddle of how it could be that someone who had once been alive has died.

Although in a way such absurd dreams involve the change from life to death, and thus a certain representation of death, the more salient aspect of them is the necessary failure of such representation. These dreams fail precisely along the axis around which they are built. The cessation of life remains unimaginable. On the other hand the evidence of death is too powerful—a body might lie in the other room—and so between this unimaginable fact of death and its all too real existence, there is a kernel of the absurd, which is represented by other means in the dream.

Father on his death-bed

The important dream in the series is "Father on his Death-Bed like Garibaldi" (Freud, 1900, pp. 427–9). Freud begins the description of the dream by stating that "after his death my father played a political part..." (p. 427). He sees his father in a crowd, standing on a chair, and recalls how, on his deathbed, he looked like Garibaldi. Freud remembers how his father had a post-mortem rise of temperature, and his cheeks became increasingly flushed. In short, he actually showed signs of life.

---

[11] There are two exceptions, one of which deals however with the death of Goethe, which represents the same characteristics of respectability, power, and admiration for Freud as the father does. The second exception is a dream ("Count Thun") where the death of Freud's father is not a theme of the manifest content, but turns out to play a role once the associations are elaborated.

Death, an absurdity

He is then reminded of another case, of a woman whose father had died, and when he was undressed, it could be seen that he had sullied his pants, i.e. passed a stool (*Stuhl* in German, which, as in English also means chair). He sums up the dream by saying that the wish that motivated it was "To stand before one's children's eyes, after one's death, great and unsullied" (p. 429). "What has become of the absurdity of the dream?" he asks, and replies decisively: "Its apparent absurdity is due only to the fact that it gave a literal picture of a figure of speech" (p. 429).

However, can we really conclude that the "absurdity is due *only* to the fact" of literally representing a figure of speech? Is the discussion of the father that soils his pants after his death, or that of the father whose temperature rises, so neutral? It seems that there is a much larger element of absurdity involved here, perhaps the greatest absurdity of all, that of our own existence. The absurd point is the ungraspable transition between life and death. The post-mortem temperature rise or flushing cheeks of Freud's father is absurd and confusing because these are signs of life after death. Not only does the bereaved Freud have to deal with the fact that his father has just passed away, but he is confronted by these signs of life that seem to throw his father's state of death into question. How can it be that a person who was present among us, talking to us, a minute ago, is now dead? Indeed, in a way at least, it cannot be so. The shift cannot be adequately represented. And the post-mortem flushing of the cheeks shakes the ground beneath our feet even more.[12]

It is, of course, more acute when the signs of life are of a less agreeable nature, as happened to the woman who saw her father's post-mortem excrement, because defecation is a sign of our mortality. It signifies the fact that we are bodies, and not only souls. For Becker (1973), nowhere is having a body more profoundly humiliating than in our excretory activity. Nachman (1981, p. 549) points out in the context of this specific dream the association between the corpse and the stool, which undergo similar processes of decomposition.

So fathers too are matter, fathers too are flesh and blood ("So you used to drink as well?," Freud asks his father in the "1851 and 1856" dream, 1900, p. 436). It is well known that Freud's self-analysis and dream book are strongly related to the death of his father. We should not forget how beyond the emotional ambivalence that the death of a father

---

[12] Cf. the remark by a patient of Leclaire (1971, p. 135), after seeing his dead father speaking to him in a dream, that the corpse itself is nothing, as compared to the in-between situations leading to it, which he deems unbearable.

arouses, beyond the Oedipal conflicts that are perhaps revived with his death, there is the issue of death itself, which the death of a father awakens to a most acute degree. This has to do with the fact that the father is an embodiment of power and authority, an emblem of strength and control. And when the father dies, there is no longer any mediator between death and oneself.[13]

The absurdity in the "Garibaldi" dream seems to have been displaced from the very fact that Freud's father, or anyone else, is dead, to the fact that he continues to be alive and politically active after his death. We must apply to this dream what Freud (1900) writes several pages later about absurd dreams, and does not apply to its analysis: "A dream is made absurd, then, if a judgment that something 'is absurd' is among the elements included in the dream-thoughts—that is to say, if any one of the dreamer's unconscious trains of thought has criticism or ridicule as its motive" (p. 434).[14] The absurd element is not the contradiction inherent to a figure of speech, but the contradiction inherent to a human figure, the transition from life to death, a central element among the dream-thoughts here.

Death: Between denial and recognition

What we have seen so far is a kind of hidden death theme running through Freud's book, in parallel and below the more manifest directions. In this penultimate section I wish to address more directly dynamics of recognition and denial of death, and deal directly with some issues regarding Freud's characterization of the dream as wish fulfillment, which seems to hamper the attribution of significance to death.

Here and there in *The Interpretation of Dreams* one stumbles upon a remark where Freud does acknowledge death as a motive, contrary to his theoretical claims. Interesting in this regard is his explication of dreams of missing a train (1900, p. 385). These dreams are anxiety-provoking, as we all know, but Freud explains that the anxiety is misleading, for these are actually appeasing dreams. Departures are a symbolic cover for death, and missing the train means avoiding this sad prospect. Therefore, although you might have missed the train you gained your life, and so the panic over not arriving on time actually hides a much deeper

---

[13] Lacan (1975, pp. 315–16; 1988a, pp. 286–7) characterizes the imaginary other, for the obsessive and for everyone, as an intermediate between oneself and death, as a small master between oneself and the absolute master.

[14] In dreams featuring dead relatives, absurdity is sometimes used to represent "a repressed thought which the dreamer would prefer to regard as utterly unthinkable," namely a death wish (Freud, 1900, 430).

Death: Between denial and recognition 93

satisfaction about remaining on the platform of life. They are actually "dreams of consolation for another kind of anxiety felt in sleep—the fear of dying" (ibid.). Another place where Freud refers directly to dreaming about one's death is in the short passage, already referred to twice above, where he discusses dreams in which a dead person is treated as alive (p. 431). In the overall theoretical context of the work, however, the presence of these isolated paragraphs, only added to the text in 1911 and 1919 respectively, testifies more to what is missing from the text than to what is found in it. The theoretical discussion of death is limited to these two short passages, these two specific kinds of dreams. Moreover, as we saw, these ideas are never applied by Freud to any of his actual dreams in the book, further evidence of the disparity between the theoretical weight death receives and the actual role it plays in dreams.

For dust thou art

Freud's (1900, pp. 205–8) dream of "The Three Fates" is utterly suffused with reminders of finitude. Freud dreams that he goes into the kitchen in search of pudding, and sees three women standing there. One of them is "twisting something about in her hand, as though she was making knödel." The dream then continues elsewhere.

The major item among Freud's associations is a childhood recollection of his first discovery of the existence of death:

When I was six years old and was given my first lessons by my mother, I was expected to believe that we were all made of earth and must therefore return to earth. This did not suit me and I expressed doubts of the doctrine. My mother thereupon rubbed the palms of her hands together—just as she did in making dumplings, except that there was no dough between them—and showed me the blackish scales of *epidermis* produced by the friction as a proof that we were made of earth. My astonishment at this ocular demonstration knew no bounds and I acquiesced in the belief which I was later to hear expressed in the words: "*Du bist der Natur einen Tod schuldig*" ("Thou owest Nature a death"). (1900, p. 205)

Poor Freud. What a cruel demonstration of this bitter existential truth. Freud says he felt a sense of "submission to the inevitable" (1900, p. 205). Through the concrete image of the woman rubbing the palms of her hands as if to make a knödel, what is actually expressed in the dream is a deep acknowledgment of the ephemeral nature of our existence.[15]

---

[15] I find Anzieu's analysis of the mother's lesson, "masturbation (rubbing *Knödel* in one's hands) is dangerous, one can die of it" (1986 [1975], p. 365) unwarranted and reductionistic.

Freud (1900) interprets the three women as the three Pharcae, or goddesses of fate. One of them, he says, "was the mother who gives life" (p. 204). It is interesting to note how he speaks only of the Fate who spins the thread of life, rather than the one who cuts it. Because while it is true that the woman/Fate in the dream represents his mother, the episode he narrates from his childhood is one that foreshadows the end, rather than representing a beginning. It is an episode linked with the dust-like and fragile nature of the living. It is as if Freud is trying to suppress the painful thought at the source of the dream, and divert it. It is not only the existential meaning that is lost therein, but also the troubling intertwinement of the mother figure and death, that is, how the mother has the power to both give life and take it away, which is salient in Freud's childhood scene and in the figure of the three fates.[16]

Via a different route, related to humorous plays on names, Freud arrives at a citation of Herder playing on Goethe's name "Thou who art the offspring of gods or of Goths or of dung," and another one by Goethe himself: "So you too, divine figures, have turned to dust!" He suddenly then says: "I noticed that my digression on the subject of the misuse of names was only leading up to this complaint. But I must break off here" (1900, p. 207), and turns to a different path of investigation. Why must Freud break off at that point? Is the subject of making fun of one's name so problematic?

Of course not. It is worthwhile examining these two citations. The second is taken from Goethe's "Iphigenie auf Tauris." It is the remark of Iphigenia when she hears of the death of numerous heroes in the war against Troy. Can we not link it to the oracular demonstration of Freud's mother, and to the verse from Genesis (3:19), "for dust thou art, and unto dust shalt thou return," which is shown by it?[17] Freud's mother shows him that the two of them are equally of dust. Everyone "owe[th] nature a death." The heroes as well, these divine figures, have turned to dust, they too have also suffered the gloomy fate of all mankind. And a private hero for Freud, Goethe, is the offspring of dung. If Freud "must break off here," as he says for no apparent reason, it might very well be because once again, while wandering

---

[16] A discussion here of the duality in Freud's thinking about the mother, or the woman, as bringer of both life and death will take us too far away from my current concerns. For an extensive treatment of the link between the mother and death, and the deathliness associated with her, see Jonte-Pace (2001). See also Bronfen (1992, p. 32).

[17] Grinstein (1968, p. 170) also does not fail to see the connection, though he does not discuss it further.

through the forest of his associations, he had stumbled upon a reminder of death.[18]

Death is always present, the "Three Fates" dream seems to communicate, always lurking behind the cheerful and vivid appearances of life. Great or meek, ambitious or not, we all turn to dust. This knowledge of finitude is not merely some dry data we possess ("My astonishment ... knew no bounds"), but causes anxiety, and has implications for our lives.

Specifically, insisting on the fact that humans are made of dust and will return to dust underlines how death is always there, always a potentiality. Not only because it awaits us all at the end of the road, but because it is there from the start, because it is implied in our structure; it is the material out of which we are made. The death that we fear is embodied in us.

This existential awareness of our transience hardly finds a place in Freud's analysis. He does though present a similar lesson to be drawn from another thread of associations: "One should never neglect an opportunity, but always take what one can ... , since life is short and death inevitable" (1900, p. 207). Poignant conclusion, no doubt, though already somewhat inclined to the positive, and using the acknowledgment of death as a source of motivation and initiative. It is as if Freud is willing to recognize—indirectly—death as underlying the dream, but not any gloomy emotions or the unpleasant consequences implied by it.

Moreover, even the existential, cautionary lesson of *carpe diem*, seize the day, is swiftly detached from the temporariness of life. It seems to resonate with another association for Freud, a remark by a young man about the good-looking wet-nurse who suckled him many years earlier, expressing regret at not having better exploited this opportunity (1900, p. 204). Freud says that what made the concealment of the *carpe diem* lesson behind a dream necessary, so as to deceive the censorship, was its sexual meanings (pp. 207–8). He thus displaces existential meanings and concerns to the sexual domain. Once again, even when death is aroused as a theme, Freud chooses to retreat to the home front of sexuality.

Such underemphasis on death in favor of sexuality is of course not unique to this dream. It occurs, among other places, in the "May Beetle" dream of Freud's patient (1900, pp. 289–92), a dream teeming with worries, death imagery, and murderousness, and where Freud's analysis

---

[18] One of the dream associations is related to a trip Freud and his wife took to Spalato, and to some Turkish cloth she bought there. As Grinstein (1968, p. 167–8) rightly comments, this trip is the same one during which the Signorelli episode, which opens Freud's *Psychopathology of Everyday Life*, took place. The Signorelli case's profound meaning is about the question of finitude, and so it supplies another link, though indirect, between death and the "Three Fates" dream.

leads to one point—the sexual dissatisfaction of the patient. It is even more salient in the analysis of Freud's childhood dream of the "bird-beaked figures" carrying his sleeping mother (p. 583), where although he recognizes the obvious allusion to death raised by this image, he dismisses it as secondary to the sexual meaning of the dream, a sort of interpretation of the dream content inside the dream, an interpretation made necessary by the anxiety that the sexual meaning aroused. A legitimate analysis of course, but it does raise two questions: First, is the death of the mother so easy a subject that one can play with it as affect-free material to be used as a blank to hide other possibilities? Second, one may ask why such maneuvers are never carried out the other way around. Why is sexuality never found to hide or cover death-related issues, or other forms of anxiety?[19]

Here and there, to sum up, death is acknowledged in the case of a specific dream, or is brought up in Freud's analysis.[20] But this is where the story ends. Almost every time Freud discusses a particular dream, he tends in the end to underplay the importance of death and deny its centrality to the construction of the dream. The theme of death is discarded in the final conclusions or deflected toward other meanings.

Freud is even more dismissive when it comes to theory. Given the many instances where he comes across an association that discloses the role of death in a specific dream, his tendency to refrain from using this as an indication of the possible role of death on the more general, theoretical level, seems clear. The theme of death fails to be developed, expanded or integrated into the overall picture of the dream constructions, unlike other "thematic" issues that do find a more suitable elaboration, such as aggression, family relationships, ambition, narcissism, rivalry, and sexuality.

Before concluding, we will look at Freud's declared theoretical justifications for his reluctance to use death to explain dreams or mental life, namely the need to locate a wish behind every dream, his major argument in the book. Once again, the "Non Vixit" dream will get us there.

---

[19] Jonte-Pace (2001, pp. 40–4) carries the theme of transforming death into sexuality in this dream a step further, raising the possibility of a murder – a fantasy of matricide so distressing that it necessitates the displacement to sexual issues.
[20] Death is recognized as the truth of a dream Freud (1900, p. 472) cites, reported by Ferenczi: A man is asleep and sees a gentleman unknown to him entering the room. The man tries again and again to turn on the light, but fails, starts laughing, and wakes up. The unknown man, Ferenczi and Freud believe, is "the picture of death as the 'great Unknown' ... The old gentleman, who suffered from arterio-sclerosis, had had good reason the day before for thinking of dying. ... It was the light of life that he could no longer turn on" (Freud, pp. 472–3).

Night of the living dead

It is within the dream itself, in the "Non Vixit" dream, that the opposition to death seems to occur. Freud points out that if murderousness was allowed in it (annihilating his friend with a look), it is in part because it had a very reassuring meaning. Everyone, the dream seemed to be saying, has a substitute. No one is irreplaceable. There are always revenants (1900, pp. 485–6). He is right I think: this is really a dream about the return of the dead. Freud's conclusion has far-reaching implications, for if everyone has a replacement, and if the individual himself is unimportant, the impact of death itself is actually softened. Death (here, the death of others) is no longer such a dreaded, irreversible possibility, for there are always ghosts. In fact, "there are nothing but revenants: all those we have lost come back" (p. 486), so runs the hidden dream-thought.

With this cyclical vision, which counters the notion of life as a linear, one-time affair, the dream takes the sting out of death. Repetition is reassuring when the very nature of what makes death threatening—that life is singular, that everything happens only once, and that the value it takes on is derived from the unidirectional flow of time—is left out of the game.

Freud (1900) describes how he thought Fliess's daughter could replace his (Fliess's) deceased sister, and how he (Freud) named his children after people he liked. "After all, I reflected, was not having children our only path to immortality?" (p. 487) he says, adding another tier to this spectral train of thought: children as a form of immortality, not just as replicates or revenants. Notably, here Freud includes himself in the general "our" (*für uns alle*).

And yet it is clear that entailed in a need to counter or oppose death, to mitigate its consequences, be it through reassurance of immortality or the idea of repetition, is a recognition of death. This recognition within the dream, in the unconscious dream-thoughts, of death as an end of life, of time as limited, of time *tout court*, of course runs counter to what Freud says in his theoretical discussions of the unconscious. This is no "dry" recognition, devoid of affect, but a highly distressing and disquieting one. There would be no need to deny death were it not also part of unconscious thought. Moreover, that "there are nothing but revenants: all those we have lost come back," is not the last word of the dream, because the revenant in the dream is only a mirage, an apparition. Under Freud's piercing gaze he turns pale, his form becomes indistinct, and in seconds he has melted away (1900, p. 421). Revenants are possibly, as Freud seems to suggest, a very comforting illusion, yet they shatter whenever they come under a critical gaze (Freud realizes logically in the dream that the person in front of him is actually dead). The dream seems to be saying that the illusion does not hold, for it reveals, underneath it, the acknowledgment of what was avoided. Freud's analysis stops short of showing this. He is content instead with uncovering the hidden wish, the wish to annul death, while failing to properly consider the unconscious acknowledgment that must underlie the wish, or the way the dream itself discloses the illusory nature of that wish. The last word, however, belongs to death, and not to vain promises of the illusion.

Anxiety and wish

This brings us to a wider question. "[A] dream is the fulfillment of a wish," Freud notoriously claims (1900, p. 121); it is the cornerstone of his dream theory. What then is the status of disturbing emotions in general, according to Freud, with regard to the wish? What if the material in the dream-thoughts is the antithesis of wish fulfillment—anxiety, worries, and painful reflections? Freud notes two mechanisms whereby the dream can deal with these elements. They can either be made into their opposite and replaced by wish fulfillment, or can be joined by another wish, whose satisfaction will be strong enough to counter the distressing feelings (pp. 487, 556–7). This allows the fulfillment of a wish to still be, from a theoretical viewpoint, the major instigator of a dream. Strangely enough, this section was added to the book in 1919, that is, already at a time when Freud's thought about anxiety dreams was beginning to expand to include traumatic anxiety dreams (1920, pp. 12–14, 31–3). At any rate, although Freud acknowledges complications he stresses the fact that a wish is always involved.[21] But if we shift attention to what the wish attempts to cover or change, a different picture is revealed:

Freud wants the wish to have the last word, yet we have encountered dreams where the jungle of associations and the thicket of wishes could not hide the bitter smile of death or its burdening consequences in the mind—anxious, depressive, mournful trains of thought. Dreams in which an unconscious wish is present, but whose entire *raison d'être* is nothing but to repudiate a certain acknowledgment of death, unpleasant to the dreaming mind. Such is the case for instance with the "Dissection of the Pelvis" dream, where instead of remaining with the fearful or

---

[21] There is a further refinement in Freud (1916–1917, pp. 213–19). In a later revision Freud (1933a [1932], p. 29) redefines dreams as only "an attempt at a fulfillment of a wish," sometimes, as in trauma dreams, an unsuccessful one.

gloomy recognition of the prospect of death, the train of thought swerves toward the glory of an Etruscan grave, and the idea of immortality through children. Freud tends, in his analyses, to be satisfied with arriving at a wish, any wish, and hardly looks further to uncover what lies underneath—the recognition of death and death anxiety.

In many such cases, the wish seems more of an awkward and transparent defensive maneuver than a true instigator of the dream. What is important for me here is that these dreams show, with or without the wish involved, that death not only can be present in the mind, represented and in some way acknowledged, but can also be a major determinant of the dream.

Other cases present a milder version of this relationship between death and the wish: sometimes the dream at its core clearly involves a wish, but that wish shows that it revolves around a certain recognition of death, in the absence of which it cannot be explained. One wishes to live longer—but only because one knows his or her time is limited, and the sand keeps falling through the hourglass.

In other cases it seems that the insistence on the primacy of wishes comes more from Freud the dream interpreter than Freud the dreamer of dreams. Such dreams where anxious feelings about death seem to be the dominant force driving the dream seem to put in question the whole theory of wish fulfillment.

My quarrel, anyway, is not with the theory of the dream as a wish fulfillment, but with Freud's doubts concerning the representation and psychic role of death. Even when we keep the dream fulfillment theory intact, the idea of death's marginality and lack of representation becomes untenable, as this chapter and the last have shown. In the very book that was written to support the idea that dreams are the fulfillment of a wish, there is a lot of material that points instead to death as a central psychic motive.

At any rate, it is precisely the acknowledgment of death behind the wish that best supports the idea that recognition of death is unconscious. Two last examples will help illustrate this. In a series of dreams which initially seem, according to Freud, to contradict the theory of wish fulfillment, Freud finds himself working again in the laboratory of the chemical institute—a time in his life which he recalls as barren and humiliating, his "gloomiest and most unsuccessful year" (1900, pp. 475–6). What seems, on the one hand, to be punishment dreams, turn out upon deeper analysis to be wish fulfillments: "So I was once more young, and ... *she* was once more young" (p. 476). The deep instigating agent for the dream was the wish for youth, says Freud, the "constantly gnawing wishes of a man who is growing older" (*ibid.*). " [T]imes were hard in the old days; all the same, it was lovely then—I was still young" (*ibid.*).

The will of an old man to be young again cannot be separated from the acknowledgment of the flow of time, and the prospect of death. In Freud's own illustration of how wishes always prevail over other moods we can only hear the wish if we admit the recognition of death and the need "to do something about it" that lies behind it.[22]

In one of his dreams, added to the book in 1919, Freud sees his son coming home from military service. Yet there is something wrong with him, and the bandages around his forehead, his gray hair and false teeth suggest that he is dead, old, or wounded (1900, pp. 558–60). The day residues in the background of the dream, Freud says, indeed consist of a deep concern that his son, from whom he and his wife have not heard for a while, might have been wounded or killed. After a short attempt by the dream work to conceal them, these concerns break through. Morbid symbols abound. The dream clearly expresses the conviction that the son is either wounded or dead. Freud guesses another motive is at work, and the key for it is an accident the son in the dream almost suffers, which reminds Freud of an accident he himself had as a child. Curiously, the son's accident elicits satisfaction rather than anxiety. How could this be?

What this dream expressed, says Freud (1900), is a satisfaction with staying alive. Narcissistic pride over one's survival is strong enough to allow itself representation in the dream, even through the death of a close and beloved person. Freud describes the impulse satisfied by the son's accident as "the envy which is felt for the young by those who have grown old, but which they believe they have completely stifled" (p. 560).

Worries alone, says Freud (1900, pp. 560–1) in the following discussion, cannot "make a dream." A wish must be involved. But can the envy, the bottom line of Freud's analysis, exist without recognition of one's inevitable fate? The unconscious ignores death, Freud claims, and recognizes it only in the case of the other (1915, pp. 292–3, 296–7). It is not at all clear if such a claim of ignorance of one's own death is sustainable, yet it is even more difficult to understand how such ignorance can be claimed in the case of envy, which involves direct comparison. Envying a person for something she has, means wanting it as well.

---

[22] For Kofman (1985) this dream and several others indicate that "nostalgia for youth ... is always nostalgia for sexual potency, just as ideas of death and old age are always connected with the idea of impotence" (p. 22). She concludes that the death anxiety found in Freud's dreams is always related to anxiety about sexual impotence. While this might be true in some cases, one should still be alert to the tendency mentioned above, among both Freud and his interpreters, to sexualize death.

Surely, the conscious mind knows that one is getting old. Yet if the unconscious envies the other, it too must have some knowledge of ageing. In the dream of the son coming back from the front, the comparison is direct. The son is about to have an accident identical to one that Freud experienced in his youth. It is a clear case of "he and not me," "he in place of me." A revolt against the way of the world, of one generation replacing another, seems to be strongly involved.

Freud seems more troubled by the thought that his son will go on (replacing him), while he dies, than he is assured of some semblance of perpetuity or continuity through him (children as a form of immortality). And to this gloomy train of thought the unconscious reacts in the only way it knows—according to Freud—with a death wish.

Thus, not only can the unconscious recognize the death of the self and not just that of the other, but such a recognition might also be involved in the death wish toward the other. It is the acknowledgment that allows for the wish.

Conclusions: Death and dreams

It is a lifelong preference of Freud—sometimes conscious, sometimes unconscious—to relegate death in his writings to a superficial influence, and to assign primacy to other motives, such as wishes, emotional ambivalence, conflicts, and drives. One of my aims in discussing Freud's dream book is to show how in Freud's own dreams, and some of his analyses, death resists this downgrading exercise and shows itself to be the more radical cause, the basic source around which revolves the whole process of dreaming at times. Freud's dreams and associations betray an unorthodox picture: they teach us that death is undeniably present. We looked at numerous examples of how death figures in dreams, sometimes centrally, sometimes marginally, but always in a way that influences other concerns.

I see no reason to go so far as to claim, with Stekel, that "the specter of death is to be found behind every dream" (a phrasing Freud resists, see Freud, 1900, p. 397), but I certainly think that some dreams are dreams of death. Freud sometimes recognizes death on a certain level of his analyses, yet more often does not. Often he acknowledges it on the surface, but claims it to be only a subterfuge or side issue in the dream, serving another, deeper motive. At hardly any point does he address death explicitly on a theoretical level.

One reminder of how this side of Freud's attitude to death, that marginalizes it, has become entrenched in psychoanalysis, is in the interpretations of the book itself. As mentioned above the pervasiveness of the theme of death and of death-related affects and thoughts in *The Interpretation of Dreams* has in general failed to capture the attention of scholars who have studied the book (we have seen above some exceptions and their limitations). Traditional readings remain focused on classic psychoanalytic issues, such as Oedipal conflicts, rivalry, ambivalence, and infantile sexuality. This is the case even among such scrupulous authors as Grinstein (1968), who, while he does not leave a stone unturned, fails to acknowledge the evident role of death in *The Interpretation of Dreams*.[23]

My focus was on Freud himself, yet the issue is of course relevant to everyone's dreams. The theme of death permeates Freud's dream book not only because Freud was obsessed with death in general (de M'Uzan, 1977 [1968]), or was allegedly going through a mid-life crisis, as Anzieu (1986 [1975]) maintains (drawing on Jaques's, 1988 (1965), concept), but because death is an essential part of psychic life. It is an ongoing and inescapable concern, which seeks expression in our dreams, and is present in so much of the rest of our thoughts and feelings. Claiming that the centrality of death belongs only to Freud's private world would seem like another attempt to repudiate death's centrality. We have occasionally seen death figuring in the dreams of people apart from Freud, and have discussed theoretical considerations that point to death's involvement in psychic life. For the most part, death in this regard is no different from any other issue in Freud's book, be it Oedipus, rivalry, the centrality of sexuality or even mechanisms specific to dreams, in its claim for generality. If those other issues are to be seen as generally human, rather than unique to Freud's life, so is death. If the dreams in the book are not only the royal road to the unconscious but also a pathway to theory, then that theory has to include death too.

The centrality of death is apparent in the material as it is given to us, and despite the fact that it has already undergone selection according to other principles. "Forbidding" the presence of death in the unconscious and its derivatives severely weakens Freud's claim to reveal the truth behind dreams. As long as death is left out of the picture, the interpretation of dreams specifically and our understanding of the human psyche in general, will only be partial.

---

[23] The problem, of course, lies not only in how Freud's dreams are interpreted, but in how dreams in general are interpreted. Grotjahn (1951) for example, while ostensibly interested in the issue of death, and lamenting the denial of death in modern culture, readily argues that: "it seems to be impossible for the unconscious to symbolize one's own death" (p. 414), going on to interpret death symbolism in dreams as hiding a castration threat (pp. 415–16) or as an expression of an infantile regression to a utopian "happy hunting ground" (p. 420).

Conclusions: Death and dreams

Freud's dreams go a long way toward working through questions of death, displaying clear knowledge of finitude in the unconscious. Death is not just apparent in them, it also lies at their source. Freud's claim is that death is irrepresentable. Suppose he is right. It would still be up to him (and now to other analysts) to supply some explanation, some theory about why, if irrepresentable, death is a motive force in dreams.[24]

The inquiry in these two chapters into the role of death in *The Interpretation of Dreams* helps to illuminate several issues. First, it shows that death seems significantly present and highly active in unconscious and preconscious life. The issue of death is crucial in psychic life generally and among the forces that form dreams.

Second, it supplies us with an example of *the ways* in which psychoanalysis neglects and reduces the issue of death. Death is relegated to secondary status on many occasions where it appears in dreams or associations. Freud's tendency is to push it aside in favor of other dream instigators such as sexuality, rivalry or ambition. Sometimes he uses other explanations, like sexuality, almost as a veil to eclipse any kind of existential concern. It is, however, true that the tendency to ignore death is an ambivalent one. Although most of the "conclusions" in the book tend to dismiss death or diminish its importance, Freud nonetheless often frankly presents associations where death does play a significant part. Had he not done so, the current analysis would have been almost impossible. There are also some scarce theoretical discussions on the role of death in dreams. This is not coincidental. It reflects a truly ambivalent attitude with regard to death, which can be detected throughout his work.

Third, the intricacies of Freud's thoughts and fantasies around death provide us with an illustration of *how* people can be occupied with death. Death is not a specific symbol or representation, or merely a localized event. As finitude, it plays a much more intricate role in our psychic world and is inextricably entangled with life and with life activities. The discussion of ambition exemplifies this: Planning of future projects and undertakings and the pondering of self-value involve the issue of finitude. Even more classic psychoanalytic notions, such as sexuality, rivalry, and narcissism involve the problem of death and acknowledgment of finitude. Isolating the issue of death, denying its importance,

---

[24] As I will explain later, I believe that the representation we do have of death is shaky, never closed and clear, and as such it necessitates the work of thought to come to terms with its inadequacies, to think it through, and dreams are one way this work is carried out. Beyond this, death alters and inflects other concerns and contents, exerting its influence indirectly.

and ignoring the relation of other issues to it, lead to a misunderstanding of much of human life. This creates a biased, partial picture of what it is to be human.

Fourth, the discussion has served to show that a recognition of the role of death may help to better explain clinical material, in this case, Freud's dreams. Discussing the clinical usefulness of an approach that does not ignore the role of death is beyond the scope of this book, but the example of *The Interpretation of Dreams* shows that such an approach is not without advantages.

Lastly, beyond death's centrality in the book, what becomes clearer is its forgetting. If death as a psychic influence is sidestepped by Freud, and later by so many other authors, when it is so widespread in his own dreams, it is hardly a surprise that it is later ignored on a much wider scale.

Death is a part of psychic life. The final chapter (VII) of *The Interpretation of Dreams* opens with a chilling dream: a man falls asleep after losing his child to a fatal illness. The dead child lies in the adjacent room. In his dream, the man sees the child approaching, fire all around him, asking, "Father, don't you see I'm burning?" He wakes up to see that the room where the child's body lies is actually on fire (Freud, 1900, p. 509). This is a perfect emblem of the whole problem we are dealing with. Death is a reality, right next to us, in the next room, and it will not be dismissed by simply superficially acknowledging it. It enforces itself. We might not see it, but it infiltrates our dreams, shows itself, covered with light and fire. Death can be rejected as secondary or dropped from theoretical discussion, but it will keep coming back. We might as well recognize it.

We began our journey through *The Interpretation of Dreams* with an observation on how its major theoretical contributions are initially merely a detour, branching out from the topic of death in dreams. Can Oedipus, rivalry, infantile sexuality, and narcissism all be merely a detour? Psychoanalysis itself, a detour from death? Perhaps the displacement—Freud's chapter on death dreams ends up with Oedipus—is not only a detour on the level of the flow of the text, but also in the analytic and emotional sense: taken, that is, in order not to discuss death. To avoid death, Freud turns to *Oedipus*, he constructs psychoanalysis. Death is there, evident, and the only thing left to do is to construct this theoretical edifice, or *Oedipus*, to prevent us from looking directly. The book that speaks of the royal road turns out to be a detour.

5 Death and anxiety

Freud, we saw, has an explicit position against the psychic influence of death, as well as a clear tendency not to focus on it when it shows up. Death, for its part, has its own take on this: it shows up, and quite often, as the excursion into *The Interpretation of Dreams* demonstrated, asserts itself and demands centrality. To understand better Freud's difficulty with death and death anxiety and to see better what happens in this encounter between theory and death, his statements and tendency are not enough. We must consider the wider framework of his thought; we must look at Freud's ideas on anxiety and see their possibilities and limitations for explaining anxiety about death; must determine, that is, what the broader model of anxiety allows or disallows with regard to death. If death is an undeniable part of the world, and if anxiety about it forms part of our experience, could Freud's psychoanalysis account for it within the models through which it normally understands the experience of anxiety?

It is well known that Freud revised his position on anxiety; from seeing it as a direct transformation of repressed libido to a view of anxiety as a signal of danger, leading to repression. The first view is represented in the "Anxiety" lecture in the "Introductory Lectures" (1916–1917), and the second in *Inhibitions, Symptoms and Anxiety* (1926).

The "Anxiety" lecture begins by distinguishing between realistic and neurotic anxiety (Freud, 1916–1917, pp. 393–4). Making the distinction, one notes, already dictates a certain position vis-à-vis the problem of anxiety about one's future death; the possibilities this bifurcation leaves us with are either actual anxiety about immediate danger faced by the organism or neurotic anxiety, whose origin is inside, and manifests itself in exaggerated forms. Little room is left for considering the kind of non-concrete, ongoing apprehensiveness regarding life's fragility, based on an acknowledgment of future death and unrelated to a specific threat. Alternatively, such apprehensiveness is explained as neurotic.[1]

Yet seeing death anxiety as realistic does not make it a significant psychic concept, because even the possibility of realistic anxiety is readily dismissed. As "Anxiety" proceeds, realistic anxiety falls out of view, becomes negligible, "neuroticized" (judged as not adapted to the situation, inexpedient, Freud, 1916–1917, pp. 394–5), and its essence is deemed a repetition of an earlier form of anxiety (pp. 395–7). Finally, it loses its realistic aspect, its primacy in face of the situation (it is not a "natural response," pp. 407–8), and becomes, in the discussion of the responses of children, completely neurotic, deriving from "unemployed libido." Alternatively, it is defined as a later acquisition, the result of education (pp. 407–8). This is also the case in the later theory of anxiety, where realistic anxiety turns out to be neurotic as well (1926, p. 168).

In the "Anxiety" lecture (Freud, 1916–1917, p. 399), neurotic anxiety in phobias is described as an exaggeration of a normal anxious response to danger. Yet in the focus on the exaggeration, the validity and nature of the normal response are almost forgotten. And still, if we remove the exaggeration, the "over" part, anxiety remains to be explained.[2] This anxiety is rarely spoken of, and when it is, it is often seen as itself neurotic. It is as if the response to danger is too natural to be theoretically interesting. The result, at any rate, is that it fails to be mentioned. What Freud did not talk about has importance and achieves significance, as a resonant absence, in subsequent developments of psychoanalysis.

The problem has to do with the nature of danger. Response to external danger is the model and analog for defense and for instinctual danger, coming from inside (Freud, 1926, pp. 92, 145, 155, 165, 167). And yet although external danger remains in the background of the discussion as a kind of threat (1916–1917, p. 401; 1926, pp. 126,

---

[1] In discussing the fear of death in *The Ego and the Id*, Freud (1923, pp. 57–8) actually says that the fear should be distinguished from both realistic and neurotic libidinal anxiety, thus confirming the view above. He hastens to do so, in my view, because he wishes to counter the claim that every fear is reducible to the fear of death, which might threaten his own ideas on sexuality as the omnipresent source of anxiety. The position Freud opposes actually presupposes the similarity between the fear of death and any other fear, and therefore, in order to contest it, Freud has to insist that death anxiety is of a different kind. He goes on, however, to describe the fear of death, as we saw, as part of a third category of anxiety, which has to do with fear of the superego, but this new category does not solve the problem indicated here.

[2] Cf. Searles's (1965 [1961], pp. 512–13) similar and pertinent remark on the analytic approach to phobias about death. Even after the symbolic meanings have been exposed and unconscious factors cleared out, death is still a frightening reality that should be dealt with.

Death and anxiety   107

155), it is obviously marginal, and is only briefly touched upon (pp. 134, 165–8) (Freud's slight reservation, p. 130 has no effect on his conclusions).

The danger Freud does speak of is inside. The source of the threat is within. In the first theory of anxiety, the threat comes from internal flooding, from an accumulation of libido, and in the second, from "a growing tension due to need" (1926, p. 137). Freud does not directly dismiss external danger, but through a series of selections, overlooks it or belittles its importance. Thus, although he mentions anxiety as a response to danger (pp. 134–5), he offers only one example, that of birth. And yet he immediately claims that although there is a real threat to life at birth, psychologically there is no such danger, because the newborn is unaware of it. Hence there remains no explanation in the text for anxiety as a response to real danger. The second theory of anxiety fares no better: For Lifton (1979, pp. 125–6), the shift in that theory, which was supposed to free anxiety from being tied to libido by redefining it as a response to danger, falls back into what he calls the "instinctual paradigm," into the link with the libido, in that the threat specified turns out to be an instinctual libidinal one.[3]

All this is much more than a bias or preference on the part of Freud about whether to place external or internal danger at the center of his discussion.[4] When one ponders the basic characteristic of a dangerous situation, wanting to know what at bottom we are afraid of when we are anxious, the seemingly very basic answer is: a threat to our existence (a Kleinian type of critique of Freud). And yet, this simple contention is not always recognized by Freud, or is recognized but refuted or its importance belittled (Freud does admit it as we saw in *The Ego and the Id*, 1923, p. 57, where he says what the ego fears is annihilation, to which

---

[3] The process of specifying and limiting what actually threatens is apparent with regard to Freud's assertion (1926, p. 137) that danger is "a growing tension due to need." It is worthwhile tracing the path of his argument. He starts with the danger of birth and asks what danger is (p. 135), going on to explore situations of anxiety in childhood, as part of a debate with Rank. He moves on to discuss childhood phobias, and claiming that most anxieties in childhood are not comprehensible, "confine[s] [his] attention" to three (p. 136): fear of being alone, being in the dark, and being with a stranger. He finds a common denominator between all of them: separation, or loss of the object. Yet he speaks of this object in terms of a longed for object, thus already looking at it from an active perspective. The longing becomes anxiety (p. 137). Then, from longing, Freud takes one part only: the idea that the object fulfills the infant's needs. And so, Freud is left with the idea that danger arises from a "tension due to need." "[N]on-satisfaction" of needs is now for him the essence of danger (p. 137), but only through cutting down, limiting, and selection.

[4] For a witty discussion of externality and internality of danger and anxiety, from a different perspective, see Weber (1982, pp. 48–60).

he quickly adds the threat of being overwhelmed). Freud hardly mentions specific mortal threats as the core of anxiety.

Freud's reluctance to acknowledge external danger leads him to the counter-intuitive implication that anxiety is not part of self-preservation and is even contrary to it (1916–1917, pp. 394–5). Freud attempts to bypass the near truism that anxiety is about one's life, by creating a split—a practical reaction (running away), and an impractical, neurotic, superfluous anxiety. Does this split really exist though? Is anxiety not part of the flight, what drives it, and part and parcel of life? Freud transforms anxiety into something very specific, insisting that anxiety is only such and such, and can only occur under such and such circumstances—but our lives go well beyond his account, and his attempt necessarily leaves out too many circumstances and anxieties, omissions that play a role in limiting it.

Freud is not even willing to acknowledge that the organism recognizes a threat to its life, and will try to avoid that threat. He speaks of the lack of fear in children (1916–1917, pp. 407–8, and in a sense, 1926, p. 136), and in this way explains away external danger as something that cannot be natural or basic. This position is not only questionable, but also incompatible with Freud's own constant reference to external danger as the model for the internal one.

Note that Freud's attempt to justify his position is quite weak. He does not speak here of the immortality of the unconscious, as he does elsewhere in explaining heroism as a simple belief that "[n]othing can happen to me" (1915, pp. 296–7). He says that children are innately unafraid, but admits that it has to do with them simply being unaware of dangers (1916–1917, pp. 407–8). This actually tells us nothing about the anxious reaction itself. Of course the knowledge that something is dangerous is required if it is to be feared, except perhaps in the case of some innate phobias. However, once it is discovered that something is dangerous, with the result that it is avoided and feared, it is this reaction of fear that must be explained, and Freud ignores it.

These issues tie into what was said earlier about self-preservation. As we saw, although Freud acknowledges the existence of instincts of self-preservation, he does not see them as a possible instinctual basis for the organism's fear of death. What, however, if not to go on living or to defend against threats, is the possible meaning of such instincts?

At a deeper level, these issues are related to a reluctance of Freud's to simply recognize life. What seems to be largely missing from his texts here is the wish of the organism to live, to perpetuate its existence. Existence itself, beyond its "existential" aspects, in its psycho-biological form of self-perpetuation, is not theoretically acknowledged. Significant in this regard, beyond the dismissal of the significance of the self-preservative instincts, is the attempt, in *Beyond the Pleasure Principle* (Freud, 1920, p. 39) to align them with the death instinct. Freud suggests that the aim of self-preservation is not to live, but to die better: to die on the organism's own terms.

It is as if rejection of the fear of death (on a more general level, of death not as a real, concrete threat) and rejection of the possible influence of death come at the price of ignoring both a much simpler anxiety, and the psychic influence of a simpler threat. To prevent a recognition of death's general influence, fear for one's existence in the face of concrete danger is put into question, and expelled from theory.[5]

With regard to the more general aspect of death (not a specific threat of annihilation), it is evident that the theory of anxiety largely neglects it. In the first theory of anxiety, as described in the *Introductory Lectures* (Freud, 1916–1917), death is simply not mentioned. In the second (Freud, 1926), it is referred to only in two short passages where, as we saw, it is explained as something that takes place between the ego and the superego, and is clearly marginal in the text.[6]

In the final lines of the "Anxiety" lecture, Freud seems still to be disturbed by having ignored that possible core of anxiety: "There is only a single point that we have found disconnected—a gap in our views: the single, yet scarcely disputable, fact that realistic anxiety must be regarded as a manifestation of the ego's self-preservative instincts" (1916–1917, p. 411). It is difficult to formulate the problem more clearly than that. This essence or grain keeps being lost and forgotten.[7] It is scarcely disputable, too obvious perhaps, but deliberately left out of the theory.

The second theory of anxiety moves in a direction that seems to open more possibilities with regard to death, especially through the idea that anxiety is a response to felt or expected helplessness (*Hilflosigkeit*).

---

[5] The difficulty with recognizing survival-related anxiety is not limited to Freud, and is still prevalent today. Thus, Hurvich (2003, p. 579), in a comprehensive discussion of the concept of annihilation anxiety, claims that it has not received sufficient elaboration or importance in psychoanalytic theories. Issues of self-preservation have also been neglected in analytic literature (p. 586).

[6] The marginality of the account of death anxiety is apparent in the fact that when Freud summarizes the list of anxieties, each according to its corresponding developmental phase, he fails to mention death anxiety (1926, pp. 146–7), as noted by Hoffman (1998, p. 45). This is also the case in another resumé of anxieties where again, fear of death is missing (Freud, 1926, pp. 142).

[7] When Freud (1916–1917, p. 430) returns to the theme in a later lecture, and insists that anxiety is the result of ego-libido, he does no more that repeat his distinction between the expedient response (flight) and the inexpedient one (anxiety).

110   Death and anxiety

The basic experience of the infant is helplessness, and what reminds us of it evokes anxiety (Freud, 1926, pp. 166–7). "[G]rowing mental development" is responsible for changes in what is felt as dangerous (p. 162), and so perhaps even some kind of mature, "existential" death anxiety could find in these ideas a theoretical model suitable for it. Many other elements that could serve to account for death anxiety are there,[8] but although the model perhaps could account for death anxiety in a non-reductive manner, it is explicitly reduced to something else, the relations of the ego and the superego.

But it is not just that the conclusion is against death. There is perhaps something misleading in the use of the idea of helplessness, and it is important to examine precisely what Freud means by it. Helplessness here does not involve confrontation with external forces, which the organism is unable to alter in its favor. The helplessness Freud speaks of is still sexual, helplessness that originates inside. The drives cannot find the object suitable for their discharge. It is a helplessness that comes from excess, from fullness, rather than from lack or void. The organism is overwhelmed from within. Separation, the absence of the external object, is only anxiety-provoking because the object satisfied needs, and without it those needs will be unsatisfied (1926, pp. 137, 155).

As it stands, this characterization of helplessness, marked by the influence of the energetic model and the idea of tension, cannot serve as an explanation for death anxiety. It is another case where the external

---

[8] Beyond helplessness, several factors in that second theory could make it a suitable explanation for death anxiety that would acknowledge fear of death as important. It would be a specifically psychoanalytic explanation, in that it would require an earlier anticipation and would create a link between the adult fear of death and the emotional world of the infant. The components are all there. The ego is now the seat of anxiety (Freud, 1926, pp. 140, 161). Anxiety is no longer a transformation of libido (pp. 140, 161), that is, directly and necessarily linked to sexuality. The move is no longer automatic (p. 140), and the mental system is thus more involved in anxiety. It is acknowledged that different danger situations result from the "changed mode of life" and from "growing mental development" (p. 162), and thus one can posit an anxiety that is formed only when the required cognitive capabilities, of abstractness and forward thinking, enable one to recognize mortal danger. Anxiety now has a Janus face: it looks both forwards to the future, and back into the past. Anticipation is an essential characteristic: ("Anxiety... is anxiety about [*vor*, toward] something," pp. 164–5). Death could now be posited as an object of anxiety and of that anticipation. Anxiety also has the character of indefiniteness (pp. 164–5). (The possible relevance of anticipation and indefiniteness with regard to death is noted by Lifton [1979, pp. 126–7], and the developmental phase-specific character of anxiety, and the idea of anxiety as a signal, by Hoffman, 1998, pp. 42–3). And yet, while it seems that this description of anxiety could very well accommodate death anxiety, it is explicitly negated in those places where it is directly discussed by Freud. While on the one hand, some of these theoretical elements really could help build a model of death anxiety, I believe Freud is not simply obstinate, and that there is a vast distance between such elements and a true consideration of death anxiety.

source of threat or danger goes unrecognized, and with it not just helplessness in the face of a specific threat, but also the kind of helplessness that could have helped account for death anxiety: the helplessness in confronting unavoidable ageing and decay, or unpredictable dangers.

Beyond the details of the theories of anxiety, the problem with regard to death lies in their general viewpoint, which is common to both theories. The whole framing of the discussion of anxiety limits in advance any serious consideration of anxiety in its more existential aspect. The discussion revolves around certain processes in the mind, the mechanics of the mental system and libidinal energy transformations, and leaves out the subjective part of anxiety and its more global place in psychic life. Treating anxiety in terms of processes, or focusing on its technical side, as Freud does, leads one to believe that anxiety could very well not have existed. It implies that there is something contingent about anxiety. Anxiety is not considered in a global manner, and related to human life in a broader sense. The theory fails to properly acknowledge the possibility that anxiety defines something crucial about human lives. It also fails to consider the potentially positive influences of anxiety on the psyche, those unrelated to functioning—libido, repression, displacements—but rather those pertaining, for example, to the planning of one's life, or to the value we attach to life. To put it briefly, it neglects the existential importance of anxiety in our lives.

One could perhaps have believed that one could do away with Freud's explicit statements against the importance of fear of death noted in Chapter 1, tear them out of the textbooks, and reassign death anxiety its proper place in psychoanalysis. We begin to see, however, that this is impossible and how they are part and parcel of a profound position. Freud's model of anxiety thus limits in advance analytic theory's potential to take death anxiety into consideration. Examples of this we saw above were the insistence on the internalization of danger and the sexual basis for anxiety, the tendency to focus on neurotic anxiety, and the disavowal of the more adult, cognitively-developed fear of death. The theory is such that if death were in fact an influential force in our psychic world, Freud would find it difficult accounting for it within his existing models of anxiety. While the explicit arguments against death have not always been very sound or convincing, the neglect of death in psychoanalysis seems to originate at a deeper level. We will pursue further the ramifications of this neglect in Chapter 13.

6   A struggle with the concept of death: "Thoughts for the Times on War and Death"

One might perhaps claim that there is no real problem in integrating death with psychoanalysis. That it has not yet been done may be seen as a theoretical accident. I will try in the following pages to look at this question, and elucidate some of the complexities and problematics of Freud's thinking about death, by dealing with his most important text on the subject, a paper written in 1915 called "Thoughts for the Times on War and Death." In the midst of the first World War, as Europe plunges itself in blood and both of Freud's sons are at the front, Freud sets about writing an account of the influence of war. He had plenty of time, after all, as patients were virtually non-existent. Behind the theoretical text, a text that brings together Freud's ideas about the war and about death, there are glimpses of a personal account, the reflections of one of Europe's finest fruits who watches his beloved continent tear itself apart. Indeed, the first part of the text, "The Disillusionment of the War," is devoted precisely to the breakdown of an illusion: that of peace between nations and universal humanism, that war has forever undermined. In the second part "Our Attitude towards Death," Freud attempts to further isolate and understand the source of the bewilderment felt by people in that period (1915).[1] Freud claims that these feelings are caused by the altered attitude toward death imposed on people by war, and he is, therefore, led to describe the ordinary attitude toward death. This is Freud's first organized attempt to deal with death and the only one (except perhaps *Beyond the Pleasure Principle*, to be dealt with in the next chapter) in which death is the main subject rather than marginally alluded to, and it outlines his future position on the subject. Examining it is both an end in itself and a sort of case study for illuminating the nature of the difficulty for psychoanalysis as a theory, and for analysts as practitioners when dealing with death.

---

[1] The English translation of the title is somewhat misguided, Samuel Weber (1997, p. 96) points out, the German original speaking of a "relation" to death. Weber superbly deconstructs the text on war and reads it as meditation on violence.

While on the whole, as I argued above, Freud's writings show little theoretical interest in the issue of death or are reductionistic, "Thoughts for the Times on War and Death" is often taken to express a different position, a more "existential" concern with death.[2] First, there is the harsh criticism found at the beginning of the article regarding modern society's attitude toward death, which Freud terms "cultural-conventional," and where his power as a cultural critic is seen to the full. Although people give formal recognition to death as inevitable, they behave as if it does not exist. They shut it out from their thoughts, and when events bring them face to face with it, they treat it as a chance event, not as the necessary outcome of life. The second indication of an arguably more existential approach to death in this text is the often-quoted final paragraph, in which Freud proposes that we "give death the place in reality and in our thoughts which is its due" (1915, p. 299). This passage is sometimes referred to as representing a view of death as an important factor in mental life, especially the closing maxim: "*Si vis vitam, para mortem*. If you want to endure life, prepare yourself for death" (p. 300). In addition to these two passages, one can find throughout the article sharp and crystallized apprehensions of the inevitability and arbitrariness of death. Take, for example, the following: " ... it is really too sad that in life it should be as it is in chess, where one false move may force us to resign the game, but with the difference that we can start no second game, no return-match" (p. 291).

At the same time, the text contains some of Freud's clearest formulations of the impossibility of representing death in the unconscious (1915, p. 296), where we are all immortal (p. 289). There is no profound reverberation for awareness of death in the mind and fear of death is viewed as secondary (p. 297).

We have here, then, two worldviews: one that finds in death a meaningful and important coordinate for human life, and another that

---

[2] Here, as earlier in this book, the term "existential" will be used to designate a certain sensibility in regard to death, and will not refer directly to the thought of a particular philosopher, theologian, psychologist, or school of thought. This sensibility, which is not uniform and which can be found in writings that are as chronologically disparate as *Ecclesiastes* and Heidegger's *Being and Time*, includes a perception of the importance of finitude in our lives and its implications. Such implications range from the relationship between finitude and perceiving and valuing life, to the psychological significance of the emotional attitude towards death, mainly in the form of anxiety thereof. The existential attitude does not reduce death to other phenomena, nor transform it, but rather underlines its inevitability, arbitrariness and place in mental life.

disregards the importance of death *per se* in our mental life; the text vacillates between them.[3]

There is much more, however, than the mere juxtaposition of two attitudes, one denying and the other valorizing death's importance. When read in the light of the entire text, the very statements which seem to belong to a kind of existential discourse are found to contradict themselves and to be devoid of any meaningful content.

This confusion is reflected, for example, in the following statement: "The fear of death, which *dominates us oftener than we know*, is on the other hand something *secondary*" (Freud, 1915, p. 297, emphasis added). Dominates us or is secondary? By closely reading the text and pointing out its various contradictions and inconsistencies, I hope to show it to be the product of two conflicting attitudes toward death. Two different positions, one akin to existential approaches and the other dismissing death as unimportant or psychically marginal, seem to be struggling for expression. Each time Freud tries to express one position the other one influences the text so that the original meaning is lost. The nature of death and its psychic implications are such that something in Freud's attempts to understand it using ordinary psychoanalytic methods and to integrate death with an analytic explanation, remains unsettled, or in a state of tension. It is this tension that will occupy us here. We shall see that the text often speaks to us in more than one voice.

Let us delve then into Freud's effort at explaining the human attitude toward death, and see how this topic constitutes an intractable difficulty, stubborn and unyielding, in the path of psychoanalysis from its very beginning; a difficulty that is still being encountered in present-day psychoanalytic perspectives on human finitude.

Giving death the place which is its due

Before we start examining the text, a brief review of the content. Freud claims that much of his contemporaries' bewilderment is caused by the effect war has in changing their attitude toward death. After describing the modern cultural-conventional attitude to death, mentioned above, Freud turns his attention to the attitude of primitive man toward death, which is also reproduced in our unconscious. He sees it as a composite of three component vectors: hate—together with acknowledgment of the death—of one's enemy; denial, in the case of oneself; and ambivalence,

---

[3] Cf. Lifton (1979, pp. 13–7), Yalom (1980, pp. 66–7) and Hoffman's (1998, p. 50) texts which stress the existence of an ambiguity or an ambivalence in Freud's overall attitude towards death.

concerning the death of someone close. Our unconscious attitude—ignoring the subject's own death, wishing for the death of others, and ambivalence in the case of people close to us—is quite remote from what Freud calls our "civilized cultural attitude toward death." The latter has been badly shaken by war. The paper ends with the following passage:

[War] strips us of the later accretions of civilization, and lays bare the primal man in each of us. It compels us once more to be heroes who cannot believe in their own death ... But war cannot be abolished; ... there are bound to be wars. The question then arises: Is it not we who should give in, who should adapt ourselves to war? Should we not confess that in our civilized attitude towards death we are once again living psychologically beyond our means, and should we not rather turn back and recognize the truth? Would it not be better to give death the place in reality and in our thoughts which is its due, and to give a little more prominence to the unconscious attitude towards death which we have hitherto so carefully suppressed? This hardly seems an advance to higher achievement, but rather in some respects a backward step—a regression; but it has the advantage of taking the truth more into account, and of making life more tolerable for us once again. To tolerate life remains, after all, the first duty of all living beings. Illusion becomes valueless if it makes this harder for us. We recall the old saying *Si vis pacem, para bellum*. If you want to preserve peace, arm for war.

It would be in keeping with the times to alter it: *Si vis vitam, para mortem*. If you want to endure life, prepare yourself for death. (Freud, 1915, pp. 299–300)

Writers on the theme of death in psychoanalysis have rightly observed that these closing lines do more than merely sum up the text; they rather contain a sort of general statement, urging the reader toward a change, toward an ethically correct and fuller life. In general one can say that this paragraph has been treated as a sort of existential pronouncement by Freud regarding the significance of death for humankind, and the need to live our life in the constantly acknowledged shadow of death. Along these lines one can understand how some writers came to the conclusion that Freud's intention here is to say that "all doctrines that deny the significance of annihilation" should be abandoned (Alford, 1992, pp. 130–1), because "[t]hese images are nothing but the denial of annihilation, and therefore denial of death itself" (Lifton, 1979, p. 14).[4] Other writers conclude by linking Freud to existential philosophical traditions, and so we find in the literature that the closing line of "Thoughts for the Times" "leads us toward some of Heidegger's own views about death" (Bolivar, 1993, p. 124. See also Kaufmann, 1959, pp. 48–9 for a similar

---

[4] Although Lifton, who advocates symbolic immortality, criticizes Freud's attitude (which he refers to as "rationalistic-iconoclastic"), this criticism is irrelevant to the current chapter.

claim concerning other parts of the article). Another writer claims that Freud is following here a psychological-philosophical tradition "that argues that one *must* appreciate death keenly if one is also to appreciate life to the fullest extent" (Kastenbaum, 1977, p. 36, emphasis in the original).

A recent writer believes Freud's last line expresses his "ethical imperative" (following Laplanche, 1976 [1970]): an imperative "to be ready for the possibility of loss and mourning, for disappointment and failure" (Carel, 2006, pp. 130–1). Even writers who focus on Freud's attitude toward death and the fear of death tend to assign supreme importance to that last paragraph. Freud is praised for calling us "to deal frankly with the psychology of death," thus "taking more into account the true state of affairs" (Wahl, 1959 [1958], p. 29. See also Ricoeur, 1970, pp. 329–30), and for expressing, "under the guise of a maxim," "the idea of the inextricable interweaving of life and death" (Eissler, 1955, pp. 28–9).

Many of these authors criticize Freud in other parts of their work for being generally disinclined to treat death as important for psychic life. One such clear example is Yalom (1980, p. 66–7), whose book contains invaluable criticism of Freud's inattention to death and its implications. Yalom articulates a more positive tone, however, toward this particular essay, "Thoughts for the Times on War and Death," where he sees Freud speculating boldly about death. He cites the entire closing paragraph, reading it as representing Freud's mindfulness "of the role death plays in the shaping of life," and laments the fact that Freud, apart from this article, remained silent on the subject of preparing for death in his other teachings for therapists.

All these writers treat the last paragraph as an integral part of the text. Laplanche (1976 [1970]), however, points out that there is something odd about these final words. While seeing them as linked to a line of thought that includes both Montaigne and Heidegger, he identifies a discordance between the last paragraph and the rest of the essay.[5]

I have noted these references in the literature to show that not only does this last paragraph sound "existentially oriented" in spirit, it has also been understood that way by a variety of authors.[6] And yet a closer reading of the essay as a whole suggests that this passage, too keenly

---

[5] It should be noted that Laplanche's main interest concerns the axis of self/other, and not an existential/reductionistic understanding of death (which is the subject of the current chapter).

[6] A somewhat amusing but indicative example of the level of discrepancy between the concluding statements of Freud's article and the rest of his paper, is Loy's (1996) slip in discussing Freud's view of death: He cites Freud's position regarding the unavailability of death to the unconscious as part of his "Thought for the Times," and in the following

praised by these authors for showing an existential understanding of death, is much less "existential" than it might seem when read as a text apart, and not in the context of the rest of the paper. Freud's dismissive approach was not renounced in it. As we shall see in the following pages, this passage and others in the text, and consequently the text as a whole, are the "compromise formation" of two attitudes, and as such actually fail to express either of them. This problem has been completely overlooked by all the authors quoted above, and so renders their interpretation incomplete.[7]

But what is the place which is death's due?

Looking at Freud's closing lines about giving death its place and preparing ourselves for death, we may become confused, because that passage, despite its confident and somewhat prophetic tone, is far from clear. If what is laid bare by war is the "primal man in each of us," and if war compels us once again to be "heroes who cannot believe in their own death," what then is meant by the appeal to "adapt ourselves to war"? Freud wants us to admit that in our civilized attitude toward death we are living beyond our means. He wants us to "give death the place in reality and in our thoughts which is its due." This statement, in itself vague, could be read existentially, as urging us to be open to the possibility of death, to bring it into constant consideration, and perhaps to accept the fear of death as a constituent part of our life. On a more abstract level this statement could indeed be interpreted as leading in the direction of Heideggerian thinking, seeing man's being as being-toward-death. But such interpretations are called into question by the second part of the sentence which asks us to "give a little more prominence to the unconscious attitude toward death" which was suppressed. Doing that would take "truth into account" and get rid of the unnecessary illusion.

Yet now is the time to recall what Freud himself describes as the attitude of primeval man and the unconscious. Interestingly, Freud's

---

paragraph says that "In *another* short essay ... Freud recommended more consciousness of death" [emphasis added], and cites the concluding lines of "Thought for the Times": "Would it not be better to give death the place ... " (p. 4). Possibly Loy means "On Transience," but in reality the two statements he cites belong of course to one and the same text.

[7] It is quite possible that other instances in the literature, which ignore this essay, are related to the fact that it has something incomprehensible and self-contradictory in it, sensed by the authors but not elucidated. How else can one understand the fact that Schur's (1972) 500-page-long book, dedicated to Freud's attitude towards death, discusses so marginally what seems to be Freud's fullest account of death?

description is far from "existential." Though recognizing death as annihilation with regard to others, our unconscious ignores the possibility of our own death. Death has no place in the reality of the unconscious, says Freud explicitly several pages earlier (1915, pp. 289, 296). Again, it is not only the cultural-civilized attitude that ignores death. The unconscious is no different in that regard. The call to abandon our comforting illusions about death and to re-adopt our "real" attitude is, therefore, misleading. Our "real" attitude, the unconscious one, ignores death no less and denies its place in reality and in our thoughts. Therefore, there is nothing to return to—no illusion-free zone in our mental life concerning death. Going back to the unconscious attitude will not help us prepare for death.

What then could Freud have meant by his concluding words in "Thoughts for the Times"? Freud's last paragraph, not an isolated example as we shall soon see, hardly makes sense. The entire paper is actually the result of a hesitation between two attitudes, with the text ultimately leaving both these conflicting positions thwarted.

It seems that part of the problem in understanding what Freud is saying arises from the fact that he leaves open crucial questions about the meaning of his claim. Among these is the difference between readopting the unconscious attitude, and recognizing it or knowing about it; whether the truth we should return to is that of death or that of the unconscious; and which of the elements in the unconscious attitude (being murderous, recognizing death as annihilation in the case of others or the denial of death for ourselves) Freud is talking about: neither does he clearly pinpoint which component of the situation renders it painful or disturbing.

Basically, all attempts to make sense of what Freud is saying in this famous paragraph run into the two basic problems already discussed, and that we will come across again in other sections of Freud's essay: the first is that actually there is no difference between the unconscious and the cultural-conventional attitudes in their denial of the existence of death, and the second is the tension between the existential tone of the paragraph, particularly the maxim "prepare yourself for death," and the other more classically psychoanalytic descriptions. Instead of proposing the full range of possible interpretations, I will only briefly outline several such interpretations, and show how none of them manages to offer an acceptable reading of the paragraph.

One reading is that it is chiefly the murderousness of the unconscious which is distressing for us, in the general nexus of war and death. It is unlikely that Freud (1915) would urge us to readopt or re-assume it, which would be in clear contradiction to the spirit of the article (see p. 296, and most of the first essay, "The Disillusionment of War"). He would rather urge us to know about it, to recognize our true nature; this will supposedly render unconscious pressures easier to endure. Yet this explanation does not make the paragraph clearer and more coherent, for two reasons: First, one cannot ignore the existence, according to Freud, of other aspects of the unconscious attitude toward death. Isolating the different aspects is misleading, because they are intertwined. One would, therefore, still have to face the difficulties raised above about the element of denial of death in the unconscious. Second, this interpretation still cannot solve the riddle of the meaning of the last line, which calls on us to prepare for death.

But if it is not the murderousness of the unconscious, what could be the source of the distress that we feel? Freud (1915, p. 289) seems to suggest that the changes in our attitude toward death that war has brought about are a serious cause for distress. But what is the precise effect of war?[8] This question is bound up with another: What is the illusion Freud is talking about in the last paragraph and why has it become valueless? Perhaps under the pressure of external reality, of war, we have regressed to our unconscious attitude, and, therefore, our conscious attitude becomes superfluous, an empty idea that we do not really believe any more. The source of our difficulty would thus be the tension between conscious and unconscious ideas, which has become accentuated because the unconscious is now closer to the surface. Or perhaps our conscious attitude, which tends to ignore death, has become a valueless illusion because war forces us to face death as a mass phenomenon (p. 291).[9] But here again we encounter the same problem: the unconscious also ignores death, i.e. the person's own death. Readopting its attitude offers no advantage over the conscious one, but merely replaces one illusion with another.

Both these possible sources of discontent—heightened conscious-unconscious tension and massive exposure to death—necessitate a diversion from standard Freudian explanations if we are to accept them. This is because "taking the truth ... into account" might mean explicitly taking into account the disturbing and unpleasant truth of the unconscious, yet the *reality* which knocks on the door in the case of death is still

---

[8] Later in the chapter it will be seen that there is more than one answer to this question in Freud's essay.
[9] Freud says (1915, p. 292) that in the context of war it is no longer possible to hold our former attitude, but a new attitude has yet to be found. He then moves on to talk about the unconscious attitude and that of primitive man. However, the impossibility of holding that earlier attitude does not explain why one should adopt the unconscious one, nor does this explanation solve the problems raised in the paragraph above.

an external one. That is, even if Freud thinks that there is some attitude of the unconscious of which we are unaware, it is actually the external reality of war in any of its possible ramifications—of death, of the accumulation of deaths—that is disturbing for us, and in a much more intensive form than merely the ruining of a fantasy. The reality itself is the heart of the problem, not the disparity between it and the fantasy.[10]

We find then that there is something about this passage that stubbornly refuses to fit. The call to give death its due place, and to live our life under the imperative *"para mortem,"* remains incomprehensible in light of the rest of the text. It is not some minor problem of logic, but rather a major difficulty. "Enough with denial, let's go back to denial," to put it schematically, is what is actually being said. What then could Freud mean here, and what can be inferred from his essay about his attitude toward death?

The highest stake in the game of living

In an attempt to answer the above question I now move to another, no less intriguing passage in which Freud tries to set out in more detail the relationship between letting death enter our thoughts, and our life. This paragraph comes immediately after Freud's discussion of the cultural-conventional attitude toward death with all its behavioral and intellectual manifestations. He then turns to an examination of the effects of this attitude on us.

He writes:

But this attitude of ours towards death has a powerful effect on our lives. Life is impoverished, it loses in interest, when the highest stake in the game of living, life itself, may not be risked. It becomes as shallow and empty as, let us say, an American flirtation, in which it is understood from the first that nothing is to

---

[10] Some authors (Alford, 1992; Lifton, 1979) seem to think that Freud, in this passage, is advocating the abandonment of all doctrines that deny the significance of annihilation. If we try to elaborate this position it would mean going back to that moment that the text describes before those doctrines appeared. This moment (to be discussed later) happened when primitive man was faced with the death of his loved one, and consequently began inventing ideologies whose aim was to mask death and deny its significance, "the significance of annihilation" (Freud, 1915, p. 293-5). Yet even if primitive man had some sudden, clear apprehension of death at that moment, it was still a very transient one, since his general attitude about his own death was to ignore it completely. He denied death, according to Freud, both before that moment and subsequently, through the invention of doctrines that promise an afterlife. This interpretation will not make giving "death the place ... which is its due" any more comprehensible. In addition, this moment involves a conscious, or perhaps a total (both conscious and unconscious) apprehension of death, and is not the unconscious attitude in itself, so returning to it will not be a return to our unconscious attitude.

happen, as contrasted with a Continental love-affair in which both partners must constantly bear its serious consequences in mind. Our emotional ties, the unbearable intensity of our grief, make us disinclined to court danger for ourselves and for those who belong to us. We dare not contemplate a great many undertakings which are dangerous but in fact indispensable, such as attempts at artificial flight, expeditions to distant countries or experiments with explosive substances. We are paralyzed by the thought of who is to take the son's place with his mother, the husband's with his wife, the father's with his children, if a disaster should occur. Thus the tendency to exclude death from our calculations in life brings in its train many other renunciations and exclusions. Yet the motto of the Hanseatic League ran: "*Navigare necesse est, vivere non necesse.*" ("It is necessary to sail the seas, it is not necessary to live.") (Freud, 1915, pp. 290–1)

Upon a close reading of the above paragraph, certain problems become apparent. "Life is impoverished," we are told at the beginning, "when the highest stake in the game of living, life itself, may not be risked." Now this imposing phrase closely resembles in tone the message conveyed in "On Transience" (1916 [1915]), written several months following "Thoughts for the Times." The article, dealing with transience in general, is also a statement concerning human transience and its effect on the value of life. Freud's stance is that the transience of things lends them more value. Freud's contention in "Thoughts for the Times" about not risking the highest stake in the game of living initially seems closely related. He seems to be saying that human finitude or the awareness of it renders life richer and more interesting. Eliminating death from life by hardly thinking about it results in shallowness and emptiness.

Thus, it appears that Freud is concerned with our intellectual and cognitive attitudes, those he characterized in the preceding passage, about the cultural-conventional attitude (i.e., not thinking about our own death, and judgments attributing death to accidental events). The message of the paragraph seems poignantly existential: as humans we tend to put death aside, banishing it from our thoughts, and this attitude has a price. We live a diminished, shallower, and emptier life.

But a sharp twist is ahead. "Our emotional ties" and the "intensity of our grief" cause us to keep away from danger. What comes next is to my mind a quite odd and unexpected list of activities that we avoid. These include artificial flight, expeditions to faraway places, and experiments with explosive substances. Not the most common activities, to be sure. We are no longer in the realm of thought, for here the text is dealing with emotions and actions. It turns out that what we miss, the way in which life is diminished, is that our activities are more restricted. The text has become quite concrete. The reader has the feeling that Freud wishes to demonstrate his earlier point, but that the demonstration is quite at odds with the claim itself (that life loses in interest).

The price we pay for our tendency to exclude death from our calculations is a restricted sort of life, one might say a neurotic life, which, under the fear of death, is not pushed to its limits. We may recall Otto Rank's (1950 [1945]) description of the neurotic, the type who restricts him/herself because of the fear of death, as one who "refuses the loan (life) in order thus to escape the payment of the debt (death)" (p. 126). But are Freud's words really similar to Rank's? Is he proposing a theory whereby fear of death is at the center of the human predicament? It hardly seems so, for the activities denied the ordinary person by not thinking about death are too far-fetched, too esoteric perhaps for this to be the case. Freud's examples are much weaker than the claim he is trying to make. "So what," one could say. Not all people, after all, are destined to be conquistadors and mountain climbers. Are these the serious consequences we are warned against? Is it really so unfortunate that we do not "court danger for ourselves and for those who belong to us"?

Why does Freud seem to lose momentum in the middle of his message? My answer is that it has been an ambivalent message from the outset, directed toward two opposing ends. For why is it that people refrain from overly-dangerous tasks? It is "the intensity of our grief," "our emotional ties," and the thought of who is to fill our place or our loved one's place if we or he dies, says Freud. But are not those behaviors precisely the clearest signs of a significant *presence* of death in our thoughts? It is precisely because we *do* think about death, because we *are* aware of this eventuality, even incessantly, and are even "paralyzed by the thought," to borrow Freud's own term, that we are careful and avoid dangerous activities. Freud actually claims the contrary in the preceding section, where he describes our cultural-conventional attitude, in which we try hard not to think or speak about death. In fact, the attitude he describes here, of avoiding danger for fear of what will happen, is much closer to the description of the continental love affair than to that of the American flirtation. We human beings bear in mind the consequences, both the possible influence our actions will have and the possibility of life—or of the "affair"– having an end. Is it because death is excluded from our calculations that we refrain from action, or because "we are paralyzed by the thought"?[11] Are we oblivious to the possibility of death or obsessed with it?

---

[11] The thought of who is to take our place if something happens to us is actually a thought about death and its consequences.

Freud evokes heroism and bravery in other places in the article (1915, pp. 291, 296–7, 299), and it is possible that this paragraph should also be read as one about courage. Ordinary people are not bold enough to risk their life performing heroic deeds. Yet this explanation does not resolve the contradiction in the paragraph: the ordinary person, the one with the cultural-conventional attitude, who is criticized for not being a hero, for not daring, not pushing his life to its limits, is impoverished because he does not think about death. But the hero, the one who dares, who will risk death to attain a cultural goal, is actually the one, according to Freud himself, who ignores death totally (pp. 296–7): he is heroic, Freud suggests, only because his unconscious, like any other, actually ignores the possibility of death. And so for the hero, the "highest stake in the game of living" may indeed be risked, but only because this game has no value for him, because he does not realize its rules. Although it is a game with only one critical move he behaves as if he can always have a rematch.[12]

This impasse is similar to the one we encountered earlier when analyzing the concluding lines of Freud's essay. There too, Freud's call to oppose the cultural-conventional treatment of death by taking death seriously, ended by turning to an attitude (that of the unconscious, of primeval man, and now that of the hero) where death is equally ignored and where one is no less blind to its presence.

This paragraph, then, is self-contradictory and gradually advances from one claim to its complete antithesis. It seems that when Freud arrives at the statement that the problem with people is that they refrain from handling explosive substances, he is not where he wanted to be. The question of what Freud *really* meant when he said that life is made less interesting when death is left out remains unanswered. We are back in an aporia.

With a sense that this aporia is fundamental to "Thoughts for the Times on War and Death," I wish now to carry the investigation further, and discuss two more of its sections. As we continue to investigate Freud's position, the aporia will reemerge with a twist, and its centrality to Freud's thought on the issue of death will become apparent.[13]

---

[12] To borrow Freud's metaphor for life mentioned earlier.
[13] In a recently discovered first version of Freud's article (1993 [1915]), one that was originally read at the meeting of *B'nai B'rith*, one can discern several differences from the final version. The paragraph I have just dealt with is one where the differences between the two versions are the most obvious. They do not, however, shed more light on the issue at hand. See Le Rider (1992), Nitzschke (1991), Meghnagi (1993), and Jonte-Pace (2001, pp. 74–98) for discussions of the differences between the two versions. See Razinsky (2005) for thoughts about the importance of Jewishness and the Jewish-atheist-Christian context for Freud's discussion of death in the B'nai B'rith version.

The direct encounter with death

Freud's description of the primeval human's confrontation with death, to which we now turn, is yet another example of Freud having more than one intuition regarding death. This example is perhaps closer to the experiential level than those already discussed. We can see his vacillation between considering death as important, giving it its due, and taking a reductionistic stance, which regards death's influence as secondary to certain psychoanalytic notions. The passage appears in the context of Freud characterization of the attitude of primeval man toward death, and concerns primeval man's first confrontation with the reality of death. It can be regarded as a kind of mythic description of the human encounter with death.

Freud (1915) characterizes the primeval human's attitude toward death as very different from ours, i.e. from our conscious-cultural-conventional attitude. We have seen that primeval man recognizes death vis-à-vis his enemies and even desires their death, but completely denies it in regard to himself. Toward those who are neither completely other, nor completely self, he is ambivalent. Freud describes the moment when primeval man stood near the body of his loved one. Primeval man was then "forced to learn that one can die, too, oneself" (p. 293). The death of the close other was painful for primeval man, but it also pleased him, for he was also an other.

Freud then mentions an unattributed philosophical view, whereby the intellectual enigma of death is what led primeval man to reflection, and thus was the "starting point of all speculation" (1915, pp. 293–4). Commenting sarcastically yet characteristically that "here the philosophers are thinking too philosophically," he declares that he would like to "limit and correct their assertion." But then the supposed limit and correction turns out to be a complete inversion of the claim, because Freud says it was the ambivalence toward the two-faced object, at once loved and hated, that caused primeval man to reflect, and not, in fact, the enigma of death. This reflection led to religious doctrines whose aim was to deny the significance of annihilation (the invention of immortality). We can see how death is subjugated to psychoanalytic concepts. The motive for inquiry is not the brute fact of the existence of death in the world, but rather an *internal* conflict; not the fact of human finitude, but "the law of ambivalence of feeling" toward objects. Psychoanalytic terms are quickly invoked to block the possibility of an existential acknowledgment of death. Death and the anxiety it evokes, as usual, are explained in psychoanalytic terms (castration, guilt, conflict), which do not fully address the issue.

Could it then be that it is also the psychoanalysts who are thinking too psychoanalytically? Perhaps, but there is no one single Freudian doctrine about death in this article. Freud (1915) is quite clear here about the law of ambivalence of feeling being the important factor. But we read otherwise in his own text. We read that when primeval man saw the loved one dead, "he was forced to learn that one can die, too, oneself, and his whole being revolted against the admission" (p. 293). Hoffman (1998) discusses this paragraph in the context of Freud's insistence on the hypothesis that death has no representation in the mind, and is, therefore, inaccessible to us. "[H]ow can it be," he asks, "that a human being's 'whole being revolted against the admission' of something that to begin with cannot be a content of subjective experience in any profound sense—something that is, rather, 'unimaginable and unreal'?" (p. 36). Carrying Hoffman's analysis a little further, one can point to the self-sufficient nature of the explanation. Let us recall: primeval man does not yet know of the fact of his finitude, does not acknowledge it. Suddenly he learns about it, in the most painful way. And—how could it be otherwise—"his whole being revolted." Note that this reaction of primeval man, as described in the text itself, is completely autonomic and self-explanatory. It needs no further elucidation. Freud adds ambivalence of feeling; but if we read carefully, the addition is superfluous; the original description is quite logical without it. Ambivalence still serves as a condition for being influenced by the other's death, because otherwise indifference could be the rule (near the slain enemy, primeval man had triumphed, Freud reminds us).[14] However, once the condition is fulfilled it is not the ambivalence that generates the response, but the pure knowledge of death, of finitude, that is responsible on the emotional level for a revolt of the whole personality. This is Freud's own description contrary to his conclusion.

It is noteworthy that we are no longer dealing with intellectual enigmas. In the intellectual domain perhaps the philosophers are thinking too philosophically but here, with primeval man's response to the death of his loved one we are dealing with an intense, immediate, and emotional response, which in psychoanalytic terms we would probably call "instinctual."[15] Here too, then, even when it seems the contrary, we find that the text speaks with more than one voice.

---

[14] As a matter of fact, it is not even ambivalence which serves as a condition, but the mere existence of love for the other. This love is what forces primitive man to face death.

[15] As opposed to "there is nothing instinctual in us which responds to a belief in death" (Freud, 1915, p. 296).

126   Thoughts for the Times on War and Death

One can also note the opposition between reacting emotionally with one's *whole* being, and having an ambivalent, split frame of mind. The emotional response to the reality of death, which we have just revealed in Freud's text, has a certain totality, an overarching influence, unlike the more psychoanalytically-oriented explanation offered in that same paragraph whose major characteristic is partiality and ambivalence.[16]

The stress on both the irruption of death into awareness, and Freud's reluctance to recognize it in that mythical moment of encounter, finds support when we look at an earlier version of the article entitled "Death and Us," read by Freud at the meeting of *B'nai B'rith* (1993 [1915]; see footnote 13). Freud says there specifically that one of the consequences born of this encounter is the fear of death (p. 28). In the later version, the one found in the "Standard Edition," this observation was deleted.

Freud's correction to the claim that speculation began for mankind with the encounter with death, actually adheres to his standard, reductionistic view of the important psychic motives. Yet we have found out that the reduction does not succeed in being complete, that another view of death stubbornly manifests itself in Freud's own text, a view that does not reduce death to any psychoanalytic notion.

The influence of war

Before concluding, let us examine one last example of the inconsistencies in Freud's essay. The essay's subject, as stated, is the influence of war, and Freud twice refers directly to the effects war has on our cultural-conventional treatment of death. We note the difference between the two references, though the context gives no reason to postulate a change of mind. The first reference to the influence of war is right after Freud describes the cultural-conventional attitude toward death and the paragraph we have analyzed about life becoming less interesting. It reads:

It is evident that war is bound to sweep away this conventional treatment of death. Death will no longer be denied; *we are forced to believe in it*. People really die ... (1915, p. 291, emphasis added)

The second time is in the concluding paragraph:

It is easy to see how war impinges on this dichotomy [between our unconscious attitude towards death and our cultural-conventional attitude]. It strips us of the later accretions of civilization, and lays bare the primal man

---

[16] See also, in another context, Hoffman's (1998, p. 52) emphasis on the "whole" in this phrase.

in each of us. It compels us once again to be *heroes who cannot believe in their own death*. (p. 299, emphasis added)[17]

Once again Freud's text leaves us perplexed about his stance. Does war force us to believe or to disbelieve in death? Did we or did we not believe in death before the war, in our normal life? It would seem unjustifiable and naïve to assume that such clear contradictions *in the very subject of the article* are coincidental or are due to Freud's inattentiveness. It seems much more likely, as I have argued throughout this chapter, that Freud has two competing views of death, whose interplay is so complex that they lead to inconsistencies, bungled writing, and contradictions.

Freud's hesitation

What we see then, when we look back at Freud's essay as a whole, is that it contains two different attitudes toward death, each one seeking expression; two attitudes—one valorizing death, the other belittling its psychic importance—which come into constant confrontation and which incessantly undermine both each other's claims and the logic of the article as a whole. The interplay of the two attitudes generates passages which are in a way a compromise formation of both. This polyphonic, or rather dissonant, text, constantly alternating between two positions, leaves us somewhat perplexed about Freud's "real" attitude toward death.

These two attitudes, which sometimes appear separately in Freud's writings, are here not only found together in the same article, but continuously alternate in a complex game of vacillation. Passages intended to express the first attitude end up as manifestations of the second, while clear articulations of the second conceal, and are undermined by, revelations of the first.

One way of looking at the problem is as a vacillation between two positions concerning the same question: why is death generally absent from our thoughts and calculations in life?

---

[17] Now, one might say that while Freud speaks about our own death in the second passage (p. 299), he deals mainly with another's death in the first one (p. 291). Yet this interpretation is not in line with the text (for example: in the immediately preceding paragraph [*ibid.*] Freud deals with the use of art as a means of experiencing a symbolic death, and speaks of *our* death through identification with the hero).

There is also no basis for assuming that Freud wants to illuminate a compound and ambiguous position that results from the influence of war: that one has to recognize death but at the same time is forced even more strongly to deny it. Here, as with the last paragraph of Freud's text, there is no indication that the two attitudes described converge, complete each other, or result from one other. There is no cross-reference between them at all.

The first position claims that we *do not want* to think about death, and thus we *avoid* thinking about it. The second supposes we *cannot* think about death. The first of these two is what we referred to as Freud's existential position, which is also a critical one. It implies that a change is needed; it regards the absence of death from our minds as problematic; it proposes that death does exist on some level or at some time in our thoughts, but that we prefer to minimize its presence. The other position is Freud's "standard" view regarding the psychic reality of death, and death-related mental products. It holds that death is not really representable for us, that all thoughts about death are epiphenomenal, and that all emotions regarding death, mainly anxiety, are secondary to other emotions. This stance is purely descriptive, and implies that there is neither a need for nor a possibility of change.[18]

Freud's problem is that he holds both positions simultaneously. He suggests that people should pay more heed to the problem of death, but at the same time claims that this is impossible. Every time he uses the first position as a criticism, he falls back on the second. We have seen this clearly in the last paragraph of the essay, where Freud insists that death should be given its due place, and the unconscious attitude more prominence, but this task can actually lead nowhere, because the unconscious ignores death no less than people do in their cultural approach. The same kind of self-contradiction is also apparent in the passage that asserts that life becomes less interesting when death is not considered or risked. There we saw that those who are most willing to risk life and limb, that is, those who ostensibly live their lives to the fullest, are actually the ones who are most oblivious to death. Finally, the same problem is evident in two passages where Freud speaks about the influence of war, one stating that war changes our cultural-conventional attitude toward death, and does not allow us to deny it, while the other asserts that war only serves to bring out more clearly our basic disregard for death on the level of the unconscious.

We note Freud's dilemma in an example taken from the very beginning of the article. Expressing the existential stance, Freud writes (1915, p. 289) that we tend to put death aside, eliminate it from life, hush it up. (It is interesting to notice the German word used: *totschweigen*, literally to silence it to death, to shut it up, thus rendering it dead. The "it" in

---

[18] This description, derived from an analysis of Freud's essay as a whole, is very much in line with Hoffman's (1998, p. 36) discussion of the question of whether the absence of death from our thoughts is the result of repression or of the impossibility of representing it. Piven (2004, p. 39) also questions, in the case of primitive man, whether he refused to believe in death as annihilation because he really "could not imagine it," or because "he wished not to."

Freud's phrase refers to death itself). Yet then he slides immediately into the other position, that of the irrepresentability of death (i.e., death cannot be thought about, represented or experienced in any way). The shift between Freud's two very different, almost contrary positions is managed swiftly, almost too naturally.[19]

It is no doubt true that while Freud's general attitude toward death tends to be reductionistic and denies the importance death has in our mental life, "Thoughts for the Times on War and Death" offers an alternative. Yet we cannot overlook the fact that this attempt to present us with a different view of death becomes entangled in a web of self-contradiction and ambiguity.

It is now clearer what exactly is at stake in trying to integrate an existential sensitivity to death into psychoanalysis. We have seen some of the deep contradictions and oppositions between the existential imperative to take death seriously and basic psychoanalytic positions and modes of understanding. What becomes apparent is the extreme difficulty Freud encounters when, equipped with intuitive knowledge about the importance of death, made more vivid perhaps by the contemporary atrocities of war, he attempts to explain death while remaining within the structure and terms of his psychoanalytic worldview.

These difficulties have not since disappeared, as we shall see in the following chapters. Theoretical discussions about death and psychoanalysis seem to not always fully recognize the depth of the problem they are trying to solve, which at times renders the solutions less sound than hoped for. Too often integrative attempts go directly to the solution without fully exploring the theoretical problems that need to be resolved.

One point still remains which might be of interest to us, and gives some hope for future perspectives. When one considers the psychoanalytic approach to death, one cannot overlook a rather interesting fact about the text at hand. In those very places where "Thoughts for the Times" does discuss death more existentially, as a fact of life, it is still undeniably very "psychoanalytic" in its spirit. Freud is, so to speak, very Freudian here. This is the Freud who comes to unveil our illusions, the lies we tell ourselves. This is Freud the "unmasker" of cultural hypocrisy (his critique of the modern approach to death is further discussed in Chapter 8). This observation may make us wonder whether the classical psychoanalytic attitude toward death (seeing it as secondary and not as

---

[19] Right afterwards in the text, there is another too-swift shift, noticed and analyzed by Hoffman (1998, p. 34), from irrepresentability as a cognitive limitation, to a universal belief in immortality in the unconscious.

constitutive in the psyche) is justified, and whether an attitude that analyzes the defenses raised in the psyche against the knowledge of finitude is not in some aspects more congruent with the spirit of psychoanalysis. Would it not be better if psychoanalysts and analytic thinkers "give death the place in reality and in our thoughts which is its due"?

7 Driving death away: Freud's theory of the death drive

The two tendencies seen in the last chapter were very hard to reconcile. Freud's attempt to give death its due place within a psychoanalytic perspective was countered by a theoretical disinclination to do so. It is now time to consider what might be characterized as Freud's most serious effort to include death in psychoanalysis, namely, the theory of the death drive. Freud's attempt to make death an organizing principle, to place it, moreover, at the heart of his entire edifice, while compelling at first, ends up a failure.

Is the death drive the one exception to an overall psychoanalytic sidestepping of death? Does this notion not place death in fact at the center of analytic theory? This claim, often communicated to me personally and cited as an argument against my claim that the analytic tradition has neglected death, also frequently appears in the literature (Eissler, 1955; Brown, 1959, pp. 87–109; de M'Uzan, 1977 [1968]; Gabel, 1974; Pontalis, 1977; Bolivar, 1993; Eigen, 1995, pp. 280, 286; Parat, 1998, pp. 1839–45; Piven, 2004, pp. 153–85; Carel, 2006; Mills, 2006). Freud's three most important biographers clearly see the theory of the death drive as Freud's personal solution to the question of mortality (Jones, 1957, pp. 301–2; Schur, 1972, pp. 344, 373; Gay, 1988, p. 394). For Gay, *Beyond the Pleasure Principle* demonstrates that the reason Freud did not publish the book he had penned on metapsychology was that his ideas until then "had not had enough about death in them," and that Freud "had not integrated what they had to say about death into his theory" (p. 394), a problem ostensibly solved with the publication of *Beyond the Pleasure Principle*. The current chapter aims at demonstrating that this claim—namely, that through the death drive psychoanalysis genuinely meets the challenge of death—is unsound.

Not only does the death drive fail to overcome the psychoanalytic problem with death, it even exacerbates it. The theory of the death drive is a fascinating attempt to grapple with death, yet in reality it does little to mitigate the reluctance of psychoanalysis to regard the emotional response to death as psychologically meaningful. This theory is yet another example of how death has been largely disregarded in analytic theory. This is not to say that the idea of the death drive is not transformative: Indeed, *Beyond the Pleasure Principle* is a remarkably complex work which adds depth and sophistication to analytic theory and which, on certain readings, might be useful as a basis for an analytic theory of death—but not in the way in which it is presented by Freud and interpreted by most of his followers.

The theory of the death drive has met, as we know, with only very limited success. Freud did not manage to persuade the analytic community of the necessity of his new ideas, and most theoreticians and analysts rejected them. The theory was, however, embraced by some schools, mainly by the Kleinians, by Jacques Lacan and his followers, and some other salient French authors such as Green. Both trends—the one that accepts the death drive and the one that rejects it—retain the belief that it is indeed an answer to the question of death. With the exception of some rare remarks in the literature, mainly those of Rank (1950 [1945]) and Searles (1965 [1961]), which are discussed later, neither trend questions the relationship between death and the death drive—the subject with which we are occupied here. Thus, those who have rejected the theory have sometimes tried to explain it away by linking it to actual cases of death in Freud's life; alternatively, Klein (1948), the major proponent of the death drive theory, sees it as the primary source of death anxiety. Either way, for both groups—those who accept the theory and those who do not—the death drive is understood to be concerned with death and the emotional response to it.

That the death drive is seen as intimately linked to the question of death is evident in Freud's (1920) introduction of this concept in *Beyond the Pleasure Principle*, and is also clear in many analytic discussions of this concept (e.g., Friedman, 1992a, pp. 192–4; Krell, 1994; Carel, 2001). Weatherill (1998), who broadly explores the theory of the death drive in Freud and in other analytic schools, equates it with coping with death in general (pp. 16, 119–49). Lowental (1981) describes the death drive as a force actually manifested in dying patients. For most other analysts, and in the general culture, that the death drive refers to death is simply taken for granted. Bibring (1941) summarizes the connection of death with destructiveness (an aspect of the death drive): "The problem of finding the original model of the self-destructive trends ... leads inevitably to the subject of death; for the question of the nature of death and its place within the scheme of life is in a sense the same as that problem and should help to solve it" (pp. 121–2). In addition, some theoreticians specifically concerned with the question of death, who would like to see more place given to it in psychoanalysis (Brown, 1959, pp. 87–109;

Bolivar, 1993; Eigen, 1995, pp. 280, 286; Piven, 2004; Carel, 2006; Mills, 2006), see the death drive as a concept that links psychoanalysis to existential thought, and interpret it as a way of taking death into account within analytic theory. For them, as well, the death drive is about death.[1]

But is the death drive actually a theory about death? Is it an existential theory of death? I argue here that it is not. My concern is neither with the suitability nor the correctness of the theory, but rather with the kind of position it puts across. What type of conceptualization of death is expressed in it? What can one say about this attempt to deal with death? The theory of the death drive is here also a test case for the way in which a theory can take on death, that unyielding phenomenon, which perhaps wholly defies comprehension or conceptualization.

The death drive and death

Introduced in 1920, in *Beyond the Pleasure Principle*, the death drive is the tendency of the organism to return to a pre-organic, inanimate state (Freud, 1920, p. 38). This tendency is inherent to life, and was born the moment life first emerged from the inorganic (p. 38). The Nirvana principle, the principle behind the death drive, aspires to zero or constant stimulation (pp. 55–6). At the basis of the death drive is a fundamental inclination to repetition. This repetition is not in the service of the pleasure principle; it persists regardless of the issue of pleasure and is manifested, for example, in the dreams of trauma neurosis. The death drive is first directed toward the self and is later deflected outward (pp. 54–5; 1924b, p. 163). It is mixed with the sexual drives, themselves repetitive as it turns out, and is not easily discernible (1923, p. 46). It is easier to detect when aimed at others and manifested as aggressiveness (these manifestations are described in Freud's later texts).

Discussions of this theory abound in the psychoanalytic literature (see especially Bibring, 1941, 1943, Laplanche, 1976 [1970], 1999 [1996], Matte Blanco, 2005 [1973], Friedman, 1992a, 1992b, Caruth, 1996, pp. 1–9, 57–72 [with a focus on trauma], Weatherill, 1998, 1999a, and Carel, 2006). Critiques of it have been voiced as well, whether regarding its adequacy in explaining phenomena, its clinical value or justification, its speculative nature or its moral consequences (see Friedman, 1992a,

---

[1] Needless to say, many discussions of the death drive do not touch the question of death at all, focusing on other aspects such as trauma or repetition. Moreover, in general, the death drive is not a common notion in most schools of psychoanalysis. Still, the death drive figures as a leading contender for an analytic solution to the problem posed by death.

pp. 189–90, and Barford, 1999, for an overview of these critiques). One of the problems is that it is not clear to what extent there is such a drive independent of three different entities, namely, the tendency to alleviate tension, innate human destructiveness (or alternatively, primary masochism), and the repetition compulsion. Also noteworthy is the empirical fact that most uses of the death drive tend to remain within its more recognizable aspect, the tendency toward destructiveness. This aspect is central to Freud's own later presentations of the death drive (1930, 1933b [1932], 1937). In *Beyond the Pleasure Principle*, however, a different picture emerges. What the essay outlines is a philosophical concept, one that is indeed, as its name implies, a death drive and not a drive to destructiveness. Freud is engaged in an immense theoretical effort to encircle death, to grasp something that keeps slipping away. The attempt ends in failure—not only because death remains, as I claim here, outside the circle, but also because no stable outcome is achieved. In the final analysis, the riddle remains. The nature of the text itself is revealing here. It is complex, confused, self-contradictory, and full of doubt. Freud's confidence in his theoretical voyage fluctuates from a view of it as a thought experiment, a sheer play with ideas (1920, pp. 24, 59–60), to a belief so strong he cannot understand how the facts have escaped him before (1930, pp. 119–20). Authors who have analyzed the text aptly point to the ways it contradicts itself on various issues and fails to advance – not even a step (Laplanche, 1976 [1970]; Derrida, 1987).

Ostensibly, with the introduction of this concept, a response has been given to the assertion—mine and others'—that death is forgotten or marginalized in psychoanalysis. Here, on the brink of old age, after many years of theorizing, Freud (1920) finally not only recognizes death's importance in our lives, but even accords death the status of a formative psychic factor, life's organizing principle ("the aim of all life is death," p. 38).

But the appearance is deceptive because, as I claim here, the death drive is an ingenious concept from a theoretical viewpoint. It seems to concern death, but what is actually discussed is almost the diametric opposite of all that the term "death" denotes. The death drive allows one to deal with death, but without having to deal with the threatening elements in it, to discuss it and at the same time to abstain from such discussion. The essence of death, the frightening element in it, is not ignored, but rather directly countered.

The concept of the death drive constitutes almost the antithesis of what we normally perceive as frightening or difficult about death. To demonstrate this, we need first to analyze death conceptually and pinpoint the frightening or demoralizing aspects of it. These aspects, which belong to death as it appears to humans, not as it "objectively" is, are interwoven. Unpicking them we can see where the death drive stands with regard to each strand. Now plausibly the death drive is not death: People do not die because of the death drive, and it is not the death drive they fear. That it is justifiable to compare the attributes of the death drive with those of death is not self-evident. However, the death drive is an attempt by Freud to deal with death, and it is a significant part of the available material when examining the psychoanalytic approach to death. Moreover, as just mentioned, the theory of the death drive is often evoked when the issue of death in psychoanalysis is raised. Furthermore, Freud (1920, pp. 38–9) indeed holds that people die because of the death drive, and Klein (1948) suggests that people are afraid of the death drive.

What then does our usual concept of death entail? Let us try to analyze the idea of death and see what meanings it encompasses and what is terrifying in it. The first, almost trivial aspect of death is that it is the negation of life, its complete reversal and opposition. Life and death are mutually exclusive; where life is present, death shall not be, and where death is, life is no longer.

Second, death is arbitrary. True, death is also the emblem of the inevitable, the inescapable. But it is arbitrary in three senses. First, it appears arbitrary as far as the circumstances or time of its arrival are concerned. Death can strike suddenly, un-announced, with no alarm signal. We may know the "what," but almost never the "when" of death. Second, it is arbitrary in the sense of it being unmotivated. There is no "reason" for it when it comes (for others), no explanation (unless we hold some specific religious beliefs). The question of why it comes is doomed to remain unanswered. We wish to understand, but the arrival of death transcends our usual mode of thought, which seeks out motives and reasons for everything. Our comprehension hits a wall, behind which nothing exists. Death, we suspect, is meaningless. Death is also arbitrary in the sense of being indifferent. It is not a punishment destined for those who have sinned, or for a specific population, but a lurking possibility for everyone.

Another troubling aspect of death is that it is external to us. Something outside of us is responsible for our death. A car may hit us, a cancerous tumor might develop and lead to our death,[2] or we may get shot in a battle. Death is always external to us as psychic subjects.

These last points, of arbitrariness and externality, can be subsumed under the title of lack of control. Death is not under our control.

---

[2] Although internal to our bodies, such a tumor would still be external to subjectivity or psychic life.

A fourth frightening aspect of death is that we actually know nothing about it. We normally treat it as the ultimate negation or the end of life, but regarding the specific nature of this negation or end we hardly know anything. We lack knowledge not only about why it comes, but on more fundamental issues as well: What is death? What kind of state is it? What does it make of us? Within the domain of theology, the theory of negative attributes (*via negativa*) has been proposed: One can only say what God is not, never what he really is. In a similar manner, the concept of death is one we can only formulate negative propositions about. It is a big question mark for us, another reason we fear it. Levinas (1987 [1979, 1947], pp. 71–2) says he fails to understand how the most essential character of our relationship with death has somehow escaped the attention of philosophers. This character is not the nothingness of death, as one usually thinks, but the appearance of something which is "absolutely unknowable" or "ungraspable."

A fifth aspect of death which makes it frightening is the erasure of individuality. The structure of one's personality, emotions, and thoughts are all lost when one dies, fading into nothingness. Rank (1950 [1945], pp. 123–4) proposes fear of loss of individuality as the motive force behind being afraid of dying. The loss of individuality in death is also exemplified in Ibsen's *Peer Gynt*. Peer Gynt is obsessed with his self throughout the play. Toward the end of the play (Act V, Scene 7) he meets the Button Moulder, a sort of angel of death, who comes to take him. The Button Moulder announces to Peer Gynt, whom he considers "a gleaming button on the world's waistcoat," that he "must be popped into [his] Casting-ladle ... So as to be melted down."

Peer Gynt rebels at the idea and says he is willing to take any other punishment, just not to be dissolved "with any Tom, Dick and Harry" in the Casting-ladle, that is, "merged into the mass":

Send me to Him with the Cloven Hoof for a certain time—say, a hundred years ... That's a thing I daresay one might put up with; ... But the other idea—to be swallowed up like a speck in a mass of strange material—this ladle business—losing all the attributes that make a Gynt—*that* fills my inmost soul with horror!" (Ibsen, 1921 [1867], pp. 206–14)[3]

A final characteristic of death is the end implied in it. Death is what resides beyond life, after life, and outside it. It is the end of life, transcendental and unique.

---

[3] Perhaps this attribute is more frightening in Western cultures, where individuality is more central. It could be that in some Eastern worldviews merging with others in death is something one aspires to, rather than shuns.

Do these characteristics subsume the image of death? Can they be said to be universal and time independent? Probably not. Conceptualizations of death can influence the way we perceive it. Promises of an afterlife, depictions of heaven and hell, and visions of reincarnation surely play a role in shaping the nature of the affective approach to death. But there is also something which I believe is universal about the fear of death; something which remains untouched by belief and ideological systems. (Such concerns about death can, in more or less similar terms, be discerned even in texts as distant as the Epic of Gilgamesh.) In fact, it is what makes these systems necessary. More important perhaps is that the aspects of the attitude toward death mentioned here are apparent specifically in a Western, secular worldview. This is the culture that psychoanalysis most often operates in, that it has arisen out of, and that serves as the relevant context for Freud's thought and formulation of his ideas on the death drive.

The above characteristics of our usual concept of death give rise to worldviews or psychological tendencies whose goal is to lessen their impact. Take arbitrariness. The inevitability of death itself is hardly ever denied. Few people really believe they will be an exception, although practices such as cryonics (freezing one's body in the hope of future revival and rejuvenation) go in that direction. What happens more often is a reconceptualization or alteration of the meaning of death, whereby it is understood as a continuation of existence. The arbitrariness of its timing is often simply ignored or suppressed in a perspective that assumes that if death comes, it is never now, but sometime in the distant future, when one is very old. Its indifference and lack of reason are dealt with in the almost automatic tendency to focus on the circumstances themselves rather than on death as an inevitability and, often, to secretly envision death as somehow fitting the specific person who died.

Where does the death drive stand with regard to these different attributes of death? First, regarding the notion of death as the opposite of life, the very term "death drive" seems almost oxymoronic. Death has become a drive, a force, a form of energy. "Drive" (*Trieb*) designates living things, a term linked with liveliness, activity, dynamism. Death is here not the opposite of life or its negation, but characterizes one of the living being's main drives, and is bound with life. The self-contradictory nature of the term "death drive" should not be taken as a "proof" of its untenable nature, but as disclosing what this construct attempts to achieve. It colors death with life.[4] Freud has made death a part of life

---

[4] Lichtenstein (1974 [1935], pp. 74–5) mentions the conceptual contradiction between drives and retrogression. The drives are the forces physical retrogression resists. Entropy

itself. Yet for him it is not as it is for Heidegger, a limit known all along or a defining principle. It is a concrete tendency of life itself, on the same biological (or nearly biological) level of the forces that construct life.

More interesting is the way the concept of the death drive deals with the issue of inevitability and the different modes of arbitrariness. The universality of death that knows no exception is preserved. The death drive is built-in and active in each and every one of us; from the moment we are born, we are compelled toward its ultimate aim, death. This hardly comes as a surprise. As I said, although this absolute inevitability of death is the most frightening fact about it, it is rarely contested. Its evidence in reality is simply overpowering. But the related, almost diametrically opposite dimension of our thoughts about death, the fact that its arrival is always arbitrary, always unexpected, is assuaged through reversal, for a tendency toward death is now found within us, and always active.

In a passage in *Beyond the Pleasure Principle* Freud (1920) points to this consoling aspect of the death drive, where death is the outcome of an (internal) necessity rather than something arbitrary: "[P]erhaps we have adopted the belief because there is some comfort in it. If we are to die ourselves, and first to lose in death those who are dearest to us, it is easier to submit to a remorseless law of nature, to the sublime Ανάγκη [Necessity], than to a chance which might perhaps have been escaped" (p. 45). Perhaps, Freud proposes, we have embraced a belief in the internal necessity of death to, as he says quoting Schiller, "bear the burden of existence." That is, Freud himself is aware of the fact that a hypothesis like that of the death drive neutralizes one of death's most frightening aspects, its arbitrariness.

Interestingly, Freud also holds, in another context, the exactly opposite view. In "Thoughts for the Times" (1915, p. 290), he describes how we habitually attribute a person's death to external contingent circumstances. For example, we might explain such a death by saying that he or she had bad luck. In doing so, we try to alleviate and suppress the universality and inevitability of death. The death drive stands in

---

is opposed to drive. The more general tension in the death drive theory, between the Nirvana principle and a drive to aggression (Carel, 2006, pp. 35–41) is also relevant to the juxtaposition of 'death' and 'drive'. For Matte Blanco (2005 [1973], pp. 1469–71) too, the movement and the stasis implied by the term are contradictory.

The objection (Choron, 1972 [1964], p. 48n.) that Freud was speaking of a drive (*Trieb*) rather than an instinct (*Instinkt*), and that only the latter, being more biological, creates a contradiction, is unnecessary. "Drive" has all the connotations of force, energy, and liveliness that are contrary to death, and it does not have to be encoded as a biological scheme, "instinct," in order to be opposed to it.

The death drive and death   139

opposition to the human inclination to interpret death in such a manner. The person died because something inborn and inherent to human existence necessitated that he die. It was not bad luck that brought about death, but a built-in tendency, integral to human life.

Thus, Freud describes two contradictory tendencies. Death is sometimes easier to handle if it is conceived as an inevitability rather than a chance occurrence that might have been averted, and yet it is sometimes easier to swallow if it is viewed as a chance event, with each case resulting from its own specific circumstances, rather than as a universal truth. These are actually two responses, respectively, to the two almost opposing attributes of death itself, that it is both arbitrary and inevitable.

In the sixth chapter of his text on the death drive, Freud (1920, pp. 45–9) suddenly turns to an enquiry of a different order. He declares a need to make a detour into biology, and explores Weismann's ideas on mortality and immortality in organisms. This detour is actually an investigation of the question of whether death is a chance event or necessary. Freud tries to find out if living beings really must die, and if mortality is inextricably bound up with life itself (pp. 44–5). He is trying to unravel the riddle. Why do we die? Is it just some bad luck that befalls us?

Laplanche (1976 [1970], p. 110) notes that when Freud discovers that his biological detour actually shows that death is not intrinsically linked to the nature of life, through the example of unicellular organisms, he "kicks over the table" and drops the whole discussion.[5]

Even before that conclusion, the very fact that Freud takes this biological detour, which is a kind of an island in the text, questions, in another sense, the necessity of death itself. It is as if death is only inevitable if it comes from inside. If it does not, it is merely an accident, something that happened to occur, but could just as well have been avoided. It is as if external death is always a mere coincidence. What is hinted at here in *Beyond the Pleasure Principle* is more explicitly stated in "The Uncanny," written around the same time, where Freud says that one reason we, as modern people, do not really acknowledge our mortality is that biology has been undecided on death's inevitability, that is, it has left open the possibility that death is "only a regular but yet perhaps avoidable event in life" (Freud, 1919, p. 242). Freud, at any

---

[5] Jonte-Pace (2001, pp. 49–50) is more explicit when she says that the chapter on unicellular forms of life, added to the text only when most of it was finished, is actually an affirmation of immortality in the heart of a book that ostensibly denies it and shows that the aim of life is death.

rate, takes the trouble of straying into biology, to search for a promise of mortality, to be assured of the sublime Ανάγκη [Necessity].

Overall, the death drive is an attempt to negate death's arbitrariness by fortifying its inevitability. The death drive also alleviates the trouble entailed in our not knowing the reason for death. The arbitrariness of death, in the sense of it being motiveless and aimless, is mitigated by a concept that attributes motivation, will, and agency to death. Death here is the work of some tangible force, the death drive, and as such, is not as incomprehensible and arbitrary as might appear in life. This is what Freud (1927) himself seems to suggest in *The Future of an Illusion*, where he describes "the humanization of nature" invented by the ancients:

Impersonal forces and destinies cannot be approached; they remain eternally remote. But if the elements have passions that rage as they do in our own souls, if death itself is not something spontaneous but the violent act of an evil Will ... , then we can breathe freely, can feel at home in the uncanny and can deal by psychical means with our senseless anxiety. (pp. 16–7)

The means we have to influence these forces are the ones we use within human society: adjuring, appeasing, and bribing them. In his description of the beliefs of others, Freud is the best critic of his own theory. The humanization of nature, which he cites as a means used by the ancients to take the sting out of death, is applicable to his own theory of the death drive as well, which sees a force, an agency behind death, rather than a complete arbitrary appearance which defies comprehension. Death, with the death drive, ceases to be meaningless.

We still need to examine the question of arbitrariness in the sense of the timing and circumstances of death's arrival, and its indifference. These will be dealt with later.

Moving to the next attribute, death's quality of being always external to us and uncontrollable, we see that the concept of the death drive introduces a challenging twist. Death is internalized: "Everything living dies for *internal* reasons" (Freud, 1920, p. 38, emphasis in the original). These internal reasons are not the decay and amortization of living tissues, but a psychically internal tendency, a drive. Death is reconceived as part of us. As a result, it becomes in a sense controllable by us (of course, if by "us" we mean consciousness or the ego, then our control of death, or the death drive, is limited, as is the case with other drives. Yet, in the same way that sexuality is part of us, although it belongs to the id, so is death, under the concept of the death drive). We are no longer completely passive in relation to it, but restored to an active role.

It is interesting to note in this context the explanation that Freud (1920, p. 39) gives in *Beyond the Pleasure Principle* regarding the self-preservative instincts. These were once one of the two poles of the dichotomy of the instincts, yet they can no longer now be seen as central, and must be reintegrated into the new dichotomy of life and death instincts. Freud's solution is surprising. It is true, he says, that we witness in the organism drives whose aim is to prolong life, but these part-instincts actually work in the service of the death drive.[6] The organism wants to die, as dictated by the death drive, but to die its own death! It tries to keep at bay any possibility of a return to the preorganic that is not immanent to itself, issuing from inside. This description makes internality a crucial thing, and shows how central it is to Freud's discussion. I will deal extensively with this idea later on.

Transforming death into something we desire counters the normal sense of it being something undesirable, yet inevitable. "Desire" here is used in a rather general sense. The death drive is not a wish for death, and yet it is a drive inside that has death as its goal. In "The Theme of the Three Caskets," Freud (1913b) states this directly: Pretending to choose death is a defense against it, a reversal of the bitter truth that we have no control over it and no choice but to meet it.

Another unnerving aspect of death, that it is a question mark, a phenomenon of which we have no positive knowledge, is also mitigated by the concept of the death drive. The death drive is something we know about—how it works, how it was created, and, to a certain extent, how it manifests itself. We know that it aspires to a minimal amount of excitation (the Nirvana principle), and to restoring the organism to its previous inorganic state. The death drive can be conceptualized; one can write about it. It does not defy understanding to the extent that death does.

The death drive also constitutes a solution to another terrifying element of death, the erasure of individuality, the blurring of all that is unique to us, all that we are, at the moment of death. If throughout our lives we have aspired to death (Freud, 1920, p. 38), if heading toward death is a tendency embodied deeply in us, then in death we finally achieve our goal. Death becomes the moment of fullest self-actualization. Only in death will we fulfill the aspiration inherent in us all along. Death will not blur our individuality, but rather will be its final proof. The explanation of the self-preservative instincts as part of the death drive makes the individualized death even stronger. It will be *our* death. I shall soon get back to this.

---

[6] The attribution of the self-preserving instincts to the domain of the death drive might not be Freud's final verdict on them, but for the purposes of the discussions here the fact that he raises it as a possibility is enough.

Death, it was claimed earlier, is an end, something beyond and after life. But the objective of the death drive is to bring us back, as aforementioned, to a primordial, inorganic state, the state from which life originally emerged. Death becomes not an unknown end to life, but a return, a restitution of an earlier more basic state: "for dust thou art, and unto dust shalt thou return" (Genesis 3:19). This return neutralizes some of the threat. Again, support for the notion that the element of return alleviates the threat of death is to be found in Freud himself. In "Thoughts for the Times on War and Death," Freud (1915, pp. 294–5) discusses the consequences of the discovery of death upon the demise of a close person. First, spirits were invented; then came the invention of the afterworld; and, finally, life was also extended backward, in the evolution of theories of reincarnation. Doctrines that prolong life backward and make life and death a series of repetitions serve, as Freud claims, to negate the meaning of death as the end of life. He adds that these ancient ideas are the starting point of our modern cultural-conventional attitude of denial of death. Freud himself admits then that a conception of life (and death) as return serves to deny the meaning of death as the end of life, that is, to deny the meaning of death. Yet, in arguing for such a return, his theory of the death drive performs just such a denial.

Repetition negates not only the finality of death, but also time orientation in its entirety. Death, an event that subjectively is always in the future, becomes the remembrance of things past, time regained.

Perhaps then, the death drive theory is still part of the modern cultural conventional view in which death is denied. Ostensibly, with the introduction of the death drive, death is posited at the center of psychoanalytic theory. In reality, much of what is threatening in it is neutralized, while only the shell of the term "death" is taken in by the theory. That being said, the theory of the death drive remains a sophisticated and challenging attempt to theorize death, even if, as I claim, it refuses the challenge of the major difficulties surrounding it.

Dying your own death

The problem of the link between the death drive and death is brought to a climax in a nodal point in Freud's (1920) text, already mentioned, where he puts forward the idea that "the organism wishes to die only in its own fashion," and will, therefore, reject dangers coming from the outside (p. 39). The idea is perhaps marginal in the text, but is to my mind of crucial importance. The drive of the proper would be stronger than life and than death (Derrida, 1987, p. 356).

Although it can be seen as pushing to an extreme the general idea of the death drive, that "everything living dies for *internal* reasons" (Freud, 1920, p. 38), this claim is still generally foreign to Freud's thought. It has virtually no history. It remains a puzzle in psychoanalytic thought, an almost singular statement, estranged from almost all the rest of the Freudian corpus and rarely embraced by other authors, even those who adopt the death drive theory, with the single major exception of Eissler (1955, pp. 104–7, 253–7). In 1938, Freud (1940 [1938]) reiterates this concept, saying that "it may in general be suspected that the *individual* dies of internal conflicts but that the *species* dies of its unsuccessful struggle against the external world" (p. 150, emphasis in the original).[7]

By focusing on this idea we can get a clearer picture of the problem inherent in envisioning the death drive as Freud's "answer" to death. Let us look at Eissler's (1955) *The Psychiatrist and the Dying Patient*, a text that wholeheartedly embraces the perspective of the death drive, and constitutes one of the only large-scale studies on the theme of death from the psychoanalytic point of view. First hesitatingly (pp. 104–7), and then without reservation (pp. 253–7), Eissler suggests that death, concretely, in reality, is the expression of one's internal tendency to aspire to it. He means that this is not only true in the case of disease, for example, but in many other kinds of death. Eissler knows his position sounds absurd but deems it worthy of examination. The justification he provides is that if we assume the involvement of internal factors in each and every one of our acts and in every experience we undergo, why should we not assume the same for death? Eissler's position is based on two assumptions: general psychic determinism and (seemingly) Freud's idea that the organism wishes to die its own death, which strangely enough Eissler does not mention in that section. In fact, Eissler is only radicalizing Freud here.

The idea of dying one's own death, or dying in one's own fashion, is a denial of death in several respects. First, these formulations further concretize the point made above about the internalization of death: the

---

[7] Another place where Freud expresses something of a belief in an innate, predetermined death is in "The Dissolution of the Oedipus complex" (1924a, p. 174): Freud mentions death as an analogy to the dissolution of the Oedipus complex, in that universality does not preclude tracing individual development: "It is also true that even at birth the whole individual is destined to die, and perhaps his organic disposition may already contain the indication of what he is to die from. Nevertheless, it remains of interest to follow out how this innate program is carried out and in what way accidental noxae exploit his disposition." This citation also discloses some of Freud's curiosity about the question of inevitability and arbitrariness in regard to death, discussed above.

idea that, on the empirical level, that is, in real life (not as a claim from some remote theoretical consideration, but in reference to actual, corporeal death), death results from some internal activity or conflict, is, for lack of a better expression, a blatant denial of death itself.

What is at stake is not a simple involvement of unconscious processes in bringing about or postponing death, but death as the thoroughgoing outcome of internal forces, as is clear from the stress put on the early, possibly innate onset of these factors. The claim is different in nature from arguing, in the case of a sick person, that his or her illness is influenced by psychological factors.[8] What Freud and Eissler are talking about is an internal involvement in every death, and as the determining factor, as Eissler plainly claims, a psychological determinism concerning death that is general, almost mythical, rather than involved only in a specific case of illness or accident, a determinism that is active and preset from the very beginning of life, rather than, for example, only in an old man wishing to finally come to rest. It is described almost as a *malediction* cast upon us.[9]

The idea of dying one's own death also denies other aspects of death. Mostly it denies death's imminence: that it is an ever-present possibility or potentiality. Freud's theory, thus pushed to an extreme, assumes a preset date of death, or at least a general scheme to be followed in advance of death. But this is not the case in reality, for death can come at any second. Now, one could argue that while the date is in fact predetermined, we are just not aware of it. However, if we theoretically construct death as the result of some internal process, a preset scheme albeit unknown to us, we clearly cancel, in this conception, not only the

---

[8] In addition to cases of illness, death may also of course be facilitated in the case of a certain class of dangerous behavior and in some kinds of psychological disorders, by unconscious motives, or result, in the case of suicide, from an internal decision. But these are all isolated phenomena. The dying-your-own-death idea offers something much more radical.

[9] Unforgettable in this context is Rilke's (1964) marvelous description of the death of old Chamberlain Brigge in *The Notebooks of Malte Laurids Brigge*. It starts with lamenting the "factory-like" deaths in the Hôtel Dieu, "[w]here production is so enormous an individual death is not so nicely carried out. ... Who cares anything today for a finely-finished death?" Malte then continues:

Formerly one knew (or perhaps one guessed it) that one had one's death within one, as a fruit its kernel. The children had a little death within them and the grown-ups a big one. The women had it in their womb and the men in their breast. One *had* it and that gave one a singular dignity and a quiet pride.

My Grandfather, old Chamberlain Brigge, still looked as if he carried a death within him. And what a death it was: two months long and so loud ... That was not the death of just any dropsical person; it was the wicked, princely death which the chamberlain had carried within him and nourished on himself his whole life long ... He was dying his own hard death. (pp. 17–23)

external origin of death, but its ongoing possibility: life is constructed as a complete unit in itself, with a beginning, an unfolding, and an end—a pre-made whole to be lived as one, regardless of the world around it.[10] This conception negates the clear possibility that the scheme will not be fully developed, that the whole might be cut short at some point in the middle. We will see in Chapter 10 other manifestations of the same error.

I mentioned earlier several senses of the arbitrariness of death. We have just seen where the death drive, through the notion of dying one's own death, stands with regard to arbitrariness, in terms of the uncertainty of its timing. The idea of dying one's own death is also opposed to another sense of arbitrariness, that of indifference. Eissler (1955, pp. 105–7, 253–7) seems to imply that an internally determined death might also be involved in cases of large-scale death, such as war. Note that he refers to the work of the death drive on the individual level, and not on the social one. Freud would not go as far as to claim this himself, but the absurdity in Eissler's position exposes another aspect that is obscured by the idea of an internal, predetermined death, namely, death's indifference. Death can hit several people at the same time, with no reference to them personally. It can wipe out hundreds, thousands, in a single minute. It is tempting to think of death as essentially personal, but this idea flies in the face of the evidence. The concept of the death drive does exactly this—it makes death a very intimate and personal issue. We die our own death. The issue is somewhat different from the fear of loss of individuality in dying discussed above. Death is not in fact an individual issue, and positing it as specific and predetermined in each person comprises an attempt to deny its impersonal character. What is frightening is not only that others die with us, rendering our death depersonalized but that death can be completely indifferent to us. What is terrifying is that we might not count, that nature itself is blind to us. The idea of the death drive goes directly against such recognition, and thus, in yet another way, denies death.

Adam Phillips (2000), in a remarkable book that presents Freud's ideas on death as a significant contribution and Freud as a mentor in mortality, puts specific stress on Freud's claim that the organism wants to die in its own way. Dying in our own way becomes our primary project, even when achieved at the price of suffering (p. 9). One of

---

[10] While it is true that the idea of dying one's own death is an ideal for Freud, and he recognizes the possibility that the forces of reality will intervene and bring about an earlier end, life is constructed here as that closed and complete unit where death emanates from the inside.

Phillips's main messages is that of death's indifference to us. "The intention that man should be happy has no part in the plan of creation," he quotes Freud as saying (p. 16). Yet it is precisely the death drive that Phillips celebrates as a sign of the anchoring of life in death and of death's indifference, that constitutes a denial of death. The concept of a death drive makes death highly personal; it denies its indifference.

A major point in Phillips's (2000) discussion is the futility involved in searching for any secure meaning, especially meaning anchored in providence or nature itself: "We are the animals who seem to suffer, above all, from our ideals" (p. 17). However, the preceding analysis leads us to think that to retain the idea that death is personal is also to keep something of the idea of providence. It expresses, as well, the idea of uniqueness in the face of nature. We have our own death, and so are immune to death until the hour of our personal death, whose coming was somewhere decided upon.[11]

Critiques of the death drive

To see more where the death drive theory stands with regard to death, it is important to refer to some prominent criticisms made of it. Among those offering critiques of Freud's theory of the death drive, a small group has addressed precisely its relationship with death. The major point made was that it does not deal with anxiety about death. Otto Rank (1950 [1945]) criticizes the neglect, in psychoanalytic literature, of the fear of death, in favor of the "death impulse" (p. 115). When Freud finally decided to confront death, through the death drive, he did so in a way that fitted well with his wish theory, and the element of fear was neglected (p. 116). Becker (1973, pp. 99–100), Yalom (1980, p. 66n), Schermer (1995), and Langs (1997, p. 214) raise similar objections, namely, that the death drive theory turns death into a wish and ignores anxiety. Breger (1981) laments the elision of aggressivity and death in one term, and suggests that the death drive "does not deal with the psychology of death at all" (p. 110).

Searles (1965 [1961]) finds that the concept of the death drive has tended "to obscure the deepest significations of the inevitability of death. ... this concept obscures the fullness of the impact which this fact makes upon us: the potential poignancy, terror, rage, and sorrow

---

[11] At one point Phillips (2000, p. 78) asks similar questions: Is Freud not seduced back into teleology by assuming that life has a project, even though it is the project of its own demise? Would life then once again not become a coherent story? However, such questions are left hanging.

which it holds are all diluted in a conceptual view which maintains that... each of us unconsciously *longs for* this inevitable event" (p. 509, emphasis in the original). Not only is the theory itself a problem for Searles, but also the debate around it, which "served to distract us from looking into the depths of poignancy ... which is aroused in us by our awareness of death's inevitability" (*ibid.*). Although Searles's description of the death drive, like those of many other authors, involves some misrepresentation of the concept, and although many authors do see the death drive theory precisely as a theory of mortality, his position is correct. What he seems to stress is the absence of the subjective dimension from the concept of the death drive.

Lifton (1979, p. 49–50) praises the unitary vision of life and death implied by the theory of the death drive but notes, as part of his general critique of the concept of instincts, how the instinctual mechanics served to hide this unitary vision. However, when the theory was rejected, the vision was lost with it, and so was the idea of death as significant for motivation.

These criticisms are, nevertheless, rare in psychoanalytic literature. In general, when the theory was rejected, it was for other reasons, and when it was accepted, these scarce remarks did not have much influence. The death drive theory was still regarded as a compelling Freudian account of death. These critiques add to the preceding discussion the important point that emotional responses to the reality of death—anxiety, rage, sorrow—have not been addressed, and are not accounted for in the death drive theory. They indicate the problem with transforming death into the object of a wish.

However, these critiques dismiss the concept of the death drive too easily. First, as I showed, death anxiety is not "neglected" (Rank, 1950 [1945], p. 115) in the death drive theory. Rather, this theory cleverly and systematically includes and resists it, and cannot simply be dismissed as unsuitable. Second, and more important, these critiques remain general and abstract, and serve more to expunge the death drive as a theory of death rather than examine it in detail.

It is not only anxiety that is missing in the death drive theory. In a sense, the whole focus on instincts in *Beyond the Pleasure Principle* is already at odds with the idea of death as a content of thought. Hoffman (1998, pp. 38–40) correctly notes that the language of blind instinctual forces does not lend itself easily to discussions about the cognitive appraisal of death and its meaning.

This leads to a crucial point. More than just a bias is revealed here in what Freud chooses to discuss or leave out. Constructing death in terms of a drive will automatically distort the concept of death. Death is not only a situation or an event. It has meaning, both in itself, and more importantly, with regards to the rest of our lives. It is erroneous to think of death as a mere end point. The language of the drive, but more importantly, the absence of a language of meaning—in other words, the discourse of death as pertaining only to the natural domain and not to the human—is significant. Death is meaningful in a way that forms part of our lives and our psychic worlds. In general, Freud's theory is occupied both with meanings and with instinctual forces, but not in *Beyond the Pleasure Principle*. The death drive cannot be the last word on death, because the symbolic side is completely missing from it.

Jonathan Lear offers another interesting critique of Freud's (1920) use of the word "death" and of his theory of the death drive. "Death" as "the aim of all life" (Freud, 1920, p. 38) functions as an enigmatic signifier, in Laplanche's terminology, introduced into the theory as a temptation, a goal, but with actually nothing behind it. It is a way of organizing experience in a meaningful way, with a teleological principle, "an explanatory end-of-the-line" (Lear, 2000, p. 85). Instead, what Freud's observations in *Beyond the Pleasure Principle* should have led him to was an acknowledgment of the lack of any working principle, a recognition of a nondirected, self-disruptive activity of the mind (p. 130). To Lear's apt description, we can now add that the same necessity of ensuring purposefulness, of having things organized, is embodied in the idea of the death drive in reference also to a different kind of lack, that of death itself. Something that is unaccountable and arbitrary, foreign to our system, which imperils it by its very nature and calls for the limit of the theory to be recognized, is now covered by another principle of functioning, and is transformed into an explainable, knowable thing and a part of the system.[12]

Some authors have sought to "explain" the writing of *Beyond the Pleasure Principle* through the biographical details of Freud's life (Ekstein, 1949; Hamilton, 1976): the loss of his brother Julius, about which he felt persistent guilt; the death of his daughter Sophie and his friend Von Freund; his advancing age and possible illness; and the influence of World War I. That is, they saw the theory as grounded in pessimism and experiences of loss. Although these explanations do help to shed light on the text, they also serve to reduce *Beyond the Pleasure Principle* to the mere expression of a personal struggle.[13]

---

[12] There is more than an analogy here, for the inner stubbornness of psychic life and the destiny of death are brought together by Freud's text itself.
[13] Note that Freud insisted that most of the book was written before his daughter died (see his response to Wittels, cited in Jones, 1957, p. 43, and his letter to Eitington of July 18, 1920, cited in Schur, 1972, p. 329).

Schur (1972) links the death drive more directly to the problem of death. He sees it as an attempt by Freud to "work through" his obsessive superstitions about death, and to "come to terms with the problem of death by treating it as a scientific problem" (pp. 342, 373).[14] It permitted him "literally to *live* with the reality of death" (pp. 332, 344). Appealing as these explanations are, they still reduce the text to an idiosyncratic formulation related to Freud's personality. Moreover, Schur does not specify how the concept of the death drive could help to come to terms with death, and instead settles for the general "work through." The "working through" turns out to be even more detached from the real problem of death, for it is Freud's wish to die and achieve peace which is worked through, in Schur's description, and not death or the fear of it.

The present discussion has tried to show in detail how speaking of a death drive is designed to mitigate the problem death poses for life. As a theory, it renders death innocuous, taking the sting out of it. It is a general, theoretical engagement with death, much more than a personal, subjective struggle.

Recasting the death drive as an existential concept

Despite, and maybe because of, the fact that the death drive theory has been seen as theoretically unsatisfying—incoherent, confused, speculative—it has also proved to be a stimulus and source of inspiration for several authors in the examination of life and death (we have already looked at Eissler's, Phillips's, and Lear's ideas).

The death drive has been seen not only as a specifically psychoanalytic approach to death, but also as representing a truly existential approach to life deep within psychoanalysis. There is something very tempting in linking the death drive to an existential awareness of death and finitude. It sometimes seems just a step from Freud's idea of the death drive to Heidegger's (1978 [1929], 1996 [1927]) conception of Man's being as being-toward-death.

But even without reference to Heidegger, we can adopt the following view of the theory of the death drive: Death is intimately tied together with life. It is embedded in the innermost layers of our being from the second we are born. From that moment on, we have only one destiny: to become dead again, to lose the life in us; we will live, grow, work, but the shadow is always there. Thus, the death drive is nothing but the

---

[14] Similarly, Jones (1957, pp. 300–2) believes the death drive theory should be explained through Freud's subjective approach to death.

expression and theoretical formulation of this most fundamental of human truths. We are creatures doomed to die.

Some attempts have been made to look at the death drive from a similar angle (Brown, 1959; Pontalis, 1977; Bolivar, 1993; Carel, 2006). However, like Laplanche (1999 [1996], p. 49), I doubt the benefit of such a perspective. Tempting as this kind of interpretation is, we must consider the following question: If, in fact, the aim of the theory is to represent our inexorable march toward death, is the specific formulation of the death drive really needed to account for it? Although the death drive theory may constitute such an account, it does not add insight into the human condition beyond, perhaps, providing an intriguing metaphor for it.[15]

Carel's (2006) thorough analysis of the death drive offers a perspective that engages Heidegger's ideas on being-toward-death. She speaks of the ethical dimension of the death drive as Freud's "ethics of finitude" (pp. 125–35). Death, a structuring element in life, is continually working within it (pp. 115–23). We must accept our finitude and that "everything we achieve may be lost" (p. 133). While I share Carel's overall conception that life and death are intertwined (p. xiii) and that death is present within life, affecting every choice, every project and plan (p. xiv), I find her invocation of the death drive problematic precisely because she does not take into consideration the manner in which the death drive is, as we have seen, a denial of death rather than its acceptance. Freud, in the death drive theory, is not a prophet of death who exposes us to death's significance. (It is, therefore, no wonder that in writing about the death drive as Freud's ethical imperative, Carel, 2006, actually has to go back to the concluding paragraph of "Thoughts for the Times" and to "On Transience" to substantiate her claim. The death drive alone cannot do so.) The death drive could perhaps be interpreted as something more philosophical, but it is important to Carel to remain close to Freud's formulations, and in so doing, her more philosophical perspective loses power: that death has a presence within life does not mean death *is* that presence. Speaking of it in these terms would be to confuse metaphorical and literal uses of the word. There is a significant difference between, on the one hand, the psychic presence of death in the form of either

---

[15] Fenichel (1945, p. 60) says that the death drive can be seen as the formulation that life is "a process leading to death." Bolivar (1993, pp. 136–40) criticizes this position as follows: The biological formulation of the death drive at best describes the simple fact that one dies, whereas finitude is important on the subjective level and is not to be reduced to the biological fact of dying. Interestingly, Bolivar, as we shall shortly see, falls into the very trap that he warns against, that is, seeing death as a destiny, albeit as a philosophical destiny rather than a biological one.

awareness or repression, or even in its philosophical guise as the fact of finitude, and, on the other, death as "a process within life ... continuously exerting its influence on life processes," (p. 46) which Carel calls, rather misleadingly, "the metaphysical and existential significance of death, captured so compellingly in Freud's notion of the death drive" (*ibid.*; see also p. 65).

Bolivar's (1993) interesting reformulation of the death drive from a Lacanian-Heideggerian perspective, which sees death as the emblem of limit in our lives—the limit met by desire, a limit that defines desire itself and is intrinsic to it (p. 133)—suffers from similar problems. The death drive for Bolivar is precisely this limitation, the limit which is the basis for all other limits, "[t]he power of negativity ... in the heart if our being" (pp. 133–4). He also refers to it as "the unconscious perception of our finitude" (p. 141), and as the freedom to embrace death (pp. 134, 145). And yet, while death is indeed always in the background of our lives, in what sense does Bolivar's conception actually refer to the death drive? Bolivar says explicitly that the concept of the death drive would have to be reinterpreted to fit his new direction. The only question is, why use the concept at all? Why say "drive" when referring to something completely different? Why bother using this concept at all when it provides neither an adequate account of what Bolivar himself means, nor of the idea of death itself?

Pontalis (1977), who notes that death is rendered internal through the death drive (p. 249), believes that it would be wrong to conceive of the death drive as a drive, and thus to inquire into its source, object, and aim. Rather, he proposes that the death drive actually mimics death. It is death in action: a process of unbinding, decomposition, fragmentation, and enclosure—psyche becomes body (p. 250).[16] It is, in Pontalis's terms, the work of death. Yet once again it seems that Pontalis's interpretation of the death drive is essentially describing what is always already taking place on the biological level: Organisms decay and die; humans live until they die. What does conceptualizing a parallel death drive add if it does no more than describe the facts of decay and the orientation of life? Even if Pontalis's more specific interpretation might present Freud's concept as less evasive than we have thus far observed, with regard to death itself it just seems to be begging the question. This "impersonator" of death is supplementary, not a substitute for death itself. How is our understanding of the psychic approach to death as an

---

[16] See Eigen's (1995) similar idea, in discussing a patient who was "a symbol and embodiment of death" (p. 281).

anxiety-generating future event enhanced by postulating death's "double" as embodied and working within us?[17]

Two other significant interpretations that link the death drive with death, that of Klein, who sees the death drive as the source of death anxiety, and that of Lacan, who sees it as related to the inherent lack of the human subject, will be discussed in later chapters.

The death drive, Freud, and death: Further considerations

Psychoanalytic discussions of death tend to cite the death drive positively as an analytic "answer" to death—a proof that death is not ignored in psychoanalysis. My contention is that the death drive is not really about death. But let us suppose that for Freud, the death drive really *is* about

---

[17] It is worth mentioning several other interesting contributions which underscore the existential aspects of the death drive. Krell (1994) for example, compares Heidegger's stress on the imminence of death to Freud's stress on the imminence of death as originating from the life processes themselves. Gabel (1974) uses the death drive to account for Sartre's "fundamental project," the subject's struggle to stabilize its continuous becoming. Elaborating on the ethics of Levinas, Critchley (1999) links the death instinct to an ethical imperative whereby, in order for an ethical relation to the other to be possible, there must be "an affective disposition to alterity" found within the subject (p. 239). Critchley locates this disposition, this dividedness, this "gaping wound" within, in Freud's death drive (*ibid.*). In a similar vein, Weatherill (1999b) also connects the death drive to Levinas's ideas, conceiving it as "the subject's total exposure to excess and ipseity" (p. 221), as innate suffering which makes the subject fundamentally and a priori traumatized (p. 225).

Piven (2004, pp. 153–85) interprets the death drive as a yearning for death whose aim is to stop pain and distress. It is a wish for regression, a flight from life, and a yearning for a blissful reunion with the mother. Death in the death drive is a fantasy of merger and union, an escape from separateness and individuation.

Finally, by reformulating the repetition compulsion, Lichtenstein (1935) turns the relationship between death and the death drive on its head. While retrogression is a linear movement backward, repetition is an attempt to bring time to a standstill (p. 69). For Lichtenstein, the aim of all drives – the essence of which is repetition – is no longer death but stopping death.

One interesting direction, though not directly related to death, is that of Grotstein, who develops the concept of "the black hole" in a series of papers (1990a; 1990b; 1990c; 1991) and links it with the death instinct. "The black hole" designates for him the basic experience of being psychotic (1990c, p. 39), a catastrophic state of "nothingness" or meaninglessness (1990a, p. 264, 275), "the ultimate traumatic state of disorganization, terror, chaos, randomness, and entropy" (1990b, p. 378). This phenomenon of the black hole is for him "the profoundest meaning of the death instinct." The death instinct is a signifier of the black hole (1990b, p. 404). "The death instinct is our preparedness to anticipate and therefore to adapt to (regulate) this ultimate horror" (1990a, pp. 258–9). Its "ultimate significance" lies "in its function as supplying signal anxiety to detect, not only dangerous, death-dealing predators both outside and inside, but also to detect the emergence of unmodulated meaninglessness and nothingness presenting as disintegration of the self from within" (1990b, p. 390).

death. If this is the case, where do we see the aftershocks, the ripples in the wider theory, the developments and the implications for that which concerns death, the psychical consequences of being mortal? They are nowhere to be found. All we have are discussions of masochism and aggression. The death drive was not expanded to include other death-related topics such as anxiety or the reduction of death anxiety to castration, nor did it enter into dialog with the ideas opposing the potential representation of death, which supposedly rule out its psychic influence.[18] This is significant. If the death drive is, as some claim, Freud's theory about death—an "answer" to death—then why did he not develop it as such?

In addition, as noted in Chapter 1, Freud's most strident objections to both the presence of death in the unconscious and the psychic validity or primacy of the fear of death occurred in 1923 and 1926—that is, later than the initial postulation of the theory of the death drive in 1920.[19] Citing the death drive as Freud's "answer" to death or to a certain theoretical lack, therefore, involves a certain degree of anachronism. If the death drive is Freud's response to death, how is it that death as an object of anxiety, as finitude, is still largely sidestepped in psychoanalysis?

A certain evasion of death can even be seen on the level of the reception and development of the death drive theory. The abovementioned tendency in interpretations and uses of the death drive to focus on the destructive element—a tendency already sometimes manifested in Freud's own writings later than 1920 (Freud, 1930, 1933b [1932], 1937)—can itself be seen as an avoidance of the death-bound aspects of it, although clearly the possibility of innate destructiveness is itself something not easily admitted by humans about ourselves.

---

[18] Klein (1948), for example, actually makes the death drive a source of death anxiety, which is itself a problematic view, but one that at least stems from a recognition that such a strong theory must be implicated in neighboring issues.

We dwelled in an earlier chapter on Freud's insistence on the absence of death from the unconscious. A reexamination of such statements in the light of the theory of the death drive is, of course, now called for. First, we have, for example, a new characterization of the drive itself. The death drive is involved in the active negation of the work of life, and Eros, its counterpart, is working continuously to counteract the work of the death drive. The death drive is also an abstract drive, as is Eros, without a specific aim or source. It involves time intrinsically and fundamentally: the drive is a process in time, going back in time in order to undo time, or, in the case of Eros, developing forward in time in order to actually restore an earlier state of things. Beyond the details, of course, Freud seems now to have the instinctual correlative he lacked earlier.

[19] *The Ego and the Id* even includes a theoretical discussion of the life and death drives, not long before the text embarks on the problem of death anxiety.

Time and again, as I have mentioned, upon presenting my ideas to audiences, the suggestion that death is neglected in psychoanalytic theory is met with the argument that the death drive makes it a central issue. There is an irony though in that the theory of the death drive is itself rejected. If the death drive is indeed Freud's "answer" to death, his one true solution, then the fact that it is generally deemed inadequate and, therefore, dismissed within the psychoanalytic literature ought to be evidence enough that a difficulty still remains.

The death drive in sum expresses the same tendency to dismiss and reduce that often characterizes Freud's theoretical consideration of death, that is, disregard for the external reality of death and the construction of death as an internal affair under our control. It does, on the other hand give expression to the struggle we have seen in the last chapter between the reductive approach and the one that acknowledges death's centrality. The reductive tendencies clearly have the upper hand again.

8 Death and culture: Death as a central motif in Freud's cultural and literary analyses

The dead and us

We have examined Freud's direct references to the fear of death and to the lack of psychic presence of death; we have looked at some texts where, notwithstanding Freud's claims to the contrary, death is revealed to be central (*The Interpretation of Dreams*). In still others Freud makes his most detailed engagements with the issue of death ("Thoughts for the Times," *Beyond the Pleasure Principle*). Yet our investigation of Freud's attitude toward death will not be complete before we look at a few additional, speculative texts where death plays a significant role, including Freud's analyses of culture (*Totem and Taboo*, *The Future of an Illusion*) and literature ("The Uncanny," "The Theme of the Three Caskets"). While in some of these texts, as we shall see, Freud's reductive approach persists in new forms, in other texts, especially in the opening paragraphs of "Thoughts for the Times," which we will revisit, and in "On Transience," we encounter significant ideas and intuitions where an awareness of death is finally expressed.

Immortality

Tension similar to that examined in the chapter dealing with "Thoughts for the Times" can actually be seen throughout Freud's work, whenever immortality is discussed (e.g., 1927, 1939 [1934–1938], pp. 19–20). A central axis of his crusade against religious belief, in texts like *The Future of an Illusion*, is linked to the idea of immortality. The belief in a hereafter or immortality of the soul, he holds, is an illusion, a childish belief that originates from the difficulty of facing reality. Yet in our unconscious, he claims, we are all immortal. Thus, on the one hand, immortality is a late construction based on illusion, and on the other hand, it is a given in the deepest strata of our unconscious. That a wish is the source of denial of or distortion of reality is nothing new yet the unconscious belief in immortality is not presented as a wish but as a constant. It is not a desire for something we do not have that forces us to distort the reality frustrating that desire. It is a mode of thinking.

Freud, at any rate, does not link the invention of immortality to the immortality felt by the unconscious.[1] A claim, therefore, that the former is but the extension, in the mature individual, of the latter—a failure to go beyond unconscious beliefs—does not seem to capture Freud's intention.

Hoffman (1998, p. 36) rightfully points out, with regard to Freud's (1915) description of the primitive man's encounter with death, that if death were "a priori inconceivable," there should have been no reason for it to be rejected. Whenever religious depictions of immortality are discussed, we can raise similar questions. How can the invention of immortality or belief in it be a distortion, illusion, or wish-fulfillment if there is no fear or apprehension of death present?[2] How can we on the one hand, disbelieve, in the deepest strata of our mind, our own death, and on the other hand, engage in desperate maneuvers to deny that very same fact of death?

In *The Future of an Illusion*, the acceptance of death as a fact of life actually holds a central place. Religion, says Freud (1927), is a story people tell themselves to alleviate the burden of existence. And a major source of misery is the fate of death looming over everything we do (pp. 16–8). This shadow is mitigated by several techniques humanity has invented to counter death. The first is the humanization of nature, already mentioned above (p. 140) regarding the death drive. Perceiving a will, albeit a malignant one, behind the arbitrariness of death, that is, attributing death to the work of some force, allows us to assume a more efficacious position, for we are no longer helpless, but can try and influence those forces, bribe or appease them.

The second is the invention of gods: "everything that happens in this world is an expression of the intentions of an intelligence superior to us, which ... orders things for the best" (Freud, 1927, p. 19). With it comes a third technique—a denial of death: "death itself is not extinction, is not a return to inorganic lifelessness, but the beginning of a new kind of existence" (p. 19). Life after death offers not only a continuation of life, which nullifies death's finality, but also a "perfection" of this world, where all that is faulty or wrong here is corrected or righted there.

The dependent relation to God, an admixture of fear and trust in protection, has its roots in the attitude of the child to his parents, mostly

---

[1] There is a link between the two ideas in Freud (1915), but as we saw, it is rather the encounter with death itself that is responsible for the invention of immortality, and not the earlier unconscious belief.

[2] Hoffman (1998, pp. 41–2) justly criticizes the same problem in Pollock (1971a, 1971b), and Money-Kyrle (1957, p. 502) mentions that one has to suppose a fear of death to justify the concern of religions with immortality.

to his father (Freud, 1927, pp. 17, 23–4, 30). It is tempting, therefore, to draw a link between the threat of death, which necessitates defense in the case of the invention of the gods, and, on an individual level, the helplessness of the child. Is there a death threat here too? This is the view held by Piven (2004), who considers the threat of death as the basic motivation for defense. The extrapolation is more than plausible, but Freud himself does not make this link. He recognizes death as a threat on the social or anthropological level, but not for individuals.[3] Is this just an oversight? I think not. It seems that Freud is much more comfortable with statements regarding death on a very general or social plane than on a psychological or individual one, where he refuses to renounce his position that death has no reign.

Thus, for example, we saw that at one point Freud (1915) provides a description of primitive man's encounter with death, which reflects a degree of existential awareness: "in his pain, he was forced to learn that one can die, too" (p. 293). Freud then describes an equivalent process in the unconscious, but omits precisely the element of awareness of one's own mortality.

In *Totem and Taboo*, to take another example, Freud (1913a) draws a parallel between the historical stages of development of systems of thought and individual libidinal development, between ontogeny and phylogeny (pp. 75–90). On the grand-historical level, an animistic phase evolved into a religious phase, before science developed in turn. On the personal level, the stage of narcissism evolved into the stage of object choice, and then on to maturity, where the pleasure principle is renounced in favor of adaptation to reality (p. 90). However, whereas the scientific worldview is characterized, *inter alia*, by the recognition or acceptance of death (pp. 88, 93), such recognition has no parallel in Freud's description of the life of the individual. Once again, then, we see that whereas Freud is highly sensitive to the difficulty death poses for existence on the general level of "Man" or "humanity," he reveals significantly less sensitivity when it comes to individual psychology, that is, where the subject of his discussion is simply "a man" or "a woman."[4]

---

[3] Freud (1927) does say that "[f]or the individual, too, life is hard to bear" (p. 16), but does not go further to explain the implications. He says civilization solves this problem for the individual, and examines various cultural techniques for countering death, described above. In addition, in detailing individual misery, Freud does not include a direct reference to death as he did for humanity.

[4] I refer here to Freud's ideas about the individual. Interestingly, when dealing with specific men and women, in his case histories, Freud does mention their death-related thoughts, emotions, associations and histories, although he does not usually build on them.

In addition, although Freud's atheistic insistence that all promises of afterlife are illusions clearly involves an acceptance of death as a brute fact, it curiously does not lead him to ask how death figures in life beyond being the source of illusions. After all, if death necessitates the invention of such elaborated symbolic systems as religion, there is clearly a reason to think it has other psychic implications as well.[5]

The Uncanny

In "The Uncanny," Freud's well-known excursion into the ghostly world of spooky feelings, we meet again the by-now-familiar dynamics of acknowledgment of death coupled with a tendency to dismiss it. The link between death and the uncanny is apparent, as Freud actually notes (1919, pp. 241–3), yet the text simply refuses to support the insight in the final analysis, with Freud seeking ultimately to establish the primacy of castration over death. Thus, in discussing what he sees as the most striking example of an uncanny feeling, the sensation experienced by many in the face of death and dead bodies (p. 241), Freud points out the strong resemblance between our modern attitude toward death and that of earlier civilizations. We have only added to the ancient approach a thin disguise of rationality, he says, and attributes this conservatism to "the strength of our original emotional reaction to death" (p. 242). Thus, Freud seems to admit a reaction that is strong and emotional. Yet the familiar rapid turnaround arrives before the end of the paragraph, where Freud retreats to his familiar position that death has no place in the psyche. The statement "All men are mortal" appears in every textbook of logic, yet "no human being really grasps it, and our unconscious has as little use now as it ever had for the idea of its own mortality" (*ibid.*). How then, if the unconscious has no use for the idea of our mortality, can we have a strong emotional reaction to it, and why should death be so uncanny?

Earlier in the text (pp. 233–6), Freud discusses the figure of the double and presents Rank's (1989 [1914]) theory, according to which the double was originally an insurance against death (the soul being the first double), but later becomes its harbinger.[6] Here too, Freud seems to affirm both a basic need to overcome death through the invention of the double and the constant threat that the double embodies. But he does

---

[5] Piven's (2004) outstanding elaboration of this point of view extends Freud's idea to many other symbolic systems.

[6] Rank's (1989 [1914]) study on the double is in fact one of the first places where psychoanalytic discussions engaged the question of death.

not stop here, and the double, without the explanation that its source is death-related being directly negated, is first linked to the phase of self-love, that is, primary narcissism, and then to the observing, criticizing agency of the ego, such that the double comes to represent no more than a case where something that belongs to an earlier stage in mental life is met again (1919, pp. 235–6). Its relation to death is pushed aside in favor of another explanation.

From its very first pages, Freud's (1919) text struggles with the evident link between death and the uncanny. It begins with a look at Jentsch's view of the uncanny feeling, which sees it as related to the intellectual uncertainty over whether a body or creature is dead or alive. Freud dismisses this explanation, in favor of another which sees the uncanny as related to repressed fear of castration (p. 233). The insistence, however, on excluding death from the picture is too obvious and forced. Jonte-Pace (2001, pp. 64–5) building on Kofman (1991 [1974], p. 160) underscores the way in which Freud's insistence on the primacy of castration in death anxiety is undermined by the recurrent obsessive references to Jentsch's idea. "Here," she says, "as in so many texts, Freud insists that castration anxiety is the foundational anxiety and that death anxiety is a secondary phenomenon, yet the priority of death is irrepressibly expressed through textual interruptions and inconsistencies." "Death ... seems to demand centrality" (p. 65).

Note that the deflection of death, by means of explicit statements or literary textual devices, manifests itself along lines we have already encountered. The reduction to castration Jonte-Pace notes is of course the most evident strategy. Yet other methods can be discerned, such as sexualization, as when Freud (1919) brings up the terrifying fantasy of being buried alive, and yet explains it, or rather explains it away, as being actually a wish "qualified by a certain lasciviousness" to go back to intra-uterine existence (p. 244) (Jonte-Pace, 2001, pp. 67–8); or concretization, by mixing fear of death and fear of the dead (Freud, 1919, pp. 241–3). By focusing on the uncanny effect of the *dead*, he largely avoids a discussion of the uncanny effect of *death itself*, and focus is deflected from death to the past relation to it (the fact that something from the past has been revived).

One way to look at the difference between Jentch's and Freud's interpretations, is to ask whether what accounts for the uncanny feeling is related to a specific content or a specific form. Jentch lays stress on a content: the uncertainty about the aliveness of someone or something. Freud, on the other hand, repeatedly gives preference to a formal explanation: something repressed is revived, something surmounted reasserts itself.

And yet despite all of Freud's (1919) aversion to it, content, content pertaining to death, inevitably reenters the game. What is repressed is of course repressed due to its threatening content, as is the case with castration. Not everything that was surmounted and revived is uncanny, and the omnipotence of thought, Freud's central example for something that having been overcome, reappears in uncanny moments, is not neutral. Examples specifically related to death keep coming up. Freud remarks that "[a]s soon as something *actually happens* in our lives which seems to confirm the old, discarded beliefs we get a feeling of the uncanny," and the example that pops up is: "it is as though we were making a judgment [..]: 'So, after all, it is *true* that one can kill a person by the mere wish!' or, 'So the dead *do* live on . . .'" (pp. 247–8, emphasis in the original). Other cases include the exploration of death as uncanny (pp. 241–3), and the not-so-neutral example of an uncanny repetition (pp. 237–8): the repeated occurrence of the number 62, which is for Freud, we have seen, a presumed age of death, which had, at the time of writing "The Uncanny," just been safely passed.

"The Uncanny" then is a text that is continuously losing itself, almost as if a theoretical price of unclarity is to be paid for the obliviousness to death.

Totem and Taboo

The pervasiveness of death and its influence on human thought and behavior is openly recognized in *Totem and Taboo* (Freud, 1913a). In his explanations of the magical world of primitive people, of the phenomena of totem and of taboo, Freud lays much stress on the role of death fears and death wishes. A long section concerns the taboo of the dead (pp. 51–63), and its overarching presence in primitive life. In other sections, Freud recognizes death (to some extent) as the threat behind the fears and acts of the obsessive personality, as the source of human thought (pp. 76–88), and as the limit of man's narcissism; death is here a limit to whose supremacy one should submit oneself (pp. 88, 93). However, here too, Freud's position is, as shown by Piven (2004, pp. 81–6), reductionistic. I will not linger on this text, but will cite instead Piven's clear and thoughtful remarks:

Freud emphasizes repeatedly in *Totem and Taboo* (1913a) that death is the most horrific fate among tribespeople, and that complex prohibitions and rituals are invented so as to avoid, contain, and ward off death ... It would seem that the fear of death is a horrific preoccupation that shadows the primitive community and suffuses every action, practice, boundary, belief, and object ... For Freud, however, this is all manifest illusion, projection, obsessive fantasy ... Beneath the taboo is repressed desire, and the desire is repressed for fear of being killed by the king, or a ghost, or a god ... The fear of death is not apprehension over the thought of nonexistence, nor of being killed by an enemy or carnivorous beast ... , but guilt over illicit death wishes and the terror of reprisal. .... Thus for Freud beneath manifest terror lurks the fear of being murdered by the parent. (pp. 81–2)

Thus, again, fear of death is concretized (reduced to the fear of the dead), rendered active and seen as a derivative or a byproduct of the death wish. The threat looms up from a concrete source: having wished for the death of the dead person, one now fears his revenge. It is a threat of wrathful murder, and not of death as an existential given or an impersonal force. (It is important to note that the above citation is indicative of only the first part of Piven's position, which on the whole lays stress on how much death itself *does* comprise a threat in Freud's analysis in *Totem and Taboo*.)

The general impression gleaned from Freud's treatment of death in *Totem and Taboo* is again one of hesitation between alternating positions, ending up with the option opposing death's significance. In this text, Freud regards death as a thought-provoking riddle and finds Schopenhauer's claim that "the problem of death stands at the outset of every philosophy" worth reiterating (1913a, p. 87); he recognizes death as the starting point for the theorization of primitive man (pp. 76, 87);[7] and he views submitting to death, rather than denying it, as a cultural achievement, one that is at risk of falling back into denial (p. 88). But he also, in parallel, ends up at the familiar bottom line of trimming death to psychoanalytically manageable size—fear of death is concrete fear of murder etc.; it is not death primitive man fears; death itself is not a cause for reflection (pp. 59–63), and other factors better account for it (pp. 92–3). The world of primitive people, readers of Freud's text might infer, is infested with death, but the author is openly and covertly reluctant to substantiate that conclusion.

Transient lives

Up to this point, we have seen that in Freud's complex and ambivalent approach to death, the tendency to minimize death's importance usually trumps the discussion. Even where death is at the center of the discussion, the reductionistic trend quickly manifests itself. Nevertheless,

---

[7] The first reference (Freud, 1913a, p. 76) to the idea might be referring to others' views of early humanity, even to be countered later (p. 78), but the second seems to adopt it without restriction.

Freud's perceptiveness does not allow him to miss death, and in several concise and sharp discussions, he sheds light on important aspects of death, to the point of offering tentative guidelines for a psychology of death, and perhaps a philosophy of death.

One such text is "The Theme of the Three Caskets" (1913b). This short essay is concerned with the recurring theme in myth and art of the choice between three women or three caskets representing women. In Freud's examples, which include Shakespeare's *The Merchant of Venice* and *King Lear*, the Greek myth of the Judgment of Paris, and other tales, the third of the women or the caskets is chosen. Her dumbness, Freud asserts, discloses her link with death. She stands for the goddess of death, and the three women stand for the three fates, the Moerae (p. 296). For Freud, this mythical theme is the result of two reaction formations to the original approach to death (pp. 299–300). Rather than as a necessity, death is portrayed as a choice; rather than being bad, death is good: the character representing death is the better one, both in her attributes (beauty, moral attitude, love) and in that when chosen she brings fortune and marriage. The myth is an attempt to mitigate the threat of death, and Freud's discussion presents death as source of distress, something in need of mitigation, something that calls for psychic work.

Further thoughts on "Thoughts"

Freud is at his best when criticizing the human approach to death. He sees through the defenses and blind spots. In *Totem and Taboo* (1913a, p. 88) he comments that in the modern world the scientific approach no longer embraces omnipotence, meekness in face of nature is recognized, and people "submitted resignedly to death." The old belief in our omnipotence, though, still survives in the trust we have in the ability of our minds to control nature.

The first pages of "Thoughts for the Times" describe the human tendency to avoid death. Freud (1915, p. 289) notes an effort, on both the psychological and the cultural levels, to push death aside and forget it. He insists on our difficulty in both acknowledging and comprehending death. I have already shown how he confuses a lack of willingness with an inherent incapacity to recognize and grasp death, but if we momentarily set aside the theoretical insistence that death is inaccessible to our minds, we can see the richness and aptness of Freud's clinical and cultural insights into the the psychology of death.

Freud's (1915) account of the reluctance to internalize death is illuminating as it insists on its complexity, far exceeding the "I don't want to know" reaction. Rather, this reluctance involves a play of recognition and denial, where recognition on one level serves as a cover for a denial at a deeper level. Thus, on the face of it we willfully declare "[t]o anyone who listen[s] to us" that we recognize death as unavoidable, as "the necessary outcome of life," that "everyone owes nature a death" (p. 289). Yet we behave as if it were otherwise, and in various manners, "eliminate it from life" (*ibid.*). The recognition is superficial and is not expressed in our behavior.

This duplicity is also manifested in our very different attitudes when it comes to our own death, on the one hand, versus the death of others. Although Freud speaks of suppressing the possibility of death in the case of others as well, it is a more superficial, rather than profound refusal. Freud's description of our unconscious attitude contrasts our own sense of immortality with our more willing recognition of the death of others. Yet also regarding the conscious acceptance of death, Freud's argument, perhaps his strongest one, that we are incapable of conceiving death because we still are present as spectators, concerns only the death of the self, in contrast with that of others, where the fact that we remain alive afterward is not necessarily a source of dissonance. Freud's (1900, p. 485) anecdote, cited earlier, of the married couple, where one partner tells the other "If one of us dies, I shall move to Paris," conveys the difficulty in applying the logic of death to oneself.

Thus, our difficulty in accepting death is hidden behind a superficial acceptance of it in the case of others, or on an abstract level. These descriptions parallel Heidegger's familiar analysis of the everyday attitude to death, in his *Being and Time* (1996 [1927]).[8] People say "one dies" quite easily, but latent in this easy acknowledgment is a deeper lack of acknowledgment. "One dies," but not me, "one dies," but not now. The recognition of death as a *general* fact of life has, as Heidegger suggests, the effect of distancing death from oneself (pp. 234–40). Accepting that "one dies" is easy. Accepting that we are included is difficult. Admitting the general case is exactly what enables us to ignore our own specific death. Plain denial would be too transparent when having to face the question directly.

Even in the general case, however, we tend to blot death out of our minds. Thus, faced with a case of death, we are always surprised, "as though we were badly shaken in our expectations" (Freud, 1915, p. 290). Even the knowledge of death we so readily admit to is easily forgotten.

---

[8] Kaufmann (1959, pp. 48–9) remarks, without elaborating though, that much of Heidegger's dense and repetitive prose is stated elegantly in these few pages by Freud.

Indeed, it also works the other way around, and rather than accepting death as general but denying its relevance to us, we accept a particular case of another's death but deny the general relevance of death to everyone: When a case of death occurs, Freud says, one tends to lay stress on the accidental factors that caused it. The person died because of an illness, an accident, or because he was too old: "we betray an effort to reduce death from a necessity to a chance event" (1915, p. 290). In the "Jewish" version of the text I mentioned earlier, he even says that this tendency is so strong that one is led to ask whether a Jew ever dies a natural death at all (1993 [1915], p. 12).

Still in this Jewish version, Freud describes yet another way to concede death and deny it at the same time, emblematized in the traditional reply to a question about one's age: "Sixty (or thereabouts) and hopefully till one hundred and twenty!" (1993 [1915], p. 12, translation changed). Here, one accepts death as a necessity, but postpones it to the very distant future.[9]

On Transience

Apart from his critique of the everyday attitude to death, Freud's appreciative approach to death is most cleverly expressed in two other related issues: the influence of death on the valuation of life, and the constitutive role of death in our lives, that is, the necessity, almost on a normative level, of acknowledging, confronting, and coping with death to lend life content and make it worth living.

"Life is impoverished, it loses in interest, when the highest stake in the game of living, life itself, may not be risked," we have seen Freud claim in a passage from "Thoughts for the Times" (1915), examined at length in Chapter 6. A life in which death is not considered is "shallow and empty" (pp. 290–1). I mentioned there how these ideas not only seem foreign to Freud's general worldview, but also that when they are read in the context of the entire text, they become shaky, almost to the point of incomprehensibility. Yet taken in themselves, these are profound claims, which tentatively suggest that the confrontation with death is an essential component of what it means to be human. Such confrontation, Freud seems to be saying, is a possibility that encourages us to live life more

---

[9] Once again Freud's approach parallels Heidegger who speaks about our usual interpretation of death as "a case of death," "a constantly occurring 'case'" (1996 [1927]), p. 234). The postponing of the possibility of death into the distant future is also implied in his analysis (pp. 234–40), just mentioned, of the everyday acknowledgment that "one dies."

fully and openly, rather than merely being occupied with survival issues or the preservation of life. Never has Freud sounded so close to George Bataille. (See my attempt, Razinsky, 2009, to more fully elaborate such a position from Freud and Bataille's texts.) One cannot disconnect life from the fact that it is ephemeral. Finitude informs every single act in our lives.

One text in Freud's writings, the short and beautiful "On Transience" (1916 [1915]), brings these ideas to the fore. In a summer walk in the countryside, Freud and two companions engage in a discussion of the ephemeral nature of all that is beautiful. For one, a poet, the thought that all the beauty surrounding them will vanish is saddening and robs that beauty of its value. For Freud, however, it is exactly the contrary: transience lends things greater value, rather than stripping them of it: "Transience value is scarcity value in time" (p. 305).

The attitude expressed in "On Transience" seems to be a very profound belief of Freud. It is echoed in a letter to Binswanger from 1912, who wrote to Freud that he was diagnosed as having a malignant tumor. Freud is grief-stricken at the news, but reminds Binswanger that he still has a chance, which he did, for he was cured and lived for many years afterward. "[Y]ou have only been reminded a little more conspicuously," writes Freud, "of the precariousness in which we all live and which we are so ready to forget. But you will not forget it just now, and life, as you say, will hold a special and enhanced charm for you" (April 15, 1912, Fichtner, 2003 [1992], p. 82). Here we have Freud's existential facet at its best. Death is always lurking around us but is generally forgotten, and a glimpse at the cold face of finitude only serves to enhance life and our affirmation of it.

Freud's position in "On Transience," although he refers to it as simple, is actually multifaceted. His objection to the position that transience reduces the value of things is maintained on two grounds: the first, just mentioned, that the effect is the exact opposite, that it lends them more value, and the second, that duration and value simply have nothing to do with each other: "since the value of all this beauty and perfection is determined only by its significance for our own emotional lives, it has no need to survive us" (p. 306). Freud's text slides from the first to the second, but the implications of each are different. In the first, death is what gives our lives value. This reflects a comprehensive perspective whereby whatever specific value something might have, part of the value derives from its uniqueness in time—from the fact it exists only once and just for a while. The second line of thought implies, based on Freud's formulation, that meanings are always necessarily human. There is no point in looking for meaning outside human life, or in something bigger than ourselves (cf. Phillips, 2000, pp. 3–31). Yet a third kind of argument, however, implicit in Freud's position, concerns nature as cyclical: "each time [nature's beauty] is destroyed by winter it comes again next year" (1916 [1915], p. 305), he notes, referring to the beauty of a flower. Here, interestingly, the meaning of transience is opposite to that just described, because individual phenomena, e.g., the foliage of trees, receive much of their meaning precisely from belonging to something above them, something larger and more permanent.

Once again, Freud's attention to death remains deeply ambivalent. While the first page or so of this short paper deals with approaches to transience, Freud moves on quickly, in the second part, to discuss the psychic determinants of the poet's approach—though not his own. Because his argument "made no impression" on his companions, he is led "to infer that some powerful emotional factor was at work which was disturbing their judgment" (1916 [1915], p. 306), and then speaks of mourning and the revolt against it.

If we recall that the issue is the approach to death, three elements are to be stressed here. First, the poet's position is pathologized. Alongside the stress Freud lays on the importance of accepting death and transience, he actually treats natural emotional responses to death, such as anxiety, despair, or mourning, as disturbances (Jonte-Pace, 2001, pp. 119, 123). Death may be acknowledged, but only as a positive influence, as something that gives life value. To mourn, or to consider death a catastrophe, or a horrible fate, is seen by Freud here to be as problematic as ever. Second, Freud regards the fact that the reaction to the prospect of death is emotional, rather than purely intellectual, as a problem in itself. And third, he treats the poet's position as in need of explanation, rather than valid in itself. A direct response to death and finitude, in Freud's view, is not something that is itself a primary psychic fact.[10]

The flip side of Freud's pathologization of the "emotional" (fearful, depressive, etc.) response to death is the heroization of the "rational" acceptance of it. It is interesting to note that the "negative" response to death is denounced, but for reasons almost diametrically opposed to those normally used. Whereas elsewhere Freud claims that death's status in the psyche is secondary, and that in the unconscious we are heroes who neither believe in death nor accept it, here he not only calls for the acceptance of death, but asserts that non-acceptance of death is a form

---

[10] If Freud's companion is indeed Rilke, as Lehmann (1966) maintains, perhaps one of the greatest minds who ever wrote about death, Freud's patronization becomes even more absurd.

of cowardice. While elsewhere Freud argues that we death can never truly accept death, he now claims that it is pathological and childish not to.

Two different interpretations of "accepting" death are at play. In Freud's general theoretical scheme, death cannot be "accepted" psychically in the sense that it has no real psychic presence, that is, it is not a "true" psychic content. Considering it, therefore, is secondary in that it hides something else. In "On Transience," on the other hand, to "accept" death means to stoically accept it as a fact, not to face it with gloom and doom and despair, not to mourn as a child, but to confront it as a mature adult.

(Piven, 2004, p. 144–7, suggests a different perspective. He argues that Freud's intention is not to denounce the existential despair (and pathologize it) but only the tendency "to condemn life and remain in a state of despondency." What is problematic and infantile, Piven says, is to fail to accept death as a part of life and to be hostile to life itself as a result, to derogate it, just because it does not conform to one's expectations, that is, just because it is not infinite.)

"On Transience" also has an ethical dimension. Often, the ethical aspect of psychoanalysis is neglected. Psychoanalytic positions necessarily suggest a certain ethics, even when unacknowledged (Blass, 2001, 2003a, 2003b): a certain view of the human being containing judgments about what is good and bad, what is desirable, and what is a healthy psychic state of affairs. One of the difficulties entailed in integrating death into the usual analytic approach is that death forces us to reconsider these values and judgments, because as I have said above, it touches every aspect of our life, every act, project, and plan. (In fact, some attempts to place death at the center of psychoanalysis fail precisely because they do not consider the ethical implications; see Stern, 1968a, Rosenthal, 1973a [1963] or Langs, 1997, to give just a few examples. They "add" death to psychoanalysis by simply inserting it into the existing models. They replace one issue with another—death instead of castration or sex—and otherwise leave the model intact.)

"On Transience" is one of the rare places where Freud does directly look to the ethical dimension. It is not by chance that in one of the few texts where he seriously considers death and finitude and acknowledges their importance, his discussion directly touches on ethics, and in its most abstract—expanded and inclusive—sense. His assertions that life is impoverished when death is left out, and that transience gives value to life, concern not the value *in* life, but the value *of* life. Freud, who once claimed (in a letter to Marie Bonaparte, August 14, 1937, E. Freud, 1960, p. 436) that the question of the value of life should not even be asked, attempts here to answer it. The issue of finitude leads to ethical questions.

"On Transience," then, supplies a kind of ethical ground for a death-sensitive psychoanalysis. Phillips (2000), drawing conclusions from such a death-based approach, presents Freud's work as an attempt to answer, or rather to dismantle, the riddle of mortality. He stresses the futility involved in the quest for any secured meanings and draws the inevitable conclusion from the declared death of God. "The death of God," he writes, "is the death of someone knowing who we are" (p. 24). Nor should we look for such an organizing principle in nature. Nature is indifferent. What Phillips urges through his interpretation of Freud and Darwin is that we renounce any idea of redemption, of perfect happiness, cure or progress, as well as forms of permanence such as God or truth, all ideas that only make things more difficult for us, and adapt to our natural human condition.

This is not as pessimistic as it sounds though, since, Phillips (2000) adds, there is beauty to be found in the ephemeral nature of things in constant flux and lacking permanence. The illusions we invent hide that beauty (p. 7). The mission is "making sense of our lives as bound by mortality not seduced by transcendence, by after-lives" (p. 12). Darwin and Freud, says Phillips, declared "the death of immortality" (p. 11). "They are not seeking stays against time. They are unseduced by monuments" (p. 12). Phillips presents Freud as a kind of instructor in the art of transience. Although he hardly confronts this take on him with other explicit or implicit positions of Freud with regard to death, his argument makes the best of available materials, such as "On Transience."

Regarding the texts where Freud deals with death, Yalom (1980) has already made the correct observation that they all lie outside Freud's formal system. They are examples of Freud feeling freer, less "a prisoner of his own deterministic system" (p. 69). The nature and marginal status of these texts are, I believe, crucial for gaining an accurate overall impression of the place of death in psychoanalysis. These sources are more literary (Freud's writing at its best from an aesthetic point of view), and explore neglected corners that are not part of the formal system.

They certainly seem liberated from the need to theorize, to use models and schemes, the need to provide a concise view of general relevance that will subsume all possibilities—all these being principles of theoretical writing. Perhaps, we might wonder, it is exactly the liberation from such needs and principles that enables Freud to deal with finitude. Freer, more open writing, which turns to literary texts, is perhaps better suited to this subject, which eludes attempts at theorization and systematization.

It is essential to point out that these texts did not make it into the Freudian canon embraced by later generations of psychoanalysts. "The

Uncanny," the most popular of them, is the bread and butter of literature departments, but is not usually part of psychoanalytic training. "Thoughts for the Times" is an almost forgotten text, except for an occasional reference to the arguments in it against the primacy of death, although it is to my mind among the most brilliant of Freud's works. And "On Transience" is also rarely referenced in psychoanalytic frameworks. This state of affairs calls for a further enquiry into the factors involved, and into the clashes between the psychoanalytic worldview and a view that sees death as a central issue.

Except perhaps in the small group of more existentially oriented authors, the several attempts by Freud to grapple directly and non-reductively with the question of finitude have not endured. His poignant insights into the dynamics of denial in the cultural-conventional approach to death and his recognition of death as the inevitable and uncontrollable lot which humans prefer to hide from, did not permeate analytic sensibility. His consideration of the value of life as directly influenced by the problem of death, his uncertain description of a potential encounter with finitude through the death of the other, and the intuition underlying his theory of the death drive, that is, death as a defining property of humanity, all these have been largely forgotten in psychoanalytic theory. The theory has thus lost some potentially very important interfaces between it and existential issues, which could serve as a basis for the development of new ideas and theoretical contributions that will deal more seriously with death and other existential concerns.

With this, our journey through Freud's writings has more or less come to an end.[11] In the next chapter, we move on to examine the analytic literature from a broader perspective, in an attempt to pinpoint in it the specific ways in which the neglect or reduction of death is carried out.

---

[11] With the exception of "Mourning and Melancholia" (1917 [1915]) that will be examined in the next chapter.

9 Avoidance and reduction of death in psychoanalysis

Pleasurable as dwelling with Freudian texts is, this book has both "Freud" and "Psychoanalysis" in its title and it is time to look into the second term. The current and following chapters, therefore, deal with a wider picture of psychoanalysis. We begin in this chapter with an overview of the reductive and marginalizing tendencies in the analytic literature, to continue in the following chapters with brief discussions of several main schools and thinkers.

The reductive-dismissive tendencies assume various, often elusive, forms. Reduction can of course be seen only when death is referred to, whereas in actual fact most of the time death is simply ignored. When not overlooked altogether, death is often marginalized, or excluded from the theoretical field. Even more common is that the concept of death is emptied of meaning: death is recognized to some extent, but is rendered something else. Like in the defense mechanism of intellectualization, death may be included in discourse, but only by virtue of the fact that it has been detached from everything terrifying. It is necessary, therefore, to uncover the ways in which death is deflated, cut down, and flattened. The different ways of disregarding or reducing death naturally overlap, and yet it is important to pinpoint them separately.

Note that many of the examples I raise here are taken from texts that do regard death as an important human issue. It is disappointing to find, time and again, reductive elements in texts which purport to lay stress on death. The very presence of such literature might create the impression that death has already been "treated," while in fact, such accounts are no more than a patch over a chronic and persistent problem. Let us examine the analytic perspectives on death to better understand this problem.

Reduction

The most basic and explicit analytic trend concerning the fear of death is its reduction into something else. Freud's explanations reduce it, as we saw, either to a manifestation of guilt, fear of castration or of losing the love of the superego, or to the result of one's own death wish. This approach was adopted by mainstream psychoanalysis almost without reservation. Fenichel (1945) is often cited as an example of reduction: "probably every fear of death covers other unconscious ideas" (pp. 208–9). Among these other ideas he lists fear of castration or loneliness and fear of punishment for death wishes against others, which we have already encountered, as well as fear of excitement, which he says is fear of orgasm, because of a traumatic view of orgasm (pp. 209, 544). Later he adds the possibility that fear of death "means a fear of a state where the usual conceptions of time are invalid" (p. 285).

I will not cite further restatements of this Freudian position; suffice to say that it is not uncommon today. It is interesting, however, to find variations of it even among authors who focus specifically on death, who examine it anew, or who even interrogate Freud's position.

Thus, for example, with reference to Freud's personal approach to death, Michel de M'Uzan (1977 [1968])—an author for whom death is a central theme, as the title of his book, *From Art to Death*, testifies— actually attributes and reduces all of Freud's changing attitudes to death to his transferential relationship with Fliess.

Hárnik (1930) suggests that the fear of death is of early origin, and that Freud should have further developed this idea (p. 486), but reduces the fear of death to the concrete fear of suffocation. Chadwick (1973 [1929]) attributes fear of death to parental threats such as banishments, being sent to one's room—threats she regards as echoing the practice of filicide in primeval cultures (p. 77). She claims that fear of death in adolescence results from the adolescent boy's first nocturnal emissions or the adolescent girl's menstrual blood that signify for them an impending death. They also revive childhood situations of masturbation and enuresis, situations where the threat of castration arises (p. 75).

The reductive tendency is sometimes almost funny. "The person with this fear of death has the unconscious fantasy of being turned into stool," claims Brodsky (1959, p. 106), and concludes—referring to adult patients—that fear of death, when it is not a disguise for castration or separation anxiety, is the "dread of turning into feces" (p. 108).

It sometimes seems that almost every possible element in psychic life can be mobilized to account for the fear of death, except for death itself. Thus, Lewin (1950, pp, 115–6) explains the fear of death as a manifestation of a fear of a sinking, yielding sensation, which is traceable to the passive relaxation that follows nursing.

Note that these explanations are not simply attempts to ground an elusive fear of death in something ostensibly more readily experienced.

They are also nullifying the very existence of the phenomenon itself. Fear of death is "the dread of turning into feces." It is not fear of *death*.

The problem has perhaps best been articulated by Yalom (1980), who cynically comments:

> one cannot but wonder why there is such a press for translation. If a patient's life is curtailed by a fear, let us say, of open spaces, dogs, radioactive fallout ... then it seems to make sense to translate these superficial concerns into more fundamental meanings. But, *res ipsa loquitor*, a fear of death may be a fear of death and not translatable into a "deeper" fear. (p. 56)

Not only is the fear of death reduced in all of the above explanations, but the psychological phenomenon itself, the fear of death, remains fundamentally unexplained. At bottom, it seems that something else is explained or described and not the phenomenon in question.[1]

One of the problems with reductionistic explanations of death is their claim to totality. It is not that analysts simply suggest that fear of death may hide something else but rather that the reductionistic explanation is the *only* one, that it completely subsumes the phenomenon of death anxiety, that death is always something else. This pretension to supply a complete explanation seriously weakens reductionistic arguments. The fact that death anxiety is always described as something else, that the thought of death, the understanding of our mortality, or a direct encounter with death, are never allotted significance in themselves, brings into question the validity of the analytic account of death.

The reduction of fear of death in the psychoanalytic literature should now be clear. One could claim, however, that it is not unique to death. It is true that at early stages in the history of psychoanalysis, reduction was the norm, and many experiences were reduced. But Freud himself was not always reductionistic, and was certainly not so in his approach to death, for the most part, in his personal life. Besides, the reductionistic tendency about fear of death has persisted across various schools in more recent authors, even when reduction was not the rule with other issues.

Another point is that death itself is unique among subjects of reductionistic analysis. It shapes and influences human life in a fundamental way, and comprises perhaps the clearest example of forces external to us and out of our control. It also may involve transcendental aspects, and surely carries meanings that go beyond the psychological domain.

---

[1] Hoffman & Brody (1957) dismiss the idea of a specific prototypical experience and suggest that "fear of death is a displacement of any internal conflict," or of an inability to tolerate any tension. The conflict involves "a wish for complete alteration" by "destruction of old parts with the substitution of a new self" (p. 437). The authors seem untroubled by the irony of attributing the fear of death to a wish for a new life.

The reduction of the fear of death could be seen as equivalent to the explicit reduction of moral values to the psychological sphere. In both cases, what was a favorite issue for philosophers is reduced to infantile psychology: the high is brought low. However, in the case of moral values, Freud leaves room for a moral psychological experience, such as guilt. Even when the discussion is stated in terms of the Oedipal dynamics of wishes, fears, prohibitions, and guilt, it still retains the essence of morality. A prohibition respected is a prohibition respected, whether the source of the respect is the code of law or a fantasized threat by the father. This is not the case, however, with the fear of death to which Freud, in his theoretical formulations, does not grant any real psychological validity. He does not refer to the psychology of the fear of death, except as an artifact.

Generalization and non-specification

Another way in which death is deprived of its significance in psychoanalysis, related to reduction, is lack of specificity in how it is perceived and explained. Aspects of death are recognized and ascribed some importance, but because death shares these aspects with other issues, it is thrown together with them. However, while death does share many properties with other things, like being external to us and beyond our control—features common to much of reality—it is also unique. It has a unique significance and meaning. It is completely irreducible to a list of properties, but if we do list some of its properties, several appear to be peculiar to death. Death is not just annihilation in some general sense, and is not an event like other possible events, but is, as Heidegger (1996 [1927], pp. 232, 242–4) puts it, our "ownmost" possibility. It is also a singular, one-time event, which we are certain will come, yet usually do not know when. It involves the flow of time and signifies it at any moment. It is both a future event and a permanent presence. Throwing death together with other psychic elements, even in a sincere attempt to explain it, involves, beyond reduction or perhaps as an aspect of it, a blurring of its uniqueness.

This problem of non-specification is apparent in the idea of death equivalences common to several analyses, namely, the idea that the experience of the fear of death is built upon earlier infantile experiences. The idea figures in Money-Kyrle (1957), Lacan (1966, pp. 186–7), Jaques (1988 [1965]), Stern (1968a, 1968b), Lifton (1979), and Piven (2004), and will be discussed mainly in Chapter 12. It differs from simple reduction in that the fear of death is seen as valid, but is explained together with earlier states. Basically, the problem is that if the psychic impact of death is explained through other experiences similar to it, like sleep, the similarity takes over and the uniqueness of the psychic response to death is lost.

For Stern (1968a) for example, the fear of death is the repetition of biotraumatic situations from infancy, by which he means early, inevitable traumata related to states of object loss. Although he speaks of the importance of working through the fear of death (p. 4), he seems to divert the object of the fear from death itself: "in fear of death we are afraid of a repetition of the mortal terror lived through in the early biotraumatic situations" (pp. 4, 12, 19). The earlier states do not just influence fear of death, they become, or rather the repetition of them becomes, the thing feared itself. Stern seeks to understand the fear of death through other things, but death itself is lost on the way.

The case can even be more pronounced when the author him- or herself does not assign death a central place in his or her analysis. In Lewin (1950, pp. 150–5) for example, "[t]he death that comes to be feared is the bad sleep that is interrupted by unfulfilled tensions and anxieties, later by guilt" (p. 153). Equivalence is established but instead of helping explain the emotional responses to death, it makes them epiphenomenal. Through equivalence, death loses autonomy and any valid psychic reality.

Sometimes death is generalized to include simply too much, and thus again loses its uniqueness. This is the case in the widespread discussion of death and rebirth in therapeutic contexts. Using the metaphor of death is fine, as long as it does not presume to be real attention to death: to the future event of death, and to transience. Psychic deadness, aptly described by Eigen (1995), is a significant and useful concept, but when analysts use it in clinical contexts, it should be clear that it is not death that is referred to but psychic death.[2]

Another example of generalization, elaborated on in Chapter 8, was Freud's (1913a, pp. 88, 93, 1915, p. 293, 1927, pp. 18–19) stress on the fear of death in Man, in the sense of humankind: Man fears death, whereas individuals never do. Again, like defensive intellectualization, death is discussed, but is too general, and is, therefore, no longer troubling.[3]

---

[2] Generalization is also at work in Carveth's (1994) depiction of the potentially positive transformative results of an encounter with finitude and death. In extending "death" to "the metaphoric or symbolic form of any obdurate limit, boundary, separation or ending" (p. 219), the encounter he refers to is actually no longer with death: "We may view 'death' as signifying ... any ultimate limit, boundary, or immutable obstacle to our will and desire" (p. 225).

[3] Lacan's ideas (see Chapter 11) about a basic lack in the subject, ideas binding together finitude and the psychic consequences of life being enrolled entirely within language, also suffer to some extent from the problems of non-specification and generalization.

Sexualization of death

Another manner in which death is side-stepped in psychoanalysis is through its sexualization. Many a time when death comes up in a theoretical discussion or in clinical contexts, it is brought down to sexual matters. Thus, Keiser (1952) regards the fear of death as the fear of orgasm, of losing the body ego or its boundaries in orgasm, and for Bromberg and Schilder (1936), the fear of death is felt, among other things, as "a fear of losing pleasure potentialities." Beyond these examples, sexualization is apparent, of course, in the theoretical primacy given to castration over death.[4]

This general tendency is obviously quite understandable given the centrality of sexuality to psychoanalysis. Uncovering the influential role of sexuality in psychical life is a major achievement of Freud. And yet it seems that sometimes the discussion of sexuality, once it has become established in psychoanalytic thought, serves as a way to avoid consideration of other issues, namely death and other existential concerns. Pontalis (1977, p. 242) puts forth a similar thought when he states that although the theme of death is, in his view, no less constitutive to psychoanalysis than sexuality, the extensive use of sexuality serves to hide the theme of death.

Jonte-Pace (2001, pp. 34–44, 52, 59, 68) notes Freud's tendency to sexualize death and thus deny it, whenever motherhood or femininity are involved.

Sometimes the problem is not direct sexualization of death-related issues but their marginalization with regard to sexual issues. Thus, although Freud (1918 [1914]) mentions the fear of death several times in the case of the Wolf Man, who "was being shaken by a dread of death" quite early in his life (p. 77. See also pp. 79, 98, 107),[5] no serious theoretical attention is given to the matter and the interpretation capitalizes on castration and sexual issues.

Even classic examples of sexual issues sometimes involve death. Such is the case of little Hans, usually taken to exemplify issues of castration, but having to do with death too (Lifton, 1979, pp. 213–19; Stern, 1968a, pp. 5–6). In that case study, the event of the fall of the horse seems to involve more than the exposure of its genitals or the aggressive wish

---

[4] For Rank (1950 [1945]), Freud's libido-based explanation is an attempt "to deny the fear of death," since "if fear arises from repressed libido, one can free libido and thus get rid of fear" (pp. 116, 122). Although Rank's position on Freud's theory might have some truth in it, it is certainly exaggerated and presents an oversimplified and too optimistic version of it. Attributing the problem to libido does not mean that it can easily be resolved.
[5] See Piven (2004, pp. 125–39) for an analysis of the Wolf Man's fear of death.

toward the father. Hans panics because he believes the horse has died (Freud, 1909, pp. 50, 52, 112, 125) or is uncertain about it. He seems alarmed by the dying itself or the transition of something living to something dead. If a strong horse can fall and die, surely so can a child like Hans. The question Hans is so preoccupied with, of how life begins, is bound up with that of how it ends. When walking on the pavement, Hans poses the question whether there are dead people buried underneath, or only in the cemetery? (p. 69).[6] None of this is brought to the fore in Freud's discussion.

Rendering death a wish and activizing the subject in death

A strategy of avoiding death related to sexualization in Freud and psychoanalysis is to turn it into a wish, discussing it through the prism of death wishes. This works on two different levels: focusing the entire discussion of death on death wishes, and using death wishes specifically as an explanation for the fear of death. Let us begin with the first level. Death wishes undoubtedly play a role in psychic economy. The assertions that powerful death wishes stir behind the moral commandment "Thou shalt not kill," and that we are really the descendants of a chain of murders (Freud, 1915, p. 296), are radical, bold contributions of psychoanalysis, which surely go against accepted beliefs. This stress on death wishes does not by any means comprise a psychology of death though. Moreover, the widespread analytic discussion of death wishes often supplants a far scarcer discussion of death. Many seem to erroneously believe that by discussing death wishes they have addressed the question of death. But it is precisely the opposite: by giving center place to the less threatening issue of death wishes, they avoid discussing the hard-to-bear meanings of death, its reality and inevitability regardless of our wishes, the terror it evokes, and its implications for life.

The focus on death wishes assumes the role of an *ersatz*, a substitute for the discussion of death. The existence of this *ersatz* is significant. Were the issue of death simply a hole in the psychoanalytic view of reality, were it completely ignored, this gap would be much more apparent, and would call attention to a need for a change (although ignoring death is still the most current mode of not dealing with it).

---

[6] Chasseguet Smirgel's (1988) analysis stressing how Hans is troubled by generational difference beyond the issue of sexual difference, and how he experiences his helplessness and insufficiency, is pertinent here. Hans recognizes his own vulnerability, as well as that of others stronger and older than him.

However, the semblance of a discussion of death in the form of a consideration of concrete elements associated with it gives the impression that things are OK.

On another level there is the actual transformation of the death fear into a death wish. The latter is often used as an explanation of the former: one fears death because one has death wishes directed toward oneself, or one fears death because one wishes the other's death and fears retaliation. A proponent of the first view would be Cappon (1973 [1961], p. 71), who believes that fear of death in the dying and in the neurotic is a defense against the wish to die, which originates in the death instinct. But if anything is defensive here it is the theoretical explanation itself. Why not simply suppose that the dying really fear death?[7]

There are numerous examples of the second instance, of which Melanie Klein's ideas (to be discussed in Chapter 10) are the major expression. Jones, to cite another example, (1951 [1926], p. 196) holds that "[d]read of death invariably proves clinically to be the expression of repressed death wishes against loved objects." Although the explanation of fear in terms of a wish is normatively psychoanalytic, applying it to the fear of death is too roundabout an explanation for something that is much more easily seen as a direct response.[8]

What characterizes this kind of explanation is that it renders the subject active in death. If what is responsible for the fear of death is one's own death wish against oneself, one becomes the active agent of the threat to one's existence rather than a passive subject. This also holds when the wish is aimed at the death of the other, and the fear of death is fear of retaliation. One is still the instigator. This is of course in sharp contrast to our normally passive position with regard to death.

Concretizing death

Beyond these difficulties, explaining death in terms of a wish also involves concretization. Aggressiveness becomes the key concept. The threat of death is reduced to its concrete manifestation in the aggressiveness toward the other or by the other. It is also personalized. One does not fear death but rather *being killed*, and not by some anonymous forces,

---

[7] Other examples are Lewin (1946, p. 431) and Lowental (1981, p. 366).
[8] As part of his discussion of annihilation anxiety Hurvich (2003) lays stress on the psychic validity of such experiences. With regard to Fenichel's formula "behind the fear lies the wish," he reminds us that sometimes "behind the fear lies a deeper fear" (p. 595).

but by a specific individual, who is not an emblem of the threat of death but is rather its direct source.

Let us examine some examples of concretization. Wahl (1959 [1958]) speaks highly of the importance of fear of death (p. 18), and is moreover concerned with how death anxiety is repeatedly described as a derivative of other issues (p. 19). However, he still sees death anxiety largely as resulting from the tendency in the human child to personify every motivation around him and from the law of the talion, namely, that if one wishes the death of the other, the same would happen to oneself (p. 24). Thus, the child becomes fearful of his death which is actually a punishment for illicit wishes, born of frustration (p. 23). Thus, fear of death is canceled as a primary state of mind and is subordinated to the existence of aggression.

Kübler-Ross (1969), in discussing the fear of death in the introduction to the theory of stages of dying, speaks of it in concrete terms only. A man who has lost his wife might then fear his own death, but because of the law of the talion (p. 3). The reason why "death has always been distasteful to man" is that, because it cannot be located in the unconscious, it was "always attributed to a malicious intervention from the outside by someone else," to a "bad act" (p. 2). As if, one might wonder, death is not distasteful enough in itself. She provides examples of the fear of the dead as manifested in rituals, which prove for her that humans have not changed, and that "death is still fearful" (p. 4). Again, it is as if only the fear of the dead and their revenge makes death fearful.

Concretization of the threat of death can occur without reference to the subject's wish. This is the case of Rheingold (1967), for whom "the maternal filicidal impulse engenders the death fear and death complex" (p. 134).

Pathologization of the psychic reaction to death

If indeed death and finitude play such an important role in people's psychic life, if they are indeed a part of our misery, the worm in our apple, what moral approach should we adopt toward the emotional response to death? It seems that psychoanalysis not only tends to reduce emotional responses to death and minimize their role, but it also tends to pathologize these subjective responses. Responses to death that could be seen as natural or inevitable are generally not accepted as legitimate in dominant strains of analytic theory. Death anxiety is regarded as neurotic and repeated reflection upon finitude as obsessive. One should be freed, it is maintained, from these thoughts and feelings. This position is sometimes explicitly stated, and can sometimes be detected in other formulations.

Treating death-related thoughts and affects as a neurotic manifestation or symptom is not in itself an indication of a serious problem in psychoanalysis, which explains many things in a similar way. Yet what psychoanalytic formulations often fail to capture is the truthfulness of people's fears and preoccupations concerning death. Accordingly, the significance of death in life is ignored. Not every anxiety should be explained away. The focus, unfortunately, is centered on the mechanism of the symptom rather than on the content, and the death-related thoughts or feelings are dismissed.

Death anxiety can of course sometimes be a symptom of certain pathologies, but certainly not always, as authors such as Fenichel (1945) seem to believe: "It is questionable whether there is any such thing as a normal fear of death," he states (p. 208), for death is inconceivable and, therefore, fear of death is only a disguise.

For Pasche (1996, p. 49), death anxiety is identified with psychotic anxiety, where the body is disavowed and one fears the complete intrusion of the "Other" (p. 52).[9]

For many, adaptation to death is judged to be crucial and healthy. Any response that diverts from the ideal of adaptation is pathological. Stern (1968a), for example, believes that fear of death is important and should be worked on, yet stresses the developmental goal of adaptation to death, suggesting that deficiency in such an adaptation results in neurosis (p. 28). Undoubtedly, coming to terms with mortality is a fundamental human task. Ascribing fear of death only to neurosis, however, ignoring its normal role in human life and maybe even its positive impact, and putting the stress on "healthy," "normal" adaptation is another way of minimizing death related responses.

Schur (1972), in a book focused entirely on Freud's theoretical and personal approach to death, nonetheless often displays reductionistic attitudes. For example, he starts out by noting that "until his last moment Freud wrestled with this problem of the 'beyond,' the meaning of death, the necessity to die and the wish to live" (p. 136), but then dismisses this struggle as a neurotic manifestation. Not only Freud's preoccupation with the date of death, but also his fear of death, are treated as pathological, as a symptom, as neurotic (p. 100), something

---

[9] Pasche (1996) distinguishes death anxiety from fear of death, which he does not deem psychotic. Fear of death signifies for him, however, only a response to an imminent threat to life, while death anxiety is the feeling that appears in states where there is no such threat (p. 49).

that has to be mastered. At times, Schur concretizes it into something physical (p. 104). He sees the age-of-death obsession as nothing but a byproduct or symptom of the loaded relationship to Fliess (p. 154)—rather than, for example, as an attempt to come to grips with the issue of finitude—and the attacks of death anxiety as an outcome of a neurotic identification (p. 103). In the final analysis, Schur interprets Freud's preoccupation with his age of death as hiding a wish to die. The wish itself is an aggression against the self, a form of punishment for aggression toward others (pp. 341–2). Schur thus falls into the full gamut of reductionistic explanations which serve to cover up death and death anxiety.

A negative moral judgment

Another way in which analytic theory tends to drive death into the rubric of the insignificant belongs to the ethical domain. One can discern on reading Freud, Jung, Kohut, Erikson, and others, a subtle yet significant moral condemnation of death anxiety and depression. This is evidenced in analyses where the negative emotional response to death is constructed as a sign of weakness, lack of maturity or as impaired psychical functioning.

The negative moral judgment regarding fear of death is also expressed through its complement: the heroization of certain responses to death. One can discern this attitude in some discussions of Freud's famous serenity about death in his senior years.[10] Freud's serenity was seen by many of his friends and pupils as heroic. Freud himself thought he knew the more profound reasons. In a letter to Binswanger (September 15, 1926, Fichtner, 2003 [1992], p. 184), he confesses that the secret behind his famous serenity, which some called courage, was a lack of interest in life brought about by the death of his grandson Heinele.

While the expressions of admiration by friends and followers, such as Schur (1972), are understandable, these approaches are still evident in later literature. Thus, for Golub, this approach is a laudable human achievement: "He coped with pain, suffering, and disfigurement in a stoic fashion" (1981–1982, p. 198), and Nachman (1981) raises this serenity to the level of a theoretical stance of Freud himself.

---

[10] Perhaps the special interest in Freud's approach to his own death is because of his professed atheistic orientation, as one of the most important modern critics of religion. In that, his case might resemble for example David Hume's death, which intrigued some contemporaries, eager to see how the declared atheist would react to his own approaching death, and whether he would repent.

A calm acceptance of death and heroic confrontation with it are considered in these examples as the highest human personal achievements. This too, is not unique to certain psychoanalytic views. It is not even unique to theory or philosophy. Heidegger (1996 [1927], pp. 235) locates a similar tendency on the everyday level, in the social pressure of *the they*—which aims at estranging the person from his or her own death—to adopt a position with regard to death of indifferent calm and refraining from anxiety.

This approach of putting serenity on a pedestal implies that any other response to death is considered less admirable. Anxiety and depression, self-mourning and terror, confusion, and despair are perhaps legitimate— but are clearly less preferable, and not because of the suffering involved. One could argue that a therapeutic approach cannot but assign calm acceptance a higher value, but it is doubtful that most analysts would explicitly do so, given their acute awareness in general of the suffering and pain that are part and parcel of being human. And yet, Freud himself expresses such a stance when he says, following his friend von Freund's death from cancer, that "He bore his hopelessness with heroic and clear awareness and was no disgrace for psychoanalysis" (letter to Eitington, January 21, 1920 cited in Schur, 1972, pp. 317–18).[11] This remark and the word "disgrace" (*Schande*), strongly exemplify the ethical judgment involved.

Finally, one can discern the same kind of unacknowledged moral judgment, with its idealization of acceptance of death, in the ideas of the perhaps most famous thanatologist, Elisabeth Kübler-Ross (1969). Kübler-Ross's theory of the dying person includes five stages, which advance from denial, through anger and bargaining, to depression, and finally to acceptance. Her theory manifests (and was probably influenced by) a tendency to depreciate anxious, raging, depressed responses, although she is clearly highly empathic to them, and to favor the calm, "dignified" acceptance in the end, as the "final word." It provides a sort of happy ending to the story, even if there is nothing happy in it, where everything rests in peace.[12]

---

[11] For Schur (1972, p. 318n), this remark shows that Freud believed that once a person has undergone analysis he "should have learned to master his fear" faced with death.
[12] The ethical dimension might have even influenced Kübler-Ross's interpretation, for it is not at all certain that progression through the stages is the usual case. Shneidman (1973, pp. 5–7) disputes Kübler-Ross's findings and observes that the more common state of things is not a staged advance towards acceptance but "a nexus of emotions," a clustering of affective states involving a hive of different responses of all sorts, continuously alternating between denial and acceptance.

How different these views are from Dylan Thomas's desperate appeal to his father (1939, p. 128):

> Do not go gentle into that good night.
> Rage, rage against the dying of the light.

Overlooking death

Whereas reduction involves some reference to death, even if it is rendered something else, there is a still more basic way by which the psychic significance of death can be sidestepped: it can simply be ignored. This is the second major characteristic of the analytic approach to death: not supplying a reductive answer, but refraining altogether from asking the question.

Death, we have seen, was generally avoided by Freud. We have encountered some attempts to deal with it in his body of work. Yet in the model of the mind, and in the etiology of psychopathology Freud presents, death is not a factor; it is absent. The theoretical disregard of death in his models is all the more striking when one considers the complex character of his writings: the precision, the wealth of considerations, the richness of associations, the multiple variations on theoretical arguments, the attention to detail, the focus on diverse clinical manifestations and implications, etc. Freud's attentiveness to the minute details of psychic life only brings to the fore how one of the most important details of all in human existence—the fact that we inevitably die, and are ever cognizant of that fact—is generally ignored. Is death really that insignificant, and finitude really that marginal?

In the writings of most other major theoreticians, Kleinians and Lacanians apart, death is rarely mentioned. When we examine the literature as a whole, we see that death is, by and large, simply not a topic. Here and there along the years an article or a book about death appears, although the overall number in more than a hundred years of psychoanalysis is not much more than a dozen or two.[13] The examples we have seen in the current chapter that do deal with death, which all display some kind of a reductive approach, and the few non-reductive ones that we will discuss in the following chapters, are but a drop in the ocean.

That the evasive aspect of Freud's approach to death has survived intact in the mainstream psychoanalytic literature, and has even become more pronounced than in Freud himself, is easily observable. It suffices

---

[13] Many of these isolated treatments of death display a critical approach.

to open any psychoanalytic text, and scan the table of contents or index, or to search a database for papers on death to realize the extent of the problem. One must shake off the usual psychoanalytic way of thinking to clearly see the absurdity of the situation. In most cases the term "death" (not to mention, "finitude," "mortality," etc.) cannot be found in indexes. If it does appear, the references are either marginal or reductive. In the body of the texts themselves, death is simply not an issue. It might be raised but quickly dismissed, or transformed, or never mentioned at all, or ignored, or repressed. Any observer willing to try the above will be left with the impression that something important was left out. Psychoanalysis is wrong to present itself as an all-embracing theory, as better suited than all other theories to explain human behavior and motivation, if it fails to include more serious reference to what is for most humans a basic source of sorrow and despair, meaningfulness and meaninglessness. I cannot over-emphasize the element of distortion embodied in the current psychoanalytic state of affairs; how remote it is from a commonsense understanding of the human being and his or her existence and suffering in the world; how divergent it is from religious, artistic or philosophical understandings of humanity, shared by virtually all cultures, and which reflect our fundamental intuition of what it is to be human.

The tendency to overlook death reflects, in part, the theoretical position that judges fear of death derivative or insignificant, but it is also a problem in itself, in that it is yet another theoretical means of repressing or belittling death's importance, and because it creates real oblivion. When an issue is raised, whatever the approach to it, it remains part of the glossary of a discipline, and often is later examined in different and innovative ways. However, when it is almost absent from a discussion, it simply falls outside the discipline, forgotten or treated as not belonging it.

Intermezzo: Dying without death—Mourning and Melancholia

Avoidance, we see, is another expression of the analytic reluctance to deal with death, Freud included. It is difficult to demonstrate such a claim, when what could support it is by definition absent from a text or a discussion, but we might try to do so through the example of Freud's (1917 [1915]) "Mourning and Melancholia." Such a demonstration is all the more difficult where the thing absent is itself a form of absence—death—and where the whole text at hand revolves around loss and absence.

"Mourning and Melancholia" brings together two emotional sets of responses or behaviors: the first, mourning, belongs to the normal sphere of behavior and the second, melancholia, belongs to that of the pathological. The two have a lot in common, including instigating factors, symptoms, and the psychological mechanism responsible for them. Both follow a loss, either of a close person or a loss of a more abstract kind (Freud, 1917 [1915], pp. 243–5). My point is that while death is clearly in the background of the text, it remains there all along, and does not form part of the text itself. This is all the more important because of the influence this article has had on the entire future development of the psychoanalytic approach to these two clinical conditions.

Let us look first at mourning. Somebody died: this is the prerequisite for mourning. Freud (1917 [1915]) carefully explains the complex dynamics of feeling in mourning, but oddly enough, his analysis of mourning has nothing to do with the most difficult thing in it: death itself. He speaks of the disappearance of the object, now no longer available for libidinal cathexis, and of the emotional ambivalence toward it. Those are concepts Freud feels very much at home with, once again subordinating death to the familiar analytic field. Thus, even when he has the opportunity to place death at the center of a psychoanalytic discussion, even when the material at hand begs for such a discussion, it is left out. Of course, here and there, one can sense in the minimalism of Freud's tone, that more than a loss of an "object" has occurred, but in general, nothing in Freud's discussion suggests that the object is not merely gone, disappeared, but that it died, ceased to exist, not only in the eyes of the ego or as a preferred destination of cathexis, but as a subject in itself, as a human being.[14]

When a loved one dies, death itself is at issue. The subject is brought into a very intimate face to face encounter with his or her own death. Yalom (1980) criticizes the inattention to death in the clinical literature on bereavement, which has "failed to take into consideration that the survivor has not only suffered an "object loss" but has encountered the loss of himself or herself as well" (p. 56), "a knock at the door of denial" (p. 64). Inattention to such aspects is, of course, detrimental to our understanding of the experience of the bereaved. Even more remote death can serve as a reminder of one's own fate. This was the case, for

---

[14] Frommer (2005, pp. 485–7) notes that the psychoanalytic theory of mourning seems to suggest that subjectively, the loss is also not real but rather resolvable. Everything can be overcome. It neglects the irrecoverable alteration of our being that might result. Through this alteration, we understand something experientially about human vulnerability.

example, for Freud, who in 1896 links his attacks of death anxiety to the death of Tilgner, a Viennese sculptor, from cardiac problems (letter to Fliess of April 16, 1896, Masson, 1985, p. 181). Freud seems to have identified with Tilgner, and imperiled as he thought he was by cardiac problems, was afraid he too would die.[15]

These dynamics of encountering death can take several paths. The death of a loved one can fracture the usual denial of death. It can involve a comparison: he is dead and I am not; a sense of guilt for having survived; unconscious triumph at having survived; identification with the dead; combinations of the above, or other processes including complications caused by hidden death wishes. Freud's dreams in *The Interpretation of Dreams* gave us many such examples.

That the death of a loved one could disrupt our usual denial of death is not only intuitive, it is also a position found in Freud himself. In "Thoughts for the Times," written almost simultaneously with "Mourning and Melancholia," yet published 2 years in advance of the latter text, Freud speaks, as we saw, of primitive man's ambivalence when a close person dies (1915, pp. 292–7). The dead one is an "other," but also himself, and this brings primitive man to recognize that he can die too. This recognition had to be dispelled immediately, and led to the invention of doctrines of immortality (pp. 293–4). Things are similar, Freud says, in the case of the unconscious attitude. Loved ones are both strangers and "components of our own ego." The conflict that ensues when they die leads, not to religion but neurosis, he says, going on to mention cases of "entirely unfounded self-reproaches after the death of a loved person" (p. 298), and death wishes.

Although the conclusion of "Thoughts for the Times" resembles that of "Mourning and Melancholia," the path that leads to it traces a different picture, which is not fully acknowledged in the text. The death of the loved one made denial impossible. One recognizes that one is not immune. And something—be it the invention of the soul or the generation of neurosis—must be done to counter it. This is missing from "Mourning and Melancholia." However, like in "Mourning and Melancholia," Freud does not go all the way, as described in Chapter 6, and inclines the description of the neurosis to the co-existence of love and hate, to self reproaches and to the death wish rather than to death itself.

---

[15] See a detailed description of the Tilgner episode in Schur (1972, pp. 100–4). Identification, which is central to Freud's essay, can function as an instigator of the fear of death (Zilboorg, 1943, p. 471), even as anticipation (de M'Uzan, 1977 [1974], pp. 157–8). Some authors (Lifton, 1979, pp. 181, 222–4; Searles, 1965 [1961], p. 495) also speak of "mimetic death" in several psychopathological disorders.

In one place in "Mourning and Melancholia," death does emerge from behind the heavy theoretical terminology. Memories of the lost object are examined, and each one of them meets "the verdict of reality that the object no longer exists." Then, almost in a whisper Freud says, "the ego, confronted as it were with the question whether it shall share this fate, is persuaded by the sum of the narcissistic satisfactions it derives from being alive to sever its attachment to the object that has been abolished" (1917 [1915], p. 255). And so death as soon as it enters the picture is quickly cut out of it again.

The death of the love object is not just an event, but a constant possibility. In that sense it is similar to the prospect of death that awaits the subject himself. The attachment to the love object stands in the light, or rather the obscurity, of future death or loss. Therefore, when a loss occurs, and there is a need, as Freud says, to decathect every single path of cathexis to the object, the process cannot be disconnected from the death itself, for the forging of every such path was done under the intimidating possibility that the attachment might end one day. Future loss is the fly in the ointment of love, we learn from Freud's analysis in *Civilization and its Discontents* (1930, pp. 76–85, 101). Seeking happiness along the path of (sexual) love he says, exposes the subject to "extreme suffering" if and when she would lose the loved object (p. 101). The expectation of mourning is what always leaves love's happiness imperfect.[16] Is this not a dimension to be analyzed, or referred to, when actual mourning is in question?

Let us now turn to melancholia. There too, "Mourning and Melancholia" remains silent on the question of death. Whereas the cultural image of melancholia is a state where, in addition to low mood and low energy, one is busy with the "big questions" of life, where death turns into an urgent concern, where the meaning of life is questioned, the psychoanalytic understanding of it, influenced, among other things, directly by "Mourning and Melancholia," presents a very different picture. The very apt insights of Freud (1917 [1915]) and other analytic thinkers into the nature of melancholia, which stress self-reproach, loss of ability to love, delusional expectation of punishment, internal conflict between the ego and the superego, all certainly have a place in the

---

[16] Cf. Freud's sorrowful words after the death of his daughter Sophie, in a letter to Pfister (January 27, 1920): "Sophie leaves behind ... an inconsolable husband who will have to pay dearly for the happiness of these seven years" (Meng & E. Freud, 1963, p. 75). The intensity of the relationship is proportional to the pain of the loss, and this is the "deal" from the very beginning. The expectation of loss can of course also be seen, in lines similar to Freud's conception in "On Transience" (1916 [1915]), as what makes one savor the relationship.

understanding of melancholia. But Freud neglects other aspects of melancholia, related to the value of life, one's existence, and one's place in the universe—to death as a prospect. As a result, the whole clinical definition of melancholia, and the ability to perceive nuances of feeling and thought, was biased in that direction. Julia Kristeva's *Soleil Noir* (*Black Sun*) (1987) is a refreshing change in reintegrating the psychoanalytic understanding of depression with more existential questions and a wide cultural perspective.

One need not go too far in search of support for criticizing Freud for ignoring these other aspects. Freud himself, in the passage from *The Ego and the Id* discussed in Chapter 1, writes that fear of death occurs either as a result of external danger, or an internal process, as exemplified by melancholia. He explains the latter case and extrapolates the explanation to the former (1923, p. 58). Thus, melancholia is seen as a condition where fear of death is active. As discussed earlier, thoughts of death are explained there as deceptive disguises of other conflicts, but at least their presence is acknowledged. Where then, is this acknowledgment in "Mourning and Melancholia"?

Freud's (1917 [1915]) text on melancholia was preceded and influenced by a paper by Abraham (1968 [1911]) on the same issue where, as Lifton (1979, pp. 184–5) argues, death imagery figures centrally. The salience of death in Abraham's text further supports the observation of its absence from Freud's closely related paper (although, it should be noted, Abraham's reference to death concerns less an apprehension of death than a symbolic imitation of death).[17]

The absence of the theme of death from the discussion of "Mourning and Melancholia" is all the more visible when we examine it in light of "On Transience" (Freud, 1916 [1915]), written just a few months later. As I mentioned, Freud's more existential understanding of death seems to be hidden in his non-canonical texts, his literary, philosophical texts, rather than being expressed in his metapsychological ones. If we accept Jonte-Pace's (2001, p. 119) proposal to read the two texts together, "Mourning and Melancholia" alongside the more minor "On Transience," we can see more clearly what is lacking in the former. Both articles, Jonte-pace notes, deal with a similar theme, the process of loss, and describe two possible reactions to "death, loss, and change" (p. 119):

---

[17] It is worthwhile mentioning Lifton's (1979, p. 185) bewilderment at the failure of most of the analytic literature to note this aspect of Abraham's ideas; his observation fits well into the overall argument here regarding the reluctance in analytic literature to examine or recognize death.

the first, healthy mourning, leading to recovery, and the second, pathological, characterized paradoxically by an inability to mourn.

What is striking to me here is the different place death has in the two texts. While in "Mourning and Melancholia" death was marginalized, almost forgotten, in "On Transience," it is the central problem: a fact known in advance that we should somehow come to terms with. Death here is troubling, a question, *the* question, we are obliged to answer; something we react emotionally to, even in advance, as prospective mourning or acceptance, and regardless of concerns of libidinal economy.[18]

Freud (1917 [1915], p. 246) summons Hamlet in his discussion of melancholia, indeed, the most celebrated of melancholics, especially in Germany, where his image possessed German romanticism. Freud mentions him, but only in reference to his obsessive ruminations. Yet Hamlet, the prototypical melancholic, is more than obsessive. In response to his father's death, he questions the value of life, the prospect of death, and poses the question—to be or not to be—which has haunted western culture ever since.

While Freud's stress (1917 [1915], pp. 248–50) on ambivalence, identification, and incorporation as a reaction to loss retains much of its explicative power, it also leaves at least some readers unsatisfied. In the words of a student in a clinical psychology graduate course, "it sounds more like the description of a bad stomachache; one has swallowed spoiled food, and now suffers from its absorption by the system," than a description of either mourning or melancholia.[19]

In sum, death is absent from "Mourning and Melancholia," and this is a significant absence. Freud himself admits, in retrospect, that "in discussing the question of mourning we ... failed to discover why it should be such a painful thing" (1926, p. 131). The insistence on a libidinal mechanistic dynamics, to the complete exclusion of death and other existential concerns, seems to be largely responsible for the failure to understand why, after all, if it is only a matter of redistribution of the ego's cathexis, mourning (and melancholia) is indeed such a painful thing.

---

[18] Hoffman (1998. p. 50) notes that with regard to Holt's (1972) distinction between Freudian humanism and Freudian mechanism, Freud's more existential views can be identified with the humanistic pole, a remark that is compatible with the divergence between his two essays on mourning.

[19] Lifton (1979, p. 189) proposes a different duality oppressing the melancholic; rather than the ambivalence stressed by Freud, he describes the duality of the sadness of loss and the protest against it.

Treating death as a problem of the ill and elderly

In much of the analytic literature then, death is simply ignored altogether. But there is a subtler, related way in which the role death plays in life is minimized. Works on death do not form a significant part of the therapeutic literature. Literature on death, however, *does exist* where the focus is on a specific population for whom death becomes more acute or distressing. One can find an abundance of such books about the terminally ill, about old people, and about the bereaved.[20] One can also find books and articles about suicides or survivors of grand scale disasters. Despite the importance of these issues the bias created by the lack of reference to death in "normal" lives, and the abundance of texts dealing with specific populations for whom death is seen as specifically relevant, is instructive. Death, it seems, is not a general human problem, but a problem of some people only. It is a problem for the very old, a problem for the terminally ill. It is a problem when someone has died and is now mourned. And it is a problem when one is subject to extreme violence or natural disasters.

But death of course is also a problem for everyone. The probability of death striking an individual in his lifetime is, everything said and done, still 100 per cent. Death is a topic to be dealt with in the life of every individual. Treating it as a problem of just some is another indication of the marginalization of death in analytic thought and the minimization of its role in life. One can even propose that the bias in the literature is an expression of a defensive tendency. If we succeed in limiting the kingdom of death to those specific populations, we can go on living as if it is not our problem. Death as the most basic given, which every one of us must face and respond to in one way or another, continues to be absent from analytic and therapeutic thought.

"So what?"

One possible objection to this work could be subsumed in a kind of "so what?" argument. Perhaps, the claim would go, death was neglected by Freud, but so were many other issues. Freud's neglect of death anxiety is of no more significance than his neglect of quantum mechanics. *Et alors?*,

---

[20] Reviewing this literature is beyond the scope of this book. Some studies about concrete death-related situations suffer from difficulties discussed here concerning death, others less so. Although such issues have been neglected for years (Rosenthal, 1973b [1957], p. 88), interest in them has been revived by such pioneers as Eissler (1955), Kübler-Ross (1969), Weisman (1972), and Shneidman (1973), among others, as part of the evolution of a new field of knowledge, thanatology.

the French would say. Death is not part of psychoanalysis, for it has other focuses, and there is no problem with it. Actually, I believe readers who have gotten so far in this work will probably not use this argument any longer. Still, let me say a few words on it here, in guise of a short summary.

The clinical presence of death-related fears and thoughts referred to in the introduction, is itself an argument against leaving death out of the theory. But there is more at stake. Leaving the psychological consequences of death outside of psychoanalysis' scope has serious implications on the status of psychoanalysis and its possibilities. It is as if psychoanalysis deliberately chooses to limit and reduce its capacity to relate to much of the psychic world. Such diminished perspective cannot be seen as welcome. Moreover, that death will be reconfigured as so many other things and yet never as what it truly is, I think, is intellectually unacceptable. At least sometimes, it seems, death should be recognized as potentially influential in itself and claiming it *never* is discloses the absurdity.

The reduction and dismissal is also much more profound than the direct claims against death's presence or influence. We also saw that not only death anxiety, but death itself, tends to be understood in a more concrete way, while elements of it are ignored, and much of its threat is neutralized. Thus, even when the theory assumes it deals with death, it actually does not.

Thus, there seems to be a price, an internal price for the exclusion, marginalization or reduction of death. This is a point worth insisting on. It was apparent in almost all of the Freudian texts examined so far in this book. The texts become entangled, confused, contradict themselves. The phenomena related to death are not explained; the passages that seek to do so finally explain something else, and the theory becomes inconsistent.

It is not the case, the current chapter demonstrates, that the analytic problem with death belongs to Freud himself, the old pioneer father, who might have paved the way, but whose ideas are by now surpassed by newer theories. Rather, approaches of newer schools (Klein, Erikson, Kohut, Jung), we shall see in the following chapters, are largely undermined by new manifestations of reductive tendencies.

10   The post-Freudians in the labyrinth of death

As the previous chapter demonstrated, the difficulty that death poses for psychoanalysis goes far beyond Freud, cutting across schools, perspectives, and generations. One manifestation of the problem, we saw, is silence about death. But not all analysts are silent about it. It is now time to look more closely into the ideas of those salient analysts, founders of schools, for whom death does assume some importance, who do approach it directly and who specifically try to offer responses to what are conceived as inadequacies of the Freudian worldview. Klein, Erikson, Kohut, Jung, and Winnicott all enrich the approach to death, but all seem to be trapped within the same difficulty of relating psychoanalytically to death. Lacan's ideas, discussed at some length in the next chapter, fare somewhat better.

The Kleinians

Within the psychoanalytic world, Melanie Klein and her followers are unique in their claim that they do in fact acknowledge death's importance (Riviere, 1936, pp. 43–5; Klein, 1948; Money-Kyrle, 1957; Segal, 1958, 1979; Jaques, 1988 [1965]; Weininger, 1996), a view sometimes shared by others like Meyer (1975 [1973], p. 83). They see death as a major source of anxiety and a dominant focus in psychic life. Klein (1948) criticizes Freud for his position regarding death, and regards death anxiety as primary, and in fact as the deepest anxiety. Her position, however, as we will see below, reveals similar flaws to those we already encountered—mostly, in a more radical form, the transformation of death into a completely internal matter.

Klein's basic building blocks are simple: first, the existence of an instinctual dualism of life and death instincts, out of which such oppositions as good and bad, and love and hate, are derived, and second, interactions between inside and outside through the mechanisms of projection and introjection. The development and vicissitudes of these building blocks shape the baby's development, its anxieties, object relations, and psychic life.

Klein is actually one of only a handful of analysts in Freud's time who have adopted the theory of the death drive. For her this does, however, entail consequences: "[A]nxiety has its origin in the fear of death"; "[I]f we assume the existence of a death instinct, we must also assume that in the deepest layers of the mind there is a response to this instinct in the form of fear of annihilation of life. ... the danger arising from the inner working of the death instinct is the first cause of anxiety" (1948, p. 116). The death instinct, she holds, in the form of sadism and destructive fantasies, exerts strong pressure on the evolving ego (1933, pp. 271–2). It is first directed against the ego itself (1957, p. 73, 1932, p. 183), and only afterward, due to the anxiety it arouses in the baby, against an object. The baby's sense of defenselessness and helplessness in the face of these destructive impulses is experienced as a great danger and constitutes, according to Klein, the deepest source of anxiety, the basis of every future anxiety (Riviere, 1936, p. 44; Klein, 1932, p. 183, 1952, p. 198, 1957, p. 22). Klein terms this feeling of defenselessness fear of death.

This primary anxiety is crucial to understanding not only future anxieties, but also the whole of psychic development. The ego is set into motion, as it were, by the need to protect against such internal threats, as is its continuing progress (Riviere, 1936, pp. 44–5; Klein, 1957, p. 61).

The infant's major mode of defending against the great anxiety provoked by the death instinct is projection of parts of the destructiveness onto objects in his or her surroundings: the mother's breast, and later the father's penis. These are now perceived as persecutory, being endowed, in the baby's fantasy, with the sadism that earlier inhabited himself.[1]

Anxiety then, for Klein "arises from the operation of the death instinct within the organism, is felt as fear of annihilation (death) and takes the form of fear of persecution. The fear of the destructive impulse seems to attach itself at once to an object" (1946, p. 296).

Klein adds that the outside diversion is never completely successful, and, therefore, "the anxiety of being destroyed from within remains

---

[1] Another defense is splitting the object and one's feelings towards it into good and bad (Klein, 1946, pp. 297–305). A parallel tendency leads to integration of both the ego and the object (Klein, 1952, pp. 208–12). The resulting "depressive position," with its mourning over the loss of the completely good object, guilt and will for reparation is more concerned with the object and less with the possibility of annihilation of the ego, and is therefore less relevant here. See however Jaques (1988 [1965], pp. 235–8), discussed below, who sees the struggle around awareness of death in the mid-life crisis as related to the level of working through of the depressive position.

active" (1946, p. 296). She holds, then, two related positions about annihilation anxiety: that it is felt inside, as anxiety over the work of the death drive, and that it is manifested as a fear of a persecutory object.

The Kleinian understanding of the fear of death

Unconvinced then by Freud's arguments against the primacy of death anxiety, Klein (1948) suggests that there is fear in the unconscious of the annihilation of one's existence. For Klein, death anxiety is not an epiphenomenon of castration anxiety but rather the primary and inevitable anxiety. In fact she shows how the fear of the superego entails in advance a fear of death.

The role of death anxiety is thus established. However, a closer examination of her position brings into question the degree to which it actually addresses death.

To begin with, fear of death, in Klein's theory, is manifested as a fear of a specific object. It is not the fear of the end of life, or of the inevitability of such an end, nor fear of a vague notion of death, but of something clear and concrete, even if distorted by the baby's fantasies. The threat of death then is dressed in the specific clothing of a persecutory breast.

The persecutory object not only has the role of giving form and name to the dread that lacks them, but is also a mediator between the baby and death. An intermediary is introduced into the fear of death.

Parallel to the concretization of the threat of death, the fear itself is concretized. The baby not only feels the possibility of its inexistence, but experiences the death instinct as an attack and persecution (Klein, 1948, p. 117). It is highly doubtful whether describing fear of death as a sense of being under attack and persecution is the best possible description of that fear. One suspects that what Klein means when she refers to fear of death is not what the term commonly denotes. In her conception, both death and death anxiety are transformed. Death for her is the possibility of inexistence, whose origin is internal—annihilation caused by the instincts—in the first stage, and external, though through a specific object, in the second stage. Death anxiety, according to Klein, is a sense of attack and persecution that does not really belong to fear of death itself as a thing in the world. Fear for life might result upon attack or persecution, but can very well exist without them. Death is something real, with an objective existence in reality, but Klein transforms it into an infantile fantasy, something inside that belongs to the psychic system.

Riviere's (1957) Kleinian formulation exemplifies the nature of the problem: "All fears come back to the fear of death: to the destructive tendency that might be called the capacity for death in oneself" (p. 356).[2] When Klein imparts such a primary status to death anxiety, her terminology is misleading, for it is not the death one normally fears that she speaks of, but "the capacity for death in oneself."

Klein can write extensively about fear of death but if what she means by it is the fear of internal destructive pressures, then apparently she does not share with most people the simple meaning of the word "death." She might very well explain something—perhaps a psychically significant something—but it is certainly not the fear of death.

The referent here is actually not death at all. In the equation "fear of death = fear of the threat in the death instinct," one could substitute any word for "death" on both sides, for there is no reference at all to reality, and it all remains a closed system.

Some Kleinian formulations (Weininger, 1996) suffer from the problem of transforming death into wish, as discussed in the previous chapter. Thus, fear of death is not only fear of the internal drive, but also a result of the wish to destroy the object and the ensuing guilt. It arises out of one's own death wishes, rather than from the fact of death.

Furthermore, Klein's ideas are open to the criticisms made earlier about the death drive theory as a theory of death. Defined in terms of a drive, a part of life, death is less the negation of life, and its arbitrariness is neutralized by its being the necessary outcome of the work of the death drive. That it comes from within reduces the anxiety involved. Death is no longer a question of which we know nothing, but a definite theoretical construct, which is inherently less threatening. And it no longer cancels our individualization, because it fulfills, as it were, an inner tendency striving to achieve its goal, thus becoming a locus of self-fulfillment. In sum, by transposing the threat from death itself to the death drive, death is rendered less threatening.

Whereas in Freud, however, this criticism applies to a theoretical concept, the death drive as a theory of death, in Klein it applies directly to her description of a psychological reality experienced by the baby.

The problem is not in linking death with inner life—clearly death is reflected in our inner lives—but rather with the link to the specific form of inner life presented by Kleinian theory, and with the fact that this inner game is all that is left of a much bigger picture. The question

---

[2] The tension between giving death centrality and immediately turning it into something else is also clear in the following formulations of Riviere (1957): "[w]e cannot escape the conclusion that an intense fear of dying by active aggression or passive neglect is a fundamental element in our emotional life" (p. 357). Fear of death is fundamental, but it is death by "active aggression or passive neglect."

concerns the complete neglect of the reality of death itself. To put things bluntly, if we were immortal, Klein could still speak in the same way about fear of annihilation due to projection of aggressiveness. The fact that we die is not part of her explanation in any way, not in itself, and not as a source of psychic work.[3]

One could present Klein's formulations as an attempt to answer the question of how in the first place the child comes to represent death. Thus, a reliance on the object as the source of threat would be seen as necessary for acquiring a representation of death. Such an understanding, I find, seriously undermines the role of construction in theory. It does not alter the fact that death is constructed by Kleinian theory as something quite alien to the nature of the phenomenon itself. Thus, for example, Schermer (1995, pp. 127–9), for whom Klein's description accurately represents how death is perceived by the child, compares the infantile representation of death "in the persona of an external bad object" to the image of the "grim reaper" for adults. This comparison is itself a case against such a view, because the two kinds of representation are clearly not the same. Probably one is really afraid of the grim reaper, but for the Kleinians the persecutory object is indeed the bringer of death. While the grim reaper is a concretized representation that stands for something else, the persecutory object is identified by Kleinian theory, and by the infant according to it, as the threat itself. Death is persecution by the object. Moreover, in Kleinian theory representation through the object is not some primary step which is later reformed or expanded, but remains valid throughout life.

When we talk about the fear of death, we often mean adults. Were it the case that Klein's explanation applied only to the mental limitations of the baby and its lack of knowledge of future death, this might have reinforced her views, but the same explanation is applied by her and her followers to the adult attitude to death.[4]

The theory's application

Thus, for example, in her paper "Fear of Death: Notes on the Analysis of an Old Man," Hanna Segal (1958) describes a successful Kleinian

---

[3] That Kleinian theory focuses on inner life does not justify its position on death. Kleinians do not claim that inner life is completely insular. In particular, it is maintained that death has an influence on it too.

[4] Kleinians and Freudians are split over the question of whether fear of death is something that the baby is capable of experiencing (Klein, 1948, p. 116; Riviere, 1936, p. 43; Money-Kyrle, 1957, p. 501), but both share the conviction that the adult attitude to death is based on infantile feelings.

analysis of a 75-year-old man, whose psychotic breakdown 2 years earlier was the result, she concludes, of an unconscious fear of death, intensified by old age (p. 178). A similar mechanism, she notes, might be at work in other cases of breakdown in old age (*ibid.*).

Throughout the article, however, when fear of death is discussed, it is as a form of persecution or punishment, to a point where death itself seems marginal. There is no consideration of the real threat of imminent death for this old man, much of whose life, we are told, had just recently collapsed, or of his encounter with his own mortality. Instead, we find plenty of discussions of his weaning at the time of the birth of his younger brother, 72 years before his current condition and treatment.

More is involved here than the familiar criticism of bringing everything down to the same set of infantile mental structures and experiences. Something in the very essence of the experience of this old person seems to have been left outside the clinic. His experience of anxiety in the face of life's termination is neither accepted nor seen as authentic. Too quickly, reasons are sought out behind it, under it, around it.

There is clearly a negative moral judgment involved, toward the patient's death concerns, as is shown in the closing lines of the paper, according to which the success of the analysis made it possible for him "to face old age and death in a more mature way" (p. 181).[5]

Another relevant contribution of the Kleinian school is Elliott Jaques' (1988 [1965]) well-known conception of the mid-life crisis, which brings to the fore death's psychic impact in adult life. Jaques links the mid-life crisis to the growing awareness of death (p. 234) but time and again equates death with destructiveness, and in fact, without sufficient reason— because he well explains why death is a problem for us, the addition of destructiveness being superfluous. In any case, for him, the acceptance of death is related to a reconciliation with one's destructiveness (p. 246). Accordingly, if death is destructiveness and its "infantile equivalent" is "[t]he chaotic internal situation [under conditions of prevailing persecution]" (p. 236), it is no wonder that Jaques comes up with a partial "solution" to the problems death arouses (a good working through of the depressive position, pp. 235–6, 242–6, which "regain[s] the primitive sense of wholeness" and "goodness," p. 245), because it has to do more with internal issues than with the reality of death.

---

[5] These critiques aside, it is worthwhile underscoring the many merits of Segal's (1958) paper. The examination of the specific attitude to his future death of one subject, and the ways in which it is part and parcel of the rest of his mental life is a great deal of what psychoanalysis has to add to other perspectives on death.

I commented above that the reductionistic tendency in the analytic perspective is not unique to the explanation of the fear of death. Beyond, however, the fact that death is unique in the influence it has on human beings, in its possible psychic reverberations, it should be recalled that Klein herself directly opposed what she saw as Freud's reduction of the fear of death to castration, and claimed fear of death should be regarded as a basic, non-reducible phenomenon. Regrettably, her theory reduces it no less.

Klein has been criticized for her tendency to find destructiveness, envy, mourning, and sorrow everywhere (see Weatherill, 1998, pp. 45–8, for a summary of critiques of her theory). The result, it is claimed, is a pessimistic analytic position, where all things are necessarily bad. Yet perhaps, after all, not that bad: as in Freud's death drive, death itself, as a major source of sorrow and anxiety, is excluded from the picture.

Erikson

With the advance of psychoanalysis and the development of new perspectives that give more weight to processes that mature after childhood, and with the growth of less mechanistic models, the perspective on death changes as well. We shall see, in the several authors we now turn to— Erikson, Kohut, Jung, and Winnicott—who grapple to some extent with death, that the theoretical place assigned to it is mitigated by newer, more sophisticated, forms of reduction, alongside renewed expressions of old ones, which blunt death's sting.

Erik Erikson's (1963 [1950], pp. 48–108, 247–74) scheme of the eight ages of man extends psychoanalytic developmental explanations to the entire scope of human life, and gives more explicit consideration to the interaction between the individual and his or her social environment. Each stage along the life cycle includes a central conflict to be resolved, with two possible outcomes. These outcomes and stages include, in ascending order, basic trust versus basic mistrust, autonomy versus shame and doubt, initiative versus guilt, industry versus inferiority, intimacy versus isolation, generativity versus stagnation, and finally, ego integrity versus despair.

At the final stage the mature individual who has gained all the other ego qualities develops "the fruit of these seven stages," "the ego's accrued assurance of its proclivity for order and meaning," and an acceptance of one's life as lived, as a necessity. One accepts one's lifestyle and the contingent cultural-historical conditions of one's life. Death thus loses its sting. The alternative, in the absence of such integration, is despair and fear of death (Erikson, 1963 [1950], pp. 268–9). One's specific life is not accepted as what should have been, as "the ultimate of life" (p. 269), and the time left is too brief to change anything. So it seems that here we have an analytic discussion of the fear of death in human life, an acknowledgment in theory of the fear of death as a valid and integral part of life. But is this truly the case?

Hoffman (1998) makes the essential point that Erikson posits integrity as a criterion of health and regards death anxiety as a "developmental failure" (p. 52), and criticizes Erikson's dichotomy of either non-conflictual acceptance of one's life-cycle or complete despair as being oversimplified.

Indeed there is simplicity in Erikson's attitude and preference for "healthy" integrity over anxiety. But the problem runs deeper. Erikson's notions are another case of the analytic tendency, discussed earlier, to pathologize death anxiety. Death anxiety is an unwelcome sign of an unsuccessful, unfulfilled life. The only ones who succumb to it are those whose lives are inadequate and who fail to achieve ego integrity. Death anxiety is condemned as weakness, or as a sign of other preceding weaknesses.

Erikson's conception of death anxiety or despair can almost be considered a variation on divine judgment. As the person's life comes to an end, her deeds, experiences, and relationships must all be evaluated. Did she lead a good life? If she did, she gets a final reward: a feeling of integrity and freedom from the poisonous experience of concern about death. But if she did not, she is condemned to suffer the fate of death anxiety. There is a moral judgment involved, evaluating one's entire life. Retroactively, a value seal is put on the life lived. Erikson's theory proposes a kind of a happy end: if development proceeds in a normative direction, death shall have no dominion, to cite Dylan Thomas, or, to put it differently, the life well-lived does not arouse pain.

Yet the most significant problem with Erikson is that he fails to distinguish ideal from reality. The integrity achieved at the cross point of life and death, together with the counterpart of despair, is an ideal. As such, it might subsume something about the imagery of life and death that is ours, but it still differs from reality. Human beings do not necessarily die in that way, given the simple fact that people do not necessarily die old. They also die young, and they die at points where the narratives of their lives have not arrived at any form of closure. They die in the middle of things, sometimes without notice, sometimes with very little notice. For many, a full narrative of life unfolded to its end is not the case. The whole conception of a nice-and-tidy life cycle is a fallacy, a denial of the imminence of death, which can rear its head at any moment. The underlying statement is not that at the end of life comes death, which is nothing more than a tautology, but that death will come only when life has reached its natural end and the cycle has been completed.[6] Such theoretical conceptions reinforce the false sense of control over death, and act in the service of defenses against it.

The crucial thing is that the *possibility* of a full, completed life cycle not being the case is ever present. There is always a chance that we will die next year, next month, the next hour or minute; we never know. This awareness of the uncertainty of death is part of the psychology of death, and should be analyzed, rather than suppressed.

Erikson's description ascribes death a place, but only for the old. Death anxiety is not part of life, except in old age. Erikson (1963 [1950], pp. 270–1) says that every stage has precursors and derivatives, but makes no reference in this context to fear of death. He even mentions that there is maturation of integrity as well as wisdom (1982, pp. 59, 65)—the strength associated with his last stage—throughout the stages, but does not mention precursors of the fear of death.

Is death a concern only for the very old? Not if we look at Erikson's own examples. His book *Childhood and Society* (1963 [1950]) opens with a description of two cases, a 3-year-old boy (pp. 25–38) and a soldier in his early thirties (pp. 38–47). In both cases we can see how death plays a significant role. The child suffers severe, epileptoid convulsions that begin 5 days after the death of his grandmother and even resemble her heart attack. He then finds a dead mole, becomes agitated, and asks his mother what death is. Judging that the answers he got were insufficient, he goes to sleep and has another attack. A third attack happens when he accidentally crushes a butterfly. The child had seen his grandmother's coffin being taken away but was not told the truth (pp. 25–7). His favorite game became building oblong boxes that resemble a coffin, and Erikson, treating him some 2 years later, comments that the child is afraid to be inside one of them (pp. 29–30). Clearly then, the child is

---

[6] Erikson (1964, p. 134) himself speaks of "closure" of a style of life that the older man represents for the younger generation. It is this idea of closure that I identify in the above passage as problematic.

The fallacy I am talking about here is part of Erikson's problematic overall conception of life: that it has a cycle, a sequence, an order; that things follow each other, are predictable. This picture is always in disaccord with reality, and nowhere more than in the final integrity-versus-despair phase.

I do not entirely disagree with Erikson's characterization of the last phase. My reference to the picture he presents as ideal captures not only its opposition to reality, but also the role of an ideal as a motivating idea and as a symbolic element that acts as guiding principle. The idea of death as completion is indeed a part of the story we tell ourselves, and any serious examination of the psychology of death should account for it as well (see Lifton, 1979, pp. 105–7 and elsewhere in his book, for the case for images of continuity, self-completion and a good death).

occupied with issues of death and is anxious. Now, while Erikson is aware of this, he interprets the case in other directions, focusing on the child's aggression and fears of retaliation, on guilt and on his fears lest his mother die from his attacks on her (pp. 30–3), in a way similar to the classical psychoanalytic interpretation of death-related concerns seen earlier in this work.[7]

Erikson's second case is that of a marine who suffers from several symptoms after having been in danger during battle. There too, the emphasis is put on other issues, but alongside them, intensive exposure to acute life-threatening danger cannot be overlooked. It should be mentioned parenthetically that the significance of the exposure to mortal danger is, in general, not sufficiently acknowledged in the psychiatric view of trauma neurosis.

Erikson's perspective suffers from a few other defaults. It assumes, for example, an approach to dying that is like making a subtotal of the life that preceded it. This notion of a mechanistic summing of prior experiences requires, to my mind, much too much coherence and allows no new independent psychical work to be done when facing death.[8] The psychic response to death in Erikson is actually not a response to death, but rather an outcome of the person's approach to his or her life as it was lived. (Note that Erikson's neglect of the possibility of creation of new frames of mind reiterates the more classic psychoanalytic stance that the approach to dying is not a result of the knowledge of death or emotional experiences related to it, but rather is determined by past experiences that do not involve death at all). Erikson also seems to neglect the importance of unconscious motives, fantasies, and conflicts in the determination of one's attitude toward death. There is a misconception in assuming that there is a whole, a bottom-line that can be reached. Psychic life is diversified and multifarious.

Moreover, Erikson's perspective on death anxiety turns it into an absence of something else (integrity), a deficiency, a lack of achievement. In the Eriksonian model, death anxiety does not contain the potential role of a motive, of something that has a psychological impact. It is not something that might result in renewed perspectives on life, a thrust toward change, toward expanding life and looking for new

---

[7] Yalom (1980, p. 77) mentions this case of Erikson as an example of death being influential for children too, but he does not mention the fact that the case is actually in discord with the theory.

[8] The idea of a summary results from Erikson's belief that the successful struggle in every stage presupposes the successful overcoming of the conflict posed by the previous stages. This is most pronounced in his view of the last stage, an overly mechanical reevaluation of life determined solely by what came before.

meanings (see Hulsey & Frost, 1995, for a discussion of how awareness of impending death can be transformative).[9]

One thing that imminent death can bring about is a change in precisely the entire view of life which itself, according to Erikson, is supposed to determine the approach to death.

Erikson's ideas, in summary, manifest various problems resulting from implicit assumptions about death. This notwithstanding, they remain important in terms of their acknowledgment of the human need to adapt to death and in the recognition of the fact that death is lurking in the shadow of everything achieved in life.[10]

Kohut

With Kohut, we are once again in a situation where a theoretician's sensitivity to death is blurred once he or she begins conceptualizing it within a theoretical system. Some rare statements by Kohut evidence sensitivity to the burden death puts on us, as well as an awareness of its centrality for the human being:

Man's capacity to acknowledge the finiteness of his existence and to act in accordance with this painful discovery may well be his greatest psychological achievement. (1966, p. 264; see also 1990 [1978], p. 306)

Kohut (1966, p. 266) also speaks of a stage of cosmic narcissism, the final transformation of narcissism in old age, when individual narcissism is transcended, and death is fully acknowledged. Kohut's idea expresses the notion of human participation in contexts—social or natural—larger than the individual himself. It pinpoints, if pushed further, a movement of gradual relinquishment of one's self, which grows from an awareness of finitude that crystallizes as impending death.

And yet things get complicated in the details. Praising the acknowledgment of transience as a developmental achievement is problematic

---

[9] In contrast to Erikson, who sees death anxiety as issuing from a subjective sense of failure, of lack of integration and individuation, other theoreticians have claimed that things are more likely to work the other way around: The more one has achieved individuation, the more one is subject to a feeling of ontological insecurity (see Firestone, 1994, pp. 236–7; Lachmann, 1985, pp. 195–9).

[10] The popular ideas of Kübler-Ross (1969) regarding the struggle of the seriously ill with death, represented in a series of five stages which such individuals undergo, display problems similar to those of Erikson's theory. In her theory we find both the insistence upon a life process going full circle, while as we have noted above, not everyone has the chance to undergo all of life's typical phases, and the implied moral judgment (see above, p. 181). For Kübler-Ross, one must come to terms with death in a manner resembling Catholic last rites, that is, things must end in reconciliation. See also Stephenson (1985, p. 93) and Lifton, (1979, p. 105n).

exactly in its denunciation of the anxiety of death and anything that falls short of calm acceptance. This is the essence of Hoffman's (1998) critique of Kohutian ideas about death. Like Erikson, Kohut proposes "an idealized, even mystical concept of healthy adaptation to mortality" (p. 33), and in preferring the ideal of adaptation to mortality, leaves no place for anxiety, conflict or grief over it (p. 56).

Hoffman's pertinent critique exposes much of the problem. I shall add below some points to his analysis. In the idea of cosmic narcissism as the final form of narcissism (Kohut, 1966, p. 266), we meet, once again, the idea of self-actualization. Death is no longer a source of threat or a limitation to life but the point of the richest and fullest self-realization, as we have seen with the notion of the death drive. Death becomes the crown of individual development. One fulfills oneself best, and is most oneself, when one dies.[11]

At any rate, there is more to Kohut's perspective on death than mere healthy adaptation. Like Erikson, he creates a link between the life "well" or "correctly" lived and death, and suggests that the person who lives properly will not be afraid of dying. But Kohut pushes the thought even further, glorifying dying itself. He speaks of a kind of heroic, triumphant death, where death becomes almost a victorious celebration of individuality and one's narcissism.

Kohut's (1977) words stand for themselves. In contrasting his view of the individual as the Tragic Man with the Freudian Guilty Man, as he sees him, Kohut says that he baptized him tragic rather than "self-expressive" because failures are unavoidable. He then adds: "Tragic Man's defeat and death do not, however, necessarily signify failure. Neither is he seeking death. On the contrary, death and success may even coincide." What he has in mind, Kohut continues, is

> a hero's *triumphant* death—a victorious death, in other words, which (for the persecuted reformer of real life, for the crucified saint of religion, and for the dying hero on the stage) puts the seal of permanence on the ultimate achievement of Tragic Man: the realization, through his actions, of the blueprint for his life that had been laid down in his nuclear self. (p. 133n, emphasis in the original)

This notion is not marginal to Kohut's work. The above citation appears, albeit as a footnote, in Kohut's (1977, pp. 132–3) description of the fundamental difference between Tragic Man and Guilty Man, a difference

---

[11] In his view that the stage of cosmic narcissism is "genetically predetermined" by the child-mother fusion in early infancy, Kohut (1966, p. 266) reiterates the analytic insistence on an earlier anticipation of the relation to death, an anticipation that impairs its independence, albeit here only to a minimal extent.

that he sees as the justification, in this context, for self-psychology. Moreover, the essence of Tragic Man is the striving toward fulfillment of the self. Yet this aspiration necessarily and inescapably encounters a limit in death, and the question poses itself. It is in response to this question that Kohut, instead of looking upon death as a limit, integrates it within life as yet another locus of self-actualization, indeed the most important one.[12]

There is nothing tragic, in fact, about the tragic man. The tragic man wants to fulfill himself, and the one necessary obstacle, instead of serving as such, is integrated into the image Kohut outlines, into the very pattern of the central self he is trying to develop.

Kohut's ideal death is theatrical, more suited to a stage hero, and less to a regular flesh and blood person. It would be comic, were it not indeed tragic. The tragic for Kohut is more than a metaphor for the human being. In fact, he explicitly sets the theatrical model of tragedy as an ideal (1985a, pp. 37–45). The essence of tragedy for Kohut is "man's attempt to live out the pattern of his nuclear self" (p. 37), and death is specifically described as integral to the essence of tragedy and to the hero's development, for only then his or her "narcissistic fulfillment attains permanence" and absoluteness (p. 38). The tragic hero's death is, therefore, not incidental, Kohut maintains, but "the fulfillment of the destiny of an innermost self" (p. 41).

Yet, if this model is the ideal, where is the discussion of everyday men and women's psychological response to death? References to death are quite rare in Kohut's work, and the few that do exist focus on the heroic form of dying.[13] Instructive in this regard is the list of examples. These include the death of a member of the resistance against the Nazis, in whom "the ultimate state of narcissistic balance" with "inner peace" was achieved, along with "even the experience of conscious pleasure" in the unification of ones ideals and personality (1985a, p. 21). Other examples are those of the Christian martyrs, cases of death "*pour la patrie*" (1978 [1954], p. 184), and the fall of the Spartan

---

[12] Kohut's (1985b, p. 263) insistence that he did not suggest a link between psychological health and lack of fear of death is unconvincing. His attempt to add nuance only leads to reassertion of the idea of heroic death.

[13] Strozier (1999, p. 329) mentions the absence of a text about death in the Kohutian corpus. For him this is because Kohut's is a theory of beginnings, development, healing and possibilities, and therefore has no conceptual place for death. Although this seems correct, to neglect the fact that aspirations and developments encounter at least one unavoidable frustration and end in death is not justified by a focus on fulfillment. What Kohut does with death, making it yet another achievement of the fulfilled life, is precisely a result of the failure to take into account the negative aspect of death with regard to development and aspirations.

soldiers at Thermopylae, who in dying might have lost their lives, but not their selves (1985b, p. 263–4).[14]

Death, when examining Kohut's ideas, is actually not painful in itself: "If an individual succeeds in realizing the aims of his nuclear self, he can die without regret" (1985a, p. 49).[15]

Kohut's approach also displays the concretizing analytic tendency with regard to death anxiety. The most fearful dangers are not those that have to do with biological death, but rather "the destruction of the self through the withdrawal of selfobject support." "[I]t is not death that we fear, but the withdrawal of selfobject support in the last phase of our lives" (1991 [1980], p. 503; see also 1985b, p. 264). When selfobjects (very broadly speaking, Kohut's term for significant others experienced as part of the self) turn their backs on someone dying, she will suffer fear. This is reminiscent of Freud's description of death anxiety as a fear of being deserted by the superego, or his characterization of helplessness as a threat that comes from the absence of the object that could have satisfied one's drives.

Jung

> Naturally we have a stock of suitable banalities about life which we occasionally hand out to the other fellow, such as "everyone must die sometime," "you can't live forever," etc. But when one is alone and it is night and so dark and still that one hears nothing and sees nothing but the thoughts which add and subtract the years ... and the slow, irresistible approach of the wall of darkness which will eventually engulf everything I love, possess, wish for, hope for, and strive for, then all our profundities about life slink off to some undiscoverable hiding-place, and fear envelops the sleepless one like a smothering blanket. (Jung, 1960 [1934], p. 405)

This citation, where death and the fear of it are capitalized on, is taken from Jung's paper "The Soul and Death" (1960 [1934]), where he proposes a coherent view of death (a similar position is expressed in Jung, 1960 [1931], pp. 398–403, as well). Jung's natural attraction to the riddles of life, and his less mechanistic view of the person in comparison with Freud incline him to see death as important in the

---

[14] Even in these heroic forms of death, one wonders if death is so easily accepted. Take for example the doubt of the martyr over whether she is indeed sacrificing her life for the right cause.

[15] This is also implied, to a milder extent, in Wolf's (1983, pp. 541–2) self-psychological description of death anxiety as expressing fear not for one's life, but for the cohesion of the self.

psychological world. And yet his approach echoes problems and biases that were pointed out here concerning other analytic theories.

Jung's basic idea is that in a manner similar to life's ascent toward a goal in the first half of life, life's descent in the second half is also directed toward a goal, one's death. He pursues the comparison further: just as we can sometimes see a tendency among young people to refuse the normal direction of life, by clinging in thought or behavior to childhood, so we can see among ageing adults a tendency to refuse the direction of life and cling to their youthful habits. Both are equally neurotic (1960 [1934], pp. 405–7). While it seems that Jung is preaching against denial of death, in fact he goes all the way in the other direction and wants the acceptance of death to be fully "rational" and devoid of fear. Thus, Jung's insights, seeming to come from a criticism of the tendency to ignore death and eliminate it from life, for example the observation that we sometimes falsely believe that "one's time of life is a mere illusion which can be altered according to one's desire" (p. 408), themselves push death out of life. In denouncing, on "rationalistic" grounds, the fear of death, they dismiss death's place in life. We meet in Jung a clear tendency to pathologize the fear of death, which he calls an "infantile resistance against the normal demands of life" (p. 405). Jung is almost condemning the old person occupied with her past for refusing the arrow-like flow of time (p. 407).

Jung's approach to death is teleological, more so than Freud's concept of the death instinct (to which Jung's approach bears surprising resemblance in certain aspects). Death is not just the meaningless end of life for him, but is its goal. Although on the one hand such a view emphasizes death and stands in contrast to views that simply dismiss it, the opposite problem becomes manifest: for when death is so imbued with teleological meaning, a refusal to recognize its meaninglessness is implied. The idea that death is what life aspires to denies death its pointless, incomprehensible, and unjustifiable nature, which lies at the heart of our misery. This problem manifests in several additional ways in Jung's approach.

As with Erikson, Jung's thoughts are another expression of the restriction of the fear of death to the old, which is actually a way of denying its presence. This leads to the manifestation of another death-belittling tendency (explored above), namely treating life as a unit with a necessary orbit (life's curve is like a parabola, Jung explains), which arrives at its conclusion only at the end, that is, only after it has traveled its full, preset path. Life ends only at the end, and death is stripped of its continual imminence. The vision of a life cycle becomes almost a guarantee of its completion.

On yet another level one could also say that Jung, who seems to embrace the religious view that the soul survives the body's demise, actually manifests a much more blatant form of denial of death. More interesting, however, is the implication that this idea has for Jung's view of death, as it relates to the living. Jung speaks of death as a goal, but this goal turns out to be more and more related to the life beyond rather than to earthly life in the here and now. He speaks of death as a goal, as the teleological end of life, yet it is not *in life* that that goal has meaning according to him, but outside it.

To sum up, Jung's position, although it apparently stresses death's importance and the necessity of ascribing it a place in our thoughts, expunges death from life.

Winnicott

Some may say that the problem with the analytic approach to death is linked to its original focus on neurosis, whereas now, with the evolving stress in analytic thought on narcissistic and borderline situations and psychotic phenomena, attention is on earlier, more abstract, vague, and total forms of anxiety. These, it might be claimed, bring us closer to an apprehension of life, to a more fundamental fragility, and so death receives its place in analytic theory.

There is some truth in this suggestion, in that these anxieties hint at a very basic level of insecurity. On the other hand, neurotic cases, such as obsession, often explicitly express concern about death, so it is not clear that the issue of death is more closely related to borderline and psychotic manifestations. Either way, the attention to such anxieties has not significantly altered the way psychoanalysis deals with death. Among other things, a generalized anxiety about vulnerability is linked to the fear of death, but the idea of death itself is not part of it. This can be seen if we look, for example, at one of these attempts to characterize the more fundamental, less developed anxieties: Winnicott's (1974) concept of the fear of breakdown.

What one is afraid of in what Winnicott (1974) calls the fear of breakdown is "the unthinkable state of affairs that underlies the defence organization" or "a breakdown of the establishment of the unit self" (p. 103). His main claim is that the fear of breakdown is a fear of something that has already occurred. The breakdown took place, but was not experienced as such and is, therefore, expected in the future (p. 105).

Dealing with the fear of death in the context of the fear of breakdown is a natural step that Winnicott himself takes, as it requires "little alteration" (1974, p. 106). The death feared is "the death that happened but was not experienced," because the patient was not mature enough (p. 106).

While Winnicott surely captures here something of experience and psychopathology, his description fails to adequately account for the fear of death for two reasons. First, Winnicott refers only to a metaphoric death, and does not account for death as a real event, which necessarily and inevitably takes place, and is neither merely metaphoric nor intrapsychic.[16]

This leads to the second problem, namely that Winnicott's description actually replicates, albeit from a different perspective, the analytic tendency to explain the fear of death in terms of the past. Not only is the anxiety reduced to an earlier one, as is usually the case, but the event feared is itself transformed into a past event. Lamentable as it might be, however, in actuality death is a future event, one that has yet to take place. So Winnicott's account might explain something, but certainly not death. I find this recurrence of the same tendencies and shortcomings within such divergent views puzzling. Again and again, we encounter the notion that only what has happened in the past is capable of having psychic influence.

The problem is also evident in Christian David's (1996) attempt to apply Winnicott's explanation to the fear of death. Sensitive as David is to death, his use of Winnicott is problematic. He applies the fear of breakdown to the fear of death in asserting that whereas in breakdown the event is a past event, in death it is a future one. This argument is fine, but what is left then of Winnicott's explanation? What is actually "applied"? The explanation is overturned, but nothing remains; all he had to say was that what was feared had already taken place. David is simply restating the fact that death is feared, without adding a theoretical explanation. Providing an analytic explanation of death, as we see once again, is not easy.

Part of the importance of examining the ideas of Winnicott and Kohut on death consists in their being representatives of an approach that is different from the classic psychoanalytic one regarding the source of difficulties, putting stress less on instincts and more on environmental failures. Such theories perhaps have the potential to deal better with the importance of death, and yet, as we have observed, their approach to death and death anxiety suffers from old and new problems and limitations, and does not overcome the analytic difficulty which death presents.

---

[16] Winnicott says elsewhere that annihilation anxiety is "a very real primitive anxiety" that appears long before death anxiety (1956, p. 303). There is no reason to dispute this view as a chronological ordering. Winnicott (1974), however, speaks directly about death, and his description that might have suited annihilation anxiety simply cannot account for death.

11 Lacan

Of all the analytic thinkers, Lacan's attempts to conceptualize death and its psychic influence are probably the richest. His seminars and articles abound with references to death. At times, he is very explicit, as for example in his analysis of the centrality of death in Freud's (1901, pp. 2–6) well-known *Signorelli* parapraxis in *The Psychopathology of Everyday Life* (Lacan, 1966, p. 379; 1975, pp. 56–9. See also Borch-Jacobsen's analysis, 1991, pp. 98–104),[1] or in saying, when commenting on Hegel, that "The human subject is nothingness, in effect, before ... death" (1966, p. 121; 1977a, p. 26). Lacan explicitly mentions encountering the reality of death as a goal of analysis: the end of analysis should confront the analysand with the human condition, with his or her helplessness faced by death (1986, p. 351; 1992, pp. 303–4. see also 1978, p. 312; 1988b, 268–9).

For many Lacanians and authors who write about Lacan, the centrality of death for the Lacanian enterprise is almost taken for granted. Bowie (1991) for example sees Lacan's theory as an attempt to "write transience back into the psychoanalytic account of the human mind" (pp. 9–10). The subject has been most extensively explored in a work by Borch-Jacobsen (1991), to which the reader is referred for more ample discussions. Here I shall explore only briefly some key points in Lacan's treatment of death.[2]

---

[1] I have included, when available, references to both the French and the English texts of Lacan.
[2] Another fine review of this topic, especially concerning the death drive, is in Weatherill (1998, pp. 73–103).

There has also been a line of critique questioning whether placing death as the central motive in Lacan's theory is justified. Barzilai (1995) for example contests that kind of interpretation, and finds that Borch-Jacobsen's book largely overemphasizes death: "From chapter to chapter [in Borch-Jacobsen's work] a unitary view becomes evident. Everything gradually converges on the negation of the subject. In effect, all of Lacan's teachings undergo a radical process of homogenization. Death is the God-term presiding over this enterprise" (p. 91). Borch-Jacobsen, says Barzilai, turns the *Écrits* into a "demotic, latter-day version of the *Book of the Dead*" (p. 92).

I shall also, however, acknowledge a gap, a very Lacanian gap, between the signifier and the signified—death—repeatedly sliding under it, and question the degree to which Lacan centralizes human temporal finitude. Lacan's "death" both brings death to the fore and pushes death aside, makes this absence present, and simultaneously renders it absent. Overall, alongside and within Lacan's creditable theoretical attention to death, he is far from having resolved the problem in analytic thinking about death.

The symbolic, the imaginary, and the real

Lacan's theory delineates three orders in reality and psychic life: the symbolic, the imaginary, and the real. In all three, death can be said to be central.

The symbolic

The symbolic order is Lacan's term for the overall influence of language, on the one hand, and social law and prohibition, on the other, which he binds together (1966, pp. 272–9; 1977a, pp. 61–8), following Lévi-Strauss's work on structural anthropology. The symbolic precedes and goes beyond individual existence. We are born into it, and die into it. The symbolic function intervenes in every detail of human existence (1978, pp. 41–2; 1988b, p. 29)

The symbolic is founded on the play between presence and absence, between being and non-being (Lacan, 1978, pp. 51, 354, 367; 1988b, pp. 38, 308, 319). In the symbolic process, non-being comes into being through speaking (1978, p. 354; 1988b, p. 308). The word is the absence of the thing, Lacan says. He does not settle for some abstract absence though. There is a link, he insists, between speech, in the overarching meaning he gives to it, and death, and this, he informs his students, is the crowning point in his seminar (1978, p. 241; 1988b, p. 206). In every speech uttered there is death.

Every use of symbolic language has a deadly element in it. Being is lost in favor of meaning. With language, one can speak about things while they are absent, manipulate them, multiply them, and give them permanence. But there is a price in that it is not the thing but its name that is left in our hand. Therefore, Lacan contends, paraphrasing Hegel, that the symbol is "the murder of the thing" (Lacan, 1966, p. 319; 1977a, p. 104). One can ask whether it is really justifiable to define the symbolic act as murder or death. Yes it is, Maurice Blanchot

(1995 [1949]) argues, in a text having the same general spirit.[3] "Of course," he says,

> my language does not kill anyone. And yet, when I say, 'This woman,' real death has been announced ... ; my language means that this person, who is here right now, can be detached from herself, removed from her existence and her presence" (p. 323). "For me to be able to say 'This woman,' I must somehow take her flesh-and-blood reality away from her, cause her to be absent, annihilate her. (p. 322)

This annihilating element of language applies to the self as well. The speaking subject is already alienated from herself in the very fact that she speaks. Lacan's (1973, pp. 127–8; 1977b, pp. 138–40) use of the known distinction between the I of the statement and the I of the enunciation (*je de l'énoncé, je de l'énonciation*) is pertinent here. The subject signified in language is not the one that utters speech. But the subject only exists in language, so this loss is inevitable.

Again, in the words of Blanchot (1995 [1949]): "Clearly, in me, the power to speak is also linked to my absence from being. I say my name, and it is as though I were chanting my own dirge: I separate myself from myself," and (Blanchot's metaphors growing increasingly morbid) become "an objective, impersonal presence, the presence of my name," which is equivalent to "a tombstone weighing on the void" (p. 324).

Something of the subject's being is continuously cut off, eliminated, and this is inevitable. While language is the only means of expressing, or creating subjectivity, it is also what makes this subjectivity inherently cut down, absent: "I identify myself in language, but only by losing myself in it like an object" (Lacan, 1966, pp. 299–300; 1977a, p. 86). The subject "loses his meaning in the objectification of discourse," and this is a source of his "most profound alienation" in modern civilization (1966, p. 281; 1977a, p. 70). Language belongs to others, to everyone, and in fact to no one, and because subjectivity is constituted in it, the individual lives in a profound alienation.

Nothingness is internal to the speaking subject. Lacan speaks of a decenteredness of the subject with regard to the ego. This decenteredness does not suggest exactly the same, familiar kind of subjectivity, simply elsewhere, unknown to us like a small homunculus that is controlling us just outside consciousness. That would be an attempt to save

---

[3] I am indebted to Borch-Jacobsen (1991, pp. 169–170, 194) for the idea of commenting on Lacan through Blanchot's (1995 [1949]) at times much clearer text (although unfortunately at other times just as laborious and baroque as Lacan's). Both Blanchot and Lacan are actually interpreting Hegel, and both do so following Kojève's reading of him.

our usual conceptions of the subject (1966, pp. 523–4; 1977a; p. 171). Instead, Lacan, through binding together subjectivity and the symbolic order, subjectivity and the Other (the dispersed, anonymous, non-personalized other), makes subjectivity itself a non-centered kind of emptiness, a nothing.

For Lacan, under the action of the signifier, the subject is "injected with a sense of death. And this is poisoning rather than inoculation. The taste of death is not something that the subject acquires through experience, ... for it has been there from the start as a perilous gift from the signifier" (Bowie, 1991, pp. 162–3). Death is there from the beginning.

The imaginary

Let us move into the realm of the imaginary, Lacan's order denoting any form of dual relationship, the involvement of image, and the fundamental experience of the creation of the ego. In his theory of the mirror stage, Lacan (1966, pp. 93–100; 1977a, pp. 1–7) describes how the human baby, upon encountering his image in the mirror, identifies himself with that image. The result is that he takes on an identity prematurely. While he is still lacking any coherence, motor control or body image, he now comes to own a self-identity without really being ready for it. The newly formed identity—the ego—will, therefore, be alienated from himself, "the armour of an alienating identity" (1966, p. 97; 1977a, p. 4). This process, which is the model for any future identification, transforms the ego formed in it into an empty, deceiving entity. Hence, the human subject becomes something always lacking.

Lacan directly asserts that the identification with the image is death, because it implies lack of change (1978, p. 278; 1988b, p. 238). The ego is the closest and most accessible manifestation of death in the subject's life (1978, p. 245; 1988b, p. 210). Something of the individual's being and nature was left out when the image was taken on as a new outfit.

From another angle, the imaginary identification is interpreted as a calming barrier against death. Ragland-Sullivan (1986) believes that for Lacan, "identity is taken on in a triumph over death cum fragmentation" (p. 111), because the infant's initial fragmentation is linked to a "metaphorical" death or "chasm in being." One place in Lacan that Ragland-Sullivan could use to support her claim is Lacan's (1966, pp. 186–7) belief that death is experienced in the primary misery of the newborn (to be mentioned below). Bowie (1991, p. 100) suggests that focusing in analytic work on the imaginary might lead to a false belief in immortality, while focusing on the symbolic would emphasize mortality, because of the death inherent to the symbolic.

Many of the references to death in Lacan's writings actually refer to obsession (1975, p. 315; 1988a, pp. 286-7, 1978, pp. 253, 311-2; 1988b, pp. 217, 268-9, 1966, pp. 314, 452-3; 1977a, p. 99). In referring to Hegel's master and slave dialectics, Lacan says that the obsessive places the master between herself and the absolute master—death. Waiting for the master's death separates her from her own (1975, p. 315; 1988a, pp. 286-7).

Thus, both in terms of the existence of the subject in language and the construction of the ego through the imaginary, one could say that there is an element of death, non-being or alienation in the subject's life. Lacan's work has uncovered these aspects of lack and alienation inherent to human life. The question remains, however, to what extent are these contributions relevant to the question of death. While I would not go so far as to claim that death is only a metaphor in them, I do believe that these Lacanian ideas regarding fundamental aspects of finitude and alienation, this limitedness inside, are not entirely germane to the question of the subject's existence in time. Associated with the subject's temporal finitude, they are still different. They do not refer to the event of dying, or to the terror it can inflict, to the necessity of that event, or to its anticipation. They do not refer to existence in time. In some sense, therefore, they are not about death or temporal finitude.

Yet there is a conflation, in Lacan's teaching, in Lacanian circles, and in texts referring to Lacan, of these conditions and the issue of death and they are many times referred to as identical. The differences are ignored or forgotten, and effects of the symbolic and of the ego's construction in the imaginary are taken to be theoretical references to death and to the person's existence in time.

An example will demonstrate. Perhaps the most explicit reference to death as a psychic explaining factor is in his paper "The Neurotic's Individual Myth" (1979), an analysis of the Rat Man where Lacan states, as if declaring a new paradigm for analytic understanding, that the triangular Oedipal constellation is not enough, and that "there is within the neurotic a quartet situation" (pp. 415-6, 420). "What is this forth element?," he asks. "Its name is death" (p. 424).

What does Lacan mean by this? (Isn't this the familiar million dollar question with Lacan?) Because of the ego's imaginary construction in the mirror stage, the premature assumption by the subject of an image, in other words because the ego is first experienced as external and, therefore, as a locus of self-alienation, the subject is "throw[n] back onto the level of a profound insufficiency" and "a rift ... a primal sundering, a thrownness, to use the Heideggerian term," is first created in him. "It is in this sense," Lacan says, "that what is revealed in all imaginary relationships is an experience of death" (1979, pp. 423–4).

Lacan's rift, however, is void. In the text, the imaginary construction of the ego does not seem to "support" or "substantiate" Lacan's declaration concerning the significance of death, which exceeds it in tone. There is narcissistic relation, there is insufficiency, alienation; but there is no death. Lacan seems to sense this himself, and adds, through reference to Hegel's dialectics of master and slave, the idea of the threat of death as a mediator of all human relationships (p. 425). But there too it turns out that he actually means the imaginary influence of death. Moreover, the way he presents this explanation does not seem to be integral to the paper. It seems to be an artificial addition.

The somewhat strange history of the publication of this text is perhaps no less significant for understanding Lacan's approach to death than its contents. The paper is originally a lecture given in 1953. It did not appear in print, and unofficial versions of it circulated in Paris. It was not included in Lacan's collection of papers, the *Ecrits* (1966), and neither did it appear in *Autres Ecrits*, the recent collection (2001) of Lacan's papers not published in 1966. A comment in the *Ecrits* (Lacan, 1966, p. 72n) promised a revision and publication of the text, which were not, however, carried out. When translated into English, Jacques-Alain Miller, the editor of Lacan's writings, felt he "ought to emphasize" that the text, "which is more than twenty-five years old," should only "be regarded as the rudiments of later developments," not much more than "first trials" (Lacan, 1979, p. 405).[4] Thus, on the one hand, we have a manifesto for the inclusion of death in psychoanalysis, and on the other, a text both neglected by its author and actively removed from the corpus, covered with apologies and warnings not to take it seriously.

This duality is characteristic of Lacan's references to death: an acknowledgment of and focus on death, accompanied by some diminution and altering of its significance.

The real

Lacan's third order is that of the real, which, broadly speaking denotes reality, both psychic and external, when not mediated by the symbolic. The real is another notion where death is sometimes seen as central to Lacan's thought. One of the earliest, most elaborate, and

---

[4] The text was printed in the French journal *Ornicar?*, Vol. 17–18, in 1978.

most cited references to the real is in Lacan's interpretation of the dream of Irma's injection, that we have already encountered in Chapter 3. Freud's gaze into Irma's throat is for Lacan (1978, pp. 186, 196; 1988b, pp. 154–5, 164) an encounter with the real. The anxiety-provoking image condenses essentially three aspects that together comprise the real: the female sexual organ, the flesh in its non-human existence, and death. The first element is related of course to femininity but also to the origin of life, the origin of the world, as in Courbet's famous painting by that name, which belonged to Lacan personally, depicting a photo-like close up of the female organ. The second is what Lacan calls "the flesh one never sees," "the other side of the head," "the flesh in as much as it is suffering" (1978, p. 186; 1988b, p. 154). I believe Lacan refers here to a level of human existence that is found below the symbolic level, that precedes our view of ourselves as subjects. It is flesh as something that is beyond our grasp of it, but is what we are, and we suffer when it suffers. The third element, death, speaks for itself. Thus, in fact, all three elements are aspects of our condition of mortality, of being subject to death. It is the source, the substance from which we were created as thinking subjects—our bodily existence—and our finitude.

Still, I believe the centrality of death to the concept of the real has been somewhat exaggerated. The Irma passage is an exception to Lacan's references to the real which in general denote that which cannot be denoted, which is impossible to be taken in by the net of signifiers. While death clearly belongs to that category, and in a later chapter I will elaborate on death's resistance to understanding and symbolization as a central factor in our approach to it, Lacan does not often mention death with regard to the real. More then than being a notion occupied with death, the real supplies us with a possible structural scheme for conceptualizing it.[5]

Let us move on to three domains in Lacan's thought: the death drive, desire, and *das Ding*, each related respectively to the three orders: the symbolic, the imaginary, and the real, where death has some relevance.

---

[5] Because the real is, by definition, outside the scope of the symbolic, resistant to symbolization, Lacan refers to it as the incarnation of impossibility. It is also what gives the real a traumatic quality (Evans, 1996, p. 160). But again, this traumatic quality is not death. It is also noteworthy that for Lacan, it is specifically the real – in contrast to the symbolic, which is characterized by games of presence and absence (Evans, 1996, p. 159) – that does not comprise any absence (Lacan, 1978, p. 359; 1988b, p. 313), and is characterized by brute presence, always coming back to the same place (1973, p. 49; 1977b, p. 49). The gap, the hole, is in the symbolic, not in the real.

Tragic paths and the death drive

Lacan is one of the only theoreticians to have adopted the Freudian concept of the death drive, but as in Freud and Klein, the death drive in Lacan is not really about death. For Lacan, Freud was obliged to introduce this concept to renovate essential aspects of his discovery that were being forgotten or flattened out, namely that in man "a profound perturbation of the regulation of life" occurs (1978, pp. 50–51; 1988b, p. 37). The need for repetition, which forms part of Freud's concept, is not related to biological regulation mechanisms and the need for equilibrium but is bound up with the function of language, the introduction of the symbol (1978, pp. 110, 113, 241; 1988b, pp. 88, 90, 206). The individual is transcended by something external and ex-centric (1978, pp. 142–3; 1988b, pp. 115–16). Within the symbolic, "Life is only caught up ... piece-meal, decomposed. The human being himself is in part outside life, he partakes of the death instinct" (1978, p. 113; 1988b, p. 90). In the final account, Lacan identifies the death drive with the symbolic (1978, p. 375; 1988b, p. 326).

Thus, while Lacan declares that Freud's death drive is to be understood as expressing the limit of the subject's historicity—that is, death—and insists that death be understood in the Heideggerian sense as that "possibility which is one's ownmost, unconditional ... , certain and as such indeterminable" (1966, p. 318; 1977a, p. 103),[6] he actually equates the death drive with the work of the symbolic. As a consequence, the death involved becomes the loss of being that the latter generates (1966, pp. 318–19; 1977a, pp. 103–4).

Lacan also elaborates on Freud's inquiry, in *Beyond the Pleasure Principle*, into the possible immortality of unicellular organisms. In fact, Lacan notes, death is the price of sexualization (1973, pp. 186–7; 1977b, pp. 204–5). Every drive is, therefore, a death drive in that it embodies death (1973, pp. 181, 186–7; 1977b, pp. 199, 204–5).

The death drive figures centrally in Lacan's interpretation of the myth of Oedipus. Oedipus' fate exemplifies for him that "the final word of the relation of man to this discourse of which he is ignorant, is death" (1978, p. 245; 1988b, pp. 209–10). He suggests that to fully appreciate the significance of this myth to psychoanalysis, one should study *Oedipus the King* together with *Oedipus at Colonus* (1978, pp. 245, 271; 1988b, pp. 209–10, 232). Oedipus there "lives a life which is dead" (1978, p. 271; 1988b, p. 232). Two key sections at the end of

---

[6] Lacan's proximity with Heidegger on that issue and some others is explored by Boothby (1991, pp. 203–14).

the tragedy attract Lacan's attention. The first is Oedipus' bitter phrase, upon learning that the people of Thebes were told he must be brought back, forgiven, and redeemed: "Am I made man in the hour when I cease to be?" (1978, p. 268; 1988b, p. 229). The second is the closing lines of the tragedy, when the choir announces the moral that it is better to die immediately, or, better still, never to have been born at all (1978, p. 269; 1988b, p. 230). What is Lacan trying to say here? If the usual interpretation of Oedipus in the analytic system locates him within an enclosed system of drives and libidinal forces, a fuller understanding of the Oedipal myth will have to include death as that which transcends this system. It will have to include death as a final goal that life is bound up with. Oedipus exemplifies Freud's death drive. Life wants to die (Lacan, 1978, p. 272; 1988b, p. 233).

Lacan sees death as the essence of tragedy. In his remarks on the tragedy of Antigone, Oedipus' daughter, Lacan does not tire in stressing how death is bound up with Antigone's life. He sees Antigone as the personification of the death drive, aspiring toward death (1986, p. 327; 1992, p. 281). He also sees her, however, as already dead in a way. For him Antigone epitomizes death's encroachment on life (1986, pp. 291, 326–7, 331; 1992, pp. 248, 280–1, 285). In her quest for a proper burial for her brother she has already traversed the line separating life from death. Her certain death manifests itself while she is still alive. Lacan develops the notions of "the second death" and the "between two deaths" ("*l'entre deux morts*") to account for her situation. The second death, a term he develops following Sade, would be a kind of death after death, the end of suffering after death (1986, p. 341; 1992, p. 295), complete decomposition of the body (2001, p. 122). Being already dead, Antigone is found between the two deaths.

The nature of desire

Desire, in its deepest essence, is, according to Lacan (1978, p. 246; 1988b, p. 211), desire for nothing. When met in a concrete form, in a dream for example, it should not be reduced to a kind of drive. We have only manifestations and elaborations of desire, as in a dream, but never desire itself. Desire is never named: behind everything named in the dream, there is the unnameable, and this unnameable, Lacan says, is akin to death (1978, p. 247; 1988b, pp. 211–12). "It is ... as a desire for death that [the subject] affirms himself for others" (1966, p. 320; 1977a, p. 105). If desire is the heart of the analytic enterprise, it could be said then that death figures centrally in Lacan's view of psychoanalysis.

Borch-Jacobsen (1991, pp. 1–19, 84–96, 198–239) addresses the question of how desire, if it is for nothing, can be experienced or satisfied. Lacan adopts Hegel's view of desire, with which he had become familiar in Kojève's (1947) interpretation, as pure negation. Desire is a negating capability. As such, satisfaction is, strictly speaking, impossible. In the Kojèvian-Hegelian system, desire's only object is another desire. It will not be satisfied with any element in nature. The other's desire is itself not part of a given reality, and as such could potentially offer some satisfaction. What Lacan takes from this system, according to Borch-Jacobsen, is desire's fundamental "non-identity to itself" (1991, pp. 91–2). As such, it cannot be satisfied by the other's desire, and its only satisfaction would be to "plunge into nothingness, to die" (*ibid.*). For Borch-Jacobsen, the engagement in the imaginary struggle, although it results in a form of death in the identification with the other, is a means to avoid the real satisfaction of desire, in death, and the confrontation with the abyss of one's own desire as desire to death (pp. 92–7). Oedipus itself, Borch-Jacobsen interprets, is but a defense.

One needs to make the distinction between desire as lack or desire for nothing, and desire for death, two meanings I find confounded in Lacan. What, it should be asked, is the meaning of desire for nothing? What is behind the easy formulations whereby death is behind everything? Does Lacan mean the structure of desire as negation? Does he mean wanting nothing? Aspiring to death? Sometimes what he has in mind is a nothingness which serves as a background to everything. He speaks, for example, of desire as "a relation of being to lack. This lack is the lack of being" (1978, p. 261; 1988b, p. 223). At other times, however, he also refers directly to a desire for death, in the simplest sense of the term, such as when commenting on Freud's *Beyond the Pleasure Principle*: "Life is ... characterized ... by nothing beyond its aptitude for death" (1978, p. 271; 1988b, p. 232). "This life we're captive of, this essentially alienated life ... , this life in the other, is as such joined to death" (1978, p. 272; 1988b, p. 233). Lacan sees this as a radical claim, which stands in contrast to what may seem to characterize Freud's theory, namely that everything, death included, is accounted for in libidinal economics. It is, therefore, beyond the pleasure principle. As claimed earlier in this work, this "beyond" has no real beyond in it. Death remains outside the system and is not brought into it. Aspiration to death, which remains part of the libidinal account, leaves out exactly what, in death, is fundamentally outside the regular business of life.

Again, however, Lacan does not easily fall into the trap, and attempts to correct Freud in his interpretation, claiming that this aspiration to death is symbolic rather that organic. What leads Freud to think that there is something beyond the pleasure principle is not the death of people, but human lived experience, as it occurs under the rule of the symbolic order (Lacan, 1978, p. 103; 1988b, p. 80). Here, however, we again reach the point that death under the symbolic is indeed not death.

Das Ding

We meet the same dynamics according to which behind everything named lurks the unnamable, in Lacan's concept of *das Ding*. This concept, which Lacan borrows from Heidegger, is elaborated upon in his seminar on the ethics of psychoanalysis (1986; 1992). It is subsequently abandoned, and in part integrated into the concept of *object petit a*.

Das Ding, "the thing" in German, is for Lacan the thing in as much as it is not related to human perception or thought. Lacan uses it to denote a fundamental level of reality that precedes its incorporation in our mind. In the mind, order and representations preside, but they are built around something that is not there, that is left out (1986, p. 65; 1992, p. 52). The laws of pleasure and unpleasure are secondary and apply to what is already present in the mind, but they are not the more fundamental level, which lies outside them and originally guides the subject's orientation. *Das Ding* remains alien to us, external, even hostile. It is toward it that we actually aspire and around which "[t]he whole progress of the subject is ... oriented" (*ibid.*).

Psychic organization begins, both logically and chronologically, with *das Ding*, and it is around it, around this foreign element, that the entire movement of representations turns and gravitates and in relation to it that our mental world is constructed (Lacan, 1986, p. 72; 1992, p. 57). From this center of gravitation psychic life always keeps a distance, which Lacan (1986, p. 84; 1992, p. 69) suggests, is the condition of speech.

Das Ding is our absolute other; it is the object we look for, but one that is by definition lost to begin with (Lacan, 1986, p. 65; 1992, p. 52). Instead, we find all the other objects that constitute our mental or psychic world, objects with attributes and names, which we can manipulate. Lacan (1986, p. 72; 1992, p. 58) links *das Ding* to Freud's idea in "On Negation" (1925) that the finding of the object is the refinding of it, and identifies it with the original lost object.

I have elaborated on *das Ding* because although in itself it does not have a great deal to do with death, it gives us a structural account that may be applied—as I shall try to do later—to the manner in which death interacts with psychic life.

Although at one point Lacan marginally mentions death in connection with *das Ding* (1986, p. 69; 1992, p. 57), death is not part of the concept, and two elements in Lacan's description incline it in other directions. First, Lacan (1986, p. 82; 1992, p. 67) at a certain point identifies *das Ding* with the mother, the original object of desire, banned by the universal law against incest. He then goes on to explain this universal law in a way that belittles the mother's importance in favor of the structural scheme he describes: the reason for this law is that without it, there will be no world of demand, and no unconscious life (1986, p. 83; 1992, p. 67). There will be a kind of short-circuiting if what is wanted is simply attained. It will render psychic life superfluous. Second, Lacan's idea of *das Ding* is that of a searching orientation, and more specifically, an active desiring orientation of the subject. I believe the concept is more useful at an epistemic level rather than applied to desire.[7] It can be useful in understanding death precisely as a kind of absence around which presences—representations in our psychic world—circulate, but that is itself not one of them: an unrepresented place, something abyssal that lies beyond.

The concrete fear of death

While Lacan recognizes finitude as a central theme, he explicitly argues against death's direct influence on us. In Lacan's view, the human world is a symbolic world, and everything human is mediated by the signifier. Now, while one would be tempted to cite fear of death as an exception, it is exactly this feeling that Lacan uses to support his claim of the ubiquity of the signifier. There is, he suggests, based on Hegel, no fear of death that is not symbolic (1975, p. 248; 1988a, pp. 223). There is nothing biological, natural or "real" about the fear of death, no effect of death that is the result of a direct encounter. Man has access, says Lacan (1986, pp. 341–2; 1992, p. 295), to the knowledge of death precisely because we are speaking subjects. As such, we become acquainted, through the use of language, with the possibility of our own demise. Now, while Lacan must assume this position to justify his claim regarding the totality of the symbolic in mediating experience, such a claim fails to appreciate the possible influence of death, the same

---

[7] For Lacan, it is neither death nor not knowing that moves everything, but the active force in a wish. "[D]esire ... is what keeps the chain of signifiers moving" (Bowie, 1991, p. 122). It is true, however, that more than is the case for other analysts, this force in Lacan is related to lack, to a fundamental incapacity to satisfy itself, and is always directed towards something that transcends what can be attained.

220 Lacan

influence that forms the basis for the lack that our symbolic existence creates, and was supposed to account for why we are fundamentally lacking. We are finite but this finiteness in itself has no direct influence on us.

Elsewhere, Lacan contends that the fear of death is "psychologically subordinate to a narcissistic fear of damage to one's own body" (1966, p. 123; 1977a, p. 28). He then suggests, in yet another text, that death, before it becomes the content of thought, is felt, experienced in the primary misery of the newborn, in the trauma of birth, in the first months (before the mirror stage), characterized by physiological prematurity, and later, in what he calls the trauma of weaning. All these are but the first in the series of separations and renunciations throughout the subject's psychic life (1966, pp. 186–7). Lacan actually here joins those authors who explain death through death equivalents. This kind of explanation entails several problems, as was explained briefly above and will be more thoroughly examined in the next chapter, and has a strong reductionistic element.

Conclusion: Talking about death

There is little doubt that among the central figures in the history of psychoanalysis, Lacan is the most acutely aware and theoretically sensitive to death. But his focus on the consequences for the human subject of living with language mitigates this concentration on death. The subject is lacking in two central respects: one is that existence is finite, and the other is that, upon entry to the symbolic order, there is a loss of being. While Lacan sees the former as the deeper cause of the latter, it is to the latter that his theoretical interest is turned, and which he sees as a fundamental human problem.

Beyond the question of focus, Lacan's much too swift oscillation between these senses is itself a problem. The mixing together of these two separate elements—time and erasure through language—gives a false impression that death is really at the center. In reality, it is only sometimes so, and many times what is actually referred to is other forms of lack.[8]

Moreover, because of this mixing between the two kinds of lack, instead of finitude's influence accounting for the cut on entry to the symbolic, it becomes the other way around. The notion of lack, fundamental for Lacan's ideas, be it those of the mirror stage, of the nature of

---

[8] To appreciate this, consider a case where death is an explicit problem. If a patient in psychoanalytic treatment suffers from fear of death, should a Lacanian analyst work with the lack implied by the symbolic order?

desire or of the symbolic world, becomes itself the center, and the original lack, the fundamental lack in human existence, even according to Lacan himself—death, finitude—is relegated to the background.

The overall impression one sometimes gets is that reference to death is so abundant in Lacan that when it is cast into discourse, it actually carries too little meaning. Many utterances include some reference to death, but seem too remote from it, almost empty. Nearly every element in Lacan's theory, we saw, is assumed to include aspects of mortality: the symbolic, the imaginary, the real, desire, das Ding, the death drive, the goal of analysis all have something to do with death.[9] The disturbing sense of a certain arbitrariness in assigning "death" to concepts is reinforced when we see, for example, that the imaginary's link to death is understood in two contradictory ways: both the assumption of the static image and the chaos that precedes it are taken to be forms of death. Mainly we see a lot of confusion; a discourse suffused with death-talk but almost as if death was an all-encompassing magical word brought to seal an uncovered hole in Lacan's own teaching.

It can seem that in Lacanian discourse the importance of death is an established fact. Moreover, this is taken to be something that belongs in advance to Freud's thought, and comprises an inherent part of psychoanalysis. Herein lies a problem, I think, because there is no direct engagement with the Freudian texts, or with other analytic texts concerning the issue of death, for example, the arguments against the primacy of death. What is lacking is an analysis of the problem of death in psychoanalysis. While Lacan has established a tradition of return to the Freudian texts, curiously this is not implemented in the case of death. The result is that Lacanians may easily claim that death is a central preoccupation of psychoanalysis, and yet they do not attempt to address the gap between their school and other schools, including Freud's thought. They even seem unaware of the existence of such a gap.

The intermingling of his references to death with those to the symbolic and the imaginary makes it difficult to extract discrete, independent positions and ideas about death from Lacan's system. You either take the whole system, insights on death included, or leave it. Given the slight diffusion of ideas from Lacanian circles to the wider public of analysts, Lacan's interest in death cannot be readily exported to the general analytic world.

---

[9] Ragland-Sullivan also applies death to the unconscious: "since the unconscious is a gap, a hole, a negation, it resembles metaphorical death" (1986, p. 296); here she is to my mind using the word death too loosely.

12   Attempts at reconciliation

Our overview of analytic thinking about death will not be complete without a brief look at some valuable contributions by more existentially oriented thinkers, some within psychoanalysis, some in close dialog with it. These contributions, by writers who are more aware of the problem of death, could perhaps help supply the framework for including death within psychoanalysis.

Rank and Becker

Otto Rank criticizes Freud for privileging wishes over fears as the crucial concern for man, and claims that the ideology behind Freud's explanations is "that man is purely instinctual and that fear is brought in from the outside," in the threat of castration (1950 [1945], p. 122).[1] He proposes an alternative view stressing fear as integral to the human being, and claims that there is an "inner fear" that "exists independently of outside threats" (*ibid.*). This inner fear later attaches itself to experiences of the outside, but this is already a means to counter the fear, because external experiences are more locatable and partial than the fear that began inside.

Rank's unlocatable fear pervades the life of the individual and has no specific object: it is a general fear of life. Fear of death appears only later, is opposed to it, and turns out actually to be dislocated from death itself. Rank's position of a generalized fear of everything, which is by the same token fear of nothing, thus paradoxically belongs precisely to those approaches that displace fear of death to other fears.

Rank's ideas gain interest in the more complex and elaborate interpretation they receive in Ernest Becker's magnum opus, *The Denial of*

---

[1] Rank does not acknowledge that it is precisely the instinctual nature of man which renders death internal, and thereby cancels it as a threat from outside, as we saw in our discussions of the death drive and Klein.

Death (1973), perhaps the single most important and influential contribution to the psychological discussion of death.

Fear of death is for Becker a primary human motivation. Virtually everything we do comprises a means of coping with it. The world, in Becker's view, is a truly dangerous, overwhelming, and frightening place to be. What helps us get along is a basic sense of narcissistic vitality, and especially the ready-made ways our culture schools us in. We deal with the world by cutting out a section of it for ourselves, and living in it (1973, p. 22–3).

What is most problematic for the human being, according to Becker, is our dual nature as both an animal and a symbolic self. We are creators of symbolic worlds, but cannot escape constant reminders of our natural essence, of our fate to decompose in the earth (1973, pp. 25–6). A godworm, Becker calls the human subject. "Consciousness of death" is, according to Becker, the primary repression, and Freud is wrong in claiming it is sexuality (p. 96). Beyond denial of death what the person tries to do within his or her limited means is be heroic in a way and transcend one's mortal condition. One is driven to "desperately justify [one]self as an object of primary value in the universe; [one] must stand out, be a hero" (p. 4).

Following Brown (1959), Becker expands on how death for us comes to signify our creatureliness and corporality. He laments, along with Brown and Jonathan Swift, the fact that we defecate as a sign of our weakness and misery (citing one of Swift's poems: "Nor wonder how I lost my Wits; Oh! Caelia, Caelia, Caelia, shits!") (Becker, 1973, p. 33, based on Brown, 1959, pp. 179–201). Without disputing the obvious relation of corporality and the body's inescapable, final decay, it would seem that bodily decay should, if anything, signify death, rather than the other way around. One sometimes gets the impression that the fact that we defecate is no less troubling to Becker than the fact that we die.

Similarly, in many of Becker's specific discussions, death issues are biased toward the question of narcissism. Death, in Becker's view, is a form of a narcissistic defeat. It humiliates us. We are not the omnipotent gods we would like to be; we do not control our fate, not even our own bodies.

Following Rank and Kierkegaard, Becker arrives ultimately at a kind of religious solution to the misery of the human condition (1973, pp. 67–92, 159–75): One should yield to the power of nature and find real transcendence in the "beyond" of religion and not in one's private projects or "beyonds." Becker believes that psychoanalysis can only go half way toward this (1973, p. 124). His conclusions deserve serious attention, but they are not just a supplement to the psychoanalytic enterprise; they replace it. If we cut out the religious solution that Becker outlines, we are still left with a problem.

Becker's position about anxiety is very different not only from usual conceptions of anxiety, particularly those of psychoanalysts, but also from those of the existentially oriented authors discussed here. What Becker writes about is not an awareness of death as important to the living because it can help us live better and more authentically, but something else, total and radical, which is reminiscent of the self-effacement of Buddhist traditions; the role of existential anxiety for him (following Kierkegaard) is to annihilate the self. Rank's conclusions, as Becker (1973) presents them, were also disposed to complete self-renunciation and surrender to the highest powers, to the "bigness of nature" (pp. 173–5).[2]

Becker's main problem seems to be one-sidedness. As rich as his explanations are, it seems wrong to subsume all human phenomena under one cause or one problematic. Reality is too complex. Death is important in psychic life, but there is no need to make it the only important thing and include everything under its title.

I find Becker's view of man too pessimistic. He neglects both the vitality of being alive, and the world as it is. We should not seek to replace this world. Becker too easily "sees through" the fallacy and futility of the world around us. Yet deconstructing everything is no less of an illusion. It is to this world, a world that is half illusory, that we should adapt.

Piven

With Jerry Piven's *Death and Delusion* (2004) this Rankian-Beckerian tradition reaches its apex. Piven's most important contribution is a detailed description of the psychic work necessitated by death, and an insistence on how avoiding recognizing death has manifestations that spread over all domains of our life. The shadow of death lies behind such issues as violence, religious beliefs, ideologies, misogyny, suicide, and cultural cohesion in groups. Piven successfully applies Freudian ideas to death: if death is a troubling concept because it creates anxiety, it should

---

[2] The Buddhist perspective, as presented by Loy (1996), transcends life-death dualism by nullifying the existence of the self. "If we can realize that there is no delineated ego-self which is alive *now*, the *problem* of life and death is solved" (p. 24). This changes the rules. If there is actually no death and no self that dies, then the very problem we are facing dissolves as does most of psychoanalysis. This being said, there are of course Buddhists who see meditation on death and preparation for death (albeit as a transition) as fundamental.

be repressed; yet repressed, the anxiety of death is not at rest, and keeps influencing our behavior, our ideas and cultural constructs, and our perception of reality. We have to create illusions, fantasies, defenses, cultural symbols, and biases in perception, to provide us with a sense of meaning to soothe the anxiety of death (p. 31).

Piven's (2004) first argument then is that death anxiety is an influential motivating force in human behavior, the awareness of which is evaded in manifold ways. A second claim is that this line of thought can be found in Freud. To my mind, Piven does a better job supporting the first claim than the second, and the evidence Piven cites from Freud concerning death as the reality to be avoided is not always as convincing. It is nevertheless true that Piven cleverly reinterprets even Freud's direct rejections of death as a psychic factor in a way that makes them more intelligible from the point of view of death's centrality in human motivation (pp. 105–7, 190; see also Ricoeur, 1970, pp. 329–30).

Piven (2004) insists on the complexity of the idea of death. Death, he says, is a fantasy, a "network of ideas and images" (p. 59). Herein he lays down the theoretical basis for a dynamic clinical method of working with death, which would include analyzing individual meanings related to death in every patient.

Piven expands on the continuity between the adult, conceptual fear of death, and the infantile relation to death. While the child, says Piven, knows nothing about the end of life, he knows very well about annihilation, injury, and separation. The child comes to fear death through an accumulation of annihilating experiences, although the link between these experiences and the concept of death is only formed later in life.

It is an intriguing and stimulating argument. On the one hand, Piven seems right in claiming that the idea of death is complex and that it is emotionally rooted in earlier experiences. On the other hand, he sometimes seems to contend that these early experiences wholly subsume death, a position which would appear to neglect the uniqueness of death. I do not accept, for example, Piven's claim that "[t]here is no *intrinsic* reason human beings must feel horrified by death" (2004, p. 44, emphasis in the original), as the terror of death needs no explanation. More on this follows shortly in the context of death equivalents.

Lifton

Robert Lifton's main focus in *The Broken Connection* (1979) is on the imagery we use to relate to and understand life and death, and on their continuity.

Lifton terms Freud's approach to death "rationalist-iconoclastic," referring mainly to his view of belief in immortality as an illusion, one to be fought, because death is total annihilation (1979, pp. 13–19). Lifton contrasts it with his own belief, namely that we "require symbolization of continuity—imaginative forms of transcending death— to confront genuinely the fact that we die" (p. 17).

Lifton is a harsh critic of the absence of death from Freud's view of human experience (1979, p. 30). "Within a libido-centered paradigm, death tends to be negated—or "de-deathified," even (especially) when it is being discussed" (p. 218).

Although Lifton deals extensively with issues of life and death, his clear emphasis is on modes of vitality rather than death, to the point that it sometimes seems he has a negative view of death-related experiences and anxiety. At times, in overstressing the need for vitality, he seems to lack sensitivity to the possibly defensive roles of imagining transcendence and symbolic immortality (Piven, 2004, pp. 229–33). Death seems less a problem in itself for him than a threat to modes of immortality.

Death equivalents

One of Lifton's (1979) central concerns is the genealogy of death imagery. As early as birth, he claims, images are formed relating to three kinds of experiences—separation, disintegration, and stasis—which serve as precursors for later feelings concerning death (p. 53). Lifton's claim is that through "imagery around death equivalents" such as sleep, cuts, pains, bruises, separation, feelings about feces, fainting, and numbness (p. 68)—one can have an experience approximating death, and that our idea of death is built upon such experiences (pp. 53–72). When the idea of death itself begins to be formed, at about the age of 18 months, it "already has a considerable history" (p. 65).

It is not that death equivalents are merely "training wheels" in the formation of a concept of death. We continue all our lives "to construct our sense of death from our separations ... ; to move back and forth in our minds between death and death equivalents" (Lifton, 1979, p. 68). Variations on this idea appear in Money-Kyrle (1957), Lacan (1966, pp. 186–7), Jaques (1988 [1965], p. 236), Stern (1968a, 1968b), Lifton (1979) and, as we just saw, Piven (2004).

Yet there is the problem: once equivalence is established between two elements, the similarity cannot be easily limited. The line between the idea of death as based on sleep, and the idea of death as more or less identical with sleep, is often crossed. Death loses its uniqueness, singularity and importance, and becomes one with experiences of disintegration, stasis, separation, sleep, fainting or any other equivalent. In a way, once the equivalence is firmly established, one starts to lose sight of what was so frightening about death in the first place. Thus, the double-edged sword of death equivalents, which was initially designed to help integrate death into psychic life, ultimately serves death's reduction. For example, it is difficult to argue for death's (and death anxiety's) central role in psychic life, as most authors who speak about death equivalents do, when death is rendered comparable to an average night's sleep.

Clearly, reduction is not the intention of Lifton's project. Nevertheless, it is part of it. One frequently gets the impression that he relates to the equivalents not as anticipations of death but rather as the issue itself. The explicative tool replaces the explained.

Formulations of the death equivalents idea tend to disregard any independent fear of death. Thus, Stern (1968a, p. 4): "The anticipation [of death] ... would not be accompanied by feelings of fear were it not conceived of as repetition of a previous situation in which the ego experienced something like its own annihilation."

If we explain death through other things, such as early annihilating experiences, is it still death that we have in the end? Have we accounted for the impact of our continuous awareness of finitude or of the inevitability of death, the irreversibility of time? Reference to the early emotional roots of the annihilating experience does not exempt one from dealing with the fact that something is added to the fear of death with the acquisition of the knowledge of finitude. There is a qualitative leap involved. Understanding the essence of death carries psychological significance in itself.

Clearly, being afraid of death, like any other experience, is colored by our emotional and conceptual world. However, why limit the influences on our fear of death to our personal histories of trauma? Why would fear of death not also be shaped by symbols and cultural concepts, like religious ideas, and other elements of psychic history, along with the specific history of impingement and loss? The understanding that death is a complex concept, which carries multiple meanings, need not entail that these meanings are always and necessarily related to personal infantile experience.

Piven's (2004) explanation of the adult fear of death as an accumulation of experiences undergone in infancy is a later, more nuanced and developed version of the idea of equivalences. Experiences of separation, injury, helplessness, trauma, and impingements all serve as *templates* for the fear of annihilation of one's existence (p. 11), because they all entail a feeling of being vitally threatened (p. 11).

That death-related anxieties and emotions have early roots seems probable. There is no reason to suspect that such emotions are foreign to our personalities. A relationship with death must have been shaped by something. The question is whether these early roots are the important thing. My point is that they are not. Early roots might contribute to our emotional experience of death, but they do not "explain" it, and are not at its center.

Yalom and clinical approaches

Irvin Yalom's *Existential Psychotherapy* (1980) contains perhaps the most thorough elaboration to date of the psychic role of death and the most serious consideration of death in clinical practice. Because, he believes, death is always active in psychic life, his clinical approach insists on seeking out death as an issue even when it does not come up spontaneously. The therapist should seize, he insists, every possible opportunity to bring death into therapy (pp. 165–73). What might be popular wisdom among therapists not to "scratch where it doesn't itch" is misguided when it comes to death because in a sense death always itches (p. 29).

Yalom uses a variety of techniques, some analytic and some not, whose aim is to foster greater death awareness in his patients, including uncovering how death anxiety is often defensively displaced onto other issues, and thus finds expression in other, more concrete fears (1980, pp. 43–8, 187–90). He also explores the patient's individual approach to death. In severe cases of experiential death anxiety, Yalom even employs behavioral techniques of desensitization to reduce the patient's anxiety.

Yalom's basic idea, congruent with positions such as those of Becker and Piven, is to apply the analytic model of defense to the issue of death. Thus, where in Freud's model the drive leads to anxiety and anxiety to defense mechanisms, Yalom (1980, pp. 9–10) proposes that awareness of ultimate concerns (specifically, death) leads to anxiety, and from there to defense mechanisms. In other words, awareness of death is terrifying and necessitates a defense against it. Psychopathology would be an exaggerated and ineffective mode of defense.

For Yalom, the model simply needs to have its content switched, while its structure stays the same. The direction looks fruitful but seems to require more work. Retaining the structure of the model while investing it with different content is a much more radical move than seems at face value. The model is specific, follows assumptions peculiar to it, and is constructed in specialized terms. Hence, one must examine these assumptions, and explore the details if one wishes to change it. How, for example, does the defense mechanism work against the existential awareness of ultimate concerns? Does the defense relegate it to the unconscious? What is the exact mechanism arousing anxiety?

Another variation of this sort of substitution with similar problems is to be found in Irwin Hoffman's *Ritual and Spontaneity in the Psychoanalytic Process* (1998), a valuable attempt to integrate death in a relational psychoanalytic approach, insisting on the significance of finitude for the construction of meaning in general. Hoffman points out allusions in Freud to how we are unconsciously very much aware of death, while consciously refusing that acknowledgment through defensive means (pp. 34–8, 41–2).[3]

How in fact does an opposition of recognition and denial come about? "Signal anxiety in response to a glimmer of an appreciation of the permanent annihilatory significance of one's own death," Hoffman (1998) writes, "could instigate defensive operations that would interrupt the development of this germ of an idea and its accompanying affect, relegating both to unconscious status while fostering a narcissistically comforting belief in immortality in consciousness" (pp. 42–3).

Hoffman (1998) claims that this model could have been available to Freud himself, that his later theory enabled it. In other words, with the concepts of disavowal and splitting of the ego (p. 36), along with the second theory of anxiety, based on the thought that different stages in life correspond to different determinants of anxiety (pp. 42–3), Freud could have considered death in a new light and assigned it a place in his work.

In fact, as has already been demonstrated throughout this study, it is doubtful whether these elements alone could have really enabled Freud to assume a different approach to death. I have shown, for example, how the theory of anxiety is much less open to providing an account of death-related anxiety than Freud's formulations seem to suggest. In insisting on the inherent difficulty in conceptualizing the psychic influence of death analytically, I claim such models always require much more than mere rearrangement of concepts and attribution of known mechanisms to new objects.

Hoffman's (1998, pp. 47–50) suggestion that we see the two alternative approaches to death voiced by the two interlocutors in Freud's "On Transience" as an intrasystemic conflict of the ego, is a case in point. Can compound ideas such as "the feeling that life derives meaning and value from the fact that it is destined to end," and "the feeling that life is

---

[3] Hoffman's claims reverberate here with work by other authors (Zilboorg, 1943, pp. 465–71; Becker, 1973).

rendered empty and meaningless by the anticipation of death," (p. 49) both of which require philosophical understanding, easily be attributed to the ego, even from the perspective of ego psychology? What does the notion of conflict add? Are all the things we know to be true of intrapsychic conflicts valid here? Casting, in this case, the ambiguity of death in psychoanalytic language would require a transformation of psychoanalysis and of the meaning of conflict, and this is indicative of the difficulties I have been pointing to throughout this work.[4]

The therapeutic question of how death should be dealt with in the clinic exceeds the limits of this book. Yalom's guidelines, namely always to scratch, seem useful. Rosenthal (1973a [1963], 1973b [1957]) also advances the idea that the patient's conception of death should be sought out and analyzed by the analyst in every therapy. Failing to do so would be "cooperating with the patient's own taboo" and would jeopardize therapeutic success (1973a [1963], p. 170) (see also Stern, 1968a, 1968b, and Lifton, 1979, p. 392).

In a somewhat idiosyncratic book, loaded with personal reflections, Langs (1997) gives a detailed discussion of therapeutic issues related to work on death anxiety. His main contribution is in linking death with issues related to the frame. Langs's theory is that modified frames arouse what he terms predatory death anxiety (anxiety related to concrete, predatory death threats) and that secured ones enhance existential death anxiety (the existential awareness of death as a general and inevitable phenomenon) (1997, pp. 106, 188–209), an observation that is of potential interest to therapists.

Facing the abyss and surviving it

One common premise about death that existentially oriented psychoanalysis can help to do away with is the idea that death awareness is necessarily and inherently negative. Death awareness has, rather, potentially positive influences, and part of clinical reflection on death is to acknowledge such influences. The encounter with death can be a transformative experience. Death awareness can install a strong sense that "existence cannot be postponed" (Yalom, 1980, pp. 161–2) and urge one to live more fully (p. 161). It could lead to what Yalom terms

---

[4] It is both interesting and disturbing, however, to find in Hoffman, alongside the awareness of death's significance, a clinical approach to death that strives to mitigate death anxiety and death awareness, to foster "a certain increment in self-deception" (p. 238–9), in what seems yet another manifestation of the old tendency to pathologize death anxiety, or at least to regard it negatively, in a text occupied with how death is integral to meaning in life.

disidentification, that is, to help distinguish core and accessory elements of one's identity. Such a process helps to alleviate anxieties related to peripheral aspects of identity, e.g., one's career and appearance (pp. 163–5). Awareness of death can contribute to "a sense of poignancy in life" and can alter one's perspective on life (p. 40).[5]

An example of a perspective the acknowledgment of our ephemeral nature may lead us to adopt is the advice by the Roman emperor and stoic philosopher Marcus Aurelius (1963): "As if you had already died and lived only till now, live the rest of your life as a kind of bonus, in accord with nature" (p. 69).

Frommer (2005) stresses how awareness of death frees us from the burden of having an established, stable identity: "reifications of identity create their own prisons" (p. 497); Being more aware of one's transience frees one to be able to think more flexibly about who one is or wishes to be.[6]

The anticipation of death and the dread that accompanies it can lead to reevaluation and transformation of the meaning of our lives, to a reassessment of our values. It might give us courage to act, because we know we cannot wait (Koestenbaum, 1971 [1964], p. 259). It might make us focus on the essentials (p. 266), to think more about what is really important to us (pp. 268, 270). In a more general manner, it can be said perhaps that the anticipation of death can help one take responsibility for one's life.

Thinking about death does not necessarily plunge one into more pondering and rumination or into depression. Fully acknowledging our finitude might also lead to a kind of immunization. The course of events, the healing processes in the mind, the flow of time, and other elements join together to submerge the sharp awareness back into oblivescence. But the effect might be that the person is more equipped to face mortality in a further station in his or her life. It is as if, once you have gazed into the abyss, you are more free to carry on with life, acknowledging what is there, without having to continuously put it out of mind.

---

[5] For Carveth (1994), an encounter with death and finitude "can sometimes facilitate ... a maturational achievement" (pp. 219–20) which consists primarily in emerging from a narcissistic egocentric subjectivity towards a discovery of the object (pp. 232–3).

[6] For Doka (1995), "the awareness of mortality may be the most significant psychological event in middle life" (p. 117), an event which carries significant implications. The perspective on time changes – time is not only measured from birth onward, but also from the point of view of the time left to live. There is a reassessment of one's identity. There is a search for symbolic immortality, and perhaps a greater sense of vitality and a renewed commitment to one's goals (pp. 114–17).

Existential psychoanalysis: Handling otherness

Rank (1950 [1945]), Brown (1959), Becker (1973), Lifton (1979), and Yalom (1980) offer us complete, large-scale theories focused on death. While all these works are deeply inspired by psychoanalysis, they actually knowingly replace it with something else. This, of course, is not a problem in itself, but if ones wishes to avoid throwing out the baby with the bathwater, one should attempt to remain more focused on psychoanalysis, and examine its constructions, possibilities, and limitations with regard to death.

Other authors more affiliated with the analytic world who have examined death often suffer, as we saw in Chapter 9, from the opposite problem of remaining too deeply within accepted modes of thought. They make an effort to explain death, but often fall back into the trap of cutting it down and reducing it to other analytic concepts, leaving some of its dimensions overlooked.[7] It does seem, however, that a psychological-psychoanalytic understanding of the psychology of death is gradually developing.

The pointed critique of psychoanalysis made by the authors discussed here has not been in general significantly integrated or internalized in psychoanalytic circles. Unlike in other areas where criticism has had a strong influence on psychoanalytic practice (for example, feminist criticism, postmodern epistemological criticism, and criticism regarding the nature of the analytic relationship), this has not happened in relation to the theme of death. If we take Lifton (1979), Becker (1973), and Yalom (1980), for example, we have to conclude that although they have written three deeply engaging books of great value, referring directly to psychoanalysis, and have influenced many people outside the analytic community, these texts have had only minor influence within analytic circles, and their common thread—the assertion that psychoanalysis is lacking with regard to death—has not become part of the psychoanalytic worldview.

For many, it seems, these authors are classified as existential psychologists, and thus not part of the analytic tradition. This exclusion comprises in itself another expression of the denial of death in psychoanalysis. If critiques pointing to a lacuna in the psychoanalytic worldview

---

[7] Eissler (1955), for example, presents a thorough discussion of the formative role of death in the structure of psychic life. Yet what are we to do with all his statements regarding the influence of death, if he so readily accepts the reduction of fears and thoughts of death to castration, as is true he claims, "almost regularly" in cases of intense fear (p. 279)? Is everything he says about death actually about castration?

have met with only little acceptance, it is because they seem to imperil common analytic conceptions. Clinicians and theoreticians alike are reluctant to make a shift in their worldview because they seem to understand that taking death seriously in psychoanalysis is not just another addition or minor modification. They see that what is at stake might be at odds with the very heart of psychoanalytic thought.

Bridges to one's past

A key problem in attempting to give an analytic account of death is the need in analytic theory to tie things into the early stages of life, when we still did not have a concept of death. Alongside the ideas we have seen so far, several other notions could be suggested, which might bridge the gap between death awareness and early psychic life, between infant and adult knowing.[8]

Self-preservation, understood perhaps as an instinct, could supply psychoanalysis with a theoretical approach to death anxiety. As a basic and natural phenomenon, it could be a route to bring fear of death into analytic theory. Zilboorg (1943), for example, believes fear of death is the affective side of self-preservation (see also De Masi, 2004, p. 50).

The experience of helplessness could also form part of an analytic model of death anxiety, and potentially be a bridge to the anxieties of the very young. Schur (1972, p. 376), for example, believes that seeing the feeling of helplessness as the core of danger could lead to the inclusion of death among the possible causes of anxiety (see also Wainrib, 1996, p. 66).

Helplessness, as we know, is central to Freud's (1926, pp. 166–7) second theory of anxiety. I have argued, however, in Chapter 5 that this helplessness is not of the kind that could also account for death anxiety because what Freud considers there is helplessness because the drives cannot be satisfied; an inner drama.

Death anxiety could be based on annihilation anxiety. It seems reasonable to posit a psychoanalytic model where very early experiences of annihilation anxiety form the emotional substratum on which a later, more elaborated death anxiety is based. This would retain death anxiety's link with the biological, as well as its basis in early development, which psychoanalysis seems to require. The degree, however, to which annihilation anxiety explains death anxiety is very limited. Death anxiety

---

[8] Other attempts at conceptualization are not always successful. Schermer's (1995) use of Bion's term "preconception" for example adds little to our understanding of death. The term is evoked, but has no explanatory value.

is different from annihilation anxiety, for the same reason that death is different from mere annihilation.

Although annihilation anxiety itself is a somewhat neglected dimension in psychoanalysis (Hurvich, 2003, pp. 579–80), it seems that with the development of psychoanalysis more and more attention is given to holistic, early anxieties, vaguer in terms of their object, anxieties that are forms of annihilation anxiety. Hurvich himself lists many examples such as "unthinkable anxiety" (Winnicott), "nameless dread" (Bion), "disintegration anxiety" (Kohut), or "dissolution of boundedness" (Ogden). These concepts, originating in different schools, tell us about the emerging sensitivity in psychoanalysis to early anxieties related to the survival of the organism: to being overwhelmed, disintegrated or losing one's boundaries.

And yet none of these anxieties are death anxiety. Moreover, the attention given to them in analytic theory serves to hide the lack of serious discussion of death anxiety. I referred earlier (Chapter 9) to the problem of the lack of specificity in the discussion of death. None of these anxieties are directly related to death. The very fact of their early onset suggests they are concerned with something else, perhaps more fundamental than the fear of death, but not replacing it. The fact that the individual will come one day to grasp his or her mortality, and that this recognition will deeply penetrate his or her thought and feelings, is still neglected in psychoanalytic thought.[9]

The concept of deferred action (*après coup*, *Nachträglichkeit*), with its center of gravity shifting between a later and an earlier event, without the earlier one completely setting the tone, could also be of help. It might account for the kind of relationship that obtains between the earlier experiences on which death anxiety is based and the acquisition of the concept of death at a later age, and allow the latter to be influential. It is true that as an infant, the child has experiences related to annihilation and separation, but when she is 5, and learns about death, these early experiences accumulate new meaning, and only then become something related to death. This kind of explanation does not allow for easy reductions of the late to the early. The early experiences would be templates, in Piven's (2004) terms, for the late, but the late response to death itself would in turn influence the early templates, alter them, and establish a closer relationship between them and death.

These attempts at integration could perhaps, especially when accompanied by other ideas examined earlier in this book, form a partial

---

[9] It is worth mentioning that annihilation anxiety is itself multiple, as both Hurvich (2003) and Gediman (1983) argue.

analytic model of death anxiety. And yet their usefulness is still quite limited. We have seen throughout this book how death is pushed away from psychoanalysis in a way that seems almost intrinsic. The next chapter will make this incongruence more explicit, and the concluding chapter will attempt a wider infrastructural clarification to help develop better analytic thinking about death.

13 Sources of the clash: The conflict between analytic ideas and concern with death

The route we have taken so far naturally leads to the thought that something about psychoanalytic hermeneutics impedes theorizing when it comes to the subject of death.

Although psychoanalysis has come a long way since Freud's early work, and recent views threaten to render some of Freud's understandings obsolete, death is still a problem for psychoanalysis, remaining marginal or negligible in analytic theory and practice. The essential position that regards death as "unpsychoanalytic" has not been fundamentally revised. Even if some groundwork has been laid for a different approach to death, the implementation of such an approach is still rare in today's analytic world. It is as if the reluctance to deal with death is more strongly entrenched than the specific arguments used to justify that rejection.

The problem stems, I suggest, from certain basic premises in analytic theory which are used no less today than in Freud's time. Fundamental analytic concepts continue to hinder theoretical attention to death. The current chapter presents a summary and discussion of such concepts. To develop a different analytic perspective on death, we must try to define where the problem lies. While some of these principles cannot be renounced entirely, some can perhaps be refined to clear the way for a different approach to death.

Where does the problem lie? Some analytic tenets that hinder the integration of death

Why is death problematic for psychoanalysis? Yalom (1980, pp. 70–4) and Becker (1973, pp. 93–124) think much of the problem is personal. Freud aspired to greatness and was eager to posit something innovative, even revolutionary, which would grant him eternal glory.[1] In Freud's

---

[1] See my paper on this issue, "Publish *and* Perish: Freud's Claim to Literary Fame" (Razinsky, 2013).

case it was sexuality. Fear of death was used merchandise. For Lifton too (1979, p. 49), psychoanalytic "neglect of death" should be attributed to the one-sidedness of the innovator, the problem being that this view was not revised by Freud's disciples.[2]

These writers' explanation captures an aspect of the psychoanalytic lack concerning death, but there are clearly deeper reasons why Freud ever adopted a stand against death, and why that resistance has been so persistent in analytic history. It is not simply the case that Freud was mistaken, and others were not alert enough, or too loyal, to notice. We have seen the vicissitudes of the tendency to dismiss death among post-Freudian theorists. Besides, too much of what Freud said has been debated, transformed, and turned upside down, for us to think of Freud as an undisputed source of wisdom for his followers. Added to this is the fact that, as we have seen, Freud was more ambivalent toward death than most of his followers; his thought about it is richer in possibilities.

The deterministic-mechanistic model

We must move on, then, to more theoretical reasons for the neglect. Yalom (1980, pp. 67–70) suggests one such reason: the complexity involved in thinking about or imagining death, which requires planning, and "projection of self into the future" is opposed, he believes, to Freud's deterministic worldview of blind forces clashing. Yalom sees this mechanistic model as something of an accident in psychoanalysis, an outmoded theory inherited by Freud from his teachers: Freud was influenced by the Helmholtzian position dominant in Brücke's laboratory, whereby behavior is determined solely by physical and chemical forces, and conceived the mind as a deterministic mechanism, a game of forces. Once we relinquish this outdated model, Yalom suggests, death will be able to assume its proper place within psychoanalysis. Yalom's analysis provides us with an initial explanation for the inattention to death in analytic theories. However, he underestimates two actually contradictory factors. First, the mechanistic worldview is much more than an accident in psychoanalysis, but lies at the heart of the analytic—or at least the Freudian—enterprise. Second, and from an opposing perspective, Freud is never fully reconciled with the mechanistic theory. He

---

[2] Freud's approach to death might have a gendered facet as well. Jonte-Pace (2001) shows how Freud's writings hint at an intimate link between death, immortality, and the feminine. The mother, she argues, plays an important role in ideas around death (pp. 45–73). The intimate link between the two heavily loaded subjects makes the consideration of each more problematic and more complex (pp. 71, 72, 147).

almost always aspires to contrary conclusions: the person as meaning-based, the mind as an interpretative matrix, desire as directed toward an object or a future outcome, and not the result of pressures. The unresolved dualism between mechanism and meaning and agency is part of what makes him such an intriguing thinker.

The focus on the past

Another theoretical building block which makes integration of death difficult is the psychoanalytic focus on the past. We have already seen many expressions of the long-standing insistence on relating death to the past, and on finding earlier experiences to explain being afraid of death, and how in consequence analytic attempts to understand death have been thwarted.

The insistence on the past in psychoanalysis has two main aspects. First, there is the focus on childhood, the belief that most of the important events in psychic life take place in the individual's earliest years, when the issue of death is relatively insignificant and undeveloped (Searles, 1965 [1961], pp. 511–12).

Second, and more importantly, there is the general quest to identify precursory experiences. Things become significant when they come back a second time. Freud's general preference for having primary and secondary stages for mental events (repression, narcissism) is of course the central example here, but it is only a more formal expression of the belief that things are hardly ever new in psychic life. Both of these manifestations of the over-emphasis on the past are detrimental to the possibility of integrating death in analytic theory, because one's own death will not only take place in the future, it is a future beyond one's own. One's death lies outside one's biography. The expectation and fear of it, and the threat it poses, are always future-oriented.[3]

The detachability of affect and content

Another place where the focus on the past is salient is Freud's (1926) second theory of anxiety, which introduces the idea of a hierarchy of anxieties. Every anxiety, death anxiety included, can be traced to an earlier one.[4] Death anxiety is a transformation of fear of the superego,

---

[3] Yalom (1980, p. 10–1) stresses that for existential therapy, the basic time is future becoming past, in contrast with the centrality of the past in psychoanalysis.

[4] The idea of hierarchy is new, but the first theory of anxiety also contains the claim that anxiety always repeats an earlier state (Freud, 1916–1917, p. 396).

which in turn is a transformation of fear of castration. Fear of castration is traced back to fear of the loss of the object, to fear of separation. Finally, separation reduces to helplessness, which in turn comes down or not, Freud hesitates, to the trauma of birth. This hierarchy, however, when examined as a whole, tells us something else about death anxiety beyond what is prior to what, and what is reduced to what. Implicit in it is the view that anxiety is free-floating, that it is not attached specifically to this or that object or content. The affect logically precedes its contents.

This, on the conceptual or developmental level, is the equivalent of what takes place according to psychoanalytic understanding on a more concrete level: the idea that affect and content are separable, that affect can wander from one object to another, an idea presented early on in Freud's work (letter to Fliess, May 21, 1894, in Masson, 1985, p. 74; Freud, 1894, pp. 52–4, 1900, p. 463). Affect is detached from content, precedes it, and has real substantive existence in the psyche, like a piece of matter that cannot be disposed of, only transformed or modified.

The detachability of affect and event or object suggests that there is no privileged status to any specific event. As such it comprises an obstacle to the integration of death in the analytic worldview, because death anxiety has a very specific and unique—albeit vague or mysterious—object. Moreover, death is something real, not a fantasy.

To some extent this problem applies equally to castration anxiety. There is a tension between the uniqueness of castration anxiety, which is a specific link between an affect and a particular idea, and the concept of affects as traveling between ideas expressed by the developmental-logical chain of anxieties. This tension seems to be in part responsible for the difficulty pointed at earlier (p. 33), with respect to Freud's (1926) text, that while castration is only a middle link in the chain, it still seems to occupy a very significant position (1909, pp. 8–9n, 1937, pp. 250–2), the concept of the hierarchy of anxieties notwithstanding. On the other hand, castration is an invented threat or a fantasy, while death is real, and is feared as a real event, and, therefore, the premise of detachability of affect and object is less of a problem in the case of castration.

The interdependence of psychic events

A notion related to the lack of specificity of affective content is the lack of specificity of psychic events. Death is a very specific, singular event in one's life, and it draws its importance from that uniqueness. There is, however, a strong premise in psychoanalysis of lack of specificity and independence. All things are interlinked: every psychic event is influenced by many others, every love relation by earlier love relations. This tension is responsible, in part, for the problems I described in the previous chapter regarding the notion of death equivalents, where the response to death is equalized with other responses, and is defined as simply another variation or manifestation of them, with the stimulus itself (for the response) being treated as insignificant. Note, however, that the interdependence of psychic events should not really comprise a problem for an analytic consideration of death, because death is, in fact, connected with the rest of psychic life: rather than isolated, it participates in and is affected by many other thoughts, feelings, and perspectives. What is needed is an understanding of death that will account for this interdependence without effacing death's specificity and uniqueness.

The instinctual model

One axis along which psychoanalysis and thinking concerned with death continuously clash is the theory of instincts. Lifton (1979) is especially sensitive to this. He portrays the dynamics by which Freud occasionally approaches a view which assigns death importance (e.g., pp. 166–7, 184, p. 218), but swiftly evokes "instinctual metaphysics" (p. 184) so as to forestall its penetration into theory. Instinctualism and libido theory "de-deathify" death (p. 218). We have also observed the tendency to divert issues of death to those of sexuality and have looked at how the concept of the death instinct itself tends to negate death, precisely by rendering it an instinct. The instinctual model may constitute less of a problem today for death's integration into psychoanalysis as many within the field reject it altogether.

The focus on presence

Another element in analytic thought that is antagonistic to an acknowledgment of death's importance is the tendency to focus on presence—on what is. There is something essentialist in most psychoanalytic currents, with the major exception of French psychoanalytic thought and Bion.[5] This tendency is not always easily discernable, and it sometimes seems the contrary: does psychoanalytic work not focus on the gaps, on the blanks in the discourse, on what was not said by the patient? This is true, of course, but only to a limited degree, for behind the gaps on one

---

[5] In France this is no doubt due to the influence of Lacan.

level, analytic thought presupposes realities on a different, unconscious level. What is a blank on the surface is a presence, is filled-in, underneath. At bottom, it is presence that is given most of the time. The defenses presuppose the presence against which and because of which they were activated.[6]

Yet death is of a different order. It is not a presence or substance of any kind but rather a form of nothingness, of non-being, and absence. The thought of death, and emotional responses to it, concern something not present and not wholly known. This complicates the analytic possibility of accounting for such thinking and feeling.

For Lacan and his followers, as well as for Green, Fedida, Kristeva, and other French thinkers, absence becomes central and accordingly they are much more sensitive to death than is usual in psychoanalysis (although, as I claim in the chapter on Lacan, sometimes this absence is so generalized that death somehow slips through the net). In fact, it is almost self-evident for them, and is indeed part of French intellectual atmosphere in the twentieth century, to place finitude at the heart of existence.

Explaining the external in terms of the internal

The focuses on the instinctual and the past, as well as the centrality of the unconscious, form part of a basic analytic tendency to explain the external in terms of the internal. This tendency has two different meanings. One is seeing the internal as causative for the external. Clearly one shapes part of one's environment through one's actions and modes of relating to the world, but psychoanalysis will often expand the scope of this influence to larger and deeper areas than those ordinarily considered the result of internal involvement. This tendency, while not universal within analytic circles, stresses the causative aspects of the unconscious and tends to look for the role of wishes and instincts in the shaping of reality. Its climax with regard to death is Eissler's idea, discussed in Chapter 7, regarding subjective involvement in the causation of death. The risk with such perspectives is that the significance of death as an external event will be lost, as happens, for example, in the psychoanalytic understanding of the fear of death as

---

[6] Similarly, I recalled earlier how what appears to be a case of absence or lack in Freud's theory of helplessness as the source of anxiety turns out to be, upon further inspection, a case of an excess presence of drives.

fear of the environment's retaliation against one's own death wishes toward it, or as a product of guilt about such wishes.

The second, much more common meaning of the analytic tendency to explain the external in terms of the internal meaning is the bracketing of the external: the analytic claim, of course, is not that external events do not exist in themselves, or are not interesting, but rather that they are not interesting in the deep sense, within analysis. There, what matters is the subject's internal life as such. This relates to the question of the analytic perspective on reality, to which we now turn.

The analytic perspective on reality

The psychoanalytic perspective on reality is one factor that makes death a difficult issue for analysis to handle. The stress in analytic theory, and even more so in treatment, is not on reality itself, but rather on what we do with it.[7] Reality is thus neglected in favor of responses to it. The latter become isolated and manageable, treatable, and the reality—less manageable perhaps, if we speak of death—is blurred into the background.

The focus on what we do with reality is problematic specifically with regard to death. This doing can mean many things, a whole range of psychic reactions, behaviors, and modes of perception and "metabolization" of reality. Reality can be loved, hated, feared, distorted; yet in all of these it is transformed or processed into something existent. Death, however, is different, in that it is not only a psychic reality, but also a powerful, independent, and unchangeable reality of another order—that is, it is not a thing at all, not a presence. Its processing into something existent converts it into something else. Death, as it were, becomes life in this manner. In analysis, when the issue of death comes up, the inquiry likely goes to how it is processed, how the person relates to it. This will, of course, help to bring out much of the specific attitude of a person toward death, but in the process something essential to death is inevitably lost. It is already converted into a form of life—mental life—and its antithetical relation to all that is life—as embodied by presence—is lost. However, death has influence not only in this metabolized form, but also as a lack, as absence, an influence that eludes many analytic mechanisms of explanation.

---

[7] Of course, the issue is much debated within psychoanalysis, as different schools vary in their evaluation of the role reality should play in our understanding of individuals. To different extents however, the problem applies to all of them.

The focus on relational aspects

A specific aspect of the analytic view of reality is its characteristic stress on the interpersonal. True, the focus of psychoanalysis is the intrapsychic, but the intrapsychic is understood as being the result of significant interpersonal interactions, as existing and functioning within relationship. Almost every substantial occurrence in psychic life is the result of some interaction with others, some perception or psychic representation of them.

The fact that we live in interpersonal, relational contexts is more of a truism than a position unique to psychoanalysis. Yet for psychoanalysis, the interpersonal world assumes a specific explanatory role. Analytic explanations will look for the other, for the relational context. Things take place, it is thought, in such interrelational contexts, even if these contexts are actually, as just said, intrapsychic, i.e. involve internalized representations. Most significantly, much of the external, non-human world is perceived, according to the theory, in interpersonal terms. Moreover a real personification of the external world is often involved, in the sense that the subject perceives it as consisting of specific human forces, or translates its perception into the internalized interpersonal world.

This has relevance for the way that death is understood by analysts, as an interpersonal issue. While empirically death can be interpersonal, it is an external reality, and specifically, one that is in a sense indifferent to any human involvement. Sometimes people kill people, and sometimes a parent can protect a child in a specific situation. Yet no parent can finally save his or her child from the fate of death. In addition, death is the most lonesome experience, even in expectation. As Heidegger (1996 [1927], pp. 221–4) reminds us, no one can take our death from us.

Recoiling from the "high": Against philosophy

On October 8, 1936 (Fichtner, 2003 [1992], pp. 211–12), Freud writes to Binswanger, his friend and pupil who has embarked on an independent road, influenced by the ideas of Heidegger. While Binswanger prefers to roam the higher floors, in the company of religion and art, writes Freud, he always preferred to stay on the ground floor, or in the basement. Freud emphasizes that, in this sense, he is the revolutionary and Binswanger the conservative, because metaphysical speculations are conservative, and attention to the bodily or the material is new.[8] This brings us back to the earlier point, namely, that death is nothing new, while sexuality is.

Yet for Freud, metaphysical speculations are not only conservative. They can also be empty or blind, examining epiphenomena, rather than basic aspects of human life.[9] Freud draws a direct opposition between the psychoanalytic view of things and that of philosophy. He contrasts his views of death directly with those of philosophy ("here the philosophers are thinking too philosophically," 1915, p. 293), and with what he sees as philosophical ideas ("The high-sounding phrase, 'every fear is ultimately the fear of death', has hardly any meaning," 1923, p. 57) or philosophical tendencies (in the analytic approach, he says, in contrast to other views, the invention of systems of ideas by primitive people was not done out of "pure speculative curiosity," 1913a, p. 78). "*[W]e* do not lay stress on the *intellectual* problem with which death confronts the living," writes Freud, but rather on "the *emotional* conflict" (pp. 92–3, emphasis in the original).[10] Fear of death as a motive belongs to a philosophical perspective. Freud wants to have it differently as if, in light of death's centrality in philosophy, it should be avoided by psychoanalysis.[11]

For Green (1983), Freud's position that death anxiety is marginal, is almost a provocation thrown in the face of philosophy. What Freud wanted to show, says Green, was that it actually took less courage to claim that man is unique among animals in being conscious of its death than to admit the limits of such consciousness, and to accept that the major instigator for thought is what lies beyond conscious voluntary control. Death, which philosophers praise so much, is but a lure; it hides castration from us (p. 256).

---

[8] Kristeva (2000 [1996], pp. 15–16) emphasizes Freud's view of himself as revolutionary in this statement, where revolution comes from being in touch with the hidden, invisible, archaic unconscious and its timelessness.

[9] An example of Freud's anti-philosophical spirit is his reaction upon reading Chestov's book, which he sees as "philosophical convolutions" to which he feels alien, a "pitiable waste of intellectual powers." Philosophers' books, he feels, are always a disguise for psychological, "or even ... psychopathological" problems (Jones, 1957, p. 148).

[10] Although Freud refers to Stekel's ideas, he seems to see them as a part of the philosophical heritage.

[11] Freud's suspicion of philosophy was, however, mixed with respect and even some envy. He wanted to become a philosopher when he was young, was quite familiar with philosophy, and was tending more and more to philosophical thinking in his later writings. I suspect some of his refusal to give death significance is related to the fact it might lead not to philosophical speculations, but to occultism. Jung (1963) tells how Freud asked him once to promise never to renounce the sexual focus in analytic theory, because it was a bulwark, and when he asked a bulwark against what, Freud replied: "Against the black tide of mud ... of occultism" (pp. 147–8).

Freud (1915) explicitly wants us to abandon what is "high" with regard to death, in favor of what is "low." It sometimes seems that fear of death is for him a philosophical construct, a pseudo-problem in metaphysical clothing.[12] To this day, clinical thought seems at times to deem death "not deep enough" and as hiding more profound motives.

While I believe this aversion of Freud and many of his followers to the high, this basic suspicion that it conceals more basic issues, is fundamental to understanding the analytic reluctance to deal with death, I also believe it is based on an erroneous judgment, because death should not automatically be seen as belonging to the domain of the purely metaphysical. Nor should metaphysical speculations be regarded as foreign to psychic life. I will come back to this later.

Generality versus idiosyncrasy I: Universal explanations

Another point which seems to have hampered psychoanalysis in integrating death as a constituting factor concerns the issue of generality versus idiosyncrasy. Psychoanalysis has a bifold tendency, seeking a general understanding of the human subject, an overall explanation of human psychic life and action, and being oriented to individual therapy, seeking to account for the specific constellation in a given person.

Death is a factor relevant to everyone, and on the same level. All men are mortal. Toward the end of *Inhibitions, Symptoms and Anxiety* (1926), Freud tries to understand the reason for the special place anxiety occupies in the mind. Because anxiety is a reaction to danger, it seems logical to look for the reason in the nature of danger. However, says Freud, "dangers are the common lot of humanity; they are the same for everyone." "What we need and cannot lay our finger on," he continues, is a factor which will explain why some people succumb to anxiety more

---

[12] Meyer (1975 [1973], p. 84) suggests that "the problem of death lures one so easily into metaphysical speculations," and that these are antagonistic to the empirical tendency of psychoanalysis.

Becker (1973) claims that Freud's major contribution is his insistence on human creatureliness, manifested in his stress on sexuality. Freud saw psychoanalysis and the stress on sexuality as a stronghold against everything that made man a spiritual being, and led him to forget his flesh and blood creaturely nature (pp. 94–7). For Becker, Freud was right in this to a large extent, but erred in failing to see that the essence of the human's creatureliness lies in his or her death.

Becker's position that mortality is part of man's creatureliness no less than sexuality is correct, and should be more commonly understood in analytic circles, precisely because it shows how something about death as a motive is compatible with the analytic perspective. Yet it is important to see how pervasive the idea is in Freud that it is exactly the contrary, that death is not a fundamental human concern and is not essentially part of the instinctual.

easily, and some are less susceptible to its influence (p. 150). Death, as perhaps the most universal lot of humanity, is thus disqualified as an important factor in the psychoanalytic theory of individual minds. Internal readiness, past experiences, constitution of drives, and familial interactions enable more individualized explanations.

The same problem can arise at the clinical level as well. There, even more than on the theoretical level, there is a need to explain the lot of one specific individual. Death can be perceived as too general an explanation. Yalom (1980), puzzled by the inattention to death in the clinical and therapeutic context, suggests that perhaps it results from a view that people die anyway, and that there is not only nothing to do about it, but also nothing to say: "Well that's life, isn't it! Let's move on to something neurotic, something we can do something about" (p. 13).[13]

The issue of generality versus idiosyncrasy, in addition to limitations, presents possibilities for the analytic approach when examining death. We will, therefore, soon return to this point.

Therapeutic pessimism

The fact, uncomfortable for therapists, that existential issues are there anyway (encouraging one to move on to something "more interesting"), also might lead to therapeutic pessimism and impotence.[14] Bolivar (1993, p. 134), for example, believes death was rejected because it supposedly does not sit well with therapeutic aims.[15]

The source of suffering in the case of death is indeed beyond the therapist's reach. One cannot protect one's patients against death any more than one can protect oneself. Anxiety is justified and realistic. Not that we should spend our lives paralyzed by the thought of death, or that the fear cannot be lessened, worked on, analyzed, and so on, but inexorable death will remain on the horizon.

Death is thus a source of suffering that on some level one is powerless against, and it can bring about despair and hamper the therapeutic process. Psychoanalysis has, however, always contained a duality between

---

[13] Yalom, of course, criticizes this attitude. The existential therapist has to explore, he claims, the individual relation to death.
[14] These are in fact claims that were raised by analytic authors against Freud's concept of the death instinct.
[15] De M'uzan (1996, pp. 46–7) also believes death might entail pessimism. There is a clash, he believes, between psychoanalysis and philosophy on the subject of death. He refers specifically to the contrast between his view stressing self-preservation and the ego's clinging to life (p. 35), and that of the philosopher Cioran who gives a higher value to acknowledging the certitude of death. That view leads, de M'uzan believes, to melancholia.

a will to explore the truth and curative, therapeutic aims. If death is psychically influential, the fact that it happens to be a "bad thing" is not a sufficient argument for its exclusion from the analytic enterprise, as will soon be discussed (and of course dealing with death might have positive therapeutic consequences, as seen in the previous chapter).

Another clinical obstacle is that death is also a problematic concept for analysts themselves as human beings, who are, like their patients, not immune to defenses and denial (Yalom, 1980, p. 58–9. See also Langs, 1997, pp. 223–33). In this regard, I believe a more open discussion of death and its psychic implications, as well as a more elaborate understanding of the role it plays in life, can serve to lessen such defenses.

Aspects of death that lie—or do they? Beyond psychoanalysis

When, in *Civilization and Its Discontents*, Freud (1930) attempts to understand happiness, he elects to leave aside abstract ideas of what happiness might be, and explore instead what really makes people happy. This is the "empirical" move in psychoanalysis. In the case of death, however, such a move cannot be made because, in philosophical terms, the awareness of death defines, in a certain manner, what a human being is. Even if only three out of every thousand people truly consider death, while all the others avoid or deny it, these three would still define something crucial for all the rest.

The encounter with death for psychoanalysis will be, more than a reference to a psychological datum, an encounter with a metaphysical reality. As such it can only be a missed encounter, a mixture of approaching and recoiling, touching and avoiding, as psychoanalysis cannot really touch death at that level. On the other hand, it cannot allow itself to really bracket or ignore it. Freud's claim that we cannot think of death or account for it in analytic terms should be understood perhaps as expressing a recognition of the centrality of death, on the one hand, and the difficulty in grasping it beyond a certain level on the other hand.

Death and the meaning of life

It is difficult to think of death as meaningful without thinking of life as meaningful. However, the meaningfulness or meaninglessness of life is not normally, in itself and with a capital M, a psychoanalytic question. Ironically, posing the question of life's meaning seems to some extent to be taken as extrinsic to life. Freud on one occasion denounces the question as unworthy of even being asked. At the end of his life, he writes to Marie Bonaparte:

The moment a man questions the meaning and value of life, he is sick, since objectively neither has any existence; by asking this question one is merely admitting to a store of unsatisfied libido to which something else must have happened, a kind of fermentation leading to sadness and depression. (letter of August 14, 1937, E. Freud, 1960, p. 436)

In "On Transience," where Freud interestingly does consider the issue of the value of things in face of transience, the position that their ephemeral nature might rob things of value is also considered ill. In a sense, the psychoanalytic position is justified. It deals with things that happen inside life, the causes and implications, the dynamic between the subject and the world, and the like. It does not ask why the subject is in the world. But people do sometimes ask these questions—what is the meaning of it all? What is the meaning of my life if I will eventually perish? What kind of meaning do I consider important and can I create it in my life?—and the questions thus become part of their lives, a psychological datum.

The thought of death and the anxiety associated with it involve the consideration of life as a whole, or in other words, a holistic perspective. One's entire existence is at stake.

The question of life's meaning does not just stay somewhere in the background. People actually ask themselves about the way they lead their lives, about changes of fate, why they exist, and what the meaning of it all is. These questions should not be reduced to something else; they are much more than merely another element in psychic life. Even if they only appear for a short time, even if they quickly subside and give way to everydayness, they still bear a crucial importance. The person might go back to her usual mode of being in and relating to the world, but in this momentary reflection on life, it is as if she has lifted her head out of the water. Perhaps we cannot live outside the water, and must dive back in. Yet in sticking our heads out for just a minute, we gain an insight into our usual condition, which was unavailable to us within the continuous flux of life.

At any rate, the intermingling of death with broad questions of meaning, somewhat uncomfortable for psychoanalysis, makes it more complicated to deal with death in psychoanalysis.

Analytic sensibilities helpful to the integration of death

Although the inclusion of death in analytic theory faces some serious obstacles, some approaches are more conducive to it.

"Freudian pessimism"

I have claimed that lending centrality to death might clash with the therapeutic aim of improving well being. At the same time, however, it must be remembered that a basic analytic tenet, which is at odds with much of the (non-analytic) therapeutic world, is that suffering cannot be wholly eliminated. Freud was never enthusiastic or naïve about the possibilities of improving one's happiness, and neither are many of his followers. Such improvement is possible only to some extent.

Truth and illusion

It is not of course that Freud or any other analyst wants patients to suffer, or is indifferent to suffering. Yet beyond the recognition of an inevitable amount of suffering, Freud and many of his followers can be said to hold an ethos where truth is supreme, and exposing it has the utmost importance, even at the price of some sorrow.

There is here the potential for appreciating the truthfulness in acknowledging one's existential condition, even when it evokes pain or anxiety. Freud and Heidegger converge here, at a point that both might have inherited from Nietzsche.

The truth of death has to be exposed specifically because it is avoided and veiled by illusions. The most valuable insights Freud offers us with regard to death are those that expose the hypocrisy of our usual attitude to it, and where his flair for uncovering illusions overcomes his tendency to dismiss death. Thus, while psychoanalytic positions both explicitly and implicitly deny death's significance, something in the analytic ethos pushes in the opposite direction, but is only rarely put into words. Psychoanalysis and existential ideas (Heidegger, 1996 [1927]) come together in their potential exposure of everyday obliviousness and denial regarding death. The only problem is that somehow psychoanalysis itself has joined in with this denial.

The question arises whether death should be brought up in analysis. Given its focus on illusions, psychoanalysis might be more inclined to do so than other streams in the therapeutic culture, which focus primarily on alleviation of symptoms. After all, truth itself, in the analytic ethos, might be curative.

Generality versus idiosyncrasy II: Idiosyncratic explorations

Whereas in one respect, death is common to everyone, in a different sense, it is also an idiosyncratic experience. This experience depends on the level of awareness of and exposure to death, on interactions between the psychic world and apprehensions of death, on life experience, and so on. Death's individual character, the fact that it carries specific meanings for each person is reinforced by the fact that death's psychic presence is interwoven with much of the rest of psychic life. Thus, the approach to it is not only subjective and idiosyncratic, but influences and is influenced by an individual's entire psychic world.

Being universal, death is problematic material for psychoanalysis; being, however, also a particular subjective experience, it falls squarely within it. The analytic inquiry, focusing on what X is for the specific patient, could be applied to death. The idea is to attempt to understand an individual's specific attitude toward death, to work on her own responses to death, and to look for her individual biases, as well as the interactions between her awareness of finitude and other elements in her psychic life. Psychoanalysis could add something to existential philosophical thought by being more specific and idiosyncratic, and by illuminating the individual complexities that underlie any idea. Yet this can be accomplished only if wider manifestations of death in life are taken into account, and if death's more general importance for human beings, and the ways it affects much of what we think and do, are acknowledged.

I described earlier how the issue of death is, for Freud, the focus of a clash between psychoanalysis and philosophy. This approach, while it may be accurate, is lamentable. Psychoanalysis might be opposed to philosophy, but instead of neglecting the issue of death, it could enrich philosophy with its unique worldview and help unravel the knot of mortality. Specifically, psychoanalysis could contribute to philosophical approaches to death by illuminating the intricate psychical motives, fantasies, wishes, and conflicts related to it—both at the general level, and more importantly perhaps, at the individual level. Every human being fears death in her own particular way. The fear is also interrelated with a host of other feelings, idiosyncratic fantasies, and unique prior experiences. The ideas of Piven (2004) and Lifton (1979) are a good start in terms of a theoretical basis for such explorations. Thus, psychoanalysis could serve to fracture the unitary and simplistic view of death anxiety into a much richer tableau. It could help us to understand how death and the knowledge of finitude affect us, both at the theoretical level, and at the level of the individual subject.

Psychoanalysis, with its focus on concrete reality, might also overcome some problems inherent to the more existential worldview. The latter puts death at the center, but sometimes refers to an overly abstract kind of death. Thus, Adorno (1973), in criticizing Heidegger's focus on death, claims: "[t]he partisan of authenticity commits the same sin of which he accuses ... the lesser people, of the They. By means of the authenticity of death as he flees from it. Whatever announces itself as "higher" than mere empirical certainty ... falsely cleanses death from its misery and stench—from being an animalistic kicking of the bucket" (pp. 156–7). In referring to Adorno's criticism, Gaitanidis (1999) claims that Heidegger, in his understanding of death, "completely ignores the body" (p. 202). In this respect, it seems that psychoanalysis, if it were to turn its gaze more to the issue of finitude and death, would probably fare better.

Thus, death's universality might be among the factors responsible for its exclusion from analytic thought, and yet, from a different angle, analytic work is quite well suited to an exploration of death, and particularly, individual meanings of death. I stress again, however, that the importance of such individual explorations notwithstanding, there is still a general, universal aspect of death, feared for exactly what it is, regardless of one's specific history or the intricacies of one's specific response to it. Clinicians should take care not to be over-subjective or particular. In exploring individual life, prior experiences, and fantasies, one should not lose death in the process.

The universality of death is not only a limit to its inclusion in analytic theories, but also an impetus to include it. While Freud is right that psychological theories should be able to account for individual differences, they also have to supply general explanations in order not to fall into the opposite trap, of explaining only specific populations and neglecting more general elements. Death is the most universal aspect of human lives.[16] It is an event different from all others, in that it is perhaps the only one that will happen to everyone, and can be expected with certainty. Any other event may or may not happen, and, therefore, there is some theoretical logic behind not putting full weight on it, lest one should be obliged to apply different theoretical explanations to different people. Freud's solution of establishing this universality through the postulation of a fantasized event—castration—seems a poorer solution than referring to the one real event that we know will happen to everyone.

In sum, we have seen here how essential elements of different psychoanalytic outlooks hamper the inclusion of death as a significant element within analytic theory and practice. On the other hand, we observed that

---

[16] Of course there are other things common to everyone. Everyone has a childhood. Yet everyone lives it differently, and the more one develops, the less evident it becomes that one can speak of things as universal, as exceptions pile up. Since death is always a future event, it is in a way the same for everyone, because it is not yet actualized in the specific.

if psychoanalytic authors were to overcome some of these difficulties, they might have some good starting points for the integration of death into psychoanalytic theory. All things considered, the obstacles seem to far outweigh the possibilities. However, psychoanalysis is a living, developing, and multifarious enterprise. Analysts and theoreticians can find ways to deal with death once the problem is better clarified. Some premises can be changed or bypassed, and new ideas keep emerging. Rather than being a source of discouragement, the current state of affairs could, when accompanied by a recognition of death's significance, serve as an incentive to improve the theory.

14 Death in life

Looking back at the path we have taken it seems that much of the difficulty in integrating death in psychoanalysis, beyond the tradition's specific claims and beyond wider analytic tenets, is related to partial and restricted understandings of death and its influence on life, and to a neglect of some of death's dimensions. Therefore, the goal of this last chapter is to examine the possible role of death in psychic life, trying to better describe dimensions that need to be addressed, as well as to offer some broad ways of thinking about how death exerts its influence on life.

The neglect of certain dimensions of death is accompanied by an overly narrow conception of its psychic influence. Throughout this study we have seen several attempts to integrate death within a psychoanalytic mode of thought, in both theory and practice. This is done *inter alia* through the theory of the death drive, the structural model, the developmental perspective, and the link with earlier annihilatory experiences. Beyond the clear merits some such attempts do have, something fundamental in many of them remains unsatisfactory. Something in the nature of the problem of death is left out. There is an aspect of death that is related to the domain of being, to how we are with death, while the theories too readily put it back into the domain of doing, of how it is processed. Too quickly the discussion is reabsorbed in the analytic discourse. Too quickly it is brought back to the mechanics of mental functioning. Too quickly one turns to the practical, to the clinical, neglecting the understructures, the ground of therapeutic work. To be sure, death can arouse conflict in the mind and is part of mental economics, but it involves more than that.

The tendency, in short, is to leave the phenomenon and go directly to the regular explanatory mechanisms of psychoanalysis. My claim throughout has been that too much of the phenomenon has been lost on the way, in the labyrinth of the mechanism.

More important than figuring out *how* to account for death within psychoanalysis is dealing with *what* is to be accounted for. We need a more thorough consideration of the kind of presence death occupies in the mind, of some of its more latent, silent aspects. To be able to deal with death theoretically or focus more attention on it in therapy, the first step is to take into account what has to be explained, that is, to deepen and widen our vision of the way in which the anticipation of our future deaths and the acknowledgment of finitude function in our lives and influence them.

Another goal of this concluding chapter is to address the claim that death is marginal and simply unimportant in psychic life. What I will attempt to show is that this view is often based on a very restricted conception of death, and, in arguing over something specific, fails to embrace much of the wider influence death has on psychic life.

Such discussion naturally has to move beyond psychoanalytic understandings to more philosophical considerations, blurring the sometimes arbitrary distinction between the psychological and the philosophical.

Death in praxis

While I hope that through an examination of existing theories and a critique of their difficulties in giving death its due place, guidelines for a more adequate understanding of death have been drawn, it is specifically not my intention here to attempt another psychoanalytic model of the response to death, and this for several reasons, worth mentioning in themselves. First, the critique, I believe, is more important here than the details of the specific model offered to deal with the problem, which will be simply added to the list of existing proposals and contributions and then adopted or not, according to its value or chance factors.

Second, within the variety of the psychoanalytic world today, it is almost impossible to propose a model that would fit all analytic schools. And yet, the problem I have pointed at is common to most of them.[1]

This leads us to a third reason, namely that divergent analytic theories—Freud, Klein, Erikson, Kohut, Winnicott, and others—have failed to conceptualize death, although their general models widely differ. We have seen, in discussing major analytic thinkers' approaches to death, how sensitivity to death, and some sporadic insights into the

---

[1] Within the psychoanalytic world, Lacanians (and perhaps in some sense French psychoanalysts in general) are more attentive to death. Hoffman's (1998) ideas offer a good integration of death within relational or interpersonal approaches, perhaps demonstrating an ongoing shift towards greater attention to death in this school (Frommer, 2005). But death can still not be said to be integral even to these approaches. In other cases, it is more a matter of personal ideas and experiences regarding death that causes a specific analyst or therapist to be more attentive to death in his or her work.

psychological work involved, have time and again been undermined by analytic understandings of death. This derives from several elements shared by most of them (though not all elements equally apply to all theories), as seen in the previous chapter, but it also has to do with characteristics particular to each model. An interesting point that comes up in retrospect is that these authors' failure to satisfactorily account for death is specifically related to the major contributions or central concepts of their theories. Freud was perfectly aware of the importance death has in life, but kept fighting it due to an insistence on *his* discovery, the unconscious, from which death is conceived as absent, and because he understood death as the goal of a drive. Klein construed death anxiety as the primary anxiety, but insisted on understanding it within her central focus on drives, with the result that death loses its meaning in her formulations. Erikson saw adaptation to death as a personal mission of every individual, but failed precisely in an overly narrow placement of death awareness within a developmental perspective, the essence of his theory. Kohut spoke of a stage, in his notion of cosmic narcissism, where death is accepted, but failed in that he conceived it as yet another narcissistic achievement, another triumph of the developing self. Even Lacan, who was most aware of death's centrality, subjugated it to the true focus of his method, the implication of humans in the symbolic order. Thus, for each theoretician, it has been the specific application of his or her theory as is to death that resulted in a failure to truly address it.

Beyond details specific to each school, the theories have failed because they have sought to understand death in terms of a worldview that fundamentally rejects the issue of death. On another level, they have failed simply because they were theories. The attempt at theorization is itself part of the problem.[2] These authors, instead of looking at death more directly, as is, dress it up immediately with a theory, and in doing so, do not allow the phenomenon itself to exist in its own problematics, in the difficulty it poses to human beings. To simply propose another model here would be to fall into the same traps once again.

It is not only that death evades modeling and understanding; the very attempt to conceptualize it changes it. We can become aware of death or grasp it for a second, but we immediately cover it again with discourse. Bataille (1955, pp. 342–3) describes a similar dynamic whereby, through the practice of sacrifice, one can get a glimpse of death, and yet cultures

---

[2] For Searles (1965 [1961], pp. 505–6, 514) language itself, in being abstract and "reality-segmentalizing," is part of what makes death less accessible to us, and specifically so in analytic literature. Searles refers to the concrete level of the complexity of the emotions aroused by death, which he finds difficult to describe.

inevitably hide death again in their explications of sacrifice, which reinscribe it in the general order of things. Discourse is immediately brought up to seal what has been opened (Razinsky, 2009).[3] In speaking of death, we are always remote from it.

My intention then is not to supply further models of the response to death. What I do wish to offer here are broad ways of thinking about death that concern its place in psychic life in general, which could supplement the psychoanalytic understanding of death.

In advance of this discussion, a brief comment is due. Without a model can death still be part of therapy? Mine is of course not a clinical book, but perhaps a few words on the clinical aspect are in place.

I believe that on a clinical level it is much more a question of correct attention than of a suitable model. What is needed is that death and its influences have a presence in the minds of analysts and therapists.[4] This awareness or clinical sensitivity should not, however, be left to the personal inclination of this or that therapist.[5] It should instead be considered part of good clinical thought.

Death and thoughts and feelings around it are such a central part of our psychic world—I do not necessarily mean in being actively, consciously ruminated—that they simply cannot be neglected. Moreover, the defenses (among therapists and patients, as among anyone else) against recognition of death are so great that unless one is deeply aware of life's inevitable end, one will fail to listen to its repercussions in the

---

[3] As we have seen, Freud too, in his description of the encounter with death in the presence of the corpse of the loved one (1915), does not end with the horror itself. He too points to this post-hoc stage, which is for him of crucial importance: it is the birth of culture. The soul, religion, and philosophy are invented out of the necessity of overcoming the encounter with death.

[4] Cf. Searles's (1961, p. 502) similar point in the case of treatment of schizophrenia, and Frommer's (2005, pp. 484–5) belief that awareness of death is really absent not only from the literature, but also from analytic training.

While my concern here is with a psycho-dynamically oriented clinical thought, it might be worth mentioning that on a clinical level, neglect of death exists in other forms of clinical thought, such as those which ignore the whole dimension of experience. The clear exception in the clinical world is of course existential psychotherapy.

In addition, I mentioned earlier that concerning specific issues related to death such as bereavement, fatal illness, death of the analyst, suicide, war neurosis and the Holocaust, there exists ample clinical literature. What is missing is attention to less clearly manifest, and more existential aspects of mortality. Moreover, not only do some of the approaches to the issues just mentioned – fatal illness, bereavement – themselves sometimes neglect existential dimensions related to them, but overall, the focus on these aspects alone serves as a further denial of death's deeper, more general involvement with human life.

[5] As pointed out in the introduction, it might very well be that the issue of death is already one of the areas where private theories are preferred over the "official" ones.

stories of others, and might, through protectiveness, neglect an issue of great importance to the patient.[6]

The "proper" attitude to death is, first and foremost, to take it seriously. Taking death seriously means, above all, recognition of death as a thing in itself, a recognition that avoids rendering death merely the aim of a death wish, social death, separation or any other understanding where death is actually no longer death.

This awareness should be accompanied by sensitivity to the ways in which death is not sufficiently present in psychoanalytic perspectives, and how current understandings of it are lacking. Uncovering the denial on the theoretical level and getting rid of some analytic prejudices concerning death, as attempted here, are crucial steps I believe in improving the clinical attentiveness to death-related issues.

In fact, because with a few exceptions (e.g., Searles, Rosenthal, Becker, Yalom, Hoffman, Piven) the analytic models of death impede more than they enable, it is perhaps better to leave them aside when dealing with death in therapy and think in a more everyday manner, yet without the defenses that are part of it. This being said, several analytic intuitions and models about death that have accumulated throughout the years, and that are discussed throughout the current study, can serve as a tentative basis. They can be joined by those basic analytic tenets that seem well-suited to guide attention to death's influence, most particularly enquiry into subjective personal representation (as discussed in the previous chapter) and the stress put on defenses (see below); these would make a good start.

Mostly, to "give death the place in reality and in our thoughts which is its due" (Freud, 1915, p. 299), we should have a deeper understanding of where exactly death's sting and its psychic presence and influence lie. We should have a wider understanding of its interaction with our lives. It is to these questions that the remainder of this chapter is devoted.

The psychic life of death

Death is a double faced entity, both an event—a future event of which we have knowledge, one that can be anticipated, that is inevitable and that can happen at any moment—and a permanent presence that permeates

---

[6] Langs (1997, pp. 223–33) describes in detail ways in which personal conflicts around death in the therapist hinder effective coping with death fears and conflicts in the patient. Frommer (2005, pp. 489) believes analysts prefer the emotional state of not being vulnerable, and therefore tend to think less about death, while Yalom (1980, pp. 204–5) stresses that therapists must work through personal death concerns.

our entire existence, for it makes us finite and transient. It becomes an absent presence throughout life. Death also influences our entire existence in time and makes life unidirectional. Any consideration of it should include all of these aspects. This might seem obvious, but, as this study has shown, this was not the case with many earlier understandings which were limited to a specific fear of a specific death, to death as a concrete threat, or which regarded the fear of death as derived from internal dynamics rather than from knowledge of the inevitable event of death itself.

Death is a future event we anticipate, the only one which we know for sure will take place. As such, it differs from just any concrete threat. To illustrate the difference: we might not be threatened by anything at all, but we will still die someday. Even if we escape cancer, car accidents, military conflict, heart attack, violent murder, or drowning in the bathtub, we still know that, say, in 120 years from now, we will be no more.

While many people die only in old age, this is never certain. Death can intervene at any moment. It is always a possibility for us. For Heidegger (1996 [1927]), this aspect of death is subsumed in the sentence, taken from fourteenth century German writer Johannes von Tepl: "As soon as a human being is born, he is old enough to die right away" (p. 228). On any given day in my life, I might die, and never see the morrow. We have no assurance against death, nothing to count on. Even if we feel young and full of life, and our bodies are strong, we cannot feel assured that there is plenty of time ahead of us. While this continuous possibility of death is, of course, ignored by most people most of the time, it certainly has much influence on our behavior. More than any other aspect of death, this imminence seems to be the one least acknowledged in analytic theory (see for example the above critique of Jung, Erikson, and of the death drive). Imminence is a fundamental element of the fear of death. Were we to know the exact hour of our death, this would create unrestrained anxiety, perhaps to a larger extent than the usual case where we do not know when we shall die, but it would be a fear of a different kind.

Death means non-being, but this non-being is not only a future; it is a background of being. Beyond the impact death as an event has on our lives, any understanding of the fact that we die must take into account the wider perspective of finitude as something that is always there for us. We are finite, we live and act on the background of vacuity. Everything we are now will cease to be. Everything we have constructed will crumble to dust. Behind our existence looms an ominous backdrop of inexistence. This shadow of nothingness is what is missing from many of the analytic texts on death. Being subject to death means being subject to it all the time.

Death epitomizes the sense in which we lack control over aspects of our lives. We plan, we endeavor, but our efforts will not necessarily end up the way we wish.

An aspect of this lack of control is related to one's own body. As subjects, we live in a body that serves us well most of the time, but that ultimately fails. As long as everything functions well, this body may be completely transparent to us, but any minor pain, temporary disease or disability is a reminder of this ultimate failure. The symbolic self (I refer here to the level of experience) aspires high, and the body pulls it down.

Death thoroughly shapes our existence in time. We are oriented toward the future, and this future is inherently limited. Death assigns to life, or rather dictates, its irreversible nature. It renders time unidirectional, a continuous flow, which cannot be reversed. We always live toward death. Time is always shortening, and with it, possibilities.[7] This is a central aspect of the limitation of reality. Death gives reality and time their limiting force. It thus functions as a limit to fantasy, in its non-psychoanalytic sense. We cannot leave all possibilities open all the time.

Alongside an orientation to time, death gives a certain quality to time. Immortality, Minkowski (1995 [1933], p. 121) reminds us, would be much more than the extension of life in time. Life under it would slow down more and more until it freezes. Life would become gray, dull, indifferent. In the words of Freud (1916 [1915]): "Transience value is scarcity value in time" (p. 305). Life is interesting because of death.

Death is a point in the timeline of our lives, and in some senses, a privileged point. It is a point beyond which nothing can be changed. Several ethical discussions and Christian traditions have tended to see the point of death as a significant one for the determination of one's happiness (Montaigne, 1998, pp. 152–5) or moral value.[8] This is, in fact, the message of the final lines of *Oedipus the King*: "Keep your eyes on that last day, on your dying. Happiness and peace, they were not yours unless at death you can look back on your life and say I lived, I did not suffer" (1978, lines 1985–9).

---

[7] From the point of view of our experience of time, Minkowski (1995 [1933]) is probably right in distinguishing two conflicting orientations within us, one that disregards death and develops, advances and aspires, and the other that acknowledges it and sees time as shortening.

[8] The famous story in Herodotus Book I (1987, pp. 73–4) tells of King Croesus who, defeated, was on the verge of being burned alive by his captors when he came to grasp the idea conveyed to him by Solon that happiness is to be determined only at the end.

To close this section, one more point is worth mentioning. I have suggested that part of the reluctance to deal with death within psychoanalysis is related to the belief that death is an abstract philosophical concept rather than "the basic substance of life" with which psychoanalysis deals. Yet, in fact, death as a symbol occupies an interesting place, at least in western culture, for it is a symbol of both the highest and of the lowest. On the one hand, knowledge of death is what defines the human as opposed to the animal, and is the source of attempts to understand the universe, and of human thought, a view Rosenzweig (1972 [1921], p. 3) expresses in the epigraph for this work. On the other hand, however, it is the most basic. How can it be maintained that death is the stuff of philosophy, while psychoanalysis deals with the basic stuff of life, when nothing defines us more as creatures that live in bodies, rather than as pure spirits, than the fact that we die? And what is more basic than the tendency in animals to run or fight for their lives when threatened? Death could, therefore, be a bridge for psychoanalysis, having one foot in basic tendencies of the organism, and the other in symbolic thought.

Death anxiety and the thought of death

The various facets of death briefly delineated above are part of the particular significance of death anxiety and awareness of death and indeed shape their nature.

Death, and anxiety related to it, throws into question life itself, its value, and significance. Does life have a meaning? Does finitude not rob it of any value? Why am I here? Even the more radical question, is life worth living? might be at stake. Such questions, which are in a way always there for us, awaiting consideration and answer, although they are sometimes left dormant for long periods, quickly return to the fore when fear of death, or thoughts of death, arise. As I have claimed above (pp. 247–8), such questions are in some sense foreign to psychoanalytic thought (of course they are touched upon in analysis in numerous ways, put in less abstract terms).

Crucial questions such as these are often related to a thought about the ephemeral nature of life, to death anxiety. Explaining, therefore, the anxiety through a defense mechanism kind of explanation alone, or as signal of a reawakening of an earlier state, is never enough. We cannot deal with it as if it is just another move in the game when the whole game is put into question.

Fear of death and the anticipation of one's future death also involve a certain self-representation. The person, as it were, attempts to cognitively grasp herself, to reflect about her entire being. Thinking about one's death is necessarily thinking about one's life. It involves a notion of who one is as a subject in time, with a history and a future. This self-representation is not generally part of the experience of other anxieties, and does not come naturally to analytic thought. It is true that the move, over the years, from a more mechanistic view of the human being to whole person theories such as self-psychology or relational psychoanalysis, a move that reflects two tendencies found in Freud himself (see Holt, 1972), certainly relativizes the above claim.

This self-representation has, moreover, a totality about it. It involves an attempt to knit life together, and spans different epochs and experiences, good and bad, the peaks and troughs of one's existence. In this too, states of mind related to death also differ from some other data normally dealt with in analytic practice.

Freud's (1915, p. 291) argument that whenever we attempt to imagine our own death we find we are still there as spectators, gives us another aspect of this self-representation. When contemplating death, our own perspective as an agent surfaces and becomes salient. We see ourselves both on the stage and in the audience.

Kauffman (1995), in his model for the phenomenology of awareness of mortality, explains how the consciousness of our own being can be the outcome of our consciousness of death. By "dislodg[ing] consciousness from its enclosure of familiarity and ordinariness," awareness of death becomes "a spiritual awakening" (pp. 78–9). The certitude we have of our future death, says Dastur (1994, p. 46), is the foundation of the certitude we have of ourselves.

On not knowing death: Defenses and distortions

How do these different aspects of death come into play in psychic life? In the following sections, I shall try to answer this question and examine the psychic presence death has, insisting that it constitutes a significant part of psychic life. Death is inextricably intermingled with life. We will begin with a quick examination of defenses against death, insisting on how, through its ubiquity, the rejection of death becomes the material life is made from. The next section portrays a specific way in which death operates in our lives, as absence, and the following one underscores how death operates through other psychic elements. Finally we will consider the manner in which knowledge of death is always active in our minds. Throughout, death is seen as a significant psychic presence, even if it works in the dark. Death is part of the texture of life itself.

Death is a threat and generates a need to push it out of life. And yet, the ways in which it is expelled and rejected from life are so widespread and fundamental that they make it an integral part of life itself.

The defense (in the wide sense) against death is ubiquitous. Psychoanalysis exposed the level of avoidance and distortion repression can cause, and in the case of death, such processes are brought to a climax.

One kind of belief that some regard as defensive is the belief in real or symbolic continuation of life or immortality. The most famous expression of this view is of course that of Freud (1915; 1927) himself: religion as an illusion of immortality, a barricade against the admission of finitude.[9]

Another line of defense is an unconscious belief in personal immortality. Here too, Freud (1915) was the first to note this defense, in describing the roots of heroism not as bravery, but as a belief in some personal invulnerability. For Freud belief in immortality is a datum, simply the way the unconscious thinks, but it is a defense as well, rooted probably in infantile narcissistic omnipotence and an unconscious feeling of control (Wahl, 1959 [1958], p. 22).

The notion of "specialness," which includes the feeling that one is unique, different, somehow exempt from the universal law, that in one's own case, things would be different, allows Yalom (1980) to much extend the scope of this defense. Especially it may also include narcissism, and life orientations such as workaholism, where the belief that one is getting ahead, progressing, and the attempt to fill time, actually serve as defenses against death (pp. 117–29). One could also point to the desire to become a self-made man or woman, to the artist struggling to produce a unique creation, and in general to the ambition to be special, to stand out, as attempts to overcome death, and sometimes to deny it.

Yalom's (1980) second major category of defense against death is that of "the ultimate rescuer" (pp. 129–41), by which he means the clinging to some powerful image, or more precisely, some image one has rendered powerful. The rescuer can be one's partner, one's therapist or a leader, but also some higher personified cause.[10]

Firestone (1994) is especially sensitive to defenses that involve destructive couple bonds. He regards many kinds of relationship as "debilitating conventional forms of safety" and security, where people

---

[9] See Becker (1973), Piven (2004), and Firestone (1994, pp. 230–1), who adds continuity through one's progeny and through one's work as other forms of immortality. A different perspective, however, on these issues is that of Lifton (1979), who argues for the crucial significance of kinds of immortality in our lives, and does not see them as illusions, but rather as expressing the continuity of life and death.

[10] Cf. Becker's (1973, pp. 139–58) interpretation of transference.

try to secure life through merger with another person (pp. 229–30) or through dominant/submissive modes of relationship, using the other as "the ultimate rescuer" (p. 232).

For psychologists working within Terror Management Theory (Solomon, Greenberg, & Pyszczynski, 1998), adherence to worldviews results from a need to counter death awareness through the channels each culture provides for imbuing the world with meaning. For Firestone (1994) and Becker (1973) not only the adhesion to a group but also conformity—to social norms, to accepted beliefs, to traditional roles—can be seen as a defense against death. One tries not to stand out, but rather to remain within the realm of the known and solid, so as to avoid the experience of existential aloneness and fear of mortality. Interestingly, we find that we have turned through 180 degrees: polar orientations to life—attempts to stand out, to do more, to count more, on the one hand, and on the other hand efforts to not stand out, to conform to norms and, as we shall now see, to limit experience—may serve as forms of defenses against death. We begin to see the scope covered by the defenses against death and how pervasive they are in life.

Another form of defense against death is holding back, limiting, and trivializing experiences. The overall pattern here is "not living in order not to die," a pattern that found its most eloquent phrasing in Rank's (1950 [1945]) definition of the neurotic as the one who "refuses the loan (life) in order thus to escape the payment of the debt (death)" (p. 126). Again, it was Freud (1915, pp. 290–1) who first pointed at the life-restricting behavior resulting from denial of death. This line of defense ranges from everyday normal behavior to psychotic symptomatology, where psychic deadness can be an attempt to defend against the real threat of death.[11] Firestone (1994, pp. 234–6) terms these "normal" forms of behavior "microsuicides": "withdrawal of feeling and energy from personal pursuits and goal-directed activity," "estrangement from loved ones and from the world," cutting off "the highs and lows of life," through emotional withdrawal from love relationships and other deep contacts, and self-denial, through an internal voice that mocks one's efforts.

---

[11] This is one of the more pathological defenses against death described by Searles (1961, pp. 495–6), who sees schizophrenia as an attempt to defend oneself against death's inevitability: deadening, or not experiencing oneself as alive, is a defense because he who is dead needs not fear death anymore. Grandiosity, an extension of the defenses described above, is another, since omnipotence is related to immortality. Note that the existence of defenses against death in severe pathologies does not in any way mean they are limited to such states. These kinds of defenses are rather frequent.

Diverting attention could be seen another general category of defense against acknowledging death. Heidegger (1996 [1927], pp. 118–22, 233–40, 250–1) describes the trivialities of the world of the normal person, the *they* (*das Man*), as a way to submerge existential concerns in a sea of banalities. Firestone (1994, p. 227–8) also speaks about preoccupation with pseudo-problems as a defense.

One especially important form of denial of death is destructiveness. Rank (1950 [1945], p. 130), Becker (1973, pp. 29–30, 99), and Piven (2004, pp. 187–217) all see the human propensity to violence and destructiveness as a fight against recognition of one's finitude. If we accept that both group belonging and destructiveness are attempts to overcome finitude, much inter-group hate and violence can be seen as expressing a struggle against acknowledgment of mortality (see Piven, 2004, for some intriguing directions), an idea supported empirically in the findings of Terror Management Theory (Solomon, Greenberg, & Pyszczynski 1998, pp. 11–9; Pyszczynski, Rothschild & Abdollahi, 2008).

In fact, the list of behaviors, modes of thoughts, and ideologies that actually serve as a defense against the recognition of death is interminable. For some, mostly those inspired by Becker's theories, there is hardly anything that is not a response to death. "[E]verything that man does in his symbolic world is an attempt to deny and overcome his grotesque fate" (Becker, 1973, p. 27).

A word of caution is due here. Death is surely avoided and defended against, but exaggeration also has its problems. Union-like love relationship may derive from other psychical needs and the meaning of religious beliefs and ideologies is far from being subsumed in the promise of immortality. Authors that focus on the denial of death often too easily degrade much of psychic, social, and spiritual life into the realm of defense.[12]

I believe a balance should be maintained. There is indeed something about genuine relatedness that often involves a common lie that through love, one will be protected from death. Creative writing often involves some illusion of immortality. Indeed, a feeling of uniqueness is a part of our sense of ourselves. Yet these are also the building blocks of life, and the pieces that make up the puzzle of meaning.

The defenses outlined here are undoubtedly indispensable in a way. Probably no one can bear to look at death with a steady eye, to reiterate La Rochefoucauld's well-known equation of death and the sun. But when much of psychic life is recruited to ensure that recognition of death

---

[12] This, as I have already said, is where I find Becker's remarkable work lacking: there is no need to claim death anxiety is the only anxiety in order for it to be important.

will not break in, the cost is high and spreads, as we have just seen, over large areas of our life. Relationships, beliefs, engagements, feelings, and thoughts, are all affected. The price we pay for keeping awareness of death at bay is considerable.

It is crucial to recognize that it is not merely an economy of psychic pain involved. Those defenses touch every corner of our life. They affect the entire approach to life, the kind of relationships we create and our sense of self. They are intrinsically linked with every aspect of our lives. Through them, death lives a human life.

Death as a dynamic absence

It is time to get to the fundamental question of the nature of death's psychic presence. Ontologically, death is an absence and non-being, almost by definition. Phenomenologically too, it is a form of lack, a black hole, as it always lies beyond our possible experience. Freud identified this lack on both ontological and phenomenological levels, but confused it with what happens on the psychological one. His arguments against the psychic presence of death transfer this lack to the psychological level. In failing to sufficiently account for the complexity of the different levels and their differences, he carried that lack intact to the psychological world without really sufficiently acknowledging his move, and then drew the wrong conclusions, claiming that death is completely absent on the (unconscious) psychological level, and, therefore, has little influence. But one could give a different, more productive account of how death's nature as lack at the ontological and phenomenological levels is reflected at the psychological level.

In seeking to understand the kind of psychic presence death has, a fundamental issue stands out: the psychic life of death is curious, first and foremost, because death lacks a clear psychic representation. As we have seen in the first chapter, it is this unavailability to thought that caused psychoanalysis to reject death as a psychic content in the first place. And yet, I suggest, it is specifically as such, as absence, as something unavailable to thought, absurd and untenable, that death has its heaviest impact on us. Death cannot be fully grasped perhaps, but it is a significant impossibility. Death is psychically active exactly in its being absent, unclear, unsettled. The nature of the idea of death—almost absent, inherently contradictory, absurd, opposed to the rest of the system of ideas—is a dynamic source of psychic work and anxiety. It certainly is not grounds for regarding death as uninvolved in psychic life, as something our system is indifferent to as such.

Freud's argument, that we cannot entertain the idea of our death because in doing so, we remain spectators, is essentially the heart of the difficulty with the idea of death. It captures the phenomenological inaccessibility of death to us and its psychological implications. The fact that when we are alive death cannot really be grasped, and the equivalent fact that when we are dead, we can no longer grasp at all, suggest together that there is something incompatible between our psychic world and the full understanding of our death. When we die, our psychic world will be no more, and while we are alive, we are always around, as living. Thinking of death means in a fundamental way, thinking of our psychological world as not being, and this, we cannot do.

The fact that death is phenomenologically beyond reach, because ontologically it is nothingness, was aptly captured by the Hellenistic philosopher Epicurus, claiming: "Therefore that most frightful of evils, death, is nothing to us, seeing that when we exist death is not present, and when death is present we do not exist" (Long & Sedley, 1987, p. 150). Epicurus' claim amounts to saying death is phenomenologically not part of life, that it is indeed "nothing to us." Epicurus offers this as a remedy to the fear of death, which he deems unjustified: if death is nothing to us, why fear it? His approach has been, however, subject to criticism since ancient times, in that death is perhaps nothing to us, but its anticipation *is* something important for us, in signifying, for example, the end of everything we like.[13]

In a similar way, yet more elaborate and pronounced, Freud puts his finger on the phenomenological unavailability of death to us, but draws the wrong conclusions from it. He translates an ontological and phenomenological absence into a psychical one, contending that death is not present psychically. Like Epicurus, he claims in a sense that death is nothing to us:[14] that the fear of death is secondary to other issues, that it is not in itself a motive in psychic life. He too maintains that fear of death is, to some extent, an error of judgment, because death is irrepresentable and thus not really part of the psychic world, and so it is not actually death we fear. In this conclusion to the spectators argument, as well as in his other arguments why death—abstract, negative, and never experienced—is unavailable to thought, he merely dresses death's nature as absence in psychological language. He lets this unavailability to thought mislead him to the (often implicit) claim that death as such is not a

---

[13] See Long & Sedley (1987, p. 152) for one critique, and Nussbaum (1994, pp. 192–238) for a discussion of several arguments against Epicurus' claim.
[14] Whereas Epicurus refers mainly to the fact that in death we are necessarily no more, Freud focuses more on how, in life, death cannot really be part of our thought.

source of psychic concern. He errs, I believe, in that this psychological-phenomenological unavailability does not take away anything of the fear of death. It is, on the contrary, its source.[15]

What then is the nature of our idea of death, and how does this specific nature interact with psychic life and influence it? "Even for us," Freud (1913a) says, the idea of death "is lacking in content and has no clear connotation" (p. 76). Essentially, the kind of idea we have of death is always deformed. We cannot be said to possess full representation of it, and it is, therefore, always lacking, absent in our psychic system. It is tense and unsettled, shaky and self-contradictory. Vague and spreading, rather than concrete and limited.[16] As such, the idea of death is anything but indifferent or non-influential: it affects us profoundly, stirring anxiety and engaging us in psychic work. It invites us to attempt to fill in the gap, and to achieve a better understanding. It imperils the rest of our psychic world, magnetizes and eludes us, intriguing us again and again. Like a black hole, its emptiness does not allow us to ignore it, and attracts everything toward it. Brushing Freud against the grain, supplying alternative interpretations to his efforts to theorize death, supports, I propose, the picture I present here, thus obliquely suggesting that it should not be considered foreign to analytic thought, but rather integral to it.

On the level of representation, death's ontological non-being and phenomenological unreachability is reflected in the fact that death remains to some extent a psychic absence. It is precisely thus—as an absence—that it achieves its strongest impact. The lack of a clear representation of death in the mind is a source of anxiety.[17] It is not as a known that death is feared, but rather precisely as an unknown. While its representation is lacking, this absence is not a simple, neutral inexistence: we know that we do not know; we know something is missing.

What is the nature of this absence? I have just suggested, through Freud's spectators argument, that there is a fundamental, irreducible incompatibility between our psychic world and the full understanding of

---

[15] De Masi (2004, p. 109) believes our "bewilderment" in the face of the idea of our death, manifested as "an absence in our thinking," hampers any chance of achieving a stable (self) integration. Death thus accompanies us throughout life.

[16] Following Burke, Bronfen (1992) argues that because death necessarily lies beyond any personal experience of any subject, it "can only be read as a trope, as a signifier with an incessantly receding, ungraspable signified" (p. 54).

[17] Piven (2004, p. 33) thinks perhaps of similar ideas when he says that the fact that death is "an undiscovered country," that it is unpredictable and unknown, makes it more frightening. Death is "an affront to reason." People cannot believe that such a horrible fate is what awaits "something so alive, so meaningful" as human life, and so they devise alternative explanations.

our death. The idea of death, which is never complete, and always inherently unstable, cannot be assimilated within the rest of psychic life. This situates it as a chasm in the heart of the system of representations, i.e. our psychic world. Death is a hole in our capability to understand the world around us. We know of death but this is always an intrinsically precarious, open-ended, and slippery knowledge, which we never really possess, because the representation we have of death is internally contradictory. We are always alive in it. This unstable, shaky nature of our idea of death is the reason why we are thrown into turmoil in trying to figure out death for ourselves. The hole death constitutes in our system of representations is the center of a whirlpool. There is an effort to seal it or divert our thoughts away from it, but, as we shall soon see, there is simultaneously an attempt to grasp it.[18]

In fact, does Freud not tell us actually that, in the final account, anxieties are about a certain lack, that of the object? The whole hierarchy of anxieties emanates from a lack of wanted presence. Here, it seems death could be put back into the picture, because when Freud disqualifies death he does so on the basis of its absence from the mind, the fact that death has no correlative in the unconscious. And yet, it is absence rather than a presence, Freud (1926, pp. 138, 167) tells us, which causes anxiety.

Or consider the notion of trauma, how something that is precisely not available to us exerts continuous influence on us, attracting and repulsing, precisely in being unattainable. This is the kind of turmoil I am talking about concerning death.

This turmoil is not only due to the unstable, absent nature of death, but also due to the continuous threat that it poses to our psychic world. The entire psychic world is fundamentally in touch with this absence that is death. A representation of death need not necessarily rank among other representations to be considered significant.[19] Placed outside the

---

[18] A concrete example of how the gap death leaves is extended to psychic life in ever growing circles is Freud's description, in *Totem and Taboo* (1913a, pp. 55–6), of the extensions, in some groups, of the prohibition against uttering a dead man's name. Within certain tribes, new names are given to people, as well as animals and objects, whose names are the same as that of the dead person, and "[t]his usage leads to a perpetual change of vocabulary" (p. 55). The avoidance extends to anything related to the dead man. Thus we have a lack that has the potential to stir the entire system of representations. It is as if the change of words is supposed to prevent the lack underneath from revealing itself.

[19] The dynamics described in this section are of course reminiscent of Lacan's *das Ding*, and indeed this is a structural basis for the current argument, as I mentioned in the chapter on Lacan's ideas. The fundamental difference however is that here the dynamics are focused on death rather than on desire. In addition, the claims here span the more abstract and the very concrete, unlike Lacan who argues only on the more abstract level.

rest of our system of representations, and foreign to it, death can act to negate all other meanings. It is not only that we do not know it directly, but this impossibility is a continuous threat to everything else we do know and possess. All other meanings are somehow interrelated, so that our psychic world in itself seems full and sufficient. But if we look not on what one has as givens—one's mental world, feelings, thoughts, and objects—but rather on oneself as a given, the fundamental absence built into the system itself, the illusion of its being closed and sufficient, immediately surfaces. It is enough to ask "what was before I was born?" and "what will happen after I die?" to bring the fragility of everything one has built to the fore.[20]

Another, more concrete manifestation of death's nothingness on the psychological level is that death is unavailable to reason as an absurdity, as a wall our mind runs into whenever it attempts to imagine its own demise or that of others in a profound sense. It is hard to digest the fact that someone was living and is now dead. It is hard to believe, for example, that falling accidentally and breaking one's neck can kill, because it seems that there is so much more involved, from the point of view of what the life-death transition means to us, than the severity of an injury. The fact that two injuries varying only slightly in degree or body location can have such radically different results—a healed wound to soon be forgotten or the irreversible cessation of life—is revolting. This terrible contingency about death is indeed one of death's most troubling aspects. Something in it always remains beyond our understanding. It seems to carry with it a great deal of meaning—after all, nothing is more significant than the question of whether someone is dead or alive—while, on the other hand, it is utterly blind and senseless.

This is the same kind of turmoil we are thrown into when contemplating our own birth, the absolutely coincidental circumstances in the absence of which we would not have been born. The unbridgeable distance between all that we are and the sheer coincidence of our

---

I wish to insist on the wall or the void one encounters whenever pondering death in general or one's own possible inexistence, and the inherent problematic nature of the idea of death.

[20] Thus, structurally, the idea of death, on some level, is not inside the system of representation, but rather outside it. "[W]hat is clearly the essence of the dream-thoughts," Freud (1900) tells us, "need not be represented in the dream at all" (p. 305). In the same way in which in the dream there is a diversion from the wish, which is not itself part of the dream, death too is present in what surrounds it. We recall here Lacan's (1978, p. 247; 1988b. pp. 211–12) aforementioned point that in the dream there are only elaborations of desire, and that behind everything named in the dream there is the unnamable, and that this unnamable is akin to the unnamable *par excellence*, death.

existence is an obstacle to any attempt to make sense to ourselves of our lives and our world.

Freud (1905, pp. 194–5, 1909, p. 133) seems to recognize the tremendous problem of the gap between life and non-life. He speaks of the great mystery for the child as to where babies come from, which he identifies with the riddle of the Sphinx. He understands that there is something ungraspable that boggles the child's mind. Here, he refers to the psychic manifestation of the ontological gap. Yet the riddle of the Sphinx (i.e., who walks on four, two, and three legs? for which the answer is the human being) is about the two poles of life, infancy and old age, *both* of which border on nonexistence.[21] The question of the origin of life constitutes a stimulus for thought, which psychoanalysis, in its focus on the importance of sexuality in the child's mind, has identified from its very beginning. In a very similar manner, the ungraspable distance between life and death provokes thought among children, adolescents, and adults. This similarity, were it recognized, should have led psychoanalysis to less reticence in accepting death as a problem in itself.

We remember that little Hans' great curiosity concerns both extremes of life, namely where children come from (Freud, 1909, p. 10) and where dead people go (p. 69). His and all children's curiosity about origins and endings is related to this fundamental question of how can someone be when he or she was not before, and how can someone who now is, cease to be.

Any meanings we attempt to assign to death crumble in the face of it. We have seen how almost any attempt Freud makes to think about death is fraught with contradictions and paradoxes. Thus, Freud observes that on the one hand, people comfort themselves with the thought of death as essential rather than arbitrary, while on the other hand, they prefer to see it as a chance event rather than as a necessity. We saw that death robs life of meaning, while also granting it meaning. We saw, in discussing "Thoughts for the Times," that Freud (1915) claims that we think of death both too much and too little, that we are obsessed with it and, at the same time, avoid it. In the "Jewish" version of Freud's (1993 [1915]) text, one can see how those who constantly avoid death are precisely those who consider it the most and actually do not avoid it, while those who face it courageously are actually those who avoid the contemplation of it (Razinsky, 2005). Freud's difficulties are indicative: death injects a

---

[21] Lifton (1979, pp. 218–20) probably means something very similar in his evocation of the riddle of the Sphinx. I use the word 'similar' because he does not mention the nonexistence at the end of life directly, except as an active force: the killings carried by the Sphinx, by Oedipus himself and the plague put on Thebes.

chaotic element into our lives. We cannot quite get hold of it cognitively; it keeps slipping away. Something about death remains fundamentally unstable, resistant to theorization, and elusive. This applies equally to the theoretician and any layperson who ponders it. Much of what we try to say about death ends in its opposite.

Freud has thus taught us much precisely through his failures, his erring, through what Laplanche (1999 [1992], pp. 147, 197–8) would call his going-astray (*fourvoiement*). These failed attempts at theorization have led us to a better understanding of death's slipperiness: it is not only that partial understandings of death reveal themselves as unstable, but that it perhaps wholly defies conceptualization, fraught as it is with contradictions.

Returning to Freud's arguments against the possibility of death's representation, we can now look at them from a different perspective. Death, Freud told us, is negative, abstract, and has never been experienced. But is it not precisely these aspects of death that make it a constant riddle for us, and not only for unconscious thought? They comprise a problem not only in terms of integration of death in the unconscious, but also in terms of integration into our thought in general. Indeed we cannot grasp death; it is too abstract to have a concrete delimited representation, and there is a fundamental negativity inherent to it, which prevents it from being clearly conceptualized. Indeed, death being a future event, we have of course never experienced it.[22] But it is exactly this leaking aspect of death, this liquidity, which makes it a focus of attention and influence rather than some marginal psychic element.

Death is a riddle, and the inability to conceive it dictates a continuous return to it. Our difficulty in understanding death does not mean we give up the effort to do so. In fact, it has a magnetic influence, which lures us more and more to understand.

Let us look again at Freud's (1915) own phrasing of the impossibility of representing death: "It is indeed impossible to imagine our own death; and whenever we attempt to do so we can perceive that we are in fact still present as spectators" (p. 291).

Freud tells us here directly that there is a limitation to the representation of death, that it is fundamentally, structurally impossible. He then draws, however, the wrong conclusions, namely, that we disbelieve our

---

[22] In mounting these arguments Freud (1923) makes a swift, but unjustified and incorrect move from the position that death "presents a difficult problem to psychoanalysis" to his claim that fear of death is essentially something else (pp. 57–8). I criticized this move in Chapter 1. Death is a problem for thought, but this problem must be faced, on the individual level, rather than used as a reason to simply forget about death. It is a riddle that persistently baffles us, since even if it is hard to grasp, we know it is there.

death, and that death has only a marginal psychic influence. Yet read closely Freud's formulation expresses an unintended possibility, namely, that this failure in representation is not an end point, but rather a starting point—a starting point for much psychic work and further attempts at representation. There is a process involved here. One should only take Freud's words literally: "It is indeed impossible to imagine ... and whenever we attempt to do so ... " Death might be irrepresentable; but why do we "attempt to do so"? What disposes us to try to figure out death for ourselves? If Freud's (1915, pp. 289–90) descriptions of how we avoid death were the sole truth, how would he explain that? The idea that there is a human *necessity* to try to integrate death into our thinking and living seems more fitting here.[23] The attempt might be unsuccessful, yet we keep at it: "*whenever (so oft) we attempt to do so.*" Why do we repeat the act if it is doomed to failure? Why do we not understand that death simply cannot be grasped? Something leaves us unsatisfied. Possibly, we only try to do so because we know we will still be around, as spectators, thereby confirming our existence and abating the anxiety. Yet it is also possible that what drives us to attempt representation is the need to come close to death.

The famous *fort-da* scene in *Beyond the Pleasure Principle* (Freud, 1920, pp. 14–17), where Freud's grandchild plays with the wooden reel by throwing it away, emitting a long o-o-o-o (standing for *fort*, gone), and sometimes rediscovering it, is a manifestation, in the concrete action language of the child, of the same thing:[24] the child attempts to represent an absence. The absence is that of his mother, we are told, but Freud's remark (p. 15n) that the child was repeating a similar game in front of a mirror, looking at himself and then crouching down so that his image disappeared, tells us that he was also trying to represent his own absence. Of course, he does not succeed. He attempts to represent a disappearance, and fails. In staging the drama of his own vanishing, he finds himself still around as spectator, the minute he raises his head to see if his image is there or not. The point is that he repeats the attempt. He throws and rediscovers, throws and rediscovers, over and over. The attempt to represent a lack is repetitive. It fails every time, and yet this failure is itself the cure. The repetition reverses the picture and makes

---

[23] Blass's (2006) reconstruction of Freud's notion of the "desire for knowledge" as a fundamental human aspect, which she locates as an integral element of the psychoanalytic worldview, is highly pertinent here.

[24] Lacan (1966, pp. 276, 318–19; 1977a, pp. 65, 103–4), in analyzing this scene, sees it as the birth of symbolic activity in the child, who switches absences for presences, a (no)thing for a name. Lacan's interpretation is relevant here, but for the sake of the current discussion, the act itself, throwing and searching, is enough.

the failure a success. He never really masters the absence, but he can live more easily with it.

Again, the equivalence with trauma—magnetizing, installing in ourselves an urge to repeat, an impetus to grasp, to attempt what is doomed to fail—is highly pertinent. Freud even says explicitly that traumatic dreams are repeated over and over in an endeavor "to master the stimulus retrospectively, by developing the anxiety whose omission was the cause of the traumatic neurosis" (1920, p. 32).[25] That is, an experience of lack in cognitive or emotional grasping or processing leads to repetition even when the repetition fails or is painful. Commenting on the concrete encounter with death in trauma, Cathy Caruth (1996, pp. 60–5) excellently brings out that even there, the source of the shock in the mind and the need to repeat is not the experience but "the missing of this experience" (p. 62), the fact that the threat was not experienced in time.

The attempt to understand death and represent it fails. We discover that we are still there. Yet the failure to represent or to imagine does not mean death is necessarily unavailable to us. If anything, it might only mean that it is unreachable through understanding. We cannot grasp it, but death is manifested to us in other ways, through feelings, anxiety, overwhelming intrusions into our life, and the fact that it constitutes a horizon to any possible projection of ourselves into the future. The attempt to imagine death, to grasp it consciously, is to try and clothe it with sense, and this is doomed to failure. Representation is already a form of understanding. It makes of what it represents a thing, an object, imbuing it with some form of existence, while death is inexistence in its essence. This is the nature of the inherent problem in psychically grasping death. A form of absence, the attempt to impose sense on it will necessarily distort death. Binding what in its nature defies representation, the pure negative, into discursive thought must result in failure. That we remain spectators is only a manifestation of the problem. Grasping it would give us something else. But this does not mean anything concerning the availability of death to us, only its availability to discursive thought or as an object of thought or imagination.

If we wish to understand death's psychic presence, we must expand our perspective. Rather than examining the idea of death in isolation, we should look at it in a broader context of other contents in mental life. Even if death itself is absent, it is present in this absence through other representations in our mind. The next section will elaborate on death's manifestation through the rest of psychic life and interaction with it.

---

[25] Because of the lack of preparedness for anxiety, the organism was not able to bind the incoming excitation (Freud, 1920, pp. 31–2).

To be with not-to-be

Because such is the nature of death, because one has no clear idea of it, we should revise the way its involvement with life is conceived. Death's psychic impact is not to be looked for in an isolated, clear-cut idea, but in its reverberations in other parts of our mental life. It is not necessarily as a unified idea that one reacts to death, but in various indirect ways. Death works alongside and through other aspects of psychic life: as a threat to the validity of other elements, as the consciousness of an end, as the feeling of time, as a sense of urgency. It is a mistake to focus on representation when trying to understand the psychic work of death, and it is likewise wrong to focus on the direct fear of death. Instead, one should look at the continuous presence of death in the mind, not only as something to be countered or defended against, but as a psychic presence that extends to much of psychic life, as a mental factor that affects our entire presence in the world, as something that we have to live with rather than only fight. We have looked at the defenses against death but they are not the only manner in which psychic life is heavily influenced by death.

Awareness of finitude is interlaced with the material of life itself. When we are ambivalent, for example, or have trouble making decisions, death might be in the background, for we know, on some level, that our possibilities are limited, and that time flows continuously in one direction, and cannot be rewound and replayed. Part of the difficulty in making choices and in being committed to them is that, in one sense, they really can have catastrophic consequences, because they are unalterable and death looms up. Nothing, in a deep sense, can be undone or redone. Death thus burdens every decision with utmost responsibility: there might be no time for a second try, and no time to waste on second best.[26] An assured future time of existence would result in different considerations. When in analysis one finds disproportionate significance attached to this or that decision, say whether or not to leave a job, such a dynamic, where death takes the stage, might be involved.

---

[26] Our existence's general directional flow and the irreversibility of time invests everything we do with responsibility, as Sartre (1957 [1943]) pointed out. This responsibility has moral and psychological dimensions.

It is true, however, that for Sartre (1957 [1943]), the subject is finite without reference to death. In contrast to Heidegger, he claims that death is strictly not any of *my* possibilities, that it is merely a contingent fact from my subjective point of view (p. 545). It should be differentiated from finitude: by merely actualizing possibilities within life we are already finite, without death being involved (p. 546). This actually makes Sartre reject death altogether: all our projects are in principle independent of death and "there is no place for [death] in my subjectivity" (p. 548).

Finitude also influences the way we experience time. Life takes place in time, and this taking place has a psychic dimension. One could experience the changing, fleeting moments, the transience, the accumulation of the past, the contraction of the future or perhaps the more abstract perspective of the advancement of time. Finitude is relevant to all of these and to any psychological or psychoanalytic understanding of existence in time.

Death also intervenes with any future planning, conscious or unconscious. In this sense, it is really part of everything we do. In all these ways, and in others described below, death is completely inherent to life, rather than an external phenomenon. We have seen, in the example of Freud's dreams in *The Interpretation of Dreams*, how death is bound up with all forms of ambition and aspiration, interacting with and inflecting every ambitious striving. We saw it linked with issues of rivalry and self-worth. Isolating death from the rest of psychic life would result in only a partial understanding of both death itself and many interrelated issues.[27]

One place where knowledge of finitude interacts with everything else is where issues of meaning and value are involved.

So many of the questions we ask ourselves regarding what we do and wish to do, finally come down to death. What are we aiming toward when we try to achieve X? Y. And why is Y important? Because it leads to Z. And why is Z important? Our final answer, involving values and commitments, often turns out to be either a reply to death, or thrown into question by death. If we wish to be happy, to do something important, or make the best use of our time on earth, we almost always, especially on the level of our more supreme goals, take transience into account, even if many times unknowingly. We make decisions on the basis of the fact that all things happen only once, and that we all perish.

The knowledge of death shakes all the rest of our knowledge, everything we think about life. Everything else is radically put into question by it. It is as if all we think, all the meanings we attach to things, all our logic, all the laws of the world are valid and applicable as long as they are *in* life. But then we realize there is another side of the court—death,

---

[27] Some analytic explanations, in reducing death to other elements, talking of its equivalents, or accounting for it in analytic terms, seem to actually do what I am describing here and relate death to other psychic elements. I have claimed, throughout this study, that these elements, the more analytically familiar meanings, are not the ones relevant to an understanding of death, and showed how instead of shedding more light on death, they often serve to minimize its influence. One should examine death's psychic presence alongside other psychic issues and elements, but with due respect to its independent status, with attention to the mutual influences and to death's actual existence (in its different manifestations: death as a real event and finitude as an ongoing presence). All these should be held in mind.

non-being—and that there things lose their meanings, on a certain level at least. "Alexander the Great and his groom," says Marcus Aurelius (1963), "are reduced to the same state in death" (p. 53). Death equalizes. It renders values equal through flattening them.

Yet death can also have the opposite influence: whatever meanings do exist, it is from death that they are derived. It is because things are finite, that they matter, or not, matter more, or less. Nussbaum (1994) argues that many of the things we value and activities we cherish in life "get their point and their value within the structure of human time" (p. 226). Many of those would not, she suggests, be available to immortal gods. Death invests things with real meaning. Death has presence, says Dastur (1994, pp. 39–40), as that which gives all phenomena their singularity, and its blackness gives them emphasis. Freud (1916 [1915]) himself, as we recall, could not agree more.

Death is inside life. Better seeing this point could both enrich and change the psychoanalytic approach to death. Analytic authors and practitioners would be open to new aspects of experience, and would be able to add layers to their analytic understanding of various issues. They would be able to treat death not as an isolated phenomenon or its psychic impact as subsumed within some specific manifestation or symptom, but rather as a much more global and constant involvement in our lives, as something that constructs and limits them, and is always there in the background. They would be able to see death more as what dictates the meaning of much of what we do, and delineates much of our psychic world, even when it does not play a part in it as a concrete element of thought. Being in time and being subject to death have a decisive impact on our lives, which is heavily undervalued in analytic thinking. To a large extent, more awareness of the involvement of death in life would only supply a theoretical basis for something that is already done in practice. Patients are always influenced by things that lie beyond their control. They have fantasies and wishes that cannot be fulfilled. Their lives are passing without their assuming responsibility for it. Awareness of death could enrich analysts' view of all this, and deepen understanding of patients' lives.

Knowledge of death and the encounter with it

While we have difficulty in grasping the nature of death, we certainly do have knowledge of death. We know death exists and we know we are finite. Such knowledge, I claim, which psychoanalysis deems an unimportant psychic factor, is always available to us, always potentially influential.

The knowledge of death is always present at some level. Suppose we do not normally think of death. Then one day our car slides on a wet road and, for half a second, we feel it go out of control. We immediately regain control over it and nothing happens, but through this local, circumscribed event, we become aware of the danger that was involved, of the "almost," and open to the understanding that death always lurks around the corner. We are always almost, we are always playing out our lives against the backdrop of the possibility of not being.

Or suppose somebody dies. The defenses might come up right away, with the usual sense of "this will not happen to me." But still, for a short time, an understanding of mortality sometimes breaks through these defenses. What these two examples demonstrate is that there is a pre-existing awareness or knowledge of death, which we were simply reminded of. It is normally not in such a moment that we grasp for the first time that we too might die. The understanding of death's universality and irreversibility, that we too shall perish, is there in the background, even if it might be dormant or not emotionally grasped much of the time.

A case of close call might result in heavy anxiety or a sense of relief in the moments that follow it. But later, at night, consciously, and afterward for a longer time, in the deeper strata of our mind, processes will sometimes act that revolve around our fragility in the world.

The knowledge of finitude is integrated into our being in the world. Transience is acknowledged at fundamental levels of our being, acting, and thinking, even if not explicitly. As Carel (2006) so well puts it:

we always make plans within the horizon of temporal finitude. One normally makes plans for—at best—the next few decades, but does not make plans for the next millennia, or take on personal projects that cannot be completed within a human lifespan. (p. 71)

Now one could maintain against this that we might have a contrary unconscious belief, where we do not really believe that we will die. One could perhaps have, for example, grandiose manic plans. But such unconscious belief, if it exists, will already take into consideration the knowledge of finitude. It will be forged against, above, or in parallel to that knowledge of finitude, but always in reference to it. This knowledge is inseparable from our being in the world.

There are thousand reminders of death—it can be the death of a close person or a hardly known one, a car accident evaded miraculously, an earthquake across the ocean, a white hair discovered in the mirror, a tooth that rots. No matter how the encounter happened, something is cracked. We have looked into the abyss. Sometimes, nothing happens at all and still we hear the voice of death, and taste the bitter taste of finitude. It can come in the most banal of life's circumstances, and without any real reminder of death. The sky is clouded in a second—and we will not be consoled. Existence might loose its meaning at once. As Koestenbaum (1971 [1964]) describes it, seeing an accident sometimes

> makes us realize—if but for a fraction of an unpleasant moment—that the world in which we live, with its goals, prejudices, and institutions, is not the solid existence that we had believed and hoped. For a moment, our otherwise secure and predictable world has disintegrated itself into total chaos. (p. 259)

The encounter almost forces us to attempt to evaluate our life. Analytic explanations simply cannot settle for what happens in early childhood, or what can be rendered in analytic terms, and neglect these kinds of experiences. One should, rather, give them a place of their own, welcoming them into the theory.

Above the specific concern of how to include a certain fear of or concern about death within the psychoanalytic worldview, what is important to recognize is how the very fact of death influences life, how the most fundamental notions of what it is to be, of having a personality and uniqueness as a human being, of life and time having a direction, of acts being singular, and of possibilities being limited, all derive their acuteness, their meaning, and their nature from the fact of finitude. In thinking psychoanalytically about death's influence, the direct fear of death as an experience is perhaps less important than the more general presence of finitude in our minds.

Even if the fear of death were not a direct issue in treatment, and were never avowed as a feeling in itself, death would nonetheless have a crucial influence on the entire psychic universe and on one's conception of the world around oneself. For we are finite creatures, and we know we are finite. We are finite in every move we make, finite in every thought and all our experiences. Finite. *Fin.*

Final thoughts

In assessing the arguments that the "Irma's Injection" dream seems to put forth to exculpate the author-dreamer, Freud (1900) cites a joke about a man who was accused by his neighbor because a copper kettle he had borrowed from him was returned with a hole in it:

> The defendant asserted first, that he had given it back undamaged; secondly, that the kettle had a hole in it when he borrowed it; and thirdly, that he had never borrowed a kettle from his neighbour at all. (pp. 119–20)

I have often had a similar experience upon presenting the ideas of the current study to analysts. Some have said that death comes up all the time in their clinical work,[1] while others have insisted that death is not an issue for psychoanalysis, and that if it comes up in treatment, it tends to be a disguise for something else. Why, they ask, is there a need to think about death in a psychoanalytic context?

There was a second divergence regarding the status of death within analytic theory, especially in Freud. Some have said that death cannot be part of the unconscious, and thus has no place in psychoanalysis, echoing Freud's explicit claims. Others have protested that my claims regarding the absence of death from Freud's thought are untrue, and that Freud dealt with death continuously.

This ambiguity and divergence of views is, to my mind, highly significant. It testifies to a deep confusion in the psychoanalytic community regarding death: Death is very important, but hardly ever an issue. It should not be part of the theory, yet it is a dominant theme in Freud's writing. This confusion is a result of a lack of theoretical clarity regarding

---

[1] In my discussion of these issues in the introduction, I mentioned that there is a significant gap between references to death in practice, perhaps through implicit theories, and the neglect of it in theory. I also claimed that, given the lack of a good theory about death in psychoanalysis (or at least given that the theories that have been offered are usually unknown to the analytic community), there is a strong question about how those who deal with death in their practice actually do so. Moreover, how do they negotiate the theory's explicit rejection of death's importance and possibility of being represented?

death, from profound ambivalence toward death in Freud, where the reductive side tends to have the final word, to neglect hidden behind superficial acceptance in later authors. The confusion is so widespread that at certain points it becomes difficult to phrase one's arguments, because it is hard to say what the common view is, and, therefore, what needs to be addressed.

Therefore, although some psychoanalytic literature that refers to death exists, what has been needed, and what the current study has undertaken, is a deep investigation of psychoanalytic theory to locate the whole scope of its distortions, problems, and biases regarding death. What of death's significance is lost in the ways it is depicted in psychoanalysis? Where do specific psychoanalytic formulations of death and of death anxiety fail? And where do the potentialities of psychoanalytic thinking about death lie?

★ ★ ★

A full summary of the path traveled in this book does not seem necessary. There is one step though, the one that opened this book, that perhaps needs to be recapitulated. The psychoanalytic neglect and rejection of death are grounded in claims against the possible representation of death, in both unconscious and conscious thought. Death is held to be absent from the unconscious because death is negative, abstract, and involves time, and because nothing like it has been experienced and it has no instinctual correlative. Looking back, my critique of these arguments can be summed up as follows. To begin with, I find some of them simply unconvincing. Then, whether convincing or not, questions always arise as to their application. Freud and his followers much more eagerly applied such criteria to death than to other phenomena, allowing for fewer degrees of freedom or room for variation. Moreover, these arguments have often not been reevaluated with the evolution of psychoanalytic theory, and plausible, available solutions, even if partial, were not used.

All this gives the impression that Freud's arguments are more of a way to justify a preexisting position than the true origin of it. The problem seems, to a large extent, to lie elsewhere.

Most importantly, these arguments are simply beside the point, in two important respects. First, death simply does not work that way. It is a mistake to see death as an isolated representation, because it works alongside and through other aspects of mental life. In general, awareness of death is much more global and subtle. Death alters and colors other psychic concerns. It influences very basic levels of our approach to life, even when not directly acknowledged. Our whole experience of life would be different without death. In setting a limit to life, death essentially enters into almost every consideration. It takes part in ambition, and in planning. It burdens and complicates decision making. It affects the experience of time, enters into ethical considerations, and influences the meanings and values we attribute to things.

Second, and lastly, the absence of a clear representation of death, captured so well in Freud's spectators argument, does not negate the possible influence of death, but actually reinforces it. Death is an absurdity we cannot really grasp that works in the psyche precisely through being a kind of unknown, a nothingness. We actually never possess a clear representation of death. The representation we have of it is always deficient, unsettled, in internal tension, and open ended. Yet it is exactly this leakiness of death's representation that makes it a source of anxiety and a dynamic center of psychic activity.

★ ★ ★

Is there a hole in the psychoanalytic kettle? The current work has been aimed at exposing a simple and curious fact: that in the most profound and intricate theory of human nature, there is a significant aspect of human life that is barely addressed—death. Death is systematically avoided, distorted, transformed, and forgotten in analytic theory.

This book has tried to make explicit, examine, and criticize certain fallacies in the psychoanalytic inattention to death. Furthermore, it has sought to identify the reasons for such inattention, seek out points of clash and possible dialog, and examine the possible role of death in the mind.

My focus was on what happens when theory meets death. We saw some explicit theoretical rebuttals of the idea that death has psychical importance. Yet we also encountered many more subtle ways in which death is ignored. The concept itself might be altered, psychical reactions to it overlooked, discussions of it biased or its meanings and consequences left untouched. We saw how the essence of death repeatedly slips out of view. Even when death is brought into the discussion it is repeatedly sterilized and smoothed over. Even in texts that supposedly focus on death, the essence of death itself is sometimes left out, while only the shell remains. In pursuit of death through what is said and not said in analytic theory, I have tried to lift the veil of silence that has been covering it.

Thoughts and fears of death, as we saw, are treated as all kinds of things—indications of guilt, separation difficulties, repressed death wishes toward an other, regression to infantile modes of thought—that is, anything except what would suggest a natural emotional response to a realistic apprehension of the deepest of all truths. Beyond this, death is oftentimes simply not considered a problem at all. An analyst or analytic author writing a book will rarely deem it important to address the psychic impact of human finitude.

One could also present things from the opposite angle: were it the case that death were important, would analytic theory be in a position to take it into account? It seems that without certain revisions, the answer is, at least partially, no. One would tend to see it as something local, concrete, and restricted.

Of course, the picture contains significant exceptions. They include Freud's insights into human death-denying practices, the doubts and hesitation accompanying his statements against the validity of the psychic reaction to death, and his attempt to give death centrality with the death drive. They include Klein's feeling that death must be fundamental to humans and Lacan's repeated stress on the existential predicament. But all these remain a secondary voice accompanying a clearer dominant melody.

Death troubles people, from childhood till old age, and on a profound psychic level, similar to the one psychoanalysis deals with. Can it seriously be maintained that it is not a relevant issue for psychoanalysis? That human beings lack a concept of death at birth changes nothing. We are born into death, a datum that precedes life itself. When knowledge of death develops, it has an impact, and this should be of concern to psychoanalysis.

★ ★ ★

Analysts might retort the claim that death is neglected by arguing that psychoanalysis is different, that in it castration and internal conflicts always have primacy over death, that death does not hold much interest for them, and that they have something else to offer. This response is perhaps unlikely, but a theoretical problem nevertheless remains. If psychoanalysis wishes to deepen and develop its enquiry, and aspires to attain the truth, one must do one's best to achieve this aim. If there is a basic problem with the theory, and significant dimensions of existence risk being left out, one should, rather than entrench oneself in old positions, attempt to integrate these aspects and understand them.

We have seen repeated inconsistencies and contradictions in analytic theory in reference to death. The theory fails to hold up, so it seems, with its current conceptions of death.

Living under the shadow of death and thinking death are a challenge. Rather than dismissing mortality as a side-effect, or a non-issue, psychoanalysis should deepen its investigation into how it affects us. Every person struggles with death; finitude has a psychic impact psychoanalysis cannot remain silent about. This would mean remaining too alienated from experience. If analytic authors wish to dismiss the psychic importance of death, they should come up with good reasons for doing so, and such reasons have not been forthcoming. The direct arguments against the psychic significance of fear of death are partial, and not very convincing. The reduction of fear of death seems exaggerated, indiscriminately wide-ranging, and almost absurd. The theoretical problem with death seems more to result from the fact that death challenges several analytic assumptions. This, however, should have been the trigger for questioning the assumptions rather than for dismissing the entire issue.

The inability to seriously account for an issue as fundamental as death, which deeply influences psychic life, should be an impetus for change. If the theory is built in such a way that it cannot account for death, be it due to assumptions that turn to infantile development for explanations or due to the emphasis on the necessary involvement of the unconscious, then where has it gone wrong?

I mean this positively. The difficulty in thinking psychoanalytically about death could lead to critical self-examination. It probes the questions most essential to psychoanalysis itself. Through this prism, psychoanalysis can test itself and evaluate its possibilities.

Alternatively, psychoanalysis can acknowledge its frontiers, its limits of understanding, and declare itself incapable of accounting for parts of psychic life. It can accept that some dimensions of human minds remain foreign to it. This possibility is complicated, for several reasons. First, patients, and people in general, will not similarly limit their psychic world to accommodate psychoanalysis. Death is too important an issue to be excluded. Not only the general account of the human being, but also the treatment of specific patients will be found to be impaired.

A second problem is that limits are too easily forgotten. There is a risk that the only explanation an analytic view will be able to supply, which will naturally see death in analytic terms, will be taken as a satisfying and exhaustive explanation, and its inherent limitedness will be forgotten. Light is shed on one face of death, for example, the fact that death wishes toward another can make one afraid to die, but then this becomes the explanation of fear of death in general, and one forgets that the fear can follow from many other threats, and more importantly, from our knowledge that life is finite.

In certain contexts, psychoanalysis has been very careful in stating its limits. It will usually declare questions of religious affiliation or political ideology, for example, outside of its scope. These, so goes the claim, are only part of analysis insofar as they are found to be deeply interconnected with the patient's neurotic tendencies. But death is very different in this regard. Existential questions are perhaps not accountable by psychoanalysis, but they are of the same nature as problems that psychoanalysis does deal with. They are integrally part of our psychic world. Death cannot be dissociated from the rest of psychic life.

Ignoring death limits the range of possibilities and situations that psychoanalysis can deal with. This can only be at the price of limiting psychoanalysis' scope.

★ ★ ★

The basic psychological movement facing the lack of clear representation of death, portrayed in the last chapter, is that of approaching and holding back, attempt and failure. Looking back at our journey through the analytic literature, this dynamic emerges as characteristic not only of the mind's grappling with death, but perhaps of psychoanalysis's very attempts to think death theoretically. It is true that for the most part the reductive tendencies have had the upper hand, but one could not ignore how this hole in the analytic understanding of psychic life repeatedly calls forth further attempts at theorization. This was perhaps clear with regard to Freud whose sensitivity to death, and basic position on its psychic importance, kept infiltrating the reductive theoretical position. This back and forth could also be seen as characteristic of the wider history of psychoanalysis: alongside many analytic explanations of death which are explicitly reductive or marginalizing and meant to explain away, we saw many more genuine attempts to grasp death analytically. Structural difficulties related to the nature of psychoanalytic explanations, joined perhaps by the more general resistance of death to theory, rendered many of these latter attempts unproductive. It was the business of much of this book to uncover the way those attempts often do injustice to death or express unwittingly reductive positions, to uncover the pattern of inclusion becoming exclusion. And yet having gone through much of the history of the attempts of psychoanalysis to account for death, the seriousness of the attempts and their persistence become manifest as well. In close analogy to the mind's unsuccessful attempts at the representation of death, the theory can be said to have strived, over and over again, to grasp death analytically and take it into account. Repeated failures and the hole left in analytic theory in what concerns death did not prevent further attempts. From Freud's cultural texts and his existential position in "Thoughts for the Times," from the consistent appearance of death in *The Interpretation of Dreams*, to Freud's heroic attempt at theorization with the theory of the death drive, and then in attempts by thinkers like Klein, Erikson, and others to bring death back into theory, in the way Lacan does and does not do it, in the way some of the more existentially oriented thinkers go a long way in bridging psychoanalysis and death (even if then at some point they hold back), it becomes clear how analytic thought refuses to leave death outside. This gives hope that more successful explanations will emerge, or perhaps that more attention will be devoted, clinically and theoretically, to death. Understanding the history of these failures, and the profundity of the analytic difficulty with death, as attempted here, is perhaps the first step.

References

Abraham, K. (1968 [1911]). Notes on the psychoanalytical investigation and treatment of manic-depressive insanity and allied conditions. In W. Gaylin (Ed.), *The meaning of despair* (pp. 26–49). New York, NY: Science House.

Adorno, T. W. (1973 [1964]). *The jargon of authenticity*. (K. Tarnowski & F. Will, Trans.). Evanston, IL: Northwestern University Press.

Alford, C. F. (1992). Greek tragedy and the place of death in life. *Psychoanalysis and Contemporary Thought*, **15**, 129–160.

Alvarado, K., Templer, D., Bresler, C., & Thomas-Dobson, S. (1992–1993). Are death anxiety and death depression distinct entities? *Omega – Journal of Death and Dying*, **26**(2), 113–118.

Anthony, S. (1971). *The Discovery of death in childhood and after*. London: Allen Lane.

Anzieu, D. (1986 [1975]). *Freud's self-analysis*. London: The Hogarth Press.

Barford, D. (1999). In defence of death. In R. Weatherill (Ed.), *The death drive: New life for a dead subject?* (pp. 12–39). London: Rebus Press.

Barzilai, S. (1995). Reading Lacan, or Harlaquanage: An essay review. *American Imago*, **52**(1), 81–106.

Bataille, G. (1955). Hegel, death and sacrifice. In F. Botting & S. Wilson (Eds.) (1997), *The Bataille reader* (pp. 279–295). Oxford: Blackwell.

Becker, E. (1973). *The denial of death*. New York, NY: The Free Press.

Bibring, E. (1941). The development and problems of the theory of the instincts. *International Journal of Psychoanalysis*, **22**, 102–130.

—— (1943). The conception of the repetition compulsion. *The Psychoanalytic Quarterly*, **12**, 486–519.

Blanchot, M. (1995 [1949]). Literature and the right to death. (L. Davis, Trans.). In *The work of fire* (pp. 300–344). Stanford: Stanford University Press.

Blass, R. B. (2001). On the ethical and evaluative nature of developmental models in psychoanalysis. *The Psychoanalytic Study of the Child*, **56**, 193–218.

—— (2003a). On ethical issues at the foundation of the debate over the goals of psychoanalysis. *International Journal of Psychoanalysis*, **84**, 929–944.

—— (2003b). On the question of the patient's right to tell and the ethical reality of psychoanalysis. *Journal of the American Psychoanalytic Association*, **51**, 1283–1304.

(2006). A psychoanalytic understanding of the desire for knowledge as reflected in Freud's Leonardo da Vinci and a memory of his childhood. *International Journal of Psychoanalysis*, **87**, 1259–1276.

Bolivar, E. (1993). The ontological grounds of the death instinct in Freud. *Psychoanalysis and Contemporary Thought*, **16**, 123–147.

Bonasia, E. (1988). Death instinct or fear of death? Research into the problem of death in psychoanalysis. *Rivista di Psicoanalisi*, **34**, 272–314

Boothby, R. (1991). *Death and desire. Psychoanalytic theory in Lacan's return to Freud.* New York, NY: Routledge.

Borch-Jacobsen, M. (1991). *Lacan: The absolute master.* (D. Brick, Trans.). Stanford, CA: Stanford University Press.

Bowie, M. (1991). *Lacan.* Cambridge, MA: Harvard University Press.

Breger, L. (1981). *Freud's unfinished journey. Conventional and critical perspectives in psychoanalytic theory.* London: Routledge and Kegan Paul.

(2000). *Freud: Darkness in the midst of vision.* New York, NY: John Wiley and Sons.

Brodsky, B. (1959). The self-representation, anality, and the fear of dying. *Journal of the American Psychoanalytic Association*, **7**, 95–108.

Bromberg, W., & Schilder, P. (1936). The attitude of psychoneurotics towards death. *The Psychoanalytic Review*, **23**, 1–25.

Bronfen, E. (1992). *Over her dead body: Death, femininity and the aesthetic.* New York: Routledge.

Brown, N. O. (1959). *Life against death: The psychoanalytical meaning of history.* New York, NY: Vintage Books.

Buxbaum, E. (1951). Freud's dream interpretation in the light of his letters to Fliess. *Bulletin of the Menninger Clinic*, **15**(6), 197–212.

Cappon, D. (1973 [1961]). The psychology of dying. In H. M. Ruitenbeek (Ed.), *The interpretation of death* (pp. 73–86). New York, NY: Jason Aronson.

Carel, H. (2001). Born to be bad: Freud's death drive as the source of human evilness. Lecture read at the 2nd global conference on: Perspectives on evil and human wickedness (March, 2001). Retrieved August 20, 2002, from Wickedness site http://www.wickedness.net/ Carel.pdf.

(2006). *Life and death in Freud and Heidegger.* Amsterdam: Rodopi.

Caruth, C. (1996). *Unclaimed experience. Trauma, narrative and history.* Baltimore and London: Johns Hopkins University Press.

Carveth, D. L. (1994). Dark Epiphany: The encounter with finitude or the discovery of the object in *The body. Psychoanalysis and Contemporary Thought*, **17**(2), 215–250.

Chadwick, M. (1973 [1929]). Notes upon the fear of death. In H. M. Ruitenbeek (Ed.), *The interpretation of death* (pp. 73–86). New York, NY: Jason Aronson.

Chasseguet Smirgel, J. (1988). Freud et la féminité: Quelques taches aveugles sur le continent noir. In *Les deux arbres du jardin: Essai*

psychanalytique sur le rôle du père et de la mère dans la psyché (pp. 41–70). Paris: Des Femmes.
Choron, J. (1972 [1964]). *Death and modern man.* New York, NY: Collier Books.
Critchley, S. (1999), Original traumatism: Levinas and psychoanalysis. In R. Kearney & M. Dooley (Eds.), *Questioning ethics: Contemporary debates in philosophy* (pp. 230–242). London: Routledge.
Dastur, F. (1994). *La Mort: Essai sur la finitude.* Paris: Hatier.
David, C. (1996). Le deuil de soi-même. *Revue Française de Psychanalyse,* **60,** 15–32.
Derrida, J. (1987). *The post card: From Socrates to Freud and beyond.* (A. Bass, Trans.). Chicago, IL: University of Chicago Press.
Doka, K. J. (1995). The awareness of mortality in midlife: Implications for later life. In J. Kauffman (Ed.), *Awareness of mortality* (pp. 75–89). Amityville, NY: Baywood.
Edwards, P. (Ed.) (1967). My death. In *The encyclopedia of philosophy* (pp. 416–419). New-York, NY: The Free Press.
Eigen, M. (1995). Psychic deadness: Freud. *Contemporary Psychoanalysis,* **31,** 277–299.
Eissler, K. R. (1955). *The psychiatrist and the dying patient.* New York, NY: International Universities Press.
Ekstein, R. (1949). A biographical comment on Freud's dual instinct theory. *American Imago,* **6,** 211–216.
Erikson, E. H. (1963 [1950]). *Childhood and society.* (2nd edn.). New York, NY: W. W. Norton.
— (1954). The dream specimen of psychoanalysis. *Journal of the American Psychoanalytic Association,* **2,** 5–56.
— (1964). *Insight and responsibility.* New York, NY: W. W. Norton.
— (1982). *The life cycle completed.* New York, NY: W. W. Norton.
Evans, D. (1996). *An introductory dictionary of Lacanian psychoanalysis.* London: Routledge.
Falzeder, E., & Brabant, E. (Eds.) (1993–2000). *The correspondence of Sigmund Freud and Sándor Ferenczi* (Vols. 1–3). (P. T. Hoffer, Trans.). Cambridge, MA: The Belknap Press of Harvard University Press.
Feifel, H., & Hermann, L. (1973). Fear of death in the mentally ill. *Psychological Reports,* **33**(3), 931–938.
Feifel, H., & Branscomb, A. B. (1973). Who's afraid of death? *Journal of Abnormal Psychology,* **81**(3), 282–288.
Fenichel, O. (1945). *The psychoanalytic theory of neurosis.* New York, NY: W. W. Norton.
Fichtner, G. (Ed.) (2003 [1992]). *The Sigmund Freud – Ludwig Binswanger correspondence 1908–1938.* (A. J. Pomerans, Trans.). New York, NY: Other Press.
Firestone, R. W. (1994). Psychological defenses against death anxiety. In R. A. Neimeyer (Ed.), *Death anxiety handbook* (pp. 217–241). Washington, DC: Taylor and Francis.

References

Fortner, B. V., Neimeyer, R. A., & Rybarczyk, B. (2000). Correlates of death anxiety in older adults: A comprehensive review. In A. Tomer (Ed.), *Death attitudes and the older adult* (pp. 95–108). Philadelphia, PA: Brunner-Routledge.

Freud, E. L. (Ed.) (1960). *Letters of Sigmund Freud.* (T. Stern & J. Stern, Trans.). New York, NY: Basic Books.

Freud, S. (1894). The neuro-psychoses of defence. In J. Strachey (Ed.), *The standard edition of the complete psychological works of Sigmund Freud* (Vol. 3, pp. 43–61). London: Hogarth Press.

(1900). The interpretation of dreams. In *S. E.* (Vols. 4–5).

(1901). The psychopathology of everyday life. In *S. E.* (Vol. 6).

(1905). Three essays on the theory of sexuality. In *S. E.* (Vol. 7, pp. 124–243).

(1908). The sexual theories of children. In *S. E.* (Vol. 9, pp. 206–226).

(1909). Analysis of a phobia in a five year old boy. In *S. E.* (Vol. 10, pp. 1–149).

(1913a). Totem and taboo. In *S. E.* (Vol. 13, pp. 1–162).

(1913b). The theme of the three caskets. In *S. E.* (Vol. 12, pp. 289–302).

(1914). On narcissism. In *S. E.* (Vol. 14, pp. 67–104).

(1915). Thoughts for the times on war and death. In *S. E.* (Vol. 14, pp. 273–300).

(1916 [1915]). On transience. In *S. E.* (Vol. 14, pp. 305–308).

(1916). Some character-types met within psychoanalytic work. In *S. E.* (Vol 14, pp. 309–336).

(1916–1917). Introductory lectures on psychoanalysis. In *S. E.* (Vol. 16, pp. 392–411).

(1917 [1915]). Mourning and melancholia. In *S. E.* (Vol. 14, pp. 239–258).

(1918 [1914]). From the history of an infantile neurosis. In *S.E.* (Vol. 17, pp. 3–122).

(1919). The uncanny. In *S. E.* (Vol. 17, pp. 217–252).

(1920). Beyond the pleasure principle. In *S. E.* (Vol. 18, pp. 1–64).

(1923). The Ego and the Id. In *S. E.* (Vol. 19, pp. 1–66).

(1924a). The dissolution of the Oedipus complex. In *S. E.* (Vol. 19, pp. 173–182).

(1924b). The economic problem of masochism. In *S. E.* (Vol. 19, pp. 155–170).

(1925). On negation. In *S. E.* (Vol. 19, pp. 235–239).

(1926). Inhibitions, symptoms and anxiety. In *S. E.* (Vol. 20, pp. 87–174).

(1948 [1926]). Hemmung, Symptom und Angst. In *G. E.* (Vol. 14, pp. 111–205).

(1927). The future of an illusion. In *S. E.* (Vol. 21, pp. 1–56).

(1930). Civilization and its discontents. In *S. E.* (Vol. 21, pp. 57–146).

(1933a [1932]). New introductory lectures on psychoanalysis. In *S. E.* (Vol. 22, pp. 1–182).

(1933b [1932]). Why war? In *S. E.* (Vol. 22, pp. 195–218).

(1937). Analysis terminable and interminable. In *S. E.* (Vol. 23, pp. 209–254).

(1939 [1934–1938]). Moses and monotheism: Three essays. In *S. E.* (Vol. 23, pp. 1–138).

(1940 [1938]). An outline of psychoanalysis. In *S. E.* (Vol. 23, pp. 141–207)

(1991). *Gesammelte Werke: Chronologisch geordnet.* London: Imago Publishing.
(1993 [1915]). Death and us. In D. Meghnagi (Ed.), *Freud and Judaism* (pp. 11–40). London: Karnac Books.
Friedman, J. A. (1992a). Freud's todestrieb: An introduction. Part 1. *International Review of PsychoAnalysis,* **19,** 189–196.
(1992b). Freud's todestrieb. Part 2. *International Review of Psychoanalysis,* **19,** 309–322.
Frommer, M. S. (2005). Living in the liminal spaces of mortality, *Psychoanalytic Dialogues,* **15**(4), 479–498.
Gabel, P. (1974). Freud's death instinct and Sartre's fundamental project. *The Psychoanalytic Review,* **61,** 217–227.
Gay, P. (1988). *Freud : A life for our time.* London and Melbourne: J. M. Dent and Sons.
Gaitanidis, A. (1999). A critical examination of Heidegger's existential-ontological account of death. In R. Weatherill (Ed.), *The death drive: New life for a dead subject?* (pp. 193–206). London: Rebus Press.
Galt, C. P., & Hayslip, B., Jr. (1998). Age differences in levels of overt and covert death anxiety. *Omega – Journal of Death and Dying,* **37**(3), 187–202.
Gediman, H. K. (1983). Annihilation anxiety: The experience of deficit in neurotic compromise formation. *International Journal of Psychoanalysis,* **64,** 59–70.
Golub, S. (1981–1982). Coping with cancer: Freud's experiences. *The Psychoanalytic Review,* **68**(2), 191–200.
Green, A. (1983). *Narcissisme de vie. Narcissisme de mort.* Paris: Les Editions de Minuit.
Grinstein, A. (1968). *On Sigmund Freud's dreams.* Detroit, MI: Wayne State University Press.
Grotjahn, M. (1951). About the representation of death in the art of antiquity and in the unconscious of modern men. In G. B. Wilbur & W. Muensterberger (Eds.), *Psychoanalysis and culture: Essays in honor of Géza Róheim* (pp. 410–424). New York, NY: International Universities Press.
Grotstein, J. S. (1990a). Nothingness, meaninglessness, chaos, and the "black hole" I – The importance of nothingness, meaninglessness, and chaos in psychoanalysis. *Contemporary Psychoanalysis,* **26,** 257–290.
(1990b). Nothingness, meaninglessness, chaos, and the "black hole" II – The black hole. *Contemporary Psychoanalysis,* **26,** 377–407.
(1990c). The "black hole" as the basic psychotic experience: Some newer psychoanalytic and neuroscience perspectives on psychosis. *Journal of the American Academy of Psychoanalysis,* **18**(1), 29–46.
(1991). Nothingness, meaninglessness, chaos, and the "black hole" III – Self- and interactional regulation and the background presence of primary identification. *Contemporary Psychoanalysis,* **27,** 1–33.
Hamilton, J. W. (1976). Some comments about Freud's conceptualization of the death instinct. *International Review of Psychoanalysis,* **3,** 151–164.
Hárnik, J. (1930). One component of the fear of death in early infancy. *International Journal of Psychoanalysis,* **11,** 485–491.
Heidegger, M. (1978 [1929]). What is metaphysics. In *Basic writings.* (D. F. Krell, Trans.) (pp. 95–112). London: Routledge and Kegan Paul.

(1996 [1927]). *Being and time.* (J. Stambaugh, Trans.). New York, NY: State University of New York Press.
Herodotus. *The History.* (D. Grene, Trans.) (1987). Chicago and London: The University of Chicago Press.
Hoelter, J. W. (1979). Multidimensional treatment of fear of death. *Journal of Consulting and Clinical Psychology,* **47**(5), 996–999.
Hoffman, F. H., & Brody, M. W. (1957). The symptom, fear of death. *The Psychoanalytic Review,* **44**, 433–438.
Hoffman, I. Z. (1979). Death anxiety and adaptation to mortality in psychoanalytic theory. *The Annual of Psychoanalysis,* **7**, 233–269.
(1998). *Ritual and spontaneity in the psychoanalytic process: A dialectical-constructivist view.* Hillsdale, NJ: The Analytic Press.
Holt, R. R. (1972). Freud's mechanistic and humanistic images of man. In R. R. Holt & E. Peterfreund (Eds.) (Vol. 1, pp. 3–24), *Psychoanalysis and contemporary science.* New York, NY: Macmillan.
Hulsey, T. L., & Frost, C. J. (1995). Psychoanalytic psychotherapy and tragic sense of life and death. *Bulletin of the Menninger Clinic* **59**, 145–159.
Hurvich, M. (2003). The place of annihilation anxieties in psychoanalytic theory. *Journal of the American Psychoanalytic Association,* **51**(2), 579–616.
Hyman, S. E. (1981). On *The interpretation of dreams.* In P. Meisel (Ed.), *Freud: A collection of critical essays* (pp. 121–44). Englewood Cliffs, NJ: Prentice Hall.
Ibsen, H. (1921 [1867]). *Peer Gynt.* (R. Farquharson Sharp Trans.). London: J. M. Dent.
Jaques, E. (1988 [1965]). Death and the mid-life crisis. In E. B. Spillius (Ed.), *Melanie Klein today: Developments in theory and practice, Vol. 2: Mainly practice* (pp. 226–247). London: Routledge.
Jones, E. (1951 [1926]). The psychology of religion. In *Essays in applied psychoanalysis* (Vol. 2, pp. 190–197). London: Hogarth Press.
(1953). *Sigmund Freud: Life and work* (Vol.1). London: Hogarth Press.
(1957). *Sigmund Freud: Life and work* (Vol.3). London: Hogarth Press.
Jonte-Pace, D. (2001). *Speaking the unspeakable,* Berkeley: University of California Press
Jung, C. G. (1960 [1931]). The stages of life. In *The structure and dynamics of the psyche.* (R. F. C. Hull, Trans.) (pp. 387–403). New York, NY: Pantheon Books.
(1960 [1934]). The soul and death. In *The structure and dynamics of the psyche.* (R. F. C. Hull, Trans.) (pp. 404–415). New York, NY: Pantheon Books.
(1963). *Memories, dreams, reflections.* London: Collins and Routledge and Kegan Paul.
Kastenbaum, R. (1977). Death and development through the lifespan. In H. Feifel (Ed.), *New meanings of death* (pp. 18–45). New-York, NY: McGraw-Hill.
Kauffman, J. (1995). Blinking: A tanatocentric theory of consciousness. In J. Kauffman (Ed.), *Awareness of mortality* (pp. 75–89). Amityville, NY: Baywood.

Kaufmann, W. (1959). Existentialism and death. In H. Feifel (Ed.), *The meaning of death* (pp. 39–63). New-York, NY: McGraw-Hill.

Keiser, S. (1952). Body ego during orgasm. *The Psychoanalytic Quarterly*, **21**, 153–166.

Klein, M. (1932). Early stages of the Oedipus conflict and of super-ego formation. In *The psychoanalysis of children* (pp. 179–209). London: Hogarth.

—— (1933). The early development of conscience in the child. In Klein, M., Contributions to psychoanalysis 1921–1945. London: Hogarth

—— (1946). Notes on some schizoid mechanisms in Klein. In M. Heimann, P. Isaacs, & J. Riviere (Eds.), *Developments in psychoanalysis* (pp. 292–320). London: Hogarth.

—— (1948). A contribution to the theory of anxiety and guilt. *International Journal of Psychoanalysis*, **29**, 112–123.

—— (1952). Some theoretical conclusions regarding the emotional life of the infant in Klein. In M. Heimann, P. Isaacs, & J. Riviere (Eds.), *Developments in psycho-analysis* (pp. 198–236). London: Hogarth.

—— (1957). *Envy and gratitude: A study of unconscious sources.* New York, NY: Basic Books.

Koestenbaum, P. (1971). The vitality of death. *Omega – Journal of Death and Dying*, **2**, 253–271.

Kofman, S.(1985). *The enigma of woman: Woman in Freud's writings.* (C. Porter, Trans.). Ithaca: Cornell University Press.

—— (1991 *[1974]*). *Freud and fiction.* (S. Wykes, Trans.). Cambridge: Polity Press.

Kohut, H. (1966). Forms and transformations of narcissism. *Journal of the American Psychoanalytic Association*, **14**, 243–272.

—— (1977). *The restoration of the self.* New York, NY: International Universities Press.

—— (1978 [1954]). Discussion of: 'Eros and Thanatos: A critique and elaboration of Freud's death wish' by Iago Galdston. In P. H. Ornstein (Ed.), *The search for the self* (Vol. 1, pp. 177–185). New York: International Universities Press.

—— (1985a). On courage. In C. B. Strozier (Ed.), *Self psychology and the humanities* (pp. 5–50). New York, NY: W.W. Norton.

—— (1985b). Stranger, take word to Sparta: here we lie obeying her orders. A conversation with Charles Strozier, July 16, 1981. In C. B. Strozier (Ed.), *Self psychology and the humanities* (pp. 263–269). New York, NY: W.W. Norton.

—— (1990 [1978]), Reflections on advances in self psychology. In P. H. Ornstein (Ed.), *The search for the self* (Vol. 3, pp. 261–357). Madison, CT: International Universities Press.

—— (1991 [1980]). Selected problems of self psychological theory. In P. H. Ornstein (Ed.), *The search for the self* (Vol. 4, pp. 489–523). Madison, CT: International Universities Press.

Kojève, A. (1947). *Introduction à la lecture de Hegel.* Paris: Gallimard.

Krell, D. F. (1994). Immanent death, imminent death – Freud's Beyond the pleasure principle and Heidegger's Being and time. In S. Shamdasani & M. Münchow (Eds.), *Speculations after Freud: Psychoanalysis, philosophy and culture* (pp. 151–166). London: Routledge.

Kristeva, J. (1987). *Soleil noir. Dépression et mélancolie*. Paris: Gallimard.
    (2000 [1996]). *The sense and non-sense of revolt*. (J. Herman, Trans.).
    New York, NY: Columbia University Press.
Kübler-Ross, E. (1969). *On death and dying*. London: Collier-Macmillan.
Lacan, J. (1966). *Écrits*. Paris: Seuil.
    (1973). *Le Séminaire, Livre XI (1964): Les quatre concepts fondamentaux de la psychanalyse*. Paris: Seuil.
    (1975). *Le Séminaire, Livre I (1953–4): Les écrits techniques de Freud*. Paris: Seuil.
    (1977a). *Écrits: A selection*. (A. Sheridan, Trans.). New York: W.W. Norton.
    (1977b). *The four fundamental concepts of psychoanalysis*. (A. Sheridan, Trans.).
    London: Hogarth.
    (1978). *Le Séminaire, Livre II (1954–5): Le moi dans la théorie de Freud et dans la technique de la psychanalyse*. Paris: Seuil.
    (1979). The neurotic's individual myth. *The Psychoanalytic Quarterly*, **48**, 405–425.
    (1986). *Le Séminaire, Livre VII (1959–60): L'éthique de la psychanalyse*. Paris: Seuil.
    (1988a). *The Seminar of Jacques Lacan, Book I: Freud's papers on technique*.
    (J. Forrester, Trans.). New York, NY: W.W. Norton.
    (1988b). *The Seminar of Jacques Lacan, Book II: The Ego in Freud's theory and in the technique of psychoanalysis*. (S. Tomaselli, Trans.). Cambridge: Cambridge University Press.
    (1992). *The Seminar of Jacques Lacan, Book VII: The ethics of psychoanalysis*.
    (D. Porter, Trans.). New York, NY: W.W. Norton.
    (2001). *Le Séminaire, Livre VIII (1960–1): Le transfert*. Paris: Seuil.
Lachmann, F. (1985). On transience and the sense of temporal continuity. *Contemporary Psychoanalysis*, **21**, 193–200.
Langs, R. (1997). *Death anxiety in clinical practice*. London: Karnac Books.
Laplanche, J. (1976 [1970]). *Life and death in psychoanalysis*. (J. Mehlman, Trans.). Baltimore, MD: Johns Hopkins University Press.
    (1992). Interpretation between determinism and hermeneutics: A restatement of the problem. *International Journal of Psychoanalysis*, **73**, 429–445.
    (1999 [1992]). *Essays on otherness*. London: Routledge.
    (1999 [1996]). The so-called 'death-drive': A sexual drive. In: R. Weatherill (Ed.), *The death drive: New life for a dead subject?* (pp. 40–59). London: Rebus Press.
Le Rider, J. (1992). Un texte retrouvé: La première version d'Actuelles sur la guerre et la mort (2e partie), *Revue Internationale d'Histoire de la Psychanalyse*, **5**, 599–611.
Lear, J. (2000). *Happiness, death, and the remainder of life*. Cambridge, MA: Harvard University Press.
Leclaire, S. (1971). Jérôme ou La mort dans la vie de l'obsédé. In *Démasquer le réel: Un essai sur l'objet en psychanalyse* (pp. 121–147). Paris: Seuil.
Lehmann, H. (1966). A conversation between Freud and Rilke. *The Psychoanalytic Quarterly*, **35**, 423–427.
Lehto, R. H., & Stein, K. F. (2009). Death anxiety: An analysis of an evolving concept. *Research and Theory for Nursing Practice*, **23**(1), 23–41.

Levinas, E. (1987 [1979, 1947]). *Time and the other.* (R. Cohen, Trans.). Pittsburgh: Duquesne University Press.
Lewin, B. D. (1946). Sleep, the mouth, and the dream screen. *The Psychoanalytic Quarterly*, **15**, 419–434.
— (1950). *The Psychoanalysis of elation.* New York, NY: W.W. Norton.
Lichtenstein, H. (1974 [1935]). Some considerations regarding the phenomenology of the repetition compulsion and the death instinct. *The Annual of Psychoanalysis*, **7**, 63–84.
Lifton, R. J. (1979). *The broken connection: On death and the continuity of life.* New York, NY: Simon and Schuster.
Loewenberg, P. (1992). The pagan Freud. In R. S. Wistrich (Ed.), *Austrians and Jews in the twentieth century: From Franz Joseph to Waldheim* (pp. 124–141). New York, NY: St. Martin's Press.
Long, A. A., & Sedley, D. N. (1987). *The Hellenistic philosophers. Volume 1: Translations of the principal sources with philosophical commentary.* Cambridge: Cambridge University Press.
Lowental, U. (1981). Dying, regression, and the death instinct. *The Psychoanalytic Review*, **68**(3), 363–370.
Loy, D. (1996). *Lack and transcendence: The problem of death and life in psychotherapy, existentialism, and Buddhism.* Atlantic Highlands, NJ: Humanities Press.
Maglio, C. J., & Robinson, Sh. E. (1994). The effects of death education on death anxiety: A meta-analysis. *Omega – Journal of Death and Dying*, **29**(4), 319–335.
Marcus Aurelius. *The meditations.* (G. M. A. Grube, Trans.) (1963). Indianapolis: Bobbs-Merrill Educational Publishing.
Masi, F. de (2004). *Making death thinkable.* London: Free Association Books.
Masson, J. M. (1984). *The assault on truth. Freud's suppression of the seduction theory.* New York, NY: Farrar, Straus and Giroux.
— (1985). (Ed.). *The Complete letters of Sigmund Freud to Wilhelm Fliess, 1887–1904.* Cambridge, MA: Harvard University Press.
Matte Blanco, I. (2005 [1973]). The four antinomies of the death instinct. *International Journal of Psychoanalysis*, **86**, 1463–1476.
McGuire, W. (Ed.) (1974). *The Freud/Jung letters.* Princeton, NJ: Princeton University Press.
Meghnagi, D. (1993). Editor's comment. In D. Meghnagi (Ed.), *Freud and Judaism* (pp. 41–56). London: Karnac Books.
Meng, H., & Freud, E. L. (1963). *Psychoanalysis and faith. The letters of Sigmund Freud and Oskar Pfister.* London: The Hogarth Press.
Meyer, J. E. (1975 [1973]). *Death and neurosis.* (M. Nunberg, Trans.). New York, NY: International Universities Press.
Mills, J. (2006). Reflections on the death drive. *Psychoanalytic Psychology*, **23**, 373–382.
Minkowski, E. (1995 [1933]). La mort. In *Le Temps vécu: Esssai sur l'aspect temporel de la vie* (pp. 121–137). Paris: PUF, 121–137.
Money-Kyrle, R. (1957). An inconclusive contribution to the theory of the death instinct. In M. Klein, P. Heinemann, & R. E. Money-Kyrle (Eds.), *New Directions in Psychoanalysis* (pp. 499–509). New York, NY: Basic Books.

Montaigne, M. de (1998). *Essais: Livre I*. Paris: Imprimerie Nationale.
Moss, M. S., & Moss, S. Z. (1983). The impact of parental death on middle aged children. *Omega: Journal of Death and Dying*, **14**(1), 65–91.
M'Uzan, M. de (1977 [1968]). Freud et la mort. In *De l'art à la mort* (pp. 49–63). Paris: Gallimard.
  (1977 [1974]). S.J.E.M. In *De l'art à la mort* (pp. 151–163). Paris: Gallimard.
  (1996). La mort n'avoue jamais. *Revue Française de Psychanalyse*, **60**, 33–47.
Nachman, L. D. (1981). Our mortal dress: Sigmund Freud and the theme of death. *The Psychoanalytic Review*, **68**, 547–560.
Neimeyer, R. A. (1997–1998). Death anxiety research: The state of the art. *Omega – Journal of Death and Dying*, **36**(2), 97–120.
Nitzschke, B. (1991). Freuds Vortrag vor dem Israelitischen Humanitätsverein "Wien" des Ordens B'nai B'rith: Wir und der Tod (1915): Ein wiedergefundenes Dokument. *Psyche* **45**, 97–131.
Nussbaum, M. C. (1994). *The therapy of desire: Theory and practice in Hellenistic ethics*. Princeton, NJ: Princeton University Press.
Owens, M. E. (2004). Forgetting Signorelli: Monstrous visions of the resurrection of the dead. *American Imago*, **61**(1), 7–33.
Parat, C. (1998). Variations sur la mort. *Revue Française de Psychanalyse*, **62**, 1821–1851.
Pasche, F. (1996). Peur de la mort, angoisse de mort, défense du moi. *Revue Française de Psychanalyse*, **60**, 49–53.
Paskauskas, A. (1993). *The Complete correspondence of Sigmund Freud and Ernest Jones 1908–1939*. Cambridge, MA: The Belknap Press of Harvard University Press.
Persinger M. A. (1985). Death anxiety as a semantic conditioned suppression paradigm. *Perceptual and Motor Skills*, **60**(3), 827–830.
Phillips, A. (2000). *Darwin's worms*. New York, NY: Basic Books.
Piven, J. (2004). *Death and delusion: A Freudian analysis of mortal terror*. Greenwich, CT: Information Age Publishing.
Poe, E. A. (1958). William Wilson. In *The Complete Poems and Stories* (pp. 277–292). New York: A.A. Knopf.
Pollock, G. H. (1971a). On time and anniversaries. In M. Kanzer (Ed.), *The unconscious today* (pp. 233–257). New York, NY: International Universities Press.
  (1971b). On time, death, and immortality. *The Psychoanalytic Quarterly*, **40**, 435–446.
Pontalis, J. B. (1977). Sur le travail de la mort. In *Entre le rêve et la douleur*. Paris: Gallimard.
Pyszczynski, T., Rothschild, Z., & Abdollahi, A. (2008). Terrorism, violence, and hope for peace. A terror management perspective. *Current Directions in Psychological Science*, **17**(5), 318–322.
Ragland-Sullivan, E. (1986). *Jacques Lacan and the philosophy of psychoanalysis*. Chicago, IL: University of Illinois Press.
Rank, O. (1989 [1914]). *The double: A psychoanalytic study*. (H. Tucker, Trans.). London: Karnac.

(1950 [1945]). *Will therapy and truth and reality.* (J. Taft, Trans). New York, NY: Alfred A. Knopf.
Rasmussen, C., Templer, D. I., Kenkel, M. B., & Cannon W. G. (1998). Indirect attempt to change death attitudes: negative findings and associated relationships. *Omega – Journal of Death and Dying*, 37(3), 203–214.
Razinsky, L. (2005). Un juif tout à fait athée ... mais cependant juif: Freud, le Judaïsme et la question de la mort. *Perspectives*, 12, 255–272.
—— (2009). How to look death in the eyes, not shunning it: Freud and Bataille. *SubStance. A Review of Theory and Literary Criticism*, 38(2), 63–88.
—— (2013). Publish and perish: Freud's claim to literary fame. Manuscript submitted for publication.
Rheingold, J. C. (1967). *The mother, anxiety, and death: The catastrophic death complex*. Boston, MA: Little, Brown.
Ricoeur, P. (1970). *Freud and philosophy: An essay in interpretation.* (D. Savage, Trans.). New Haven, CT: Yale University Press.
Rilke, R. M. (1964). *The notebooks of Malte Laurids Brigge.* (M. D. Herter Norton, Trans.). New York, NY: W.W. Norton.
Riviere, J. (1936). On the genesis of psychical conflict in earliest infancy. In M. Klein, P. Heimann, S. Isaacs, & J. Riviere (Eds.), *Developments in psychoanalysis* (pp. 43–44). London: Hogarth.
—— (1957). The unconscious phantasy of an inner world reflected in examples from literature. In M. Klein, P. Heimann, & R. Money-Kyrle (Eds.), *New directions in psychoanalysis* (pp. 346–369). New York, NY: Basic Books.
Rosenthal, H. R. (1973a [1963]). The fear of death as an indispensable factor in psychotherapy. In H. M. Ruitenbeek (Ed.), *The interpretation of death* (pp. 166–179). USA: Jason Aronson.
—— (1973b [1957]). Psychotherapy for the dying. In H. M. Ruitenbeek (Ed.), *The interpretation of death* (pp. 87–95). New York, NY: Jason Aronson.
Rosenzweig, F. (1971 [1921]). *The star of redemption.* (W. W. Hallo, Trans.). London: Routledge and Kegan Paul.
Sandler, J. (1983). Reflections on some relations between psychoanalytic concepts and psychoanalytic practice. *International Journal of Psychoanalysis*, 64, 35–45.
Sartre, J. P. (1957 [1943]). *Being and nothingness: An essay on phenomenological ontology.* (H. E. Barnes, Trans.). London: Methuen.
Schermer, V. L. (1995). Intimations of mortality from recollections of early childhood: Death awareness, knowledge, and the unconscious. In: J. Kauffman (Ed.), *Awareness of mortality* (pp. 121–151). Amityville, NY: Baywood.
Schimek, J. G. (1975). A critical re-examination of Freud's concept of unconscious mental representation. *International Review of Psychoanalysis*, 2(2), 171–187.
Schur, M. (1972). *Freud, living and dying*. New York, NY: International Universities Press.
Searles, H. F. (1965 [1961]). Schizophrenia and the inevitability of death. In *Collected papers on schizophrenia and related subjects* (pp. 487–520). New York, NY: International Universities Press.
Segal, H. (1958). Fear of death: Notes on the analysis of an old man. *International Journal of Psychoanalysis*, 39, 178–181.

(1979). *Klein*. Glasgow: William Collins Sons/ Fontana.
Shneidman, E. S. (1973). *Deaths of man*. New-York, NY: Quadrangle/ The New-York Times Book Co.
Solomon, S., Greenberg, J., & Pyszczynski, T. (1998). Tales from the Crypt. *Zygon*, **33**(1), 9–43.
Sophocles. *Oedipus the king. (S. Berg, & D. Clay, Trans.)* (1978). New York: Oxford University Press.
Stephenson, J. S. (1985). *Death, grief, and mourning: Individual and social realities*. New York, NY: The Free Press.
Stern, M. (1968a). Fear of death and neurosis. *Journal of the American Psychoanalytic Association*, **16**, 3–31.
——— (1968b). Fear of death and trauma – remarks about an addendum to psychoanalytic theory and technique. *International Journal of Psychoanalysis*, **49**, 457–461.
Strozier, C. B. (1999). Death and the self. In A. Goldberg (Ed.), *Progress in self psychology* (Vol. **15**, pp. 321–342). Hillsdale, NJ: The Analytic Press.
Thomas, D. (1939). *The collected poems*. New York, NY: New Directions.
Thorson, J. A., & Powell, F. C. (2000). Death anxiety in younger and older adults. In A. Tomer (Ed.), *Death attitudes and the older adult* (pp. 123–136). Philadelphia, PA: Brunner-Routledge.
Tomer, A., & Eliason, G. (2000). Attitudes about life and death: Toward a comprehensive model of death anxiety. In A. Tomer (Ed.), *Death attitudes and the older adult* (pp. 3–22). Philadelphia: Brunner-Routledge.
——— (2005). Life regrets and death attitudes in college students. *Omega – Journal of Death and Dying*, **51**(3), 173–195.
Wahl, C. W. (1959 [1958]). The fear of death. In H. Feifel (Ed.), *The meaning of death* (pp. 16–29). New-York, NY: McGraw-Hill.
Wainrib, S. (1996). Peur de la mort, angoisse de mort, défense du moi. *Revue Française de Psychanalyse*, **60**, 49–53.
Wangh, M. (1989). The evolution of psychoanalytic thought on negation and denial. In E. L. Edelstein, D. L. Nathanson, & A. M. Stone (Eds.) (1989), *Denial: A clarification of concepts and research* (pp. 5–15). New York, NY: Plenum Press.
Weatherill, R. (1998). *The sovereignty of death*. London: Rebus Press.
——— (Ed.) (1999a). *The death drive: New life for a dead subject?* London: Rebus Press.
——— (1999b). Facing the death drive. In *The death drive: New life for a dead subject?* (pp. 207–237). London: Rebus Press.
Weber, S. (1982). *The legend of Freud*. Minneapolis: University of Minnesota Press.
——— (1997). Wartime. In H. De Vries & S. Weber (Eds.), *Violence, identity, and self-determination* (pp. 80–105). Stanford: Stanford University Press.
Weininger, O. (1996). *Being and not being: Clinical applications of the death instinct*. Madison, CT: International Universities Press.
Weisman, A. D. (1972). *On dying and denying. A psychiatric study of terminality*. New York, NY: Behavioral Publications.
Winnicott, D. W. (1956). Primary maternal preoccupation. In *Through paediatrics to psychoanalysis* (pp. 300–305). London: Hogarth Press.

(1974). Fear of breakdown. The *International Review of Psychoanalysis*, **1**, 103–107.
Wolf, E. S. (1983). Discussion: Transience or nothingness? *Psychoanalytic Inquiry*, **3**, 529–542.
Yalom, I. D. (1980). *Existential psychotherapy.* New York, NY: Basic Books.
Zilboorg, G. (1943). Fear of death. *The Psychoanalytic Quarterly*, **12**, 465–475.

Index

Abraham, Karl 187
Adorno, Theodor. W. 250–1
Age and death
  Childhood and infancy 23, 38–9, 46, 175–6, 178, 191–5, 199–200, 225, 270
  Midlife 196
  Old age 189, 195–6, 197–9, 201, 205
Alford, C. Fred 115, 120 n. 10
Alvarado, Katherine A. 7 n. 3
Ambition 47–8, 55, 75–89
Annihilation anxiety 20, 27, 109 n. 5, 233–4
Anthony, Sylvia 23
Anxiety 32–3, 105–11, 191–3, 222, 238–9, 273
  in dreams 92–3, 98–101
Anzieu, Didier 48, 49 n. 3, 53, 55, 58, 60, 66 n. 14, 79, 93 n. 15, 102

Barford, Duncan 134
Barzilai, Shuli 208 n. 2
Bataille, Georges 165, 255
Becker, Ernest 3, 6, 9, 12, 24, 30, 31, 43, 52 n. 4, 88, 91, 146, 222–4, 228, 229 n. 3, 232, 236, 245 n. 12, 257, 262 n. 10, 263, 264 n. 12
Bibring, Edward 25, 133
Binswanger, Ludwig 165, 180, 243–4
Bion, Wilfred R. 233 n. 8, 234, 240
Blanchot, Maurice 209–10
Blass, Rachel. B. 167, 272 n. 23
Bolivar, Eduardo 115, 131, 150 n. 15, 151, 246
Bonaparte, Marie 167, 248
Bonasia, Emanuele 3 n.1
Boothby, Richard 215 n. 6
Borch-Jacobsen, Mikkel 208 n. 2, 210 n. 3, 217
Bowie, Malcolm 208, 211, 219 n. 7
Breger, Louis 9, 41, 48 n. 3, 68, 146
Brodsky, Bernard 17, 32, 171
Bromberg, Walter 175

Bronfen, Elisabeth 6, 30, 94 n. 16, 267 n. 16
Brown, Norman O. 3, 9, 30, 52 n. 4, 131, 150, 223, 232
Buxbaum, Edith 48, 60

Cappon, Daniel 177
Carel, Havi 116, 131, 133, 138 n. 4, 150–1, 277
Caruth, Cathy 133, 261–73
Carveth, Donald L. 174 n. 2, 231
Castration 17, 18, 22–3, 31, 33, 159, 171, 175, 193, 232 n. 7, 239, 251
Chadwick, Mary 30, 31, 171
Chasseguet Smirgel, J. 22 n. 13, 176 n. 6
Choron, Jacques 30 n. 18, 41 n. 1, 138 n. 4
Cioran, Emil 246 n. 15
Critchley, Simon 152 n. 17

Dastur, Françoise 261, 276
David, Christian 207
Death, arbitrariness of 135, 137, 138–40, 143, 156, 205, 269
Death, clinical aspects of 9–12, 190, 225, 228–30, 246–7, 250, 256–7, 263 n. 11, 276, 279 n. 1
Death, conceptual analysis of 134–7, 236–52, 255–6, 257–78
Death, concretization of 18, 34, 138, 159, 161, 171, 177–8, 180, 193–4, 195, 204
Death, the direct Encounter with 120 n. 10, 124–6, 157, 184–6, 256 n. 3, 276–8
Death, the idea of dying one's own death 142–6
Death, imminence of (and its denial) 144–5, 198–200, 201 n. 10, 205, 258
Death's interrelatedness with other concepts and the rest of psychic life 79, 87–9, 103–4, 147–8, 167, 240, 249–50, 265, 273–6, 277, 278, 280–1

299

See also: Ambition; Death and meaning/value of life
Death, knowledge of 23, 38–9, 136, 141, 234, 258, 260, 262–78
    See also: Death anxiety, defenses against
Death of others 19, 20–1, 50–6, 57–8, 65–6, 89–92, 100, 163, 183–8, 277
Death, overlooking 182–9
Death, people's approach to 113, 115–23, 158, 162–4 See also: Death anxiety, defenses against
Death's, positive impact in life 200–1, 230–1, 259
Death, rendering internal 140–1, 143–4, 151–2, 242
Death, representation of 97–8, 99–101, 113, 195, 225, 265–76
    See also: Death equivalents; Death and absence; Death interrelatedness with other concepts and the rest of our psychic life
    Arguments against 15–30, 152 n. 18, 271, 280–1
Death, sexualization of death 68–9, 175–6
Death and absence 28–9, 89, 209–11, 218–19, 240–1, 242, 265–73, 281
Death and individuality/subjectivity 136, 141, 142–6, 198, 202–3, 250
Death and meaning/value of life 66, 77–8, 120–3, 126–7, 164, 169, 197–9, 201–4, 205–6, 230–1, 247–8, 260–1, 268–9, 276
Death anxiety/fear of death 6, 34–6, 40–1, 105–11, 114, 137, 147, 177, 178–80, 191–3, 197, 206, 219–20, 222–3, 228–9, 246, 260–1
    Reduction of 30–9, 114, 124, 160–1, 170–3, 190, 193–7, 239 See also: Castration; Death equivalents
    Negative moral judgment toward 180–2, 198, 200–1, 205 See also: Heroization of "healthy" death adaptation; Pathologization of the response to death
    Defenses against 156, 162–4, 192, 223, 225, 228–9, 256–7, 265
Death drive 19–20, 131–54, 192–5, 215
Death equivalents 173–4, 225, 226–8, 240
Death wishes 20–1, 36, 54, 55, 57–8, 60, 77, 92 n. 14, 101, 149, 160–1, 171, 176–7, 180, 194
Deferred action 234
Derrida, Jacques 134, 142
Doka, Kenneth J. 231 n. 6

Double, the 56, 158–9
Dreams 46–104
    Dreams, concern for others in 67–73
    Absurd dreams 89–92
    Dreams and death-theoretical considerations 46–50, 92–103
    Dreams by Freud
        Castle by the sea 59–62
        Irma's injection 69–73
        'Non vixit' 52–5, 56–8, 68, 77–8, 97–8
        Dissecting my own pelvis 62–4, 81–2, 98
        Botanical monograph 83–5
        Father on his death-bed like Garibaldi 90–2
        1851 and 1856 dream 64–7, 86–7
        Hall with machines 67
        News of son from the front 68, 100–1
        Bird-beaked figures 68–9, 96
        May beetle dream 69, 93–5
        Otto was looking ill 69, 82–3
        Uncle with the yellow beard 76
        Rome series 78–81
        Three fates 93–5
        Laboratory dreams 99–100

Edwards, Paul 27
Eigen, Michael 30, 131, 151 n. 16, 174
Eissler, Kurt R. 116, 131, 143–5, 189 n. 20, 232 n. 7
Ekstein, Rudolf 148
Epicurus 266
Erikson, Erik H. 87 n. 8, 197–201, 202, 255, 284
Evans, Dylan 214 n. 5

Falzeder, Ernst 41 n. 2, 42
Feifel, Herman 7 n. 3
Fenichel, Otto 32, 150 n. 15, 171, 177 n. 8, 179
Fichtner, Gerhard 165, 180, 243
Finitude 103, 150, 164–9, 212, 257, 258–9, 274–5
Firestone, Robert. W. 201 n. 9, 262 n. 9, 263, 264
Fliess, Wilhelm 40, 41, 42, 54, 57–8, 73–4 n. 14, 78, 83, 84–5, 88, 171, 180, 185, 239
Fortner, Barry V. 7 n. 3
Freud, Ernst L. 79, 167, 248
Freud, Sigmund
    The neuro-psychoses of defence (1894) 239

Index

The interpretation of dreams (1900) 23, 46–104, 239, 269 n. 20, 275, 279, 284
The psychopathology of everyday life (1901) 20, 86 n. 7, 95 n. 18, 208
Three essays on the theory of sexuality (1905) 270
The sexual theories of children (1908) 18, 22 n. 13
Analysis of a phobia in a five-year-old boy (1909a) 18, 22 n. 13, 33 n. 21, 175–6, 239, 270
Totem and taboo (1913) 157, 160–1, 162, 174, 244, 260, 268 n. 18
The theme of the three caskets (1913) 63, 73, 141, 162
On narcissism (1914) 26, 56
Thoughts for the times on war and death (1915) 1, 15, 16, 19, 20, 23 n. 14, 26–9, 30, 46, 61, 108, 112–30, 138, 142, 150, 156 n. 1, 157, 162–5, 169, 174, 176, 185, 238 n. 4, 244, 245, 256 n. 3, 257, 261, 262, 263, 270, 271–2, 284
On transience (1916 [1915]) 88, 121, 150, 169, 186 n. 16, 187–8, 248, 259, 276
Some character-types met within psychoanalytic work (1916) 88
Introductory lectures on psychoanalysis (1916–1917) 98 n. 21, 105–11
Mourning and melancholia (1917 [1915]) 35 n. 23, 169 n. 11, 183–8
From the history of an infantile neurosis (1918 [1914]) 175
The uncanny (1919) 139, 158–60, 168
Beyond the pleasure principle (1920) 98, 109, 131–54, 215, 272–3, 273 n. 25
The ego and the id (1923) 1, 15, 16, 19, 23 n. 14, 24 n. 15, 27, 30, 33–7, 106 n. 1, 107, 133, 153, 187, 244, 271 n. 22, 272–3
The dissolution of the Oedipus complex (1924) 143 n. 7
The economic problem of masochism (1924) 37, 133
On negation (1925) 16, 34, 218
Inhibitions, symptoms and anxiety (1926) 1, 15, 19 n. 8, 22, 23 n. 14, 30, 32–3, 36–7, 105–11, 153, 188, 233, 238–9, 245–6, 268,
The future of an illusion (1927) 63, 140, 155–7, 174, 262
Civilization and its discontents (1930) 134, 153, 186, 247

New introductory lectures on psychoanalysis (1933 [1932]) 18, 98 n. 21
Why war? (1933 [1932]) 134, 153
Analysis terminable and interminable (1937) 134, 153, 239
Moses and monotheism: Three essays (1939 [1934–1938]) 155
An outline of psychoanalysis (1940 [1938]) 20, 143
Death and us (1993 [1915]) 123 n. 13, 126, 164, 270
Freud's personal life 40–5, 148–9, 179–80, 184–5, 186 n. 16, 236–7
   See also: Dreams
Freud's numerical calculations on the end of life 41–2, 65–6, 85–6, 87, 160, 179
Freud's ambivalence toward death 3, 37–8, 40–4, 113–14, 117–23, 126–30, 154, 161, 166
Friedman, John A. 133
Frommer, Martin Stephen 10, 184 n. 14, 231, 254 n. 1, 256 n. 4, 257 n. 6

Gabel, Peter 131, 152 n. 17
Gaitanidis, Anastasios 251
Galt, Cynthia P. 7 n. 3
Gay, Peter 131
Gediman, Helen K. 234 n. 10
Golub, Sharon 43 n. 5, 180
Green, André 132, 241, 244
Grinstein, Alexander 48, 62 n. 9, 77 n. 2, 80, 81 n. 4, 94 n. 17, 95 n. 18, 102
Grotjahn, Martin 102 n. 23, 152 n. 17
Grotstein, James S. 152 n. 17

Hamilton, James W. 148
Hárnik, Jenö 18, 32, 171
Hegel, Georg Wilhelm Friedrich 17 n. 2, 28 n. 17, 208, 209, 210 n. 3, 212, 213, 217, 219
Heidegger, Martin 6, 29, 42, 115, 116, 117, 138, 149–51, 163 n. 8, 164 n. 9, 173, 181, 215, 219–20, 243, 249, 250–1, 258, 264
Helplessness 109–11, 156–7, 192, 227, 233, 241 n. 6
   Helplessness (or lack of control) in face of death 63, 135, 156–7, 259
Herodotus 259 n. 8
Heroization of "healthy" death adaptation 180–2, 201–3 See also Death anxiety, negative moral judgment toward
Hoelter, Jon W. 7 n. 3

Index

Hoffman, Francis H. 147, 172 n. 1
Hoffman, Irwin Z. 3, 4 n. 2, 9, 17, 20, 24, 27, 109 n. 6, 110 n. 8, 114 n. 3, 125, 126 n. 16, 128, 129 n. 19, 149, 156 n. 2, 188 n. 18, 198, 202, 229–30, 254 n. 1, 257n
Holt, Robert R. 185 n. 18, 261
Hulsey, Timothy L. 9, 201
Hurvich, Martin 20, 30, 109 n. 5, 177 n. 8, 234 n. 9
Hyman, Stanley Edgar 82 n. 5

Ibsen, Henrik 136
Immortality 155–8, 262
Immortality, unconscious belief in 16, 17, 26, 108, 113, 117–18, 123, 156, 158, 262, 277
  Symbolic immortality 43, 77–8, 82, 85, 86, 87–8, 97, 236, 262

Jaques, Elliott 102, 173, 191, 192 n. 1, 196, 226
Jones, Enest 40, 43, 79, 131, 148 n. 13, 149 n. 14, 177, 244 n. 9
Jonte-Pace, Diane 4, 94 n. 16, 96 n. 19, 123 n. 13, 139 n. 5, 159, 166, 175, 187, 236 n. 2
Jung, Carl Gustav 85, 204–6, 244 n. 11

Kastenbaum, Robert 116
Kauffman, Jeffrey 261
Kaufmann, Walter 115, 163 n. 8
Keiser, Sylvan 32, 175
Klein, Melanie 3, 30, 132, 135, 152, 153 n. 18, 177, 191–7, 192 n. 1, 194 n. 3, 195 n. 4, 255, 284
Koestenbaum, Peter 231, 278
Kofman, Sarah 48, 49 n. 3, 82 n. 6, 100 n. 22, 159
Kohut, Heinz 201–4, 207, 234, 255
Kojève, Alexandre 210 n. 3, 217
Krell, David Farrell 152 n. 17
Kristeva, Julia 187, 241, 244 n. 8
Kübler-Ross, Elisabeth 178, 181 n. 12, 180–1, 189 n. 20, 201 n. 10

Lacan, Jacques 48, 72–3, 92 n. 13, 132, 151, 152, 173, 174 n. 3, 208–21, 226, 240 n. 5, 241, 254 n. 1, 255, 269 n. 20, 272 n. 24, 284
  Das Ding 218–19, 268–9 n. 19
  The symbolic 209–11
  The imaginary 211–13
  The real 72–3, 213–14
  Desire 216–18

Lear, Jonathan 148
Loss 183–8
  Object loss 17, 174
Love 35, 52, 100, 120–2, 184, 185–6, 262–3, 264
Lachman, Frank M. 3, 9, 201 n. 9
Langs, Robert 9, 146, 167, 230, 247, 257 n. 6
Laplanche, Jean 50, 116 n. 5, 133, 134, 139, 150, 271
Le Rider, Jacques 123 n. 13
Leclaire, Serge 9, 91 n. 12
Lehmann, Herbert 166 n. 10
Lehto, Rebecca H. 7 n. 3
Levinas, Emmanuel 136, 152 n. 17
Lewin, Bertram D. 18, 171, 174, 177 n. 7
Lichtenstein, Heinz 137 n. 4, 152 n. 17
Lifton, Robert Jay 3, 4, 9, 30, 43, 107, 110 n. 8, 114 n. 3, 115 n. 4, 120 n. 10, 147, 173, 175, 186 n. 15, 187 n. 17, 188 n. 19, 199 n. 6, 201 n. 10, 225, 226, 232, 237, 240, 250, 262 n. 9, 270 n. 21
Loewenberg, Peter 42
Long, Anthony A. 266 n. 13
Lowental, Uri 177 n. 7
Loy, David 116 n. 6, 224 n. 2

Maglio, Christopher J. 7 n. 3
Marcus Aurelius 231, 276
Masi, Franco De 9, 232, 267 n. 15
Masson, Jeffrey Moussaief 40, 41, 42, 54, 73–4 n. 14, 78, 88, 185, 239
Matte Blanco, I. 17, 133, 138 n. 4
McGuire, William 85
Meghnagi, David 123 n. 13
Melancholia 35–6, 183–8, 246 n. 15
Meng, Heinrich 186 n. 16
Meyer, Joachim E. 3, 9, 30, 42, 191, 245 n. 12
Mills, Jon 131
Minkowski, Eugène 259 n. 7
Money-Kyrle, Roger 30, 156 n. 2, 173, 191, 195 n. 4, 226
Montaigne, Michel de 259
Moss, Miriam S. 66
M'Uzan, Michel de 48, 102, 131, 171, 185 n. 15, 246 n. 15

Nachman, Larry David 43–4, 48, 49 n. 3, 91, 180
Narcissism 21, 26, 34–5, 50–2, 53, 56, 100, 103, 157, 159, 160, 201–4, 220, 223, 231, 262
Neimeyer, Robert A. 7 n. 3

Index

Nitzschke, Bernd 123 n. 13
Nussbaum, Martha C. 266 n. 13, 276

Oedipus 50, 52, 60, 104, 212, 215–16, 259
Ogden, Thomas 234
Owens, Margaret E. 64 n. 11

Parat, Catherine 131
Pasche, Francis 179 n. 9
Paskauskas, R. Andrew 43
Pathologization of the response to death 35–6, 166–7, 178–80, 198, 205, 230 n. 4 See also: Death, negative moral judgment toward
Persinger, M. A. 7 n. 3
Pfister, Oskar 186n, 3
Phillips, Adam 43, 145–6, 166, 168
Philosophy 124, 243–5, 260
Piven, Jerry 4 n. 2, 9, 20, 23, 37, 39 n. 25, 48, 49 n. 2, 128 n. 18, 131, 152 n. 17, 157, 158 n. 5, 160–1, 167, 173, 175 n. 5, 224–5, 226, 227, 228, 234, 250, 257, 262 n. 9, 264, 267 n. 17
Poe, Edgar Allan 56
Pollock, George H. 25, 156 n. 2
Pontalis, Jean-Bertrand 131, 150, 151–2, 175
Pyszczynski, Tom 264

Ragland-Sullivan, Ellie 211, 221 n. 9
Rank, Otto 3, 9, 122, 132, 136, 146, 147, 158 n. 6, 175 n. 4, 222–4, 232, 263, 264
Rasmussen, Christina 7 n. 3
Razinsky, Liran 28 n. 17, 29, 84, 123 n. 13, 165, 236 n. 1, 256, 270
Rheingold, Joseph C. 21 n. 12, 178
Ricoeur, Paul 116, 225
Rilke, Rainer Maria 144 n. 9, 166 n. 10
Riviere, Joan 191, 192, 193–4, 194 n. 2, 195 n. 4
Rosenthal, Hattie 9, 30, 31, 167, 189 n. 20, 230, 257
Rosenzweig, Franz 1, 260
Rivalry 51, 53–5, 56, 68, 77, 100, 103

Sandler, Joseph 11
Sartre, Jean-Paul 152 n. 17, 274 n. 26
Schermer, Victor L. 146, 195, 233 n. 8
Schimek, Jean G. 17 n. 3, 18 n. 6
Schur, Max 36, 40, 41 n. 1, 41 n. 3, 43 n. 5, 48, 49 n. 3, 53, 117 n. 7, 131, 148 n. 13, 149, 179–80, 181 n. 11, 185 n. 15, 233
Searles, Harold F. 3, 9, 106 n. 2, 132, 146–7, 185 n. 15, 238, 255 n. 2, 256 n. 4, 257, 263 n. 11
Segal, Hanna 191, 195–6, 196 n. 5

Self-preservation, instincts of 18, 21, 25, 108–9, 140–1, 233
Sexuality 79, 95–6, 103, 175, 237, 270
Shneidman, E. S. 181 n. 12, 189 n. 20
Solomon, Sheldon 7 n. 3, 263, 264
Stephenson, John S. 5, 201 n. 10
Stern, Max M. 4, 9, 30, 31, 167, 173, 174, 175, 179, 226, 227, 230
Strozier, Charles B. 203 n. 13
Superego 33, 34–7

Terror Management Theory 5 n. 3, 263, 264
Thinking one's own death 120–3, 162–3, 260–1, 265–73
  Freud's spectator argument 26–30, 61, 272
Thomas, Dylan 180, 198
Thorson, James A. 7 n. 3
Tomer, Adrian 7 n. 3
Trauma 133, 200, 268, 273

Unconscious
  Unconscious approach to death 15, 100–1, 115, 117–20, 125, 157, 185, 192–5 See also: Death, representation of; Immortality, unconscious belief in
  and negative content 16–17, 25–6
  and time 17–18
  and abstract concepts 18–19
  and prior experience of death 22–3
  Unconscious correlative of death 19–22, 153 n. 18, 193

Wish 54, 98–101 See also: Death wishes
Wahl, Charles. W. 3, 116, 178, 262
Wainrib, Steven 233
Wangh, Martin 43
Weatherill, Rob 133, 197, 208 n. 2, 152 n. 17
Weber, Samuel 29, 107 n. 4, 112 n. 1
Weininger, Otto 191, 194
Weisman, Avery D. 189 n. 20
Winnicott, Donald W. 206–7, 207 n. 16, 234
Wolf, Ernest S. 204 n. 15

Yalom, Irvin D. 3, 6, 9–10, 23, 24, 30, 51, 114 n. 3, 116, 146, 168, 172, 184, 200 n. 7, 228–9, 230, 232, 236, 237 n. 3, 246 n. 13, 247, 257 n. 6, 262

Zilboorg, Gregory 21 n. 12, 51, 185 n. 15, 229 n. 3, 233

For EU product safety concerns, contact us at Calle de José Abascal, 56–1°, 28003 Madrid, Spain or eugpsr@cambridge.org.

www.ingramcontent.com/pod-product-compliance
Ingram Content Group UK Ltd.
Pitfield, Milton Keynes, MK11 3LW, UK
UKHW020453090825
461507UK00007B/214